BEHIND THE
THISTLE

PLAYING RUGBY FOR
SCOTLAND

DAVID BARNES AND PETER BURNS

WITH JOHN GRIFFITHS

POLARIS
PUBLISHING

The edition first published in 2015 by
ARENA SPORT
An imprint of Birlinn Limited
West Newington House
10 Newington Road
Edinburgh
EH9 1QS

in association with

POLARIS PUBLISHING LTD
c/o Turcan Connell
Princes Exchange
1 Earl Grey Street
Edinburgh
EH3 9EE

www.arenasportbooks.co.uk
www.polarispublishing.com

First published in 2010 by Birlinn Limited

ISBN: 978-1-909715-03-5
EBOOK ISBN: 978-0-85790-601-4

British Library Cataloguing-in-Publication Data
A catalogue record for this book is available from the British Library

Designed and typeset by Polaris Publishing, Edinburgh

Printed and bound by Livonia Print, Latvia

CONTENTS

SELECTED BIBLIOGRAPHY

Barbarians Football Club 1890-1955
BBC interview with Doug Davies, SCRAN: 1987
Behind the Rose: Playing Rugby for England, Stephen Jones & Nick Cain
Bells' Life, London: 8th December 1870
Broon from Troon: An Autobiography, Gordon Brown
Chocolate and Gold: One Hundred Years of Rugby Glasgow High Kelvinside RFC
The Essential History of Rugby Union: Scotland
Football: the Rugby Union Game, London: Cassell, 1892
'The day Scottish rugby ran scared', Tom English, *The Scotsman*, 29 January 2012.
Edinburgh Academy Chronicle, 1903
Edinburgh Academy Chronicle, 1907
Edinburgh Academy Chronicle, 1909
The Edinburgh Academical Football Club Centenary History, 1958
England v Scotland 1953 Official Programme
England v Scotland 1955 Official Programme
Eric Liddell: Pure Gold, David McCaslund
'Dutch of class: Frans ten Bos on playing for Scotland', Richard Bath, *Scotland on Sunday*, 11 November 2012
'Finn Russell on his rapid career rise', Duncan Smith, *The Scotsman*, 15 August 2015
'Finn Russell relishing challenge', *The Scotsman*, 02 February 2015
'Frans ten Bos fled Nazis to star for Scotland', Aiden Smith, *The Scotsman*, 20 March 2015
The Game Goes On
'Grand Slam hero David Leslie remains undaunted', *The Scotsman*, 09 November 2013
Great Rugger Players
The Grudge: Scotland V England, 1990, Tom English
'He took his fork, picked up my steak and ate it . . .' *The Herald*, 14 January 2014
The History of Scottish Rugby
The Independent, 25th September 2004
'Interview: Iain Paxton, former Scotland forward', Aiden Smith, *The Scotsman*, 23 November 2013.
'Interview: John Jeffrey, former Scotland forward', Aiden Smith, *The Scotsman*, 2 October 2015.
'Jon Welsh: We got a bad break but you can't do anything about it now', Alasdair Reid, *The Times*, 25 November 2015
L'Equipe, 17th January 1949
L'Equipe, 13th January 1958
L'Equipe, 12th January 1959
Newspaper cutting from *The Weekly News*, Auckland: 1950
Newspaper cutting from *The Edinburgh Evening News*, 18th May 1935
News of the World, 27th February 1955
No Borders: Playing Rugby for Ireland, Tom English
'No ordinary Joe', Mark Palmer, *The Times*, 18 October 2015
'Nutter who made Jim Telfer's class of '84 finest of all', *The Rugby Paper*, January 2014

'My Life in Rugby: Dave Hilton', *The Rugby Paper*, September 2012
Private notebook of W.R.Sutherland, Hawick: 1912
Rugby Football Today, 1931
Rugby in Wales, Swansea & Llandybie, 1970
Rugby World, November 1960
Rugby World, December 1960
Rugby World, February 1961
Rugby World, June 1961
Rugby World, April 1962
Rugby World, June 1963
Rugby World, March 1968
Rugby World, September 1975
Rugby World, October 1975
Rugby World, April 2013
Rugby World, October 2013
Rugby World, December 2013
Rugby World, February 2014
Rugby World, April 2014
Rugby World, December 2014
Rugby World, February 2015
Rugby World, March 2015
Rugby World, April 2015
Rugby World, May 2015
Rugby World, June 2015
Rugby World, July 2015
Rugby World, September 2015
Rugger: The Man's Game, 1944
'Scotland weeps for Borders' wasteland', Alasdair Reid, *The Scotsman*, 22 February 2014
'Scotland's 1984 grand slam', *The Herald*, January 2014
Scotland v France 1954 Official Programme
Scotland v New Zealand 1954 Official Programme
Scotland v Ireland 1955 Official Programme
Scotland v England 1966 Official Programme
Scottish Sport, March 1894
Scottish Sunday Express, 6th February 1955
A Speech at Edinburgh Academicals F.C. Jubilee Dinner, Edinburgh, 1908
The Story of Scottish Rugby, T N Foulis
The Thistle: A Chronicle of Scottish Rugby, Allan Massie
Undated newspaper cutting from *Athletic News*, Manchester
Undated newspaper cutting from *Scottish Athletic Journal*
Wales v Scotland 1954 Official Programme
The Western Mail, 29th January 1900
The Western Mail, 4th February 1957
West of Scotland Football Club 1865-1965, 1965
'When Arthur was king of Murrayfield', *The Scotsman*, 13 February 2015
'Why the All Blacks Triumphed', *Associated Newspapers*, 1906
The World of Rugby, BBC Publishing, London: 1979
The Year of the Thistle: Scotland's Grand Slam 1983-84, Norman Mair

ACKNOWLEDGEMENTS

I am under no illusions as to how fortunate I have been to spend my career being paid to watch rugby matches and to speak to sporting legends. During that time I have been constantly impressed by the down to earth intelligence and humour of the international stars I have met – and I have often wondered how their achievements on the rugby field have coloured their lives.

This book is an attempt to get under the skin of these giants of the game so that we can understand what makes them tick and appreciate the individual qualities a character needs in order to successfully play rugby at the highest level.

Every Scottish rugby fan has wondered at some point what it would be like to join that exclusive club of Scotland internationalists. Alas only a very small number of us ever get to realise that dream while the rest can only stand on the sidelines and marvel. This book is a celebration of those who have pulled on the blue jersey, but also a tribute to the rest of us who live in the slipstream of our sporting heroes.

This book is also for Johanne Simpson, our children, Maisie and Robbie, and in memory of Russell Bruce and Frank Coutts, who both contributed to this book but passed away before its publication.

David Barnes, November 2015

I remember the first time my father took me to Murrayfield. It was 17 February, 1990 and I was eight years old. I can still vividly remember the scent of cigar and pipe smoke mixing with the sweet tang of alcohol on the breath of those sitting near us and the waxy smell of Barbour jackets in the air (that combination of smells a staple of the East Stand in those days). There was such a palpable sense of energy in the ground as the stands and terraces filled before kick-off that utterly entranced me, and I can still remember the roar that went up when a train raced along the track behind the south terrace and sounded its horn in salute, followed a few minutes later by further cheers as a cockerel was released onto the pitch.

We stood in respectful silence for *La Marseillaise* as ripples of French support sang their hearts out and then the ground seemed to erupt as the band broke into *Flower of Scotland*; I had never heard anything like it before – it was a deafening cry to arms that reverberated right through me. The players composed themselves for a moment . . . and then we were off. And in those few minutes, from passing through the turnstiles to the moment the kick-off was struck, Murrayfield, the Scottish jersey and everything about that rarefied, mesmeric version of the game I already loved had captured my heart forever.

While I loved listening to every story told to me during my interviews, I was most struck by a comment made by Simon Webster. 'You have to remember something, Burnsy,' he said, shortly after we had finished lunch one afternoon in Edinburgh, his voice quieting. 'While we play for Scotland, we're really just fans who are lucky enough to be playing.'

No other player said that to me – but talking to each of them over the past six or seven years, I know they all feel the same. They love the team just as much as we do – even more so – and they all know just how special it is that they have been the ones to take to the field with that thistle on their chest.

I'd like to dedicate this book to my father, who instilled his love of the game in me from an early age; to my mother, who has long endured my obsession with it without ever really understanding why it makes me feel the way it does; and, most importantly, to my children, Isla and Hector, who will no doubt love something else entirely.

Peter Burns, November 2015

The authors would like to thank everyone who has given their time so generously to assist in the preparation of this book. Those whom we interviewed are too many to name individually but their thoughts are included in the pages which follow.

Thanks also to Tom English for his permission to use extracts from *No Borders: Playing Rugby for Ireland* for the section on the abandoned Five Nations matches of 1972, and from his wonderful book *The Grudge* for the 1990 Grand Slam chapter.

Finally, thank you to all those at Arena Sport for their fine work and wonderful support.

THE AUTHORS

David Barnes is a freelance rugby journalist and the co-author of Jim Renwick's autobiography, *Centre of Excellence*, and of the bestselling *Behind the Lions: Playing Rugby for the British & Irish Lions*.

Peter Burns is the editor for Arena Sport and the author of *White Gold: England's Journey to World Cup Glory* and a contributor to *Behind the Lions: Playing Rugby for the British & Irish Lions*.

John Griffiths is Britain's foremost rugby historian and author of numerous books on the subject. He was consultant historian for *Behind the Rose: Playing Rugby for England* and *Behind the Lions: Playing Rugby for the British & Irish Lions*.

INTRODUCTION

On 27 March 1871, twenty players representing Scotland took to the field at Raeburn Place in Edinburgh to face twenty from across the border in England in the world's first international rugby Test match. In the history of the sport, the importance of the occasion was second-only to the fabled instant when William Webb Ellis allegedly picked up the ball during a football match at Rugby School and ran with it.

When umpire Hely Hutchinson Almond signalled the start of the game, he also signalled the start of an astonishing journey that would see Test match rugby stretch its influence into virtually every corner of the globe. From that day to this, the game has undergone such seismic change that, should we be able to watch that first match, it would be unrecognisable to the sport that is played today.

The modern game, even at school and junior club level, is a world away from what it was in the nineteenth century and the early decades of the twentieth century. Contemporary Test match rugby is in a different universe altogether – even to that played as recently as the 1980s and early 1990s, let alone a hundred years before that. Amateurism at rugby union's elite end is also now long consigned to the history books, just as the great alcohol-fuelled international rugby tours that could stretch on for months at a time are a thing of the past. But while the levels of athleticism and skill, strength and fitness, analysis, nutrition, sports science and medicine, not to mention the global profile of the game, are stratospherically different to the early years of the sport, two constants have endured throughout: the pride of wearing the blue jersey emblazoned with a white thistle, and the unbreakable bonds of a brotherhood.

Scores of books have been written on the history of the sport and of the teams and players within it. Invariably these have been written from the outside looking in. This book, in contrast, looks to tell the history of Scottish international rugby in the words of the men who have been there and done it, told from within the rarified atmosphere of the changing room and the field of play, filled with glorious recollections from tours and away fixtures, from the after-match dinner tables and, somewhat hazily, from bars in Buenos Aires and Cape Town, Auckland, Sydney, Paris and all points in between

Like a fantasy dinner party, it would be wonderful to be able to sit down with all the greats who have donned the dark blue jersey from across the ages and hear them reminisce about their experiences of playing at Murrayfield and at all the great Test match venues, large and small, around the world. That scenario is of course impossible – but perhaps this book is the next best thing. There have been over 650 Scotland Test matches across a span of nearly 150 years, and the country has been represented by almost 1100 players. This is their story.

And it begins at Raeburn Place.

ONE

THE BULLDOG AND THE HIPPO
1871-1888

International rugby came about as the accidental sequel to an association football match organised by the London-centric Football Association. With total disregard for Scottish sentiments, the FA arranged a fixture between 'England' and 'Scotland' in November 1870, selecting both teams from the London area for a game which England won 1-0. The staging caused a stir north of the border. The players representing 'Scotland' had only tenuous bonds at best with the country, connections that were, in one writer's words 'imagined rather than real'. One player's link was an annual visit to his Scottish country estate while another's was merely a liking for Scotch whisky. The Scots claimed the Rugby code was their game and a month after the soccer defeat they challenged England's rugby fraternity to accept a 'return' match under Rugby rules.

England's public schools had promoted team spirit and muscular Christianity in parallel during the nineteenth century. The doctrines of Dr Thomas Arnold, the headmaster of Rugby School, spread rapidly through the educational establishments of the four kingdoms of the British Isles and by the mid-1850s Rugby football was established as the main winter recreation at Edinburgh Academy, whose pupils were to shine the torch for Scottish rugby for most of the next fifty years. Foremost among the early rugby-playing Academicals was the Hon. Francis Moncreiff, who put his name to the challenge issued to the English rugby fraternity, lighting the blue touch paper that set international rugby ablaze and captaining Scotland's first international team against England on the Academy's own grounds at Raeburn Place in 1871 in front of a crowd estimated to be 4,000 strong.

Until the 1880s, matches could only be decided by a majority of goals, rendering tries worthless unless converted. Scotland won that first match by converting a try that was hotly disputed by the English team.

R W 'Bulldog' Irvine (Scotland 1871-1880, 13 Caps): For some years previous, an annual match had been played in London – an International match it was called – according to the laws of the dribbling game. England usually won [and the] match attracted only a sort of curiosity in Scotland [until] the idea dawned: 'If there is to be an International match, let it be a real one, and don't let the relative merits of England and Scotland in football matters be decided purely by Association football, let us ask them to send a Rugby team north and play us on our native heath.'

A H Robertson, F J Moncreiff, B Hall Blyth, J W Arthur, J H Oatts [representing the interests of Scotland's rugby fraternity]: There is a pretty general feeling among Scotch football players that the football power of the old country was not properly represented in the late so-called International Football Match. Not that we think the play of

Opposite: Bill MacLagan

the gentlemen who represented Scotland otherwise than very good – for that it was so is amply proved by the stout resistance they offered to their opponents and by the fact that they were beaten by only one goal – but that we consider the Association rules, in accordance with which the late game was played, not such as to bring together the best team Scotland could turn out. Almost all the leading clubs play by the Rugby code, and have no opportunity of practising the Association game even if willing to do so. We therefore feel that a match played in accordance with any rules other than those in general use in Scotland, as was the case in the last match, is not one that would meet with support generally from her players. For our satisfaction, therefore, and with a view of really testing what Scotland can do against an English team we, as representing

Robert 'Bulldog' Irvine

the football interests of Scotland, hereby challenge any team selected from the whole of England, to play us a match, twenty-a-side, Rugby rules either in Edinburgh or Glasgow on any day during the present season that might be found suitable to the English players. Let this count as the return to the match played in London on 19th November [1870], or, if preferred, let it be a separate match. If it be entered into we can promise England a hearty welcome and a first-rate match. Any communications addressed to any one of us will be attended to.

Bulldog Irvine: A team was selected without wrangle and without jealousy, and invitations were sent to the team to play in a great match, and responded to with alacrity. The first team was selected from Edinburgh Academicals, Edinburgh University, Royal HSFP, St Andrews, Merchistonians, Glasgow Academicals and West of Scotland. The men were requested to get into training, and did it. It was twenty-a-side, and the Scotch forwards were heavy and fast. We were ignorant of what team England would bring, of what sort of players they had, and of how they would play; and though assured by Colville, a London Merchistonian – and a rare good forward, too – that we would find their size, strength and weight not very materially different from our own, many of us entered that match with a sort of vague fear that some entirely new kind of play would be shown by our opponents.

The day of the match soon settled that uncertainty. The English twenty were big and heavy – probably bigger and heavier than ours – but not overpoweringly so. Before we had played ten minutes we were on good terms with each other. Each side had made a discovery – we that our opponents were flesh and blood like ourselves, and could be mauled back and tackled and knocked about just like other men; they that in this far north land Rugby players existed who could maul, tackle, and play-up with the best of them.

Scotland's first international team.

Hely Hutchinson Almond (Scottish Umpire: Scotland v England 1871): Let me make a personal confession. I was umpire, and I do not know to this day whether the decision which gave Scotland the try from which the winning goal was kicked was correct in fact. The ball had certainly been scrummaged over the line by Scotland, and touched down first by a Scotchman. The try was, however, vociferously disputed by the English team, but upon what ground I was then unable to discover. I must say, however, that when an umpire is in doubt, I think he is justified in deciding against the side which makes the most noise. They are probably in the wrong.

Bulldog Irvine: There was one critical time during the match. Feeling was pretty highly strung. It was among the first no-hacking matches for many of the players on both sides. Now, hackimg becomes an instinctive action to one trained to it; you hack at a man running past out of reach as surely as you blink when a man puts his finger in your eye. There were a good many hacks-over going on, and, as blood got up it began to be muttered, 'Hang it! Why not have hacking allowed? It can't be prevented – far better have it.' The question hung in the balance. The captains (Moncreiff and Stokes) both looked as if they ought to say 'no' but would rather say 'yes', and were irresolute, when Almond, who was umpire, vowed he would throw up his job if it were agreed on, it was forbidden and the hackers were ordered to be more cautious.

The match was won by Scotland by a goal and a try to a try – the Scotch goal being placed by Cross (not Malcolm, but his big brother) from a very difficult kick – and though many matches have been played since then between the countries, there has not been one better fought or more exciting than this, the first one.

The Scotsmen were exultant, and the winning ball hung for many a day in the shop of Johnnie Bowton at the Stock Bridge, adorned with ribbons like the tail of a Clydesdale stallion at a horse show. With this match and victory the life of rugby football as a national institution faily commencd.

Scottish rugby football may be said to have sprung up from boyhood to robust manhood with the first international match in 1871.

England gained revenge at The Oval in 1872 through a dropped goal and the 1873 game, played in difficult conditions in Glasgow, ended in a draw – a match that, it was said, did little to promote rugby in the city. It was a memorable affair for one of the Scottish pack. Peter Anton, a divinity student at St Andrews, described it years later as being 'as hard an international as has ever been played.' Immediately after that match a landmark initiative driven by a group comprising leading players from the Edinburgh Academicals, Merchistonians and Glasgow Academicals clubs resulted in the formation of the Scottish Union with a remit to select future international teams, a task that was greatly helped by the launch of the Glasgow v Edinburgh 'Inter-City' match the same season.

The early internationals were staged on Mondays and played between teams of 20-a-side comprising thirteen forwards, three halves, a single threequarter and three fullbacks. This was the shoving age. Forwards converged around held players and formed primitive scrummages by leaning or pushing against opponents. Heads were kept up, forwards barging or kicking the ball through. Halves acted as the first line of defence, with the sole threequarter and back-three in support to catch punts ahead, land field goals or claim marks to kick for territory.

Peter Anton (Scotland 1873, 1 Cap): What a proud man I was that day marching out of the little pavilion at Hamilton Crescent through a dense and greatly admiring and cheering crowd, and 'lined up' in front of the English! Did we not understand then the feelings of our sires at Bannockburn?

The game was not without its humours. If a dispute should arise, it was suggested that Joe Arthur should champion the Scottish side. Joe had an irresistible 'talking over' way with him, and seeing he was not in the team, it was thought some recognition should be made of his special powers!

Again, seeing the ground was to be sloppy, the English team went into a cobbler's to get leather bars fixed to the soles of their boots. I presume the cobbler was nothing worse than a 'Scots-wha-hae' patriot. When the job was done, the boots and feet could not be got to correspond. The players [had to] put on dress shoes on the bootless feet.

Bulldog Irvine: The third International match was played in Glasgow at Partick. The ground was a quagmire, and the match ended in a draw, after a game which must have been monotonous to a degree to the onlookers, and must have had a great deal to do with de-popularising the Rugby game in Glasgow. It was one succession of weary mauls, broken by an occasional rush. The impression left was that of a muddy, wet, struggling hundred minutes of steamy mauls.

Peter Anton: Owing to the nature of the atmosphere, so soon as the packs were formed, a great column of steam rose right up from the scrummage, and bent eastward with the wind. The pressure [the English forwards] brought to bear on us was of the strongest. [They] worked with desperate resolution and they were within an ace of succeeding.

They compelled us to form a maul within three yards of our goal-line. It was evident the game had reached a crisis, and the excitement was wound up to the highest pitch. Almost by instinct the Scotsmen allowed their St Andrews representative [Anton himself] take the centre of the scrummage.

For some time there was not a single movement either way. The pressure was tremendous. The English then pressed the Scotsmen a foot or two to the rear. Goaded to their utmost, they stopped their backward movement, and after a space we found ourselves gaining. Inch by inch we pressed them back and the St Andrews man, who to prevent heeling had kept the ball between his boots the whole time, was able to snatch it up, and make a very creditable run, and so ended in a draw as hard an International as has ever been played.

Ninian Finlay (Scotland 1875-1881, 9 Caps): I was too young then [on debut v England in 1875] to do anything more than enjoy the game keenly. I remember being struck by Hay Gordon's play. My admiration may have been partly due to his being new to me. He played his club matches in England, while most of the others were familiar to me either as Edinburgh Academicals or as opponents whom we often met in club matches.

Of the players, the most familiar name to me is Irvine, familiarly and universally known as 'Bulldog.' I am sure he contributed more to Scotland's holding her own in the match than would appear from reports.

Bulldog Irvine: The International of 1875 was played in Edinburgh, and was a draw – as usual, Scotland fully holding its own forward. The number of shaves the Scotch goal had from the dropping of Pearson and Mitchell that day no Scotsman playing will ever forget. A draw in favour of England.

Ninian Finlay: In those days the forwards had to carry the maul ('scrum' as it is now called) towards their opponents' goal and, when the players came through, the dribbling in loose scrum was most scientific and pretty to watch. 'Bulldog' excelled in the maul and, but for his play and the play of others like him, the forward rush towards the opponents' goal would not have come off.

W E 'Bill' Maclagen (Scotland 1878-1890, 26 Caps plus 3 Caps for the Lions): The game has changed very much in appearance, but, as a matter of fact, it is very difficult to point to any great difference that has taken place. There are really very few, although they have had considerable effect. First of all, coming down from twenty to fifteen made an enormous difference. After that there was the growth of less foot and more hand, which was very gradual and probably reached its height of excellence in Harry Vassall's Oxford years (1879-1882), and has since then probably been a little overdone.

Bulldog Irvine: 1877 saw a change. An agreement had at last been come to regarding the fifteen-a-side, and it was to be tried this time. Scotland routed Ireland at Belfast. In this match Ireland showed much good material, but it was raw. If Scotland had the best of it on the field, the vanquished were the victors at the social board. Flushed with this victory, Scotland met England full of confidence a fortnight after in Edinburgh. The match was fast and furious to a degree never before seen in an International. Within five minutes of 'No side', Graham got the ball and chucked to Malcolm Cross [who], quick as lightning, dropped at goal. The match was won and we felt that our long struggle for fifteen-a-side had not been in vain.

Ninian Finlay: Malcolm Cross, who played threequarter back, was a familiar figure beside me in Internationals. He was magnificent. We always dropped in those days. Punting became more usual [later] and came to stay. There was more individual effort in running with the ball, not so much passing – or 'chucking' as we used to call it.

The strength of early Scottish rugby was forward play and two Edinburgh Academy alumni, Robert 'Bulldog' Irvine succeeded by Charles 'Hippo' Reid, were ever-present in the Scottish international packs from 1871 until 1888. Irvine, a red-headed forward capped as a teenager, played throughout Scotland's first decade of International rugby before passing the baton on to Reid, who entered the Scottish pack in 1881 while still at school. The Academy had the curious distinction of providing two of their boys for the Scotland-England game at Raeburn Place that year. Frank Wright, a boarder from Manchester, was pressed into action against his form-mate when an English half-back missed the train to Edinburgh. Harry Stevenson, who would go on to play fifteen matches for Scotland between 1888 and 1893, was present for Assembly in the main hall at Edinburgh Academy the following morning. He later recalled that: 'Hippo and Frank came in with their class just as Tommy [Harvey, the rector] did to say prayers. There was no prayers that day! We cheered and cheered and cheered – and Tommy gave it up!'

Drawn matches have peppered rugby's oldest international fixture. To this day there have been more between Scotland and England than between any other countries. There were four in the 1870s, including the 1879 match at Raeburn Place – the first to be played for the Calcutta Cup, which had been presented to the Rugby Football Union in London on the dissolution of the Calcutta club in India. Ninian Finlay, another Academy former pupil who had been first-capped as a schoolboy, was an established part of the Scottish back division by then and his drop-kick levelled the scores at a goal each that day. Irvine's play as captain at the heart of the pack and Bill Maclagen's defence as their sole fullback had much to do with Scotland sharing the trophy.

Oxford and Cambridge meanwhile were in the vanguard of change, experimenting in 1875 by altering sides from 20- to 15-a-side, a move that was supported in Scotland because reducing numbers made it easier for clubs to field teams. Backs, moreover, had more scope to display skills and by 1877 international teams had followed suit. Scotland reaped the benefit, overwhelming Ireland in the first match between the nations (in Belfast) and beating the old enemy by a Malcolm Cross drop-goal to nil.

The game quickly evolved from the shoving age. Mauls and 'scrummages' became less protracted with fewer players in the packs. Students at Oxford University exploited the possibilities. Many were from Scottish schools where, it has been said, the 'passing' game first developed in the late 1870s. Oxford had a particularly successful side that regularly included several former pupils of Loretto and, under the influence of their captain, Henry ('Harry') Vassall, perfected a passing game that later extended to international teams. Two of Vassall's leading lieutenants became Scottish internationalists: forward James Walker and, behind the scrum, Grant Asher, who later formed Scotland's first established half-back pairing with 'Bunny' Don Wauchope.

Walker made his Scotland debut in the 1882 Calcutta Cup match in Manchester when 'Hippo' Reid and the Scottish pack were described as 'one of the finest forward divisions that ever played.' Scotland won by two tries to nil, a change in the scoring system now allowing a majority of tries to prevail when no goals were scored. It was the first time that the visiting side won the Scotland/England fixture.

Scotland met Wales for the first time in 1883 and a side that had won seven of its eight previous internationals faced England in 1884 in a game that was viewed as the showdown of the season. Internationals now took place on Saturdays and a record crowd approaching ten thousand made its way to Blackheath to see the visitors, with Don Wauchope and Grant Asher firmly in harness at half-back, lose by a conversion. The try from which England kicked the winning goal, however, caused controversy.

A Scot had 'knocked back' in the move leading to England's try – an infringement under Scottish rules. England supported the referee, a respected former Irish international, saying his decision was final. Besides, why should Scotland profit from their own mistake? The Scots wanted settlement by an independent adjudicator and a lengthy wrangle ensued, resulting in cancellation of the 1885 Calcutta Cup match.

The Irish Union intervened suggesting a meeting to consider forming an International Board to resolve disputes. The concept of a Board crystallised in Dublin in February 1886, Scotland later conceding the 1884 match to England on condition that the RFU join a Board comprising an equal number of members from each of the Four Nations. Scotland could argue from a position of strength on the field. Between 1884 and 1888 they played *nine international matches and were never beaten, with only drawn matches against England in 1886 and 1887 blotting their copybook. Sensing the Board would become the game's sole law-makers, however, the RFU in London rejected Scotland's ultimatum. 'Hippo' Reid, leading Scotland for the last time, bowed out of international rugby on a low-key in 1888 by suffering defeat by Wales for the first time before scraping home with a narrow victory over Ireland.*

Charles 'Hippo' Reid

Charles 'Hippo' Reid (Scotland 1881-1888, 21 Caps): Give me a forward team like we had at Manchester in 1882 and I don't care how many three-quarter backs you have; we could go through them. We dribbled very close, and one backed up the other so well they could not get away, and they had fliers like Bolton against us. Dribbling and tackling are the characteristics of the Scottish forwards, and on them we depend to win.

A R 'Bunny' Don Wauchope (Scotland 1881-1888, 13 Caps): I played in the [1884] match and I know the [dispute] subject pretty well. The ball was thrown out of touch, an appeal was made, the umpire on the touch-line held up his stick, all the players, with the exception of four Englishmen and two Scotsmen, stopped playing, and England scored a try. The only question of fact decided by the referee was that a Scotsman knocked the ball back. This, according to the Scottish reading of the rule was illegal, and the whole question turned on the interpretation.

The point that no Englishman had appealed was never raised at the time, and to judge by the fact that eleven of the English team ceased play, it would appear that their idea was that the game should stop. I do not know of any other point of fact on which the referee decided the try was valid.

Bulldog Irvine: After the lapse of two years we renewed hostilities [with England in 1886], and at Raeburn Place had a great game which resulted in a scoreless draw. This, in our opinion, was one of the best matches in the series, and we very narrowly missed winning it.

It is doubtful if C.Reid ever played a better game than he did on this occasion. He was the forward of his time. There was no man to compare with him in England Scotland, Ireland or Wales. Neither was there before nor has there been since. His football at all points was perfect. His speed was much above that of the average forward, and in many matches he made as big runs as the backs. In fact, [against England in 1886] his run in the second half was the best performance of its kind of the day.

Roughness has been imputed to him, but the charge is almost groundless, and if on occasion he did use his strength, it must be remembered in extenuation that he had to put up with all manner of annoying attentions, often from aspiring individuals who would have preferred the distinction of having knocked down C.Reid to the honour of half a dozen International caps.

Alexander Clay (Scotland 1886-1888, 7 Caps): ['Hippo' Reid] played hard, but he always played with characteristic good

A R 'Bunny' Don Wauchope

nature. Perhaps the best test is that Reid was universally popular amongst the players of opposing teams. He may not have had the irresistible dash of forwards of the type of the Ainslies in Scotland, but no one could gain more ground with the ball at his feet than Reid, and it was no uncommon sight, even in International matches, to see him dribble through nearly all the opposing backs.

Bulldog Irvine: During 1888 the 'unfortunate dispute' in another phase cropped up again, and robbed us of our great match [against England]. Our pride was much hurt by Wales beating us at Newport. On that occasion we played three centre threequarters, HJ Stevenson, MM Duncan and WE Maclagen with CE Orr and CFP Fraser as our halves. The latter division were blamed for our defeat, but no section of the team played above itself.

TWO

FORWARD DEBATE
1889-1907

Forward muscularity had been the strength of Scottish rugby in its first two decades of international matches, every bit as fundamental to their approach to the game as was the muscular Christianity that had shaped the public schools that spawned the Rugby Union code of football in the earlier part of the century. An honest, straightforward approach to forward play that matched the national character had become well-established, an essential part of Scotland's early rugby legacy. By the end of the 1880s, however, change was in the air.

The passing game practised so effectively by the Oxford sides of the early years of the decade had been extended to passing among half-backs, and even threequarters were beginning to throw passes as their roles evolved from defence into opportunities for attack. Forwards, too, were experimenting in a way that diluted the effectiveness of traditional Scottish pack play. In the other Home Unions, forwards were beginning to use 'winging' forwards to break off scrummages, while heeling the ball back – rudimentary 'hooking' of the ball – was emerging as an alternative to the shoving game.

This was anathema to dyed-in-the-wool Scottish forwards. To them, scrummages were about keeping heads down and pushing, about driving the ball through the opposition before forcing it free to initiate dribbling attacks when scrums broke up. 'Feet, Scotland, Feet' was the exhortation born from such a tactic, but with the development of winging and hooking, approaches required change.

The Welsh had taken matters further than most. Between 1886 and 1888 they explored reducing their packs from nine to eight by inserting the extra man in the threequarter line. Their pioneering of the so-called 'four threequarter' system was the single biggest development of the late nineteenth century that transformed the game into the one it most closely resembles today.

Scotland were resistant to change. The idea of 'winging' forwards detaching from the scrum and not pushing was viewed with contempt, as was the concept of making forwards subservient to backs by heeling the ball back for the halves to launch attacks. 'Bulldog' Irvine and 'Hippo' Reid took a stand supporting the old-style game, and for some time resistance paid off.

England, after a three year expulsion, finally buried their differences with the other Home Unions over representation on the International Board in 1890, rejoining the round-robin of matches comprising the International Championship, an entirely unofficial tournament which owed its name to an invention of the press. Scotland, under the veteran Bill Maclagen's captaincy, opened their season with convincing wins against Wales and Ireland before losing a Championship-decider to England at Raeburn Place. England, who had earlier suffered a freak defeat to Wales in Dewsbury, thus shared the unofficial title with the Scots.

Opposite: Paul Clauss

The year later, Scotland won their first Triple Crown – the game's Holy Grail of beating the other three Home Unions in the same season. 'Saxon' McEwan was an old-school captain who led a settled pack that skilfully applied time-honoured Scottish forward methods. Gala's Adam Dalgleish, the first player capped from a Borders club, a roly-poly forward named John Boswell with an unusual penchant for dropping goals from short range, 'Judy' MacMillan, Bert Leggatt, Jack Orr, Ian MacIntyre, George Neilson and Fred Goodhue completed as fine a nine-man pack as any Scotland fielded.

Scotland wracked up thirty-eight points without reply that season, before England managed a late consolation score in the Triple Crown game. Scotland registered landslide victories over Wales and Ireland and had the Calcutta Cup match at Richmond sewn up at 9-0 before conceding their only score of the campaign ten minutes from time.

Among a talented back division were the former Edinburgh Academy boy Harry Stevenson, who was regarded as the outstanding kicker of his day, an expert at the snap dropped goal and a deadly place kicker whom The Scotsman described as 'the greatest football player in the world.' Lining out with him among the backs were three of the best in the Home Unions: Gregor Macgregor, the threequarter with the fly-paper hands who kept wicket in Test cricket for England, Charles Orr (younger brother of Jack) and Paul Clauss, a prolific try-scorer of German descent on the wing.

The Home Unions took turns to claim the Triple Crown between 1891 and 1894, but arguably the most significant success of the period was Wales's in 1893. They finally

The Scotland team that played England in 1891.
Standing: GT Neilson, JD Boswell, JE Orr, HTO Leggatt, WR Gibson, RG MacMillan
Seated: FWJ Goodhue, HJ Stevenson, MC McEwan (captain), CE Orr, I MacIntyre
In front: G MacGregor, DG Anderson, PRA Clauss, W Neilson

demonstrated the value of their eight forwards, four threequarter system by carrying all before them, and the rest of the national sides were so impressed that they all converted to the Welsh system the year later.

Scotland, despite fierce criticism from the diehards, quickly adapted to the new formation and adopted new concepts in forward play to regain the Triple Crown in 1895 when MacMillan (now as captain) and Neilson were still at the heart of a forward effort which had been joined by Willie McEwan (younger brother of 'Saxon') and Tom Scott, the first in a long line of Hawick forwards to establish himself as a fixture in Scottish packs.

Rugby was growing in popularity and increasing public demand for admission to big matches meant that the Edinburgh Academy playing fields at Raeburn Place were no longer suitable for staging international rugby. The Scottish Union took the initiative and began looking for a new home. The last Scottish international to be played on what has been called 'the mother of international rugby grounds' took place in early March 1895, a 6-0 win against Ireland in the second leg of the Triple Crown season. The Scottish Union staged home matches at Glasgow's Hampden Park and the Powderhall Gardens in Edinburgh in the three seasons that followed, before in 1899 unveiling a spanking new stadium of its own, specially designed to host international rugby.

Harry Stevenson: [In the late 1880s] 'Hippo' Reid used to come out of the scrum, when we were just inside [opponents'] twenty-five – the most dangerous part of the ground – and stand behind our halves and in front of me [playing centre], either to one side or the other. He was splendid there [acting as a proto-'wing forward']: he had a chance of scoring himself or passing back to me. When 'Hippo' was out, I always closed near him. It got us tries and wins.

Bulldog Irvine: The English international of 1890 was a very bad one for us. A great surprise was sprung upon the country in the selection of W.E.Maclagen. Our half-backs were blamed for losing the match [but] where we really lost the game was in the scrummage, where the English took possession of the ball, and held our forwards while [the English halves] nipped it back to their [threequarters]. The match taught us this species of attack most impressively, and when our team went to London in 1891 and scored our greatest victory, the English press complained that we had learned it too well. Our forwards undoubtedly won us this match, and our backs were seen to great advantage. Our threequarters, W Neilson, G MacGregor, and P Clauss, were scoring men and behind winning forwards were all that was wanted.

Harry Stevenson: Long before I got to the first-class football stage I came to the conclusion that there was nothing to compete with an old pair of ordinary black walking boots, or shoes. They had been made to fit you, were comfortable from use, light and bendable, and their soles were thin. Thick soled boots or shoes for football is, I think, a mistake. Just the opposite of cricket.

I always had two thin and narrow bars, straight across the flat of the foot – no bar

Brothers George and Willie Neilson.

on the heel. Others also wore everyday boots. I think Bill Maclagen did. Another reason in my opinion for light, thinnish soled boots or shoes for football is you feel the ground better. You are never still for two seconds, or oughtn't to be, and the ground is generally softer and more springy [in winter] than is the rule at cricket.

Bunny Don Wauchope: I have always been a strong opponent of this 'new' game. Beat them well forward, and you have the game won. Many forwards play as if the threequarters were the only real players on the side; consequently they never do their own share of the play. Swing the scrummage, then it is that the backs get a real chance, and then it is that the opposing backs are run over by the forwards. If our Scottish forwards will play their own good game I should not have any doubt. Forwards who are continually trying to play for their backs will invariably be beaten.

Bulldog Irvine: HJ Stevenson, MC McEwan, CE Orr, and RG MacMillan are the prominent men of the last three years [1889-1892]. Orr, in the true sense of the word, is one of our best all-round halves, McEwan is one of our great forwards, a powerful player, strong in all points of the game. Of Stevenson it has to be said we never had a more versatile player. His defence at threequarters in 1890 materially kept down the score [against England], and when the Union saw fit to place him at fullback in 1891 and 1892 he filled the position as adequately as any man ever we had. Centre, however, is his true place, and in it he has never been known to play a poor game, a fitting testimony to the merit of one of the most remarkable players the country has produced, and a back who will be remembered along with N.J.Finlay, W.E.Maclagen and A.R.Don Wauchope.

Harry Stevenson: When I dropped a goal in 1891 against Wales I am afraid I can't say [whether I wore] shoes or boots. I don't think it matters for dropping, for I think it is the spot on the ball where the impact comes, also the angle of the ball and timing, which gives it direction and distance, which counts. You punt with the instep, but I have seen my old friend JD Boswell drop goals from his instep, from very short distances of course, inside the twenty-five.

Bill Maclagen: Then there was the change introduced by Wales, called by most people the four threequarters. I think that is probably the proper name for it; but it took several years for it to find favour; and in my humble opinion it might never have found favour, might absolutely have died of inanition, but for the introduction and permission of heeling out. I advisedly say permission, because I am not quite satisfied in my own mind that it really is legalised to this day [long applause].

RG 'Judy' Macmillan (Scotland 1887-1897, 21 Caps plus 3 Caps for the Lions): As to the influence of the Welsh system on Scottish forwards, I consider it will be deteriorating, as they will lose all their old dash. I don't say there should be no heeling out, but as the game stands at present the attention of the forwards is entirely given up to it. The older players may be able to stick to the old genuine game which they learned at the schools, but the younger ones will not be taught to put down their heads and shove, and will shirk and become loafers.

HTO 'Bert' Leggatt (Scotland 1891-1894, 9 Caps): My opinion of the four threequarter system generally is that it is much showier, and, therefore, more attractive to the spectators. The passing is easily spoiled when the tackling is determined and vigorous. I prefer the Scottish style, undoubtedly, for this substantial reason: Watsonians, who play essentially a Scottish game, played, under unequal conditions, the strongest Newport fifteen, who are acknowledged to be facile princeps in the four threequarter game, and morally beat them [in January 1894]. I think the Scottish forwards would lose their strong points, rushes and footwork, if they adopted the Welsh system.

Dedicated followers of Scottish rugby could take pride in events on and off the field as the old century closed and the new one began. A new state-of-the-art ground with its own press pavilion and accommodating more than 20,000 spectators – the first owned by any of the Four Home Unions – together with four outright Championship titles and a resounding success against the first Springboks were the highlights of the seasons that heralded in the Twentieth Century. Scottish rugby supporters had plenty to relish.

James Aikman Smith, the honorary secretary/treasurer who was to serve both the

Union and International Board as an administrator committed to the true-blue ideals of amateurism, was the official responsible for realising the potential of Inverleith on a site in the north-east of Edinburgh. His vision of a home for Scottish rugby took barely two years to reach fruition and by 1899, thanks to his financial acumen and organisational powers, the ground was ready to stage its first international.

There was an inauspicious start. The intention was to open the ground for the Welsh match in January, but the weather intervened causing a postponement. As a result, the Irish became the first visitors in February, spoiling the Union's topping-out ceremony by defeating Scotland 9-3 on their way to a Triple Crown. When Wales, however, finally pitched up for their rearranged fixture a fortnight later, Scotland completed their first international season at the ground with a stylish 21-10 win – their most emphatic victory over the Principality since the adoption of the four threequarter system.

CD 'Charlie' Stuart (Scotland 1909-1911, 7 Caps): The Scottish Union realised it was imperative they find a ground of their own and in season 1898-99 Inverleith, capable of accommodating 25,000 spectators, was opened.

England appeared there for the first time the following season [when] Scotland were led by that great forward, Mark Morrison. Incidentally this was the first time the National Anthem was played at [a Scotland] international. The game ended in a pointless draw. On the whole Scotland had the better of matters but had no reason to complain about the result.

Andrew 'Jock' Wemyss (Scotland 1914-1922, 7 Caps): Wales should have been the first country to visit Inverleith. The reason for Ireland playing the first game there was said to be that the Scottish Union feared that the grass on the new pitch was too young to withstand trampling and tearing by Welsh boots, but that in another week or two it would be stronger. Wales, of course, were not happy about the change of date, but they chortled when Ireland made their 'first-footing' a memorable occasion by winning and going on to gain the Triple Crown.

TM 'Tom' Scott (Scotland 1893-1900, 12 Caps): It was a hard game throughout, and we were fairly beaten on the merits of the game.

Mark Morrison (Scotland 1896-1904, 23 Caps plus 3 Caps for the Lions): The long and short of it is the Welsh team was too good for us. We were beaten in every department of the game. Even in the first half the Welsh forwards controlled the scrummages sufficiently to enable them to get the ball every time, and in the second half the Welsh forwards completely overran us. I might say, however, that our forwards were not so well trained as they might have been. We were also well beaten at half, at threequarter, and at fullback.

Scotland produced a clutch of inspirational captains and pack leaders at the turn of the century. Tom Scott, the first Border forward to command automatic selection over a long international career (1893-1900), Mark Morrison and David Bedell-Sivright could

The Scotland team that faced Ireland in 1899.

Standing: HO Smith, RC Stevenson, A Mackinnon, WMC McEwan, MC Morrison, RT Neilson, JM Reid

Seated: T Scott, JT Mabon, JH Couper, WP Donaldson (captain), GC Kerr, GT Campbell, L Harvey

In front: DB Monypenny

inspire teams to play beyond their potential. Indeed, it was often said south of Hadrian's Wall that Scottish packs of these times were worth considerably more than the sum of their parts. Morrison had become captain for the 1899 win against Wales at Inverleith and went on to captain Scotland fifteen times until 1904, missing only two games through injury. He led quietly, but his record spoke volumes. He carried out his duties unobtrusively but extracted the best from teams that were happy to follow his shining example.

Jock Wemyss: Mark Morrison, Scotland's famous captain at the beginning of [the 20th Century], heads my brief list of great Scottish players. He was one of the greatest forwards the game has seen with a [then] unequalled record as a captain. In fifteen of his twenty-three internationals he led Scotland and his name is inscribed five times on the Calcutta Cup.

Mark Morrison: Now, in the 1901 Triple Crown season, I used to tell my players before each game that there were just three things they had to do. The first was – get the ball. The second was – get the ball. And the third was – get the ball. And if they didn't know what to do with it when they had it, then they had no right to be there.

Jock Wemyss: I never saw Mark [Morrison] play, though I knew him well in my playing days and after, but from his contemporaries and others I have heard what a really outstanding forward he was.

There are many stories about his blunt forthrightness. Once, when Mark had been

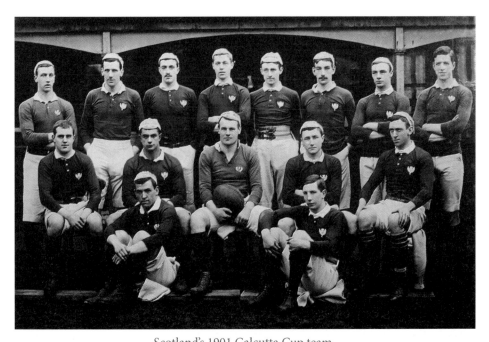

Scotland's 1901 Calcutta Cup team.

Standing: WH Welsh, AB Flett, AW Duncan, RS Stronach, Phipps Turnbull, JA Bell, A Frew, JM Dykes
Seated: JI Gillespie, DR Bedell-Sivright, MC Morrison (captain), AN Fell, AB Timms
In front: J Ross, RM Neill

delayed in reaching a scrum, he dived into the back-row and, as an urge to greater endeavour, shouted: 'Come on now, boys, somebody's not shoving. Who is it; who is it?' The immediate loud retort in unison was: 'Mark Morrison.'

Charlie Stuart: During the stay at Inverleith Scotland were very strong particularly from the opening year till 1908. If Mark Morrison was the greatest of all forwards there were others who ranked almost equally high, J.M.Dykes, W.E.Kyle, J.C.MacCallum, D.R.Bedell-Sivright, J.M.B.Scott and W.M.C.McEwan, and there was almost an embarrassing richness behind the scrum. E.D.Simson could claim to be regarded as the greatest half-back who ever put foot on a Rugby field, and J.I.Gillespie, R.M.Neill, Pat Munro, John Knox, F.H.Fasson and L.L.Greig would have been internationalists in any generation. Of the threequarters, Phipps Turnbull, A.B.Timms, W.H.Welsh, the brothers MacLeod, A.N.Fell, J.E.Crabbie, G.A.W.Lamond and A.L.Purves were truly great.

The early years of the 20th century are invariably known as the First Welsh Golden Era, but in truth Scotland shared the honours with the Principality, at least between 1900 and 1907. Morrison's men were beaten but not disgraced by four tries to one at Swansea in their opening match of the new century, but revenge against the Welsh at Inverleith in 1901 and

1903 was distinctly sweet, setting up memorable Triple Crown seasons. In his last year at the helm, in 1904, Morrison and his band had to come to terms with a heavy defeat at Swansea before recovering to win the Championship title outright with wins in Dublin and at home to England. Morrison was arguably the Geoffrey Chaucer of Scottish rugby's equivalent of Poet's Corner – a trailblazing skipper whose record was nine wins and a draw from fifteen matches in charge. In between, he also led the British/Irish Lions to South Africa in 1903 while Bedell-Sivright, his able lieutenant and the man they called 'Darkie' on account of his swarthy complexion, captained the Lions to Australia and New Zealand the following summer – the only player in Lions history to make tours in successive years.

Old-timers like Charlie Stuart and Andrew 'Jock' Wemyss, Scottish internationalists from the early 1900s who later became respected critics, used to say their older colleagues rated the Scottish side of 1901 as the best of the pre-Great War era. It was certainly one of the youngest sides to represent the country and opened the campaign with eight new caps against Wales, whose pack had dominated the Scots the year before. To counteract Welsh forward power, Scotland's selectors chose a team capable of attacking from all quarters. There was a fast, young back division featuring five Edinburgh University students complemented by two mature Edinburgh Academicals, Phipps Turnbull, a polished centre, and Johnnie Gillespie, a wonderful all-round player, at half-back. The mix of youth and experience proved a winning formula, the latter pair creating openings for the young guns to run riot. Wales, the reigning Triple Crown holders, were sent home to contemplate an unexpected 18-8 (four-tries-to-one) defeat – a real thrashing by the conservative scoring values of the day. There was no holding Morrison's team after that and the Triple Crown came north of the border when England were overrun 18-3 at Blackheath, three of the visiting three-quarters crossing in what remains the biggest Scottish winning margin against the auld enemy on English soil.

It is a curiosity of British rugby that so often a team winning the Championship has completely failed to repeat its success the next season. 1902 was a case in point. Scotland, with virtually an unchanged fifteen, lost all three games, albeit narrowly, before regaining the Triple Crown in 1903 and sending Morrison into retirement in 1904 celebrating another Championship title after a 19-3 win against Ireland in Dublin and a tight 6-3 verdict over England at Inverleith.

Andrew Flett (Scotland 1901-1902, 5 Caps): Johnnie Gillespie [was] one of the best and most efficient and original half backs Scotland ever had. He was always in command of the game however tense the situation might be. He handled the ball beautifully and his defence was clever and effective, while his unorthodox methods kept his opponents in a state of bewilderment. In the Welsh match of 1901 Scotland was pressing Wales in their twenty-five and the forwards heeled quickly. Gillespie, instead of passing out to his threes as was expected, kept the ball on the ground and like a flash dribbled right through his opponents and scored between the posts. His footwork was exceptional and he could dribble like a soccer professional. He scored the first try in each of the three matches in that champion year.

Charlie Stuart: Scotland scooped the pool [in 1901] and it was a fertile argument at the time whether the team of 1891 or of 1901 was the greatest Scotland ever put on the Rugby field. However, if the latter side reached the heights in 1901 it touched the depths the following year. Practically unchanged they lost all three internationals, a thing which had never happened previously.

Andrew Flett: Phipps Turnbull [was] a star of the first magnitude, an incomparable centre threequarter, certainly one of the most polished who have ever played the game. Tall and not very robust, he was a fearless tackler and his handling of the ball was unsurpassed, but it was as a runner that he excelled. With a very long stride, he seemed to glide through the opposing defence at high speed, apparently without effort.

JE 'Jack' Crabbie (Scotland 1900-1905, 6 Caps): It is really best for the same half always to take the base of the scrum, and the other always to stand back and hand on to his threequarters.

Jock Wemyss: D.R.Bedell-Sivright was another of the many great forwards early in the century. He gained twenty-two caps, captained Scotland in the famous match against the first All Blacks at Inverleith, and, like Mark Morrison, captained a British Touring team. 'Darkie' Sivright was a very, very hard player of immense strength whose fiery determination on the field so often led to the accusation that he was 'over-zealous.'

David 'Darkie' Bedell-Sivright (Scotland 1900-1908, 22 Caps plus 1 Cap for the Lions): When I go on to the field I only see the ball. Wherever it goes, I go too, and if someone gets in my way that is his look-out.

Jock Wemyss: Johnny Dykes, who was SRU President in my last year in the team; WP 'Bummer' Scott; AG'Sox' Cairns and Hugh Monteith were all in the class of Morrison in the early years of the century.

Tactically Rugby football was evolving. Welsh Triple Crowns of 1900, 1902 and 1905 that alternated with Scotland's successes were put down to clever forward play backed by fast threequarter lines. Welsh packs were more scientific in their approach to the game than elsewhere in the Home Unions. Strong forwards, products of the physical ways of life of the working communities of South Wales's heavy industries, perfected the art of heeling the ball out for fast, imaginative backs to exploit openings and create overlaps for wings to score tries.

Specialisation at half-back began there with the pioneers of specific stand-off and scrum-half roles emerging in the late 1890s. The practice slowly spread to the Scottish clubs through their ties with their leading Welsh counterparts and, by the mid-1900s, the debate over specialisation was raging. It was a debate that was given added impetus by the visit to Europe of the first major touring side from overseas, the Original All Blacks of 1905.

The New Zealanders had swept through the land like a gale of hurricane force before reaching Inverleith for the opening Test of their tour against Scotland in mid-November. Their focus was on constant backing-up of the player and they had specialist positions for half-backs behind forwards who packed in a fixed diamond-shaped, 2-3-2 scrum formation with a detached wing-forward or 'rover'. This 'loose' man had a dual role. Because the ball was heeled by the two New Zealand front-rankers kicking it back with their outside feet, possession emerged so swiftly that an auxiliary half-back was needed: one fed the scrum, the other gathered it as it emerged from the tunnel. On the opposition put-in, the rover blocked and obstructed to his heart's content, effectively putting extra pressure on the opposing side's backs. The rover, it seems, was the hybrid of a modern scrum-half and blind-side flanker.

David 'Darkie' Bedell-Sivright

Scotland's selectors faced a conundrum. How should they select their team to face the New Zealanders? At first they plumped for five threequarters with only seven men in the scrum. It was a recipe for disaster predicted old internationals in the match previews. Then, on the eve of the game, Dr Nolan Fell, a New Zealander who had been a dashing Edinburgh University wing in the 1901 and 1903 Scottish Triple Crown sides, declined to play against his countrymen and caused a last-minute change to plans. The Scots replaced him with an extra half-back barely an hour before kick-off, but stuck to their original decision to field seven forwards, thereby matching the New Zealand pack formation.

The match was surrounded by dramatic incidents. The Scottish Union originally refused to recognise it as a cap international and clearly underestimated the pulling power of the tourists. Such was the demand for admission to the ground that the attendance set a new Inverleith record with the entire gate money going to the New Zealanders. Apart from the late withdrawal of Fell, Scotland also had to make a late pack change when Hugh Monteith was injured. Then the charabanc carrying the Scottish side from the team's hotel to the Inverleith ground crashed when one of the horses drawing it slipped on an icy surface.

The great match eventually kicked-off on a frost-bound surface. Scotland, with seven new men, made a lively contribution to a thrilling match. They were far from disgraced by the all-conquering invaders from New Zealand and actually led 7-6 until five minutes from time, before the All Blacks maintained their unbeaten tour record with two late scores to win 12-7. All agreed they were deserving winners, but 'Darkie' Bedell-Sivright led his side with courage and enjoyed the plaudits of the All Blacks who were particularly impressed by Pat Munro, Ernest Simson and Louis Greig, the three Scottish half-backs, by John MacCallum – a try-scorer – among the pack, and by the 17-year-old debutant, K.G. (Kenneth) MacLeod, in the threequarter line.

Charlie Stuart: Scotland commenced with rare dash and New Zealand had to defend for all they were worth. After fifteen minutes' play Greig passed to ED Simson who dropped a goal. Five minutes later New Zealand scored an unconverted try and the struggle developed in intensity [and] GW Smith got a try in the corner. Just before the interval LM MacLeod kicked ahead. Instantly the forwards were up and touched down, KG MacLeod failing to add the extra points.

The second half was crowded with incident and was fast and furious. Five minutes from the end it looked as if Scotland might win. LM MacLeod tried to drop a goal. The ball went wide to GW Smith who ran the whole length to score a wonderful try. New Zealand scored again in the closing minutes and thus ended one of the fastest and best matches ever played. Scotland took great credit from the game [holding] the All Blacks to the closest result [12-7] of their tour to that date.

George Lamond (Scotland 1899-1905, 3 Caps): The wing forward game, as we have seen it played here during the [New Zealand tour], has not been a very edifying spectacle, nor one of instruction either. There can be no doubt that more than half the job a wing-forward is on the field for is to wilfully obstruct, but till the New Zealanders arrived here one has never seen any who wilfully obstructed the opposing half-backs. The formation of our visitors, if copied, will do a lot to throw all our sides hopelessly out of gear for the next couple of seasons.

MacLeod was the hero of Scotland's win against the Original Springboks exactly a year later. This time the Scottish Union were fully prepared for the Box Office draw of the early tour sides and rented Old Hampden Park in Glasgow for the occasion. A record crowd of 30,000 turned out to see a watertight defence flanked by wings of genuine pace behind a vigorous pack launch the most successful rugby season in Scotland's thirty-six-year rugby history. The tourists were beaten by two second-half scores in muddy conditions and the try by MacLeod, who according to legend had been first considered for Scottish honours as young as 15, came from a clever cross-kick by Pat Munro. Showing tremendous speed 'K.G.' caught the kick and danced across Hampden's muddy terrain for what one journalist described as an 'impossible try.' Scotland added the Triple Crown later that season with half-back pairings drawn from Greig, Munro and Simson taking turns to direct Scottish victories in which Alex Purves on the left-wing crossed for tries in each match.

MacLeod, idolised across the Home Unions, retired aged just twenty-one shortly afterwards at the request of his father, a decision precipitated by the tragic sudden death from appendicitis of his brother L.M. (Lewis,) who was also an internationalist. 'KG's' brief career had lit up the game like a bright meteor on a clear night, but with his passing from the scene Scottish rugby slipped into darkness.

Jock Wemyss: Many who saw him will claim that KG MacLeod was Scotland's greatest threequarter in this century, and he had a unique record. Capped against New Zealand in 1905 before he was eighteen years of age, he played ten times for

Scotland and retired before he was 21. He will always be remembered for the historic try he scored against South Africa at Hampden Park in 1906 when he took a high cross-field punt in full flight and raced past the Springbok fullback, Marsburg.

Charlie Stuart: The match [between Scotland and the first Springboks] will be remembered when most others are forgotten. Scotland won by two tries to nil. K.G.MacLeod's wonderful try tends to obscure all else in the game, particularly the play of Scotland's forwards, which has never been surpassed.

Jock Wemyss: That was South Africa's only international defeat in four visits to Europe. Scotland had a powerful team when that memorable triumph was achieved. Against South Africa nearly every forward could be rated a 'giant' of his day, in ability if not in stature, and most of the backs were great players.

In the pack were such formidable scrummagers as 'Darkie' Bedell-Sivright, WP 'Bummer' Scott, Ian Geddes – he always ceremoniously took off his scrum-cap when taking a kick at goal – John MacCallum and Louis Speirs, while behind them were KG MacLeod, Tennant Sloan, Pat Munro and Alec Purves.

Playing the typical Scottish forward game of long ago, the home forwards wheeled and dribbled their side to victory on a wet pitch which suited them admirably.

The highlight of the game was a classic try scored by MacLeod, a Cambridge Triple Blue and an 'even-timer' on the track. He took the ball going full out and just beat an attempted tackle by the South African fullback who, like one or two colleagues, had suffered injury in attepting to check the fiery rushes of the Scottish forwards.

Tennant Sloan (Scotland 1905-1909, 7 Caps): Oh, I saw it [Pat Munro's cross-kick for the try against the Springboks] all right and ran for it but couldn't get near it. It was only MacLeod's tremendous pace that allowed him to get under the ball and then he caught it safely at full pace.

A scene from the 6-0 win against the First Springboks in front of a huge crowd at the old Hampden Park ground in Glasgow.

THREE

CONTROVERSY AND DECLINE
1908-1914

As the new century rolled towards double figures, Scotland's rugby stock declined. Their administrators were sidetracked by disagreements relating to payments made to touring teams and there were divisions over selection of overseas students, while the entries on the playing record up to the war showed more defeats than victories in a period that was devoid of Championship titles. It was a miserable time to be a follower of Scottish rugby.

The Scottish Union, sticklers to rugby's guiding tenets outlawing professionalism, harboured reservations about the financial aspects of touring. They had handed over considerable sums to the Original All Blacks and Springboks in 1905 and 1906 as part of an agreement for staging the international matches, but when the accounts for these tours were eventually published by the London-based Rugby Union (in 1908), eyebrows were raised at the amounts given to the visitors for personal expenses. Such payments, the Scottish Union contended, were contrary to the principles of amateurism and the Union dug its heels in: no Scots (or Irish players) took part in the British tour to Australia and New Zealand in the summer of 1908 and when the Wallabies made their maiden visit to Britain in 1908-09, no fixtures were offered by Scotland (or Ireland).

The Scottish Union brought issues with the Rugby Union to a head by threatening to cancel the 1909 Calcutta Cup match. At length, the matter went to the International Board and the dispute was resolved barely a month before the match was due to take place, the Board creating a Four Home Unions Committee whose remit was to deal with administrative arguments and future touring matters.

The political controversy, it was said, heightened interest in the England-Scotland match at Richmond where Scotland enjoyed one of their best days, winning 18-8 and bringing to six the number of successive wins on English soil. The day was one of personal triumph for the West of Scotland half-back, James Tennent. He scored two of the Scottish tries and, with his partner and skipper, George Cunningham, completely dominated the match. Scotland's run of success in England was at an end however, for two years later, on their first visit to the Rugby Union's new ground at Twickenham, they were beaten by a resurgent English side. Scots will not need reminding that only four wins have been achieved there in the hundred-plus years since, rendering the RFU's headquarters nothing less than a graveyard for Scottish rugby hopes.

Charlie Stuart: J.M. Tennent played for Scotland in all internationals [in 1909]. I was capped against Ireland and was travelling reserve against Wales and England. It was a great season for Tennent. It was largely through his individual brilliance that England were beaten at Richmond. Not only did he score two wonderful tries, but time and again he bottled up the English attack.

Opposite: One of the great characters of Scottish rugby, Andrew 'Jock' Wemyss. Capped as a forward before and after the Great War – in which he lost an eye – he was later a well-known critic, writing regularly on Scottish rugby between the late 1920s until his death in 1974.

Jock Wemyss: It is impossible to single out a 'best-ever' [forward] over a long period in which there have been so many changes in method and style of play, but the greatest I have seen before specialisation became the vogue was John MacCallum of Watsonians. [He} was Scotland's most-capped forward with twenty-six international appearances before John Bannerman created the native record in the 1920s, and he had only three games against France. He was an outstanding leader and a man of few words: 'Harder, boys,' was the most he ever said.

Bill Kyle and Jock Scott were also great forwards prior to 1914. Some Borderers maintain Kyle ranks as the finest forward ever produced by the district. He was a particularly good lineout player and a grand dribbler.

Jock Scott was the finest footballer playing forward in my early days. He could run like a top-class threequarter. I saw him, when I was a callow youth watching at Inverleith, run nearly the length of the pitch through the Ireland side – when he was playing as emergency fullback.

Walter Sutherland makes a break during Scotland's first visit
to Twickenham in March 1911.

France had popped their rugby heads above the international parapet in 1906, kicking off their Test record by going over the top against the All Blacks and later England. Wales engaged them for the first time in 1908, Ireland followed in 1909 and Scotland were the last of the Home Unions to offer them a fixture, in 1910, making the annual round-robin of international matches a Five Nations tournament for the first time. Scotland's attitude to the early French matches was patronising to say the least. The Scottish Union refused to recognise the early matches as having cap status and the annual January fixtures were originally considered as nothing more than an extra 'trial' game for the more demanding rigours to come against the Home Unions. 'Charlie' Stuart remembered the first game with France as being notable for 'the latitude' the referee showed the novices, but the year later those so-called novices turned experts, springing the biggest upset of international rugby up to that time by beating another experimental Scottish team 16-15 in Paris. It was France's first international rugby win.

The next Scottish visit to Paris two years later ended in tumult. The partisan French crowd became so incensed by the English referee's decisions during a 21-3 defeat in which Bill Stewart scored a hat-trick of tries that a riot developed at the end of the game and the much-abused official had to be escorted from the ground by mounted police. The incident caused such a furore that the fixture for 1914 was cancelled.

In between, Scotland had failed to repeat their glorious win of 1906 against the touring Springboks. A South African team which won all five of its European Tests on their tour during the winter of 1912-13 – the first overseas side to enjoy such a Grand Slam – beat the Scots 16-0 at Inverleith. A four-tries-to-nil defeat hardly told an accurate story of the match, for by all accounts the visitors were a much faster outfit than their hosts and only 'Wattie' Sutherland showed that he had the pace to match the speedy Springboks. It was his tackling in defence that limited Scotland's margin of defeat.

All the matches against Wales from 1908 to 1914 were lost, and only three were won against both Ireland and England in the same period. Many of the English matches, however, were memorable affairs. Even in his dotage Charlie Stuart remembered the first Scottish visit to Twickenham in 1911. The ground was then in the middle of nowhere, he recalled, and it was only after a mystery tour through garden allotments and the remains of the orchard from which the RFU had developed it that the Scottish team finally found an entrance. History might have taken a different turn, too, had George Cunningham not lost his pants in a tackle when the English goal, a certain five points and a drawn game were but a dive away. But Scotland lost 13-8 and Twickenham remains a bogey ground to this day.

John MacCallum, in the last of his record-breaking twenty-six matches for Scotland, was the toast of his nation in 1912 when he inspired his side to their last Calcutta Cup win for thirteen years. Late in the game Charles Usher, who was making his debut, capitalised on a poor English pass to pounce for the winning try that MacCallum converted for an 8-3 win. More than 25,000 crammed in to Inverleith for a match that 'Wattie' Sutherland described as the most exciting he ever played in for Scotland, and the same number attended at Twickenham the year later when England carried off their first Grand Slam with a 3-0 win against Scotland. Despite the tight score-line, Scotland were outplayed and only luck and the outstanding defensive skills of Sutherland (again) saved Scotland from a bigger defeat.

Charlie Stuart: Scotland was the last of the home countries to take the field against [France]. Negotiations, however, had been going on and on 22 January 1910 France came to Inverleith. There was much speculation as to how the French would fare but the Scottish selectors took no chances and chose a strong side. That 'caps' were not awarded did not lessen the importance of the meeting. The Union for some peculiar reason was carrying out a principle laid down earlier when it was decided 'caps' should go only to those who played against the home countries.

The football shown by the French was a trifle disappointing, the forwards did not play as a team and the passing behind was slow and mostly ineffective. Redeeming features were the keenness and pace of the whole team, but all were prone to get offside and tackle opponents who had not the ball. They were allowed a lot of latitude which later raised the question whether it is better to permit a team to ignore the laws of the game with the idea of making a more equal match or be severe in order to teach them more speedily what must be learned sooner or later.

All [our] forwards, however, had much to commend them and proved too skilful and powerful for the Frenchmen who were beaten 27-0.

Walter Sutherland (Scotland 1910-1914, 13 Caps): Season 1909-10: I played in all the Scottish Trial Games, and was chosen for the Scottish team against Wales and England. The game against Wales was my first, and my clubmate W.E.Kyle's, his last. He was the oldest and I was the youngest player in the side. I played right wing to A.W.Angus in Wales, and left wing to J.Pearson against England; we were beaten in both games.

Jock Wemyss: On New Year's Day, 1911, France created the biggest surprise this century by beating Scotland. To be sure, it was only by the narrowest possible margin, 16-15, but the result shook the other countries at home and abroad. I can recall that shattering blow by France and when the result first appeared in the papers all Scotland was convinced it was a misprint.

No one would believe that such a catastrophe could happen, even in Paris! Maybe the Scottish side was not regarded as particularly strong but, with such great players included as W.R.Sutherland, J.Pearson, P.Munro, J.C.MacCallum, J.M.B.Scott and F.H.Turner, it hardly seemed possible that France could win.

Walter Sutherland

Jock Wemyss: For my early education as a young player I owed a lot to Wales. The first I saw of Welsh rugby was the international at Inverleith in 1911 which Wales handsomely won 32-10. Maybe it did not provide my first inspiration to try and become a reasonably good player – after all, when I had switched from soccer the previous year I had seen Scotland's home games, the first internationals I had watched, against France and England.

However, the first thing I remember about that Welsh victory was that Scotland with three new caps in an experimental back division as a result of a shock defeat by France in Paris were soon handicapped by injury.

J.M.Macdonald, one of the new wings – the other was a schoolboy, D.M.Grant of Elstow – went off for good, so with J.M.B.Scott taken from the pack to fill the vacancy the powerful Welsh forwards got completely on top and the backs went on the rampage.

Scotland had recalled the once-great Pat Munro as stand-off to the new scrum-half, Frank Osler, a South African. But Munro had been overseas for five years and the Scottish pair behind beaten forwards were completely outplayed.

With one quarrel settled, the Scottish Union soon found itself drawn into another, a domestic issue this time. The high academic reputations of Glasgow and Edinburgh's University medical and dental schools, like those of the London hospitals, made them magnets for Commonwealth students. South African, Australian and New Zealand medics converged on the leading cities. It was not surprising, then, that those with Scottish blood connections and possessed of natural talent for rugby soon caught the eyes of the Scottish Union's selection committee. Frank Osler, whose nephew Bennie became a famous Springbok after the First World War, 'Beak' Steyn and 'Mike' Dickson, the Oxford Rhodes-scholar, were noted South Africans capped; while Bill Stewart from Tasmania, who ran Hawick's Walter Sutherland a close second as Scotland's fastest wing of the period, and New Zealanders Colin Gilray, Andrew Lindsay and Donald Macpherson were London-based students similarly honoured. But their selection, often at the expense of home-grown talent, created division among the country's rugby clubs, particularly in the Borders.

Hawick, Gala and Melrose, no longer fledgling clubs, were now turning out high-calibre players and challenging the dominance that Edinburgh, Glasgow and London Scottish had enjoyed in the early years of the game in Scotland. Tom Scott and Bill Kyle of Hawick were as good a pair of forwards as any produced by Scotland at the turn of the century, while Sutherland, the Hawick flyer, was Scotland's best all-round threequarter in the lean years leading up to 1914. Why should imported talent be recognised ahead of home-grown brilliance, Border men enquired. It was a conundrum that was never properly solved and rumbled on for the best part of the next forty years.

The debate was most intense early in 1913 when 'Wattie' Sutherland, the darling threequarter of the Borders and by then a fixture in the Scottish line, was inexplicably omitted for the Welsh match. The Borders press railed against the SRU, calling their decision to slight Sutherland as 'nothing short of contemptible.' George Will, a Cambridge student, and Stewart, the Australian medic studying at the London Hospital, were the original wing choices. Even the capital's Edinburgh Evening Dispatch *didn't pull its punches. 'Not since the 1890s has there been so much indignation raised in Hawick as has this week been provoked by the omission of W.R.Sutherland from the Scottish side to play Wales,' it thundered. The storm eventually blew over when Will cried off injured, Sutherland was reinstated and went on to enjoy what he later called his best season as an international player.*

Walter Dickson (*left*) and 'Beak' Steyn (*right*), two South Africans who became Scottish
internationalists during their time studying in the UK. Both fell in the Great War.

*Despite the disputes and disappointments, Scotland still managed to produce players
worthy of a place in any team of all the talents. Jock Wemyss of Gala was a forward in the
Border tradition who, with his West of Scotland contemporary Charlie Stuart, became a
noted writer on Scottish rugby and whose recollections illuminate this period of the nation's
rugby history. Packing down with them were illustrious players such as John MacCallum,
a respected captain who eschewed iron fist leadership to encourage his packs with a velvet
glove; his successor as captain Freddie Turner who was Scotland's earliest specialist hooker;
Charles Usher, a forward of immense strength and courage; George Maxwell, the tallest
man to play for Scotland before the Great War; and 'Jock' Scott, who stood out for his rare
handling skills at a time when Scottish forwards were still primarily expected to shine with
the ball at their feet. Scott's traits were attributed to his education at Sedbergh School in
the Lake District where, it was reasoned, he was more likely to be expert at the English
forward game. The detail didn't seem to trouble the Scottish selection panel, for he was a
regular fixture in the national side between 1907 and 1913.*

*By 1911 Scotland were regularly choosing specialist half-backs and among the earliest
experts were Pat Munro (as a stand-off after a chunk of his rugby career had been lost
to civil service overseas) and Eric Milroy (at scrum-half). To the quick as lightning
Sutherland and Stewart in the threequarter line could be added snappy runners like
Hugh Martin, 'Gus' Angus, 'Jimmy' Pearson, Bill Purves and George Will, while Douglas
Schulze, Dickson, despite being profoundly deaf, and William ('Willie') Wallace exuded
coolness under pressure to shine out as beacons of dependability as the nation's leading
fullbacks of the period.*

Jock Wemyss: The first South African I saw play for Scotland was FL Osler, the Edinburgh University scrum-half, who appeared against France and Wales in 1911. Osler's selection at a time when Eric Milroy was a star player caused quite a rumpus, and so did the capping of S.S.L.Steyn against England in 1911 and Ireland the next year.

WM Dickson [of the South African Collegiate School] gained seven caps at fullback in 1912 and 1913, and he played against the Second Springboks.

There is an amusing story about Dickson, who was deaf. At the end of the 'riot' match in Paris in 1913, which resulted in Scotland severing relations with France, the crowd swept round the players in an attempt to lay hands on the referee. Dickson, who thought their yelling and whistling was acclaiming Scotland's 21-3 win, said to Charles Usher: 'Jolly decent of them to take their licking so well.'

Charlie Stuart: Our first visit to the RFU's new ground at Twickenham in 1911 was my last game for Scotland. We were unable to find the entrance to the ground and eventually wandered through allotments and scrubland before gaining access!

Jock Wemyss: For Scotland teams, Twickenham has been a 'Flodden Field'. But for a strong English hand and a yielding pair of white flannel shorts there might have been no bogy as far as Scotland is concerned.

When the first Calcutta Cup match was played at Twickenham [in 1911] England won 13-8. That was how the score stood when the incident I mention occurred. In a strong Scottish attack, George Cunningham who was playing centre, broke clean through towards the goal-posts. It was an almost certain five points for Scotland but for that tearing grip. In those days players' dress was not as complete as it is in modern times, and as the Scot did not feel he could proceed to glory in only a jersey and stockings, he discreetly, as one might say, 'went to ground'. Scotland were thus beaten on their first visit to Twickenham.

The next match [at Twickenham in 1913] was a thriller which England won by a try to nothing. Scots remember that game for the wonderful defensive play by WR Sutherland. An injury compelled a helpless Loudon-Shand to move to the wing. Sutherland played centre and how he accomplished the tremendous task of covering such a great wing as Poulton-Palmer and Coates is a story told by old men to young boys in Hawick to this day.

Charlie Stuart: As a player, [John] MacCallum has never been excelled in any country; he was the complete footballer and as much at home in the threequarter line as in the pack. JMB Scott was almost equally good. At an early age he went from Edinburgh Academy to Sedbergh and on his return was a footballer more of the English than the Scottish type, in that he was abler with his hands than his feet.

Jock Wemyss: Another great forward was Charles Usher. In his first international he scored the winning try against England at Inverleith in 1912 and, if memory serves,

John MacCallum, playing in his last game, converted it from a wide angle.

Walter Sutherland: 1911-12: I was captain of Hawick that year and had a good season. I played for Scotland against France, Wales and England. I played right wing to Angus against France and Wales, and right wing to W.Burnet against England. I scored twice against France, and once against England. We beat France and England, and lost to Wales. The game against England was most the exciting ever played in. MacCallum and Scottish forwards won the game.

Jock Wemyss: On November 23, 1912, Billy Millar's Springboks amply avenged [the 1906] defeat, for they won at Inverleith 16-0. Douglas Morkel, giant forward and famous kicker, made the Inverleith crowd gasp when he took a penalty shot at goal. The mark was ten yards inside the South African half and close to the touch-line near the Press Box, and the kick was taken towards the Ferry Road end.

The ball just missed the posts high up, sailed over the crowd out of the ground and landed on the road! It was the most colossal kick I have seen and the carry must have been not an inch less than 90 yards.

Almost the only memory of Scotland's vain struggle in that game was a great run by Wattie Sutherland.

Walter Sutherland: 1912-13: That was my best season. I captained the South of Scotland against the North and I played for Scotland against South Africa, France, Wales, Ireland and England – I was the only threequarter to play in all the Internationals.

Jock Wemyss: It was at Cardiff Arms Park, with three others who like myself were just out of their 'teens I was one of nine new caps in the 1914 Scottish team to play Wales in our first match of that season.

Because of our lack of experience we got a lesson all right and were trounced 24-5. There was, however, some excuse for our heavy defeat. The half-backs originally chosen, E.Milroy and T.C.Bowie of Watsonians who were internationals, had to be replaced by new caps A.S.Hamilton and A.T.Sloan. That was unfortunate enough since Hamilton and Sloan hardly knew each other and had never played together before. But the selectors who at that time were the entire Union Committee of seven and who had sprung a surprise when those chose Wattie Sutherland of Hawick, a first-class experienced wing to play for a first time at centre, made a quite astonishing late change in the pack.

Shortly before noon on the day of the match J.B.McDougall stood down because of a chill. We had lunch and changed in our hotel, and at a brief team-talk before walking across to the ground Roy Gallie of Glasgow Academicals was stripped and ready to fill the vacancy. But, to my amazement at least, when we got to the pavilion there among us was Archie Symington, the Cambridge forward, and not Gallie.

Yet despite all the uncertainty about the team we made a wonderful start. Only minutes after the kick-off we heeled from a scrum, the ball flashed along the threequarter line to W.A.Stewart, the Tasmanian sprinter, who rounded Jack Bancroft [the Welsh fullback] and other defenders at a great pace and scored behind the posts. A.D. 'Podger' Laing converted and we saw visions. But not for long. Quite soon Sutherland badly sprained an ankle. He was moved to the wing and J.G.Will came in to the centre. Maybe our captain David Bain made a mistake in allowing Sutherland to remain on the field for he was completely crippled, and also in switching Will, for he had no experience as a centre.

Anyway, although Wales did not manage to cross the Scottish line before the interval, they played on our weakness in the second half and piled up the points.

What remains in my mind was the hectic forward battle and I had never been in anything like it. The Welsh pack led by the Rev Alban Davies and known as 'The Terrible Eight' was, I think, the toughest I ever played against. I remember at the interval watching in astonishment while they all had their faces liberally sponged with cold water as if being brought back to life. They did not need reviving, and a lesson I learned as the result of an incident in which I was involved just before half-time was that a prudent thing for me to do for the rest of the game would be to shelter as much as possible behind our huge George Maxwell who was bigger than any of our opponents. But I count it as something that I played against 'The Terrible Eight' and survived.

The 1914 Calcutta Cup game was the last international staged in the UK before the war and was considered the most exciting of the series played up to that time. England, on course for back-to-back Grand Slams, appeared at 16-6 to be coasting to the Triple Crown before Scotland staged a miraculous recovery and nearly snatched the match out of the fire before finally going down 16-15. Five months later came War and with it a six-year gap in international battles as the Home Unions, France and the Dominions linked arms to face a bigger battle that would change the world.

Charlie Stuart: The 1914 [Calcutta Cup] game, the last match prior to the war, was one of the finest ever played. Poulton-Palmer and J.H.D.Watson, who was reserve for Scotland in the 1911 game at Twickenham, were magnificent in the English centre.

Jock Wemyss: A great Calcutta Cup match was played at Inverleith [in] 1914, still regarded by those who saw it as a classic, and memorable because of the fighting finish by Scotland who, after apparently being well beaten, only lost 16-15.

England had a splendid team [and], with the end drawing near, led 16-6. Then Scotland rallied and from a pass whipped out by E.Milroy to his partner T.C.Bowie, the stand-off added four points from a dropped goal. There followed the most thrilling score of the match. Bowie went on the blind-side and sent J.G.Will away near midfield with C.N.Lowe [his marker] in close pursuit. What a race, but it was a try for Will, and F.H.Turner's conversion left England winners, but only by the narrowest margin.

"This is not the time to play Games" *(Lord Roberts)*

RUGBY·UNION·FOOTBALLERS
are
DOING·THEIR·DUTY
over 90% have enlisted

"Every player who represented England in Rugby international matches last year has joined the colours."—Extract from *The Times*, November 30, 1914.

BRITISH ATHLETES!
Will you follow this
GLORIOUS EXAMPLE?

FOUR

THE GREAT WAR
1914-1919

Scottish rugby players showed little hesitation volunteering to serve King and country when War broke out in August 1914 and their clubs were to pay a particularly heavy price. Historians of the Gala, Hawick, Heriot's FP, Jedforest and London Scottish clubs have reckoned that more than 750 of their club members signed up for active service, of whom nearly 200 were either killed in action or died of wounds before 1919 – a staggering attrition rate.

International players, too, featured prominently among rugby's war-dead; of the thirty who had taken part in the Calcutta Cup match of March 1914, the last international played on British soil before the outbreak of War, eleven made the ultimate sacrifice. In all, thirty-one Scotland internationalists – more than any other rugby-playing country – were killed in action, lost or died of wounds.

Among them were Ronnie Simson, a London Scottish centre who had scored a try in Scotland's first visit to Twickenham in 1911 and who was among the first division of servicemen to leave England for France in August 1914. He was an Edinburgh Academy pupil who embarked on a military career at the Royal Military Academy at Sandhurst as a teenager in 1910. He subsequently became the first rugby international from the Home Unions to perish, killed in action – 'before a trench had been dug,' noted one writer years later – when a shell exploded near him on the Aisne in September 1914. He had celebrated his twenty-fourth birthday only the week before he died.

The 1914-18 conflict was the first to feature extensive aerial warfare and among the earliest students to volunteer for active service was the patriotically named William Wallace, the holder of four Scottish caps when he vacated his study at King's College, Cambridge, gazetted to the Rifle Brigade in August 1914. Some sources state that he was the first undergraduate to volunteer. After ground service on the Aisne and in the notorious Ploegsteert Wood he was assigned to the Royal Flying Corps as an observer and died when he was shot down by anti-aircraft gunfire at Sainghin, near Lille, in August 1915. The noted rugby critic of the day, E.H.D.Sewell, described him as having 'no superior as a fullback in the United Kingdom during 1912-14,' a glowing reference to a player whose opponents would have included experienced double Grand-Slammers Bill Johnston (England teams of 1913 and 1914) and Jack Bancroft (Welsh sides of 1909 and 1911).

Wallace was one of half-a-dozen Scottish caps in that 1914 Calcutta Cup match killed. Among the other legends in that fifteen who lost their lives were the skipper Eric Milroy, a victim of the Somme in July 1916, and pack-leader Freddie Turner who had captained Scotland the year before. He was lost at Kemmel in France in January 1915, prompting his old Oxford University and Liverpool club colleague Ronnie Poulton-Palmer, who had been England's captain at Inverleith in 1914, to write of Turner's role in that epic game

Opposite: A First World War recruitment poster.

as follows: 'Those who saw last year's Scotland v England match could realise what an anxiety to his opponents his peculiarly infectious power of leading was. His play was hard and straight, and never have I seen him the slightest bit perturbed or excited, and in this fact lay the secret of his great power of control.' Poulton-Palmer, too, fell in action barely three months after his old friend.

Wattie Sutherland missed the Inverleith match of March 1914 through an ankle injury sustained against Wales at Cardiff a month earlier. It ruled him out for the rest of the internationals, but by August 1914 he was fighting fit and ready to enlist in the Lothians & Borders Yeomanry before later transferring to the Argyll & Sutherland Highlanders and serving in France. He survived a bout of dysentery but, returning to the front with a commission in the Seaforth Highlanders, was killed at Hulluch in October 1918 – the last of the thirty-one Scottish internationalists to die in action.

Much has been written about the players who gave up their lives in the so-called 'War to end all Wars,' and quite rightly, too, but one hears little of the war experiences of men like John MacCallum, Scotland's try-scorer against the 1905 All Blacks and the man who

Scotland's last team before the First World War. They lost 15-16 in a titanic struggle with England at Inverleth in March 1914.

Back Row: WM Wallace, ET Young, IM Pender, AW Symington, RM Scobie, JL Huggan
Seated: JG Will, CM Usher, FH Turner, E Milroy (captain), AW Angus, AR Ross, GHHP Maxwell
In front: AD Laing and TC Bowie

Wallace, Young, Huggan, Will, Turner and Milroy died on active service during the First World War.
Usher, Angus and Maxwell survived to take their places in the Scottish team after the War.

A lineout is contested during the 16-15 defeat by Englnd at Inverleith in March 1914

led them to victory in the 1912 Calcutta Cup match. His was the story of a conscientious objector who seems to have been completely shunned by the Scottish Union after the War.

MacCallum was a son of the manse and became a doctor by profession. He qualified from Edinburgh University as the most distinguished surgery graduate of his year and after stints in Edinburgh, Liverpool and London became Medical Officer for Health in Argyllshire. But in 1916 he refused to serve and for his strong moral stance against the conflict, a belief 'born of genuine humanitarian beliefs' according to a contemporary, he went to gaol in Perth for more than a hundred days before he was released to undertake labouring duties on a Home Office scheme.

It was customary for distinguished former Scottish internationalists to be elected to the Union once their playing days were over, and many former captains –many with less exalted playing records than his – later reached high office as members of the Union. Not so Dr MacCallum who led his country five times and held the Scottish cap record for more than a decade: his name is noticeably absent from the list of distinguished former players on the Presidential roll.

ROLL OF HONOUR 1914-1918

SIMSON, Ronald Francis ('Ronnie') (Scotland 1911) KIA in the Battle of the Aisne, September 14, 1914.

HUGGAN, James Laidlaw (Scotland 1914) KIA in the Battle of the Aisne, September 16, 1914.

ROSS, James (Scotland 1901-03) Missing presumed KIA killed in action at Messines, October 31, 1914.

ROBERTSON, Lewis (Scotland 1908-13) Died of wounds at Ypres, November 3, 1914

TURNER, Frederick Harding ('Freddie') (Scotland 1911-14) KIA near Kemmel, France, January 10, 1915.

PEARSON, James (Scotland 1909-13) KIA at Hooge, Belgium, May 22, 1915.

BAIN, David McLaren (Scotland 1911-14) KIA at Festubert, France, June 3, 1915.

YOUNG, Eric Templeton (Scotland 1914) KIA at Gallipoli, June 28, 1915.

CHURCH, William Campbell (Scotland 1906) KIA at Gallipoli, June 28, 1915.

BLAIR, Patrick Charles Bentley (Scotland 1912-13) KIA at Ypres, July 6, 1915.

WALLACE, William Middleton (Scotland 1913-14) Killed near Sainghin, France, August 22, 1915.

BEDELL-SIVRIGHT, David Revell ('Darkie') (Scotland 1900-08) Died of blood poisoning at Gallipoli, September 5, 1915.

DICKSON, Walter Michael ('Mike') (Scotland 1912-13) KIA Loos, September 26, 1915.

DODS, John Henry (Scotland 1895-97) Killed on HMS *Natal* when it blew up at Cromarty, December 30, 1915.

HOWIE, David Dickie (Scotland 1912-13) Died of wounds, Gallipoli, January 19, 1916.

ROSS, Andrew (Scotland 1905-09) KIA Flanders, April 6, 1916.

WILSON, John Skinner (Scotland 1908-09) Killed on HMS *Indefatigable* when it was sunk in the Battle of Jutland, May 31, 1916.

ABERCROMBIE, Cecil Halliday (Scotland 1910-13) KIA when HMS *Defence* was blown up during the Battle of Jutland, May 31, 1916.

FRASER, Rowland (Scotland 1911) KIA on the Somme, July 1, 1916.

MILROY, Eric ('Puss') (Scotland 1910-14) KIA on the Somme, July 18, 1916.

WILL, John George (Scotland 1911-13) Missing presumed killed near Arras, March 25, 1917.

NELSON, Thomas Arthur (Scotland 1898) KIA at Arras, April 9, 1917.

FORREST, Walter Torrie (Scotland 1903-05) KIA at Gaza, April 19, 1917.

WADE, Albert Luvian (Scotland 1908) KIA at Arras, April 28, 1917.

HENDERSON, James Young Milne (Scotland 1911) KIA at Flanders, July 31, 1917.

CAMPBELL, John Argentine (Scotland 1900) Died of wounds in Germany, December 2, 1917.

STEYN, Stephen Sebastian Lombard ('Beak') (Scotland 1911-12) KIA in Palestine, December 12, 1917.

LAMOND, George Alexander Walker (Scotland 1899-1905) Died in Colombo from illness contracted in Mesopotamia, February 25, 1918.

HUTCHISON, William Ramsay (Scotland 1911) KIA at Arras, March 22, 1918.

GORDON, Roland Elphinstone (Scotland 1913) Died of wounds, France, August 30, 1918.

SUTHERLAND, Walter Riddell ('Wattie') (Scotland 1910-14) KIA at Hulluch, October 4, 1918.

FIVE

CHARIOTS ON FIRE
1920-1924

Peace, and with it longing for home and a return to civilian life, dominated the hopes of the young men who suffered the hardships of life in the trenches, at sea and in the air during the Great War. When the Armistice came, the pursuit of leisure activities returned to engage young minds and soon the rugby men of Scotland were back in action. For veterans like Charles Usher, 'Jenny' Hume, Gus Angus and Jock Wemyss, who had all been capped before the war, international rugby matches were familiar rituals and they relished renewing old friendships and establishing new ones with the young players that had kept rugby in Scotland going between 1914 and 1918.

The match results of the post-war years were immaterial; that rugby rivalries at international level were resumed with Scotland's match in Paris against France in January 1920 was reason enough to celebrate. For Scottish supporters there was the pleasure of seeing their team emerge as Grand Slam contenders in that first Championship season after the war. A defeat at Twickenham was the only blot on Scotland's copybook and three wins were sufficient to guarantee a share of the first post-war Five Nations title in a season.

Jock Wemyss: By the time the First World War had ended and internationals were resumed in 1920, past differences between Scotland and France had been forgotten. In those days the two countries played the first fixture in the Championship on New Year's Day. Scotland, waiving her right to play at home, won by a goal to nil. Before the match there was an appeal in the papers for better behaviour by the spectators, particularly towards the referee who was F.C.Potter-Irwin of England. He, of course, like most of us who were playing, had heard how John Baxter [the referee in 1913] had to be whisked away to safety. As soon as Potter-Irwin whistled the end of the game the crowd surged across the pitch towards him. I was standing quite near, and if he didn't turn quite as white as an English jersey he certainly looked a bit apprehensive, for not all his decisions had met with approval. But all was well. Just as we Scottish players were about to rally round we could see what the intention was. Potter-Irwin was hoisted shoulder high and carried off to loud applause. Irrepressible Charles Usher turned to me and said: 'They must think that he won the match, not us.'

Despite his prisoner-of-war experience Usher returned to the game in 1920, fiery as ever, and led Scotland many times. As a captain, he was brief and to the point in any remarks he made to the team. I remember one of his typical observations in the Irish match at Inverleith in 1920. Right in front of the stand there developed some lively exchanges between the sixteen forwards, who were all fighting furiously for the ball or any unfortunate player holding it. The referee, John Baxter, called Usher and W.D.Doherty, the Irish captain, and uttered a few well-chosen words to the forwards.

Opposite: Eric Liddell, the Scotland winger who became an Olympic legend in 1924.

He thereafter ordered play to resume from a scrummage, whereupon Usher turned to his forwards and said: 'All right, boys; take off the kid gloves.'

It was a campaign that saw Finlay Kennedy become the first player capped from the Stewart's FP club. A goal-kicking forward, converted the only goal of the match with France in Paris, landed two match-winning penalties in a tight match on his home ground at Inverleith against Wales and placed three more there against Ireland before Scotland packed their kit for Twickenham and the Championship showdown with England.

Jock Wemyss: My only appearance in a Calcutta Cup match was at Twickenham in 1920. It was a vital game – we were poised to win the Championship title and the Triple Crown. The Royal Family were in attendance. What I vividly recall about the presentation ceremony were the remarks to us as our officials followed the King. The late Sir Louis Greig [Scotland 1905], Equerry to Prince Albert, was among them and exhorted us to 'beat the blighters!'

I always thought that our skipper, Charles Usher, made a slip before we went on to the field. We were given two new balls from which to select, one with the usual four panels and the other with eight. The latter was taken, though I urged that it was of no use to our expert goal-kicker, Finlay Kennedy, who had been our match-winner against Wales with two magnificent penalty goals. He had two comparatively easy kicking chances, but he did not hit that eight-panel ball truly, and each time it wobbled past the posts like a demented butterfly.

There were memorable meetings with Wales, too, in the early post-war seasons. Crowds for international matches were growing and, as a consequence, the 1921 match at Swansea suffered, becoming probably the longest international ever staged. Several times the capacity crowd over-spilled boundaries causing the referee to interrupt the game. There was a fifteen-minute stoppage in the second-half when the players had to leave the pitch to enable the police to clear the playing area. It was a break that worked to Scotland's advantage. Wales were eating into Scotland's lead and promising to finish stronger when the game was suspended, but the visitors returned refreshed and closed it out with a late score.

Nerve-wracking finishes were the features of the next two matches in the series. Wales rescued the 1922 game at Inverleith from the jaws of defeat to earn a nine-all draw with a last-minute dropped goal that was met with stunned silence. Fortune went Scotland's way at Cardiff in 1923 when Leslie Gracie, a polished centre with a stunning swerve and subtle change of pace crossed for a last-minute winning try to snatch a rare 11-8 win in the Principality's capital. The Welsh spectators impressed their visitors with their sportsmanship in defeat that afternoon, carrying Gracie shoulder-high from the field as a mark of respect for his winning performance.

Gracie was one of several threequarters who set Scottish back-play alight with their exceptional speed and talent in the 1920s. Foremost among the pacemen was Eric Liddell, the original 'chariot of fire', whose achievements on the track overshadowed his talents as an international rugby wing. He retired from rugby in 1923 to concentrate on athletics after scoring three tries in only seven appearances for Scotland, and enjoyed his finest sporting hour winning Gold at the 1924 Olympics. His last international was at Inverleith against England in 1923 when each side was unbeaten and playing for the Triple Crown. The Scottish Union were overwhelmed by requests for admission to a match attended by more than 30,000 including the Duke of York (later King George VI) and his fiancée, Lady Elizabeth Bowes-Lyon (later the Queen Mother). The visitors rained on Scotland's parade, winning 8-6 in what one newspaper described as 'a titanic game' in which 'never for a moment did the interest flag.' It was the eighth Scottish reverse in nine matches with England, but no one blamed Liddell. Indeed, the same reporter was unstinting in his praise: 'Liddell was magnificent. He thrilled over and over again.'

An even more prolific strike force who would thrill with sensational effect succeeded Liddell and Gracie in 1924 when the Oxford University threequarters, Ian Smith, George Aitken (a former New Zealand captain), Phil Macpherson and the Australian AC 'Johnnie' Wallace (who later captained the New South Wales Waratahs) were selected en bloc to face Wales at Inverleith. They were blooded after Scotland had lost unexpectedly in Paris under Gracie's captaincy. A quartet well-served by its pack and fed by positive halves in Herbert Waddell and Willie Bryce perfected quick, efficient passing movements to create overlaps for the wings to use their pace and power to score tries. Smith, barely a shade behind Liddell for pace, crossed for a hat-trick on his debut and there were tries by Wallace on the other wing and Macpherson, a maturing centre, in a staggering 35-10 victory. Waddell, a rising star at stand-off, was outstanding against Ireland with two tries in a 13-8 win that set up another Triple Crown occasion with England. Twickenham, though, remained Scotland's bogey ground and a team of considerable potential was spooked 19-0 – arguably the most disappointing Scottish result of the inter-war period.

A roll-call of legends toughened Scotland's scrum in these years. Charles Usher, a natural leader who commanded the respect of players and selectors, George Maxwell, a dominant line-out expert and the ebullient Jock Wemyss formed the nucleus of the pack who laid the foundation for the 1920 Five Nations title. They were forwards in the finest Scottish tradition – hard-working, good with their feet and as hard as nails. Wemyss had lost an eye in the war but always maintained with ironic humour that he played better with only one than he had in 1914 with two. Among the emerging generation, John Bannerman, who entered the lists in 1921, had no superior for robust forward play in the UK and kept his place in the national side for nine seasons, playing thirty-seven successive internationals to create a new Scottish appearance record. He had the knack of driving his colleagues to play above their potential. Typical among these was Doug Davies, a teak-tough Borders farmer who was a natural genius at dribbling the ball and never failed to lift his game when playing at international level. Finally, at a time when the only concessions to forward specialisation were in the middle of the front-row and on the side of the back-row, David Bertram (as hooker) and Jock Lawrie (as a wing-forward) were early experts in a scrum that was encouraged to wheel and break away with the ball at its feet, upholding the conservative but effective traditions of Scottish forward play.

And 'conservative' was the adjective regularly used to describe the Scottish approach to rugby after the Great War. Jock Aikman Smith still ruled the Union with a rod of iron – particularly when it came to matters professional. Players had to pay for their jerseys and when Neil Macpherson, a useful Scottish international forward, was the recipient (like his club-mates) of a gold watch after Newport enjoyed an invincible season in 1922-23, the Scottish Union politely suggested that Macpherson return the present. He didn't and was promptly suspended from Scottish rugby circles. Scottish clubs, moreover, were banned from playing Newport. Aikman Smith brought the matter to the attention of the International Board who outlawed valuable presentations as acts of professionalism before the Scottish Union lifted the suspension on Neil Macpherson. But he was never again invited to play for his country.

Even big, bluff Jock Wemyss couldn't escape censure in the 1920s. His 'transgression' was writing articles about the game, another contravention of the laws relating to professionalism, but when he claimed he had retired from active play, no action was taken. Arguably, though, the biggest blunder made by the Union came in 1924 when they refused to grant any fixtures with the touring All Blacks. Relations were still strained from the expenses row that surrounded the 1905 New Zealand visit and, as a result, Scotland missed a box-office opportunity as well as a genuine chance to create history. The New Zealanders, who won every match of the tour, said their best game was against Oxford University and those fabled Scottish threequarters. Later that winter, Scotland went on to register their first Grand Slam leaving everyone to ponder what might have been had the best two international sides of the year met.

Jock Wemyss: When Scotland beat Wales in 1921 by 14-8 it was the first Scottish win in Wales for twenty-nine years [and] was a big surprise to all Scots. Only a week or two earlier Scotland had been beaten at home by France for the first time, the score at Inverleith being a try to nothing. Not much confidence was felt in the team and there was certainly no expectation that a long run of defeats in Wales would be ended.

It was, however, in a most remarkable game memorable for the then unprecedented crowd scenes. There was plenty of space inside St Helen's [at Swansea] but the terracing was inadequate, and no sooner had the game begun than the spectators swarmed on to the pitch. Several times play was stopped for as long as five minutes while onlookers were moved back from the touch-lines and in-goal areas. Later there was another long stoppage. The teams left the field and the referee consulted with 'Jenny' Hume and Tommy Vile, the captains, about abandoning the game. Eventually, the match was played to a finish, and although Scotland were deserving winners it is a fact that the crowd robbed Wales of a good chance of saving the match.

At half-time Scotland led 11-0 [but] Wales retrieved the position immediately they got the wind [and] Albert Jenkins dropped two goals which then counted four points each. One more and they would have taken the lead. This, however, was too much for the misguided spectators and there came that long second-half break. It gave the hard-pressed Scots a much-needed breather and near the end A.T.Sloan clinched matters with a scoring run down the wing, but he only got the try by diving among the onlookers who were packed right along the line.

That, however, wasn't the end of a hectic day for the triumphant Scots. As was the custom then they were going back direct to London after the match. So they had only time to grab their clothes, rush into their bus and catch the train. And on the train they did their washing and changing.

JR 'Jock' Lawrie (Scotland 1922-1924, 11 Caps): I started to play rugby after the First World War. I played as a 'loose' forward. I suppose I would be called a wing forward. We didn't always adhere strictly to our allotted positions in the set scrums. Except for the hooker it was sometimes 'first up, first down'. Those were the days of forward foot rushes. We forwards didn't handle the ball. That was the job of the backs. There was none of the smuggling of the ball, and second phase possession. Rucking as such was unknown. I remember one forward, Tom Voyce [the England wing forward], who handled more than he kicked but 'Feet, forwards, feet!' was always the cry.

Jock Wemyss: I recall [Phil Macpherson's] beginning because I played with him for Edinburgh Wanderers. At the beginning of the 1921-22 season he played three games for us before going up to Oxford. As I still then had ideas [about playing for Scotland], I chipped in to say: 'I'll see you in Paris on January 1'. And I beat the selectors to it – because I did! He was chosen to play against France with seven other new caps, among them were Eric Liddell, Jock Lawrie, David Bertram and Doug Davies.

Leslie Gracie and Macpherson were our centres and, while our teenager showed the greatest promise, there was no real sign that he was to become such a wonderful player. Nevertheless, he played his part in the attack which enabled Scotland to open the scoring. His inimitable jink made the half-opening, and Gracie gave Arthur Browning just enough room to get outside [the French defence and score.]

As Macpherson had shown he was neither too young nor inexperienced, he played in the other internationals that season, and the selectors showed their confidence in him by picking him as fly-half against Wales and Ireland and then returning him to centre, where he was to make his name.

DS 'Doug' Davies (Scotland 1922-1927, 20 Caps plus 4 Caps for the Lions): You didn't get a cap for playing against France [in 1922], so I didn't get a cap until the Welsh game. 'Jenny' Hume was the scrum-half and Charlie Usher was the captain and a very good captain. I thought an awful lot of Usher. He was Army trained and he had all the players as fit as they possibly could be.

Jock Wemyss was playing. [A Frenchman] had lost an eye in the war and Jock lost an eye in the war. [At the dinner after] John Bannerman and I were sitting across the table and Jock said to the Frenchman: 'I'll drink you under the table in ten minutes.' And this silly fellow, he thought Jock was drinking French wine. He was drinking whisky! Jock won the challenge.

Jock Wemyss: Lubin, one of the French forwards and myself in the Scottish pack had lost an eye in the war. We became close friends. When we were opponents in Paris in 1922 we had a bit of fun over our handicap. Lubin was a big, strong chap and good at the line-out. I suggested to Charles Usher that I might try to keep an eye on him. As we had lost opposite eyes, on one side of the field it was easy to watch the ball and man. On the other, our blind-sides were adjacent, so when watching the ball we had to use other means to ensure there was no sudden switching to another position. We mainly employed our elbows to keep contact. However, the unusual operations in which Lubin and myself were indulging attracted the referee's attention early in the game and, turning to Usher, he asked: 'What's this, Charles?' 'Just leave them,' replied our skipper. 'It's a private arrangement: they're both half-blind.'

JCH 'Jimmie' Ireland (Scotland 1925-1927, 11 Caps): On [Eric Liddell's] last visit to Scotland he stayed the night with us in Glasgow. He was a delightful fellow. He wasn't at all a Holy Willie. He was just a nice, good man. He wouldn't play on the Sabbath but he didn't make a great deal of it. That was just the way he was and everybody respected him for it

Jock Lawrie: I had quite a short International career but one game still haunts me. It was against Wales at Inverleith in 1922. Wales were favourites to win. We were leading 9-5 when just as the referee was taking a breath to blow the final whistle Wales dropped a goal – four points – and the result was a draw. I can still hear the deathly hush which lay over the whole pitch as we walked off.

Leslie Gracie: The finest game I've ever played in was between Wales and Scotland in 1923 at Cardiff. It was early on a cold wet Friday morning that I joined the remainder of the Scotland team at Paddington. It poured with rain all the way down. Scotland had not won at Cardiff for thirty-three years and I remember wondering whether Cardiff Arms Park would live up to its reputation for a big match, and, if so, how our young team, particularly the forwards, would fare against a strong Welsh pack on a slippery ground.

Wales led 3-0 at half-time and it was not long after that Scotland drew level [when] Eric Liddell, zooming along the horizon, picked up the ball at full speed without the slightest check, and ran over in the left corner.

With twenty minutes to go, Wales led 8-3 but from now on Scotland took the upper hand. L.M.Stuart, our youngest forward, had the honour of touching down for a try after working the blind side from [a] scrum [but] Arthur Browning had evidently left his kicking boots behind. Thus the score became 8-6 in the Welshmen's favour and remained so for nine of the remaining ten minutes.

[Then], running diagonally to the left to between Arthur Cornish [the Welsh centre] and 'Codger' Johnson [his wing], I saw in a flash that the latter was in two minds – whether to go for me or run between me and Liddell and prevent me passing to the latter. Up to now, I had always passed to Liddell when the ball went towards the left wing, and an Olympic record-breaker in the making had to be watched!

As I went on, the way opened up for me. I was just able to swerve round my opposite number and all I had to do was carry on over the line. But here I nearly spoilt everything. In trying to touch down [nearer] the posts I recklessly ran along the dead-ball-line, [scoring] short of my objective. Dan Drysdale took the kick and, by goaling, converted the one point lead into three. Thus ended the finest game I have ever played in: Scotland 11, Wales 8.

Eric Liddell (Scotland 1922-23, 7 Caps): It was a jolly good game, and one of the finest international matches I ever played in.

Ted Mclaren (Scotland 1923-24, 5 Caps): Never once did Eric [Liddell] show the slightest sign of bad temper or bad sportsmanship on the field; both, it seemed to me, were utterly foreign to him. Many a time he was lain for by his opponents, whose tactics were at least doubtful, but never would he repay them in their own coin – his method was invariable – he merely played better rugby and made them look like second-raters.

Leslie Gracie: The Welsh crowd forgot their great disappointment, and gave a truly remarkable display of sportsmanship by swarming on to the ground and selecting me for the honour of being carried shoulder-high off the field. Even the poor little boy spectator who was sitting near where I scored and had some teeth knocked out by my boot was reported to have said that he did not mind, as he was a Scot himself.

My final memories of the game were handing over [my] jersey 'as a souvenir for the Mayor of Swansea.' Mark you, I was later presented with a new one free of cost by the Scottish Union!

Jock Wemyss: We were changing for the 1920 game against France in our hotel in Paris and gathered in one room to receive the jerseys. Our secretary was handing them round while I was putting on my boots. He passed me, so I said: 'What about me?'

He replied: 'You don't need a jersey.'

'Why not,' I retorted. 'Aren't I playing?'

'You've got one already,' he said. 'You played in 1914.'

George Aitken (Scotland 1924-1929, 8 Caps plus 2 Caps for New Zealand): I went to Oxford on a Rhodes Scholarship in 1922 and remember it as a place where you could get all the rugby you wanted. Every afternoon could be devoted to sport or recreation – it was possible to play or practise six days a week.

I won my Blue in my first year, taking my place in a threequarter line which also included GPS Macpherson, AM David and AC 'Johnnie' Wallace. With the substitution of Ian Smith for David, this was the basis of the 'Oxford-Scots'

The Scotland team that faced Wales in Cardiff in 1923.
Standing: EH Liddell, E McLaren, AK Stevenson, DS Kerr, D Drysdale, LM Stuart
Seated: DS Davies, JM Bannerman, DM Bertram, AL Gracie (captain), A Browning, JCR Buchanan, JR Lawrie
In front: SB McQueen, WE Bryce

threequarter line which was chosen in its entirety for Scotland in 1924.

It wasn't until the debonair Ian Smith came into the picture that we came into our own. Ian Smith, six feet tall, very fast and with a raking stride, was a rugby freak. From his prep school he had gone to Winchester, where rugby was not played. In his first term at Oxford he played soccer, but was captivated by the spectacle of the University Rugby match at Twickenham and vowed, in spite of his complete inexperience of rugby, that he would play in it the following year.

The story current among Oxford men at the time was that his father spurred him on by betting him a case of champagne to nothing that he could not do it. He showed an instinct for the game, and with his great speed and fine physique went on to play thirty-two games for Scotland.

Jock Lawrie: In a game against Wales [in 1924] with the legendary Ian Smith playing on the wing an almost clockwork tactic developed – scrum, heel, ball right along the threes to Smith, score. I think he did it three times.

GPS 'Phil' Macpherson (Scotland 1922-1932, 26 Caps): We had been trounced by

England at Twickenham [in 1924] by 19-0; everything had gone wrong for us but even during the game I felt that we could beat the English side four times out of five.

George Aitken: As a player I followed the principle that a centre's principal function is to make play for his wing threequarter. When we played [as the Oxford line] for Scotland we got the ball to the wings at every opportunity.

For internationals at Inverleith we usually arrived in Edinburgh the morning of the match and put down a scrum in the dressing room before taking the field. 'First up, first down' was still the rule among the forwards.

There were twenty on the Scottish selection committee. The dominant figure, however, was 'Jock' Aikman Smith, a gentleman whose approach to the game was somewhat conservative, although his love of it was unsurpassed.

Phil Macpherson: Wallace, Aitken, myself and Smith had great knowledge of each other's play and confidence in our ability to keep contact on the break-through and to turn defence into attack. We stood close in echelon to draw the defence in and give the wing room, and we aimed to keep the ball in play in the belief that with our discipline in formation, speed and opportunism we were likely to exploit informal situations better than the opposition. We expected to have to go hunting for the ball, for in those days the result of set scrums was far less certain.

Ian Smith (Scotland 1924-1933, 32 Caps plus 2 Caps for the Lions): Philo Macpherson gave me at least half-a-dozen scoring chances in every match, and I managed to take one or two of them.

Jock Wemyss: Few will dispute that Ian Smith was Scotland's greatest scoring wing. In his first match, which was against Wales at Inverleith in 1924 and in which he scored three tries, he astonished everyone by opening the scoring almost the first time he got the ball, his tremendous stride and great pace taking him clear of all defenders. He completed the scoring with his third try in Scotland's 35-10 win. That was the first time the Oxford line – Smith, Macpherson, Aitken and Wallace – played together.

The Welsh left-wing, who simply could not get near Smith, asked to be introduced after the match as he explained he had not had an opportunity of seeing him during the game.

SIX

THE MURRAYFIELD ERA
1925-1939

Rugby had flourished in the mid-1920s. Before radio and television broadcasts enabled the masses to follow games live, newspapers and magazines devoted thousands of words of coverage to the big games. Internationals aroused huge interest, so much so that the clamour for admission to the big occasions made the SRU, realising a need for bigger premises, vacate its own Inverleith ground for pastures new across the city at Murrayfield. Today the stadium is a towering bastion of concrete and steel girders, one of the great arenas of the modern rugby world. It has had many faces since it first opened in March 1925, but at its heart the field of battle has remained a constant. When the land was purchased from the Edinburgh Polo club and financed with a debenture issue, a stand was built on the west side of the pitch and three embankments were raised to the north, south and east to pen in this new theatre of dreams. It was finished just in time to host Scotland's final game of the 1925 Five Nations Championship, where a last-gasp Herbert Waddell drop-goal overcame England 14-11 to secure Scotland's first Grand Slam in front of a world record-breaking crowd of over 70,000 spectators.

Jock Wemyss: The French match of 1925 was the last international played at Inverleith, a ground with intimate associations for the onlookers. Who can forget the promenade in front of the stand where the stewards, and a favoured few, followed the game back and forward along the broad cement steps in the august company of the members of the Union, who were not then pinned down to a particular pew?

What never changed while Inverleith was Scotland's international ground was that the dressing rooms had six wash basins but no hot water and no bath. In many ways we did much better in our hotel.

Jimmie Ireland: There were no replacements in those days. You were a reserve but once the team had got to the ground and they were all fit and well then your part in the exercise was over. I recall that after it had been confirmed that I wasn't required [as reserve against France in 1925], I sat in the enclosure with the girl I was to marry.

John Bannerman was a club-mate and he phoned me up after the French match and told me that I would be in the side to play Wales. Then there was a postcard from the Union confirming my selection.

I had a great pal in Hawick, Doug Davies. He was a lifelong friend due, I think, to the fact that the very first international I played in, somebody belted me and Doug who was a very old hand said, 'Leave the laddie alane,' and when Doug said that you tended to do as you were told.

Opposite: GPS Macpherson, captain of Scotland's first Grand Slam side in 1925.

Jock Wemyss: Many who recall things of note, apart from the glamour of surrounding an all-conquering season, will perhaps agree that 1925 was Scotland's greatest year. Scotland's famous Oxford threequarter line, in rear of the equally celebrated Glasgow Academical half-backs [Herbert Waddell and Jim Nelson], with D.Drysdale, an outstanding fullback, behind them all, will certainly go down in the history of the game as a combination comparable with any.

Waddell was prevented by illness from turning out in the first two matches in 1925, and, while changes were regrettable, it was fitting that one of our soundest outsides – J.C.Dykes – should have his opportunity. He ably filled the vacancies created by the withdrawal of Waddell [as stand-off against France and Wales] and Macpherson [as centre against Ireland] and took part in the season's triumphs – a well deserved distinction.

Jimmie Ireland: When I was playing for Scotland I was just under six feet and weighed twelve stone eight pounds. The likes of Scaly Paterson – JR Paterson – a magnificent wing forward would be no more than five foot eight inches or thereabouts and not a very heavy fellow at that. Even allowing for the fact that people generally are far bigger now than they were then, the size of rugby players now is absolutely remarkable.

Jock Wemyss: The forwards selected for the first game [in 1925] were barely adequate for their task against France. Ian Smith's brilliant running for his four tries delighted everybody and greatly impressed at least one of the French players. Late in the evening he asked the Scottish wing in how many seconds he could run the hundred metres. Not particularly attentive at the moment owing to other distractions, Smith, who thought the question referred to his scoring achievement, nonchalantly replied: 'Oh, four or five, I think.' Registering considerable astonishment, the Frenchman could only gasp: 'Mon Dieu! Mon Dieu!'

In the remaining matches, when they seemed likely to have the worst of the struggle against what were generally thought to be stronger packs, the forwards did splendidly. As individuals, nearly all compared favourably in skill, though usually conceding something in the matter of physique, with their opponents, and in the Calcutta Cup match there was the clearest evidence that they outstayed, in remarkable fashion, the strong eight led by Wavell Wakefield.

Three intended changes among the forwards for the game against Wales were reduced to two, 'Buckie' Buchanan's withdrawal allowing Scaly Paterson to remain in the pack. Waddell was still unfit, and the back division was unchanged. At Swansea, Scotland started where they had left off in the French match. Macpherson and Smith [who again scored four tries] were in terrific form, and brilliant back-play resulted in eighteen points being scored in the first twenty-five minutes. The Scottish forwards, with Jimmie Ireland hooking remarkably well in his first international, played splendidly.

As Gillies could not play, Buchanan returned for the Irish match. Waddell at last turned out, so Dykes stepped into Macpherson's place, and Drysdale captained

Scotland. All the excitement in a great game at Lansdowne Road, Dublin, was packed into the last ten minutes. There were only three minutes left when Waddell dropped a goal which meant that Ireland had to score twice to win.

Jimmie Ireland: I was working in the accounts department for Singer's of Clydebank and when I asked for the Saturday off to play for Scotland [against England in 1925] they asked if I was sure that I needed the whole day. A chap in the accountancy office wondered if I would be OK with just a half day. He hadn't the power to say that I could take the whole day off and he had to put it to his boss. Eventually, they said it was all right but they weren't impressed at all that I was playing rugby for Scotland.

On the morning of the international the Glasgow chaps got the 11 o'clock train from Queen Street to Waverley Station. We would arrive in Edinburgh about 12 o'clock and have lunch in the North British Hotel. The team would have lunch together and then go to the ground. For the game against England the dressing-rooms at Murrayfield weren't ready and so we togged in the hotel and went to the ground by bus.

For the bus ride from the North British Hotel to Murrayfield we got a police outrider escort. That was very impressive, I thought. Murrayfield was the last word. It was a huge modern stadium.

Doug Davies: They were still working on the place when we got there. The smell of freshness was everywhere and there were still bits and pieces to be finished off.

Phil Macpherson: Memory is pretty selective after so many years, yet certain events and feelings are extraordinarily vivid in recollection. There was a flurry of snow in the morning but the day became fine and sunny with little wind. The ground looked perfect but as it had never been played on, the top of the turf tended to shear off on a side-step.

Jimmie Ireland: When we came out on to the pitch we saw one of the biggest crowds that had ever been at a rugby match. There were 70,000 or thereabouts in the ground. I got a real thrill about that. From the pitch all you could see were acres of faces but I remember picking out Margaret [wife-to-be] sitting in the stand. You know, we didn't know a thing then about playing for something called the Grand Slam. To beat England: that was the thing. The Grand Slam was just something invented later.

Phil Macpherson: We had the benefit of the good hands and clever running of the two halves, Herbert Waddell and Jim Nelson, whose ideas and style of play conformed to our [threequarter game].

In the event England got more of the ball and the game moved more along one side of the field so that Smith, our left wing, who had scored eight tries in the three earlier internationals, had no opportunities in attack. The Scottish forwards had some glorious foot rushes led by Bannerman and MacMyn and the game was played at great pace.

England took the lead with a penalty goal after five minutes' play, and the lead changed hands five times before Scotland won. I remember Nelson having backed up a break-through in the centre running twenty-five yards, many of them fending off a clutching pair of hands, to score between the posts; and Wallace scuttling round his opponent to dive in to score at the corner flag overwhelmed by defenders, and the superb kick by Gillies to convert; and Waddell's [winning] dropped goal as the English forwards closed in on him.

Jimmie Ireland: The game seemed to go on for ages. It was a real struggle. I would say that we were pretty fit. Five of the Scottish forwards who played that day could do the hundred yards in just over eleven seconds. That was dashed good going. It was a pack which could really get about the field and the backs were a different class too.

But nearly everybody was almost out on his feet by the time the final whistle went. John Bannerman's greatest pleasure was to see half a dozen Englishmen lying down on the ground out for the count. That pleased him more than winning the game. He said we had played the Englishmen into the ground.

Jock Wemyss: And then the end. Waddell, who had just missed dropping a goal, was successful with a second attempt, and Scotland led by three points. The lead proved to be barely sufficient, for with the last kick of a wonderful match Holliday [the English fullback] nearly dropped a goal. So, for the first time since 1912, Scotland defeated the Auld Enemy and regained the Calcutta Cup. Our great year had ended England's dominance of the game.

The Scotland team that faced England for the Grand Slam in 1925.
Standing: DJ MacMyn, JW Scott, AC Gillies, JCH Ireland, R Howie, IS Smith
Seated: GG Aitken, DS Davies, JM Bannerman, GPS Macpherson (captain), D Drysdale, AC Wallace, H Waddell
In front: JB Nelson, JR Paterson

Ogden's Cigarette cards: Stars of the 1925 Grand Slam.
From left to right, Dan Drysdale, John Bannerman, Ian Smith, Herbert Waddell, and David MacMyn.

Phil Macpherson: In the closing minutes of the game with Scotland in a tenuous lead a scrum was ordered. As I passed open-side wing-forward Paterson I warned him that Myers the English stand-off would have a go, and I repeated this to Waddell. From a perfect English heel there was Myers charging flat out straight for the line; Paterson and Waddell hit him head on and three exploded upwards – a terrific tackle.

Jimmie Ireland: Phil [Macpherson] was simply a wonderful captain. He was a super chap and a marvellous player. John [Bannerman] was consistent: he was capped thirty-seven times for his country and, so far as I was concerned, it was a joy to play with him. He was so full of enthusiasm. The crowd ran on to the pitch at the end and we had to struggle to get back to the stand.

At the dinner in the Freemasons' Hall in George Street, John Bannerman and I sang Gaelic songs – John was something of an authority on Gaelic culture. After the dinner we went dancing, so we couldn't have been that tired.

We didn't think very much about the Grand Slam or the Triple Crown, I must say. The only thing that worried us was beating England. The importance of a Grand Slam or a Triple Crown didn't seem to matter in those days like it does in the modern era.

The Grand Slam was a triumph that heralded a successful period for Scottish rugby. Between 1925 and 1938 they won the Triple Crown three times and were champions on six occasions. In 1926, a Scottish side that included the core of the previous season's Grand Slam pack finally exorcised the Twickenham demons to become the first Home Union to win there (17-9),while Murrayfield became a stronghold against the English who had to make seven visits before recording their first success there in 1937.

The Scottish approach to rugby – on and off the field – remained cautious. The one concession to scrummaging technique was that by the late 1920s Scottish forwards had fixed positions for the set-piece. But only begrudgingly. As late as 1935 Mark Morrison, the forward who had skippered his country with honour at the turn of the century, was urging a return to the old traditions of first up, first down. Old habits died hard and he, like many of his contemporaries, viewed specialisation as a fleeting fad. Another development that exercised minds was scrum formation. By the late 1930s, South Africa's 3-4-1 pack system had won converts among the other Home Unions, but this really was a red-line for the Scottish selection committee. The foot-rush was a traditional skill of Scottish forwards, best exercised by wheeling and shearing away from the conventional 3-2-3 scrum with the ball at the feet. The tactic was especially cherished north of the border as an effective method of attack. The scrum formation that the Springboks had evolved, with only one player in the back-row, simply did not lend itself to the mechanics of wheeling. Setting up a dribble with four players packed into the second-row was physically impossible.

Meanwhile the firm hand of Aikman Smith behind the scenes upheld the game's amateur principles. Players remained in awe of him as an administrator yet retained great personal affection for him and when he died suddenly on active service – in his saloon on the train taking the team to Cardiff to play Wales in 1931 – there was a fond outpouring of grief from Scotland's rugby community.

Even King George V had received short shrift from the great man on the occasion of the maiden Scotland win at Twickenham in 1926. The International Board had adopted a relaxed position over the numbering of players, expressing the opinion that it should be a matter for individual Unions. England and Wales began the practice in 1922 for international matches and Ireland adopted it shortly afterwards. Scotland, however, while recognising its uses for identifying players taking part in trial matches, steadfastly refused to follow suit for international games. When RFU officials primed His Majesty to enquire why the Scots weren't numbered at Twickenham in 1926, the King received a stern response from Aikman Smith to the effect that rugby matches weren't cattle markets. Indeed, although Scotland experimented with numbered jerseys for their Paris visit in 1928, it wasn't until 1933 that they finally fell into line with the other Home Unions.

Happily, the concerns of the Scottish Union regarding allowances to touring sides had been resolved shortly after their refusal to host the 1924 All Blacks and in 1927 Johnnie Wallace, who had returned to Australia from Oxford to practise as a lawyer, led the New South Wales Waratahs in a thrilling match at Murrayfield. Scotland won 10-8 and only narrowly failed against Bennie Osler's Springboks four years later, going down 6-3 in a storm after taking an early lead. Then, in 1935, New Zealand made their first appearance north of the Tweed for thirty years when a side led by Jack Manchester won 18-8 against a young Scottish team for whom Charles Dick, a powerful centre, and Ken Fyfe, a nippy wing, scored tries.

The big city clubs supplied the heart of the successful Scottish 1925 Grand Slam side that claimed Championship title-shares in 1926 and 1927. Beetle-browed John Bannerman, ever-present between 1920 and 1930, and Jimmy Ireland, an indestructible hooker, came from the Glasgow HSFP club; the city's Accies club gave Scotland its first notable half-back pairing, Herbert Waddell and Jim Nelson, while Max Simmers and Jimmy Dykes from the same stable were consistent home-bred threequarters who filled the positions vacated when Johnnie Wallace and George Aitken of the Oxford-Scots line departed.

If Bannerman was the dominant force in the Scottish packs of the 1920s, then his counterpart among the backs was Phil Macpherson who played for Edinburgh Academicals after going down from Oxford. He was the outstanding British centre of the era, a rugby genius who could create overlaps with a perfectly-flighted pass. Ian Smith, the flying Scot who was his regular wing for Scotland, used to say that Macpherson gave him about half-a-dozen scoring passes every time they played together, and that on average he managed to convert one or two a game. It is a measure of Macpherson's effectiveness that, in all, Smith chalked up twenty-four Test tries, the world record until Australia's David Campese passed him more than fifty years later.

The Heriot's FP club were a rising force in Edinburgh club rugby between the wars. Dan Drysdale, equally at home as an attacking stand-off or centre, settled at fullback to forge a reputation that was without equal in the Home Unions during the 1920s. His club-mates Roy Kinnear (centre) and Dan Kerr in the pack, and Sandy Gillies, a goal-kicking forward from Watsonians, and 'Jumbo' Scott (Stewart's FP) were other indispensable regulars from the capital's clubs when Scotland were joint-champions in 1926 and 1927.

Doug Davies (Hawick), Jimmy Graham (Kelso) and John Allan (Melrose) were among a generation who strengthened the Border reputation for tempestuous forward play and the district's proud traditions were maintained in the 1930s by Jock Beattie (Hawick) and Jack Waters (Melrose) who were the bulwarks of the 1933 Triple Crown pack.

The most versatile back in the Home Unions in the 1930s was Wilson Shaw. He possessed enough pace to be an effective wing, the position in which he first won international honours, but his instinct for the game and his ability to beat an opponent with a step or a sudden burst of acceleration brought him recognition as the team's pivot. Shaw and Ross Logan, a strapping Edinburgh Wanderers scrum-half, became Scotland's most effective half-back combination of the decade before the Second World War. They were paired at short notice against Cardiff during a Barbarians Easter tour, but complemented one another so perfectly that the Scottish selectors adopted them as their first-choices for the next two seasons.

Shaw became an inspiring Scottish captain and enjoyed his finest hour at Twickenham during the 1938 Championship campaign. He revelled in dry conditions on a sunny March day and scored two rip-roaring tries in the tensely-fought 21-16 crowning win against England. Duncan Macrae and Charles Dick were the skilful supporting cast in a threequarter line whose wings, John Forrest and Bill Renwick carried off the try-scoring Oscars in Scotland's last Triple Crown season before war interrupted international rugby again in 1939.

Jock Wemyss: When an Irish team first appeared at Murrayfield in 1926 Scotland had won six games in succession, including victories over England and Wales. At that time all the home countries had, since 1910, failed to lay the 'Twickenham bogy'. In Scotland we hoped that, after those two initial successes, a 'Murrayfield bogy' would defy all comers for an equally long period. Ireland shattered those hopes with a dramatic last-minute victory.

Heavy rain right up to the start resulted in the pitch being churned into such a sea of mud so that in the second half the players had difficulty in distinguishing between friend and foe. I remember one Scot breaking dangerously with the ball and then passing to an opponent! What probably decided the game was the dramatic incident only a minute or two before the vital score. In a bid to break through the Irish defence Waddell came into a violent head-on collision. As the ball went loose play proceeded while Waddell, who was bleeding profusely from a head wound, crawled about on hands and knees. Waddell was taken off. Scotland moved Dykes to stand-off, Simmers to centre and J.R.Paterson was withdrawn from the pack to play on the wing. The Irish forwards at once made the most of their advantage and after they led a storming attack, some quick passing to the left gave Jack Gage his chance [to score the winning try.]

It is worth mentioning that the big disappointment was forgiven and forgotten when three weeks later Scotland trampled on the 'Twickenham bogy' with a victory by 17-9. Scotland were splendidly served by Drysdale at fullback. Always an astute captain, he quickly spotted Holliday [his opposite number] was shaky and it was by playing on to him that the three Scottish tries were scored.

Dykes put up four points with a dropped goal. Ian Smith broke away from the Scottish twenty-five and kicked into midfield. Holliday was beaten by the bouncing ball, so Smith arrived, gathered, and sent Waddell over for a try which the stand-off converted himself. Holliday again fumbled and Smith scored for Waddell to again add the goal points and a diagonal kick by Simmers allowed Smith to score again and ensure a famous victory.

Herbert Waddell (Scotland 1924-1930, 15 Caps plus 3 Caps for the Lions): In 1926 we were the first team ever to win at Twickenham. The ground was bone dry and to everyone's astonishment John Bannerman insisted on wheeling the tight scrums and having loose rushes – and this proved unexpectedly successful because the pack contained some superb dribblers, such as Bannerman and MacMyn in the second-row, and in the back-row JW Scott, Jimmy Graham and Scaly Paterson. This was a great day and a great triumph for John Bannerman and the forwards.

Jimmie Ireland: The great thing, always, was to beat England. I was lucky. I played them three times and we won three times.

Norman Mair (Scotland 1951, 4 Caps): Scotland had always been masters of the foot-rush away from a wheeling scrum. It was a very good attacking manoeuvre. A defender had to fall to check the rush, and if the forwards then heeled from what they used to call a loose scrum, their backs automatically had a man over. The dribbling was brilliant. One of the great forwards of that time was a doctor named MacMyn. He used to go out practising dribbling and his dog tried to get the ball off him by nosing it away. MacMyn used to keep the ball very close to him by using the outside of his foot so that the ball spun back. He had terrific control. The game has always been aimed at trying to create a situation on the field where the attacking side had a man to spare and Scotland did it by making defenders fall on the ball in front of a foot-rush. The balls were rounder then, too, and easier to dribble than when they became more pointed.

Jimmie Ireland: The art of dribbling is worth talking about. And it really was an art. You could dribble the ball away from a loose scrummage, but the real, proper time to think about dribbling was when you wheeled away from a set scrum – the second-rows would take the ball on with their feet. We would be packing down in a 3-2-3 formation and the second-rows would break away and charge upfield with the ball at their feet. It was a grand feeling to be involved in a dribble. It took an awful lot of stopping. We did a lot of practice. It was a recognised part of the game.

It was a controlled thing. You didn't just kick and chase the ball. You controlled it with the feet just as they used to do in soccer. John Bannerman was a super dribbler but he couldn't pass the ball whereas Ludovic Stuart had perfected the art so much that he could sweep the ball from one foot to the other – cross-dribbling it was called.

It was always a great thrill to play for Scotland but, even more than that, it was great fun meeting your team-mates again. We were all very pally. Compared to nowadays it all seems so low-key but on the morning of an international match there was the same excitement in the air that there is today. There was no coaching, though, or squad sessions or anything of that sort. Basically what happened was that John Bannerman would tell you what to do, although he wouldn't really go into the specifics. John wasn't much of a tactician. But somebody like Dan Drysdale might point out that the opposition fullback was a bit dicey and that we were going to try him out with a few high kicks early on. He might say that the left-centre was a bit weak in defence. Let's have a go at him. But no more than that. Other than that there was no detailed game-plan as to what you should do and so on. The tactics were very much unstructured.

Jock Wemyss: I think two of [Ian Smith's] greatest tries were scored against England at Murrayfield in 1929. Each side had scored two tries and there was only about ten minutes left to play. Twice Scotland got the ball about midfield and it went quickly out to Macpherson. Each time there was that famous jink and break, and Smith was sent flying for the corner. The English fullback was in position to guard his line both times. But Smith, with no room to swerve, simply hurtled into the fullback like an express train and each time got his try for Scotland to win 12-6.

Jock Wemyss: The Scottish team, led by Max Simmers, put up a great fight against Bennie Osler's Springboks at Murrayfield in January 1932 [losing 6-3]. There was a sensational start, for almost from the first scrum Harry Lind intercepted and scored at the posts. There was, however, such a gale and driving rain behind Jock Allan that this splendid kicker missed an easy chance to add goal points. Scotland fought with great heart against the storm during the second half and would have scored twice had the ball been put out quickly to Ian Smith.

Smith's great career ended in 1933 when Scotland won the Triple Crown by beating Ireland at Dublin in April. The original fixture had been postponed because of the memorable storm voyage from Glasgow. He was captain of the team and as relations with France had been suspended, Scotland's opening game was at St Helen's. Eight new caps were in the team and, as Wales had at long last gained a first win over England at Twickenham, nobody in Scotland thought our team could win.

The young Scots led by Smith rose splendidly to the occasion, however, and despite a shaky start they settled down confidently. Smith inspired them by opening the scoring after good handling by H Lind and HDB Lorraine. Although some of his great pace had gone, the Scottish skipper ran with all his old determination.

Next KC Fyfe, one of the new caps, kicked a penalty and then converted a try by KLT 'Kiltie' Jackson to make the interval score – Scotland 11, Wales 0. Smith was away on another run when Jackson scored. Wilf Wooller stopped Smith though he could not prevent the scoring inside pass to Scotland's stand-off. It was in this game that Scotland wore numbers for the first time against one of the home countries.

Ross Logan, who was one of the outstanding international players in the decade before the Second World War, was one of the biggest and most powerful [scrum-halves.] He could stand up to the biggest forwards, and I recall Watcyn Thomas [the Welsh captain that year] held Logan in the highest esteem, paying tribute to his indestructibility: 'Ross is like a ninth forward,' he said.

Logan played a prominent part in the postponed match in Dublin. To the chagrin of all Irishmen, Scotland won that game by two dropped goals [four points each then] to two tries [only three each]. Ireland's scores came at the beginning of each half, Scotland's at the end of each – and what a dramatic end it was!

Just before the interval Logan's accurate pass enabled Jackson to score the four points which gave Scotland, who had Ian Smith injured, a lucky lead. Near the end Logan threw a long pass direct to Harry Lind playing in the centre, and the latter's fine kick from an angle won the game and the season's honours.

Logan and Wilson Shaw became a half-back partnership for the first time in 1934 [on a Barbarians Easter tour to Wales] and were partners in five international games. It was the year Shaw was capped as a wing threequarter. The idea that Shaw might make a great stand-off came from the astute minds of Phil Macpherson and Herbert Waddell. The experiment was a huge success. Some Scots did not believe it till [in 1938] they saw that famous try at Twickenham which ensured victory for Scotland in 'Shaw's match.'

Lindsay Lambie (Scotland 1934-1935, 7 Caps): I won my first cap against Wales at Murrayfield in 1934 and a year later at Cardiff Arms Park nearly missed the game because I looked so young. Having been separated from the rest of the team on the way to the ground, I was heading for the players' entrance when a helpful Welsh official directed me to the boys' gate: a typical Welsh trick to make our chaps feel small! Vivian Jenkins added insult to injury by dropping a very speculative goal late on in the match to pinch victory.

Jock Wemyss: Scotland's victory over Ireland at Murrayfield in 1938 marked an

Ogden's Cigarette cards: Heroes of 1929.

Top, from left to right: Jimmy Dykes, Dan Drysdale, Charlie Brown, William Berkley, John Bannerman and Jock Allan
Bottom, from left to right: Bob Smith, Ian Smith, Max Simmers, John Paterson, Phil MacPherson and Harry Greenlees

important step in the Triple Crown and International Championship success. While the Scottish forwards did not by any means find matters going too well for them, the pace of Shaw, Dick and Macrae in midfield told heavily against Ireland. Scotland's 23-14 win in a spectacular game was in the end a matter of goal kicking, Ireland scoring try for try and obtaining three to two in the second half.

The 1938 Calcutta Cup match which Scotland won 21-16 was the most thrilling and spectacular of all. None can have been more exciting to watch for the play was punctuated by scoring – twelve in all – and not until RW Shaw got the last with a brilliant run just two minutes from the end was a Scottish victory certain. This was the Scottish captain's second try and his side had five in all. But it seemed that every time Scotland scored, the English fullback chalked off a try by kicking a penalty goal.

In 1938 when Scotland won the Triple Crown and Championship I rate Bill Young (Cambridge University), Laurie Duff (Glasgow Academicals) and Wilfred Crawford (Royal Navy) as the best back-row we have had.

SEVEN

THE SECOND WORLD WAR
1939-1945

There was no shortage of volunteers from the Scottish rugby community when, for the second time in barely a quarter of a century, the call to arms to serve King and country came in September 1939 and the Five Nations Championship slipped into hibernation during the Second World War. Murrayfield was converted into a supply depot for the Royal Army Service Corps and, until 1944 when it was derequisitioned and the home tie in the annual Scotland versus England services internationals was played, the turnstiles lay still. Between 1942 and 1945 the armed services played these games over two legs, home and away, and before the return to Murrayfield in 1944, the first two home matches were staged at Inverleith.

In all, eight internationals took place across the four war-torn seasons, England winning five to Scotland's three. With many top-notch rugby players from the Commonwealth stationed across the United Kingdom, qualification rules were relaxed. Thus Ronald Rankin, an Australian Test fullback, could turn out in an English jersey against the Scots at Wembley in 1942 and Rod McKenzie, who had locked the scrum for the All Blacks against Scotland at Murrayfield in 1935, was in blue for the last two games of the series in 1945. The matches provided important practice for seasoned players and helped many younger ones establish their credentials as potential post-war internationalists. The fixtures, moreover, proved welcome diversions from the everyday tensions of the war for the thousands of spectators who turned out to watch them.

Although the toll was not as great as it was in the First War, Scotland lost a generation of players to the Second, with fourteen capped internationalists alone killed in action, nearly half of them while serving in the RAF. An unexpected bonus of the war was an armistice between the rugby codes, Union and League administrators suspending old animosities. The foremost Scot returning to the 15-a-side format was a veteran of the 1924 British Lions tour to South Africa, Roy Kinnear, who shortly after helping Scotland to share the 1926 Five Nations title had turned professional with Wigan RL. He played in a League Test for Great Britain against Australia in 1929 and was serving as a corporal stationed at Uxbridge when he died suddenly at the age of thirty-eight while playing in a local Service match in September 1942.

The roll of honour included the renowned rugby wing and fabled Olympian Eric Liddell, who had gone to the Far East as a Christian missionary in the summer of 1925. He died near the end of the war in an internment camp in Weihsien, China, where he was a prisoner of the Japanese. Pat Munro, the former Scottish half-back, was killed when a bomb exploded whilst he was taking part in a Home Guard exercise in Westminster where he was an MP and Jim Ritchie of Ian Smith's 1933 Triple Crown side died of fever contracted on active service in the northern Punjab. Four members of the 1938 Triple Crown back division – fullback George Roberts, wings John Forrest

Opposite: Murrayfield Stadium's War Memorial.

and Bill Renwick, and scrum-half Tom Dorward were among the younger casualties. It was some consolation to his relatives, perhaps, that the Dorward name would live on in Scottish rugby through the fifties when his younger brother, Arthur, maintained the family's rugby honour as a pugnacious scrum-half and inspiring captain.

ROLL OF HONOUR 1939-1945

MacKENZIE, Donald Kenneth Andrew (Scotland 1939) Killed in a training flight crash south of Edinburgh on June 12, 1940.

DORWARD, Thomas Fairgrieve (Scotland 1938-39) Died of wounds in Castle Bytham, Lincolnshire on March 5, 1941.

ROSS, William Alexander (Scotland 1937) Died serving as a pilot in North Africa, 28 September, 1941.

MUNRO, Patrick (Scotland 1905-11) Killed on Home Guard duty in Westminster on May 3, 1942.

RITCHIE, James McPhail (Scotland 1933-34) Died of fever in Rawalpindi on 6 July, 1942.

FORREST, John Gordon Scott (Scotland 1938) Killed in an aircraft crash on September 14, 1942.

KINNEAR, Roy Muir (Scotland 1926) Died playing in a Service match at Uxbridge on September 22, 1942.

ST CLAIR-FORD, Drummond (Scotland 1930-32) Missing presumed drowned after the submarine *Traveller* was lost in the Gulf of Taranto in December 12, 1942.

ROBERTS, George (Scotland 1938-39) Died as a PoW of the Japanese on August 2, 1943.

PENMAN, William Mitchell (Scotland 1939) Died when his Lancaster went missing on a raid over Kassel, Germany on October 3, 1943.

GALLIE, George Holmes (Scotland 1939) KIA at Minturno, Italy, January 16, 1944.

McNEIL, Alastair Simpson Bell (Scotland 1935) KIA at Anzio, Italy on 26 January, 1944.

RENWICK, William Norman (Scotland 1938-39) KIA at Bolsena in Italy, on June 15, 1944.

LIDDELL, Eric Henry (Scotland 1922-23) He died in a PoW camp at Weihsien, Shantung province, China on February 21, 1945.

EIGHT

LIGHT FROM THE SHADOWS
1945-1949

When, at last, the war ended, international rugby resumed with a series of Victory Internationals held in the 1945-46 season among the Home Nations and the touring New Zealand Army side – the so-called Kiwis – before the Five Nations Championship, with France restored as full members, was revived in 1947. Returning to life in a country ravaged by the horrors of war and reeling from its impact, Scotland's rugby players found solace in the game that they held so dear. Pulling on the dark blue jersey, even if it wasn't in a full international, was still the greatest honour to be bestowed to a Scottish player – and one that many individuals would go to great extremes to realise.

The great restorative for British rugby as it emerged from the war years was the visit of the Kiwis – the 'Khaki All Blacks' of the Second New Zealand Expeditionary Forces stationed across Europe and Northern Africa. The tour's objects were to revive interest in the game in Britain, help services' charities and provide representative experience for potential All Blacks of the future. That they wore the all black kit of New Zealand, were led by Charlie Saxton the pre-war All Black and were committed to playing bright, open rugby added to their drawing power.

The Kiwis gave a tremendous fillip to the game in the Home Unions and several of their back division – notably Bob Scott at fullback, Fred Allen at five-eighth and Wally Argus, Johnny Smith and Eric Boggs among the threequarters – went on to become famous post-war New Zealand international players. The side undertook thirty-three matches on a European tour that lasted from late-October 1945 until the end of March 1946, losing only twice: against Monmouthshire at Pontypool and to Scotland in a thrilling match at Murrayfield in mid-January.

Ian Geddes led Scotland, all in white, from the fullback position and his side came from behind in the second half to lead 8-6 with time running out. Ian Lumsden and Russell Bruce had combined to send John Anderson over in the corner before Bill Munro scored for Doug Smith to add the conversion. In a tense finish Anderson, a real flyer on the right-wing, sealed Scotland's first (and only) victory over a New Zealand representative team to date by sprinting to the corner to touch down after Russell Bruce had fired wide with a drop at goal. Straight after the match Anderson, who had spent three years of his service life as a prisoner-of-war in Czechoslovakia, was lost to the rival code, signing professional forms for Huddersfield RL.

Scotland emerged from that win as the team to beat in the Victory Internationals against the Home Unions in the next two months. Travel difficulties from the mainland to Ireland meant that none of the British sides visited Dublin, so the post-war series lacked the completeness or symmetry of the Five Nations round-robin. Moreover, with many servicemen still abroad, Unions found it impossible to field full-strength sides and, for that

Opposite: Scotland and England line up for the anthems for the first post-war Twickenham cap match in 1947.

reason, no caps were awarded. That was a pity for Scotland's players because they twice defeated Wales, overcame Ireland and England at Murrayfield, and met their only reverse away to England at Twickenham. A high standard of combined play was the feature of their performances and it was for good reason that the Scots were hailed as the team of the series.

Russell Bruce (Scotland XV 1946 & Scotland 1947-49, 8 Caps): I played in several of the service internationals during the war, and when the war finished I captained the Rhine Army side until I was demobbed in February 1946. During that period, I also came home quite often to play for the British Army because they didn't have a stand-off in the country which suited them.

So I got a very nice trip home from France every couple of weeks in a first-class sleeper, which was set aside for me with all my papers in it. The number of times Generals or Field Marshals came along and said, 'Who's this Major Bruce occupying a sleeper while I can't get one?'

But one time they changed the starting terminus from Genapp to somewhere else, which meant I went to the wrong place and missed the connection. I was stranded. Then my driver said, 'Why don't we just motor overnight to Calais?'

I said, 'What a wonderful idea – but I doubt we'll have enough petrol to get all the way there.'

'Don't worry,' he said, 'I know a depot where the Canadians have got petrol – we'll go and bribe a jerry can from them – that should see us to Calais.'

So we headed over to the depot and did a deal with these Canadian chaps and then headed off. We drove all through the night in this open-top jeep; it was quite an adventure and we really had to hare it along all these winding roads in the pitch dark, but it was worth it. It meant an awful lot to get back and play in those games.

But when we eventually got to Calais I was put under arrest because my papers explaining that I was on leave to go and play rugby in Bristol for the Army against the touring New Zealand Army had been on the train and I didn't have anything to prove that what I was telling them was true. Fortunately, they put me on the ferry and when I got to Dover they phoned up the Army Sport Control Board, and were told, 'Yes, we're expecting Major C.R.Bruce – we thought he would be here last night.' So they finally released me and I was able to head off and join up with the rest of the team.

It was quite interesting because having spent a night in a jeep then the next night under arrest I was a bit of a write-off against the Kiwis – which was quite beneficial when they played Scotland later in the tour. Billy Munro, who was at inside centre, and I played particularly well in that game and we won 11-6. A few years later, when I played for the Barbarians alongside the New Zealand half-back [five-eighth] Fred Allen, he told me that when they were discussing the Scotland team before the match they had written me off as a no-hoper because I had played so badly for the Army. We were the only [international] team to beat the Kiwis on that tour, which was quite an achievement – especially when you consider that Scotland have never beaten

New Zealand in all the years since then. That result really stands out and should be remembered more than it is, because it was a special victory and it was wonderful to be part of it.

The Kiwis were a great team – full of power and pace, and they were all monstrously big and fit, and because they were on a tour they were much better prepared than we were. But we really stuck in as a team and were cheered on wonderfully by the Murrayfield crowd; we wanted to enjoy ourselves whenever we played for Scotland, so we attacked whenever we could and at times we looked like the touring team because things just worked so well between the players.

We had played against rugby league players in the army at that time because during the war the two codes joined forces and played under union rules. Things soon went back to normal, with the two codes once again separated [in 1945-46].

An aerial view of Murrayfield during the Scotland-England
Victory International match in 1946.

Angus Black (Scotland XV 1946 & Scotland 1947-1950, 6 Caps plus 2 Caps for the Lions): I played a couple of wartime services matches against England as an officer cadet in between studying as a medic at Edinburgh University. Ian Geddes, the fullback, was our captain and he led us again in the series of Victory Internationals straight after the war.

I played scrum-half to Ian Lumsden who later went off to live in Australia. I remember John Anderson of London Scottish playing on the wing and scoring a try against the New Zealanders. He was the fastest player of our time.

The first big game I played in was the 1945 Services International against England at Leicester and we wiped the floor with them. There was a Welsh rugby league chap playing fullback, Ernie Ward, and I got away from a scrum about halfway up the pitch, and went up the blindside dribbling the ball. It was going quite well and there was only this one bugger to beat, and it would have been the simplest thing in the world to either kick it to the left or the right of him, or even through his legs, but I swear that chap looked at me and hypnotised me and I kicked the ball right into his arms.

That was exciting, and it had a quality of its own, as did the game against Kiwis in 1946, and when we beat the hell out of Wales in 1946 down in Swansea, and these three games stand-out – because of the quality of the rugby, really. But after that, apart from university rugby and the occasional Barbarians tour, nothing – including the 1950 Lions tour games – stood out as memorable rugby experiences. Which, in retrospect, I find rather disappointing.

Douglas Elliot (Scotland XV 1946 & Scotland 1947-1954, 29 Caps): [After leaving school at sixteen in 1940 to work on the family farm] I played no rugby for two years because travel was difficult and there was little petrol for private use. But I'd had a very good grounding in the game, having been at St Mary's, Melrose before Edinburgh Academy, while, playing alongside players of the calibre and experience of Gordon Watt and Ian Henderson in the Accies/Wanderers [a war-time club amalgamation], I was never short of good advice.

Norman Mair: In his third season in club rugby [Douglas Elliot] made his debut for Scotland in the unofficial international with the Kiwis. Scotland's historic victory that day launched [him] on a career which saw him captain Scotland and win twenty-nine caps without ever being dropped, though he did miss a year through a hernia.

In the Victory Internationals, in the course of which Scotland lost only to England at Twickenham, but trounced Wales 25-6 at Swansea, Elliot had as his fellow-flanker, John Orr, with Wallace Deas at No 8, a back-row fondly remembered by the Murrayfield cohorts.

Ken Scotland (Scotland 1957-65, 27 Caps plus 5 Caps for the Lions): There was no real sporting pedigree of any distinction in my family but I was born within a stone-throw of Goldenacre, and from a very young age I have memories of playing there with either a cricket ball or a rugby ball. All my interests at that stage were sports related. It seemed as if I was at Goldenacre every Saturday watching Heriot's play, but they used to still play a lot of big games at Inverleith, and I remember going along there to watch those matches too. However, I think the key moment as far as my early rugby development was concerned came in 1946 when my father took me to watch Scotland beat the New Zealand Army at Murrayfield. From then on I wanted to play for Scotland. It really concentrated the mind – that became my central focus in life. Years later, when I made it into the Scotland team, I was happy to discover that the vast majority of the team had a similar sort of mindset. Over the years I think that has been the defining thing about the way Scotland play, and it has helped us punch above our weight for so long.

Frank Coutts (Scotland XV 1946 & Scotland 1947, 3): When I was first selected for Scotland, for our Victory International against Wales in March 1946, I was stationed in Denmark and I honestly think I would never have found out I had been picked were it not for a Corporal in Copenhagen who rang through and told me. He said he had taken the liberty of booking me a plane to Prestwick on the Thursday and that the fare was about £33 . . . It took me eighteen months to get that refunded. I don't think the SRU were mean, they were just canny.

There were five men – 'Donnie' Innes, Ian Henderson, Ralph Sampson, Copey Murdoch, William Young – who played for Scotland both before and after the war, and the famous story is that when they turned up to play for the first time since hostilities had ceased, they each found that there was no strip for them to put on, and Harry Simson, the secretary, said, 'You got your jerseys before the war.'

When they first re-introduced the National trial after the war we all turned up at Murrayfield and the great innovation was that we all had to have our height and weight measured. So I stepped up onto the weighing machine.

'Where's your penny, Mr Coutts?'

I had to pay a penny to be weighed. Harry Simson certainly liked to keep a tight ship!

I played in the last of the Victory Internationals, which was against England at Murrayfield, and it was a marvellous experience – we won 27-0 and you could really feel the crowd pressing in around the pitch. Whenever we scored the whole place went berserk; you could actually feel the noise throbbing through you.

Russell Bruce: I played in the six Victory Internationals and despite the number of players we lost during the hostilities, we gave a very good account of ourselves. We

The players in action during Scotland's momentous
victory over the New Zealand Army.

won five of the matches – against the New Zealand Army, Wales in both Swansea and Edinburgh, Ireland and England at Murrayfield and only lost to England at Twickenham. I scored four tries during those games, so was very satisfied with how it had all gone.

Angus Black: The first official cap international was against France on the 1 January 1947. We travelled to Paris by train and boat via Dover and stayed at the Hotel Lutetia which had been the Paris headquarters for the Gestapo during their war-time occupation. They'd cleaned the blood from the floors before the SRU party arrived. It was palatial.

I remember Cyril Gadney, a well-known referee from before and after the War, was in charge of the match. Early on we had a scrum and I put the ball in at forty-five degrees to the tunnel. The Paris crowd made a loud hissing noise when there was no penalty. Gadney whispered in my ear, 'Let's have it in straighter next time. Don't do it again,' but allowed play to continue.

What struck me about the French was their innate ability for the game. They had been out of international rugby since 1931, but their kicking, passing and backing up were fast and accurate. We did well to hold them and only lost narrowly.

They had two very big second-rows – Moga and Soro. They were off the planet. I remember one holding me while the other kicked me in the groin. I had a swelling the size of a tennis ball for days after. I don't know why people find it so amusing when you have a testicle like a big jaffa orange which is hurting like hell. The commentator was a chap called Rex Alston, who was a very perfect Englishman, and he had warned the people back home that I had been injured by a kick in the stomach – which must have been the established euphemism.

When I got back to Dunfermline, I went to see the doctor on the Monday morning. His name was Bobby Lind, who played for Dunfermline and was the brother of Harry Lind, who was capped on the wing for Scotland. He started laughing as well – which just about sums it up.

Russell Bruce: When we played that game we found that their professionals were there playing as amateurs again. So we asked them why they had decided to come back to union, and they told us it was more lucrative.

It had been a different story in Scotland, where they remained very strict about keeping union and league apart, despite what went on elsewhere during the war. In 1944 the Army Sport Control Board decided to organise a special game in Bradford for the amateurs against the professionals, and I was lucky enough to be asked to play at fly-half for the amateurs, alongside the great Haydn Tanner of Wales. But I got a letter from Frank Moffat of the SRU telling me that if I played against the professionals I would never be considered for Scotland again.

Hopes were pretty high then when Scotland travelled to Paris to meet France for the first time for sixteen years to launch the first post-war Championship season in 1947. Geddes remained as captain of a side comprising fourteen new caps, though many had gained unofficial recognition in the wartime services and post-war Victory internationals. Scotland were beaten, but for the young men who had experienced the austerity of the forties, the hospitality and fare offered in Paris were ample compensation for their loss.

The Scots were disappointed to finish with the Wooden Spoon in 1947, whitewashed in the Five Nations, and lost to a strong Australian tour side later that year. The Wallabies' line was crossed in only one of their five Tests – by France in Paris – and they had a dynamic back-row that featured a young Sydney doctor, Doug Keller. After the tour Keller remained in Britain to further his studies at Guy's Hospital and joined the London Scottish club from where he later played Test rugby for Scotland.

George Cawkwell (Scotland 1947, 1 Cap): I had played games – I naturally gravitated to the louts [at Oxford University where he was a New Zealand Rhodes Scholar]. It was wartime, anyone who was any bloody good had gone away.

I wouldn't have dreamt of [playing for the All Blacks], it was too divine a calling. I had a very Scottish upbringing. My mother used to play the piano and on Sunday nights we sang Scottish songs after dinner. [After the Varsity Match at Twickenham in December 1946] people came round and asked who we wanted to be considered for, and I said Scotland because of my mother.

I can't say I saw any [bloodstains in the Hotel Lutetia] but I remember people getting bloodied on the field. There were only five points in it, so it was not one-sided at all. I don't remember their forwards being much better. Maybe I was puffing around the field too much. I was assigned a job. If I'd known about it, I wouldn't have taken it on. France had two very heavy forwards, Alban Moga was one of them, and there was a danger of them coming round in the lineout. They had to be marked. If they moved forward I had to move forward with them. Moga broke through and I think I was blamed for it.

The dinner was very splendid. If we were having a rugby dinner in this country it would have been beer and some basic food, but they had wonderful food and wine. Another time, I played in Paris with the University and they really liked to do things well there. I don't know what they thought of life in this country when they came over here.

Frank Coutts: We hadn't played France since 1931 because there had been a fall-out over the issue of France fielding professionals, and this was the hand of friendship after fighting together in the war. So we all ploughed over to Paris for January 1 and I was a reserve, which meant I didn't even have to strip off; but I had my bag-pipes so I was able to lead the team onto the field. We had a lovely dinner that night in the Eiffel Tower and enjoyed the hospitality immensely – so much so that I was a bit worried by the end of the evening that a few of the boys might fall over the edge.

That was a great occasion because things had been so grim for so long and it was just wonderful to be in this magnificent city, playing rugby and enjoying life. It was sad because you found yourself thinking of all the players who were no longer with us that might have been there, and you could argue that I would never have been capped had so-and-so not been killed in the war. But that was the life we had and I was thrilled to be involved. I actually should have been in the Palestine with my regiment but the army insisted I stay behind because I had a chance of being capped.

Angus Black: The ex-military men in the team had taken wise provision against any threat of an alcohol drought and brought the wherewithal to make champagne cocktails back in the hotel. So all of us were pretty merry by the time we got to the Eiffel Tower, and the French thought they had done well because they released a lot of fine wines from the Germans, and that was all there as well.

I personally had no previous experience of wine, and set about drinking glasses like half pints of beer. So by the time we sat down for dinner, I think I got halfway through the *hors d'oeuvre* when I realised the end of the world was coming and fell under the table. I was picked up and unceremoniously dumped on the parapet round the dining area. It was the first of January, so it was bloody freezing – and, of course, I was sick all over myself.

I was told afterwards that the chap I had been sitting next to – Ian Henderson, who played in the front-row – had finished his *hors d'oeuvre* when he was struck by this overwhelming desire to give us a tune on the pipes, and he managed to get the bag under his arm and give it a squeeze when he was sick, then passed out and was dumped on the parapet as well.

The trip home by boat and train was an absolute nightmare because as long as I was out in the cold my clothes didn't stink. But as soon as I got into a warm atmosphere they began to steam, and it was very distressing to see people moving away from me so determinedly.

Frank Coutts: One of my favourite recollections is of Gordon Watt of Edinburgh Academicals, who was one of my army buddies. He was also in the Scottish side, and he took me aside before the England match at Twickenham [in 1947] and said, 'We're all being lined up to meet the King, then the whistle goes and we're off. But I've got false teeth and I don't want to meet the King with my teeth out.' So I said, 'You stand early on in the line and after you've met the King take your teeth out, wrap them in a handkerchief and pass them down the line to the touch-judge. 'It wasn't the most sophisticated plan in the world, but he was happy enough with it and when it came off without a hitch, he was very pleased.

Russell Bruce: I captained the team when we played England at Twickenham in [our] last game of the Championship – and I moved in from centre for that game to play at fly-half. That then became my new position and although I didn't play for Scotland in 1948, I was back in the team for the 1949 Championship and played all the games at fly-half. We won our opening game down in Colombes, which was a fantastic result against a good French team and Doug Elliot scored a try, as did Peter Kininmonth on his debut. We beat Wales in Edinburgh for our other victory that season, and I remember Doug Smith scoring a wonderful try on the wing in that game. My final two caps came against Ireland and England and although we lost both, which was a disappointing way to finish my Scotland career, I am so thrilled that I was given the opportunity to play in that blue jersey for all those matches, especially when you think about all the poor chaps who we had lost in the war. But for those of us who made it through, it really was a wonderful experience.

The 1948 Championship brought narrow Murrayfield wins against France (9-8) and England (6-3), leaving Scotland in mid-table, but there was a bright start to 1949 with an unexpected Paris win against France (8-0) followed by a well-planned victory over Wales (6-5) at Murrayfield. Keller was among six new caps – and captain to boot – when the Scots won at Colombes. Douglas Elliot and Peter Kininmonth, his back-row colleagues, were the try-scorers there and combined effectively with Keller in tactics that bottled up the Welsh at Murrayfield three weeks later. A defensive trap comprising the Scottish halves and back-row repeatedly snared the Welsh backs before attacking moves could be launched and eventually the home side, despite limited possession, managed to eke out a clever one-point win through tries from Doug Smith and Laurie Gloag.

Central to the team's early post-war endeavours was the great Border warrior, Douglas Elliot. He made his Scotland debut in the non-cap 1946 Victory International against the Kiwis, delivering a powerful performance that contributed significantly to Scotland's victory against the touring New Zealanders. He was blessed with pace, stamina, the hands of a threequarter and the strength of a prop, and became the outstanding Scottish rugby player of the immediate post-war years.

Norman Mair: So often in a Scotland jersey in the post-war decade Douglas Elliot seemed to be playing the enemy almost on his own. He was undeniably a great occasion player.

At 6' 2½" and fourteen stone in an era when forwards were generally smaller than they are today [he] was often taller than Scotland's recognised line-out specialists. Yet all too little was made of him at the tail.

Those who said that Elliot wasn't fit had never trained with him in the build-up to an international, albeit much of his training was done on his own and some of the conditioning simply in the course of his work, humping 16st barley bags. The farm [became] his responsibility that Saturday in January, 1949, when his father died, having just heard over the wireless his son scoring the opening try in Scotland's 8-0 defeat of France at Colombes.

NINE

THE FICKLE FIFTIES
1950-1959

Vince Lombardi once paraphrased Confucious when describing the true spirit of sporting triumph as 'being knocked to your knees and then coming back; that's real glory.' He was also famed for saying: 'confidence is contagious; so is lack of confidence.' If ever there were two phrases that encapsulated the fluctuating fortunes of the Scotland rugby team during the 1950s, it would be hard to look beyond Lombardi's concise analyses. It was a decade when several players carved their names in Scottish rugby history and when some extraordinary victories were posted; but it also saw many bleak years, years when supporters would wonder if they would ever see the thistle in glorious flourish again.

The 1950 season saw wins at home to France and England countered by defeats in Swansea and Dublin. In 1951, Murrayfield bore witness to one of the all-time great Scotland performances and one in which Douglas Elliot and Peter Kininmonth – 'Peetah' his colleagues called him on account of his immaculate English intonation – established themselves forever in Scottish rugby lore. Wales arrived in Edinburgh for the game on 3 February as 1950 Grand Slam champions and on the back of an impressive 23-5 victory over England in their opening match of the 1951 Championship. Their team contained eleven players who had toured New Zealand and Australia with Karl Mullen's Lions the previous summer, while Scotland had suffered a 14-12 defeat to France in Colombes on their opening weekend, had a young and inexperienced team – with none of the backs older than twenty-two – and in No.8 Kininmonth the only Lion in the squad (Elliot had been unable to tour owing to farming commitments). The result, it seemed, was a foregone conclusion.

In the build-up to the match, Elliot made the decision that he and Robert Taylor would abandon the usual back-row system of playing left and right flanks. Instead, Elliot would play exclusively on the open-side – he wanted to hunt the Welsh backline from every scrum and lineout. He had studied their play and had identified one of the keys to their attack, remarking with ominous simplicity: 'I know which way Glyn Davies sidesteps.'

Such was the effectiveness of Elliot's assault on the Welsh stand-off that John Gwilliam, the captain, moved centre Lewis Jones into the pivotal position to try and combat the maelstrom that Elliot was unleashing on Davies. It had little effect. As the Welsh sought to launch their attacks from further afield they found their efforts closed out in midfield by Donald Scott and Donald Sloan, who were taking a lead from their talismanic flanker's defensive efforts. As the final quarter of the game approached, Scotland were leading 3-0. A wild defensive clearance kick by the Welsh was gathered by Kininmonth, who let fly with a speculative drop-goal. He caught it perfectly. As the ball sailed high between the posts, the men in blue seemed to grow visibly. With Elliot and Kininmonth at their lead, Scotland overwhelmed their visitors in the closing minutes, scoring one try through prop James Dawson and a brace more through wing Bob Gordon, who was making his debut.

Opposite: Douglas Elliot, the flanker was considered by many as Scotland's outstanding post-war forward.

Donald Scott (Scotland 1950-1953): In 1950 Scotland beat France at home but then lost 12-0 in Wales. Meanwhile, I had gone off to do my National Service so hadn't had a pair of boots on for five weeks. I was sitting in the NAAFI having a cup of coffee with a mate, and he was reading the paper. He said, 'You're interested in Scottish rugby aren't you? Well, they're making a change to the Scotland team for Saturday. They've dropped DA Sloan and picked a guy called . . . good God, this is you . . . DM Scott.' And that was the first I heard of it. I was posted down in Winchester and the letter would go from Murrayfield to my parents' house in Langholm. They must have put it to one side thinking it wasn't that important.

It was quite difficult in those days because you had to get a visa and a passport to go across to southern Ireland and I had nothing like that. I wasn't allowed to be photographed in my army uniform but all my other kit had been sent home. I managed to get hold of a dark shirt which still looked quite military – but that seemed to be okay and I got over there and played.

DWC Smith, this big Aberdonian, was on the wing. Before the match, he came out onto the pitch for training wearing a pair of spikes. I said, 'What are you doing with those on? You'll cause real damage if you stand on someone.'

He said, 'I'm kind of slow compared to some of you guys so I need all the help I can get.' He was sprinting up and down the pitch with spikes on and, of course, nobody would go anywhere near him. We were thrashed 21-0 in the rain that day – the ground was really wet and I found it hard to keep my footing.

Angus Black: Both of Ireland's first choice centres had been injured before the match, and then one of the replacements went down with illness. The replacement's replacement was a guy called Hex Uprichard – who had been in the RAF – and he had the game of his life, as they ran out 21-0 winners.

That was the second consecutive weekend I had been in Dublin. The previous weekend I had been playing for the Combined Services, and walking the streets of Dublin on that first occasion we got spat on fairly regularly because we were British troops; and the contrast between that experience, and the following week when the Scots were there, was astonishing – suddenly we were all buddies.

Donald Scott: Fortunately, I managed to keep my place for the next game against England, when Tommy Gray popped over a conversion at the very end for a 13-11 victory. I still maintain that Donald Sloan and I scored half a try each in that match. We closed after this ball and I'm pretty sure I scored, and he might say the same. When we were trotting back towards the halfway line, I put my hand on his shoulder and said something along the lines of, 'Great, we made it. We can win this game.' And it came out later that the people watching thought that was me congratulating him, so he got the credit.

Norman Mair: We won the Calcutta Cup in 1950 and we were still within a couple of games of England over all the matches played since 1871. We beat Wales 19-0 [in 1951]. That was a bit of a freak, certainly, but at the same time, we had scored try for try with all the other countries and up till then, things hadn't gone too badly. Nobody really thought of Scotland as being weak.

Donald Scott: In 1951 we beat Wales 19-0 at Murrayfield. Their team had eleven players who toured with the British Lions in New Zealand the previous summer, and they had thumped England a fortnight earlier. The game was played in front of a record crowd at that time. They stopped letting people in, then hundreds more surged through a gap in the railings and climbed over the walls and turnstiles. The game was delayed for a little bit, and lots of supporters were brought in and sat on the grass in front of the schoolboys' enclosure, which meant that opposite the West Stand you had the touchline and then supporters only a couple of feet back. It was quite intimidating – you felt like you were in a real cauldron.

The first-half had been pretty tight and we were piling on the pressure at the start of the second-half but only leading 3-0 when their fullback, Gerwyn Williams, sent a clearance kick in my direction. I was standing there ready to gather it when I heard Peter Kininmonth's voice saying, 'My ball.'

Well, he was my captain and he was bigger than me, so I decided to leave it to him. He caught the ball, pivoted and sent over the most perfectly struck drop-goal I had ever seen, from twenty-five yards out close to the touchline.

I think he'd played in the back division at school – so might have dropped a few goals back then – but he was 6' 4" and had moved into the forwards. His kick was the turning point and we went on to beat them 19-0.

I got a bit of a laugh afterwards because someone asked me what I would have done if Kininmonth hadn't been there. I said, 'Quite simple, I would have caught the ball, skipped past the Welsh defence with a couple of sidesteps and scored between the posts. The conversion would have made five points . . . Kininmonth only got three points for his drop-goal!'

Later in the match I went through the middle and as I got closer and closer to the try-line I could sense this shadow coming up on my left shoulder. I was very tense because the last thing you wanted in those days was to be tackled in possession when you were in the clear. So with about three or four steps to go, I flicked it to Bob Gordon who was on my right. For years afterwards I always said I gave him the pass with five yards to go, and he insisted that he got it twenty-five yards out. In the end we had to compromise.

Douglas Elliot: The Scotland matches I enjoyed the most were against England in 1951 and Wales in both 1949 and 1951. I was never in a winning side against Ireland so I'd be reluctant to say that I enjoyed myself chasing Jack Kyle round the broad acres of a rugby field! As far as my own best performance, I am inclined to feel that it was in the memorable match of 1951 when we created havoc among the Welsh ranks to the extent of a 19-0 Murrayfield defeat.

Between that glorious February day and the corresponding fixture in 1955, Scotland suffered seventeen consecutive defeats, scoring just eleven tries, six conversions, and four penalties in five years for a paltry total of 57 points, and endured humiliation at the hands of the Springboks in November 1951 in the 'Murrayfield Massacre', going down 44-0. One of the reasons for this catastrophic demise in fortunes has been attributed to there being little or no consistency in selection between Tests during this terrible run, making it nigh on impossible for the team to develop any momentum. In 1953 alone, thirty-one different players were selected over four matches, and 39 new caps were awarded over only three seasons.

Scotland flanker Robert Taylor tries to shake off three
Welsh tacklers as Douglas Elliot looks on.

Throughout these years, however, Douglas Elliot remained consistently brilliant and often seemed to be the only man capable of dragging Scotland through the mire to victory. During the 1954 encounter with the All Blacks his colossal efforts almost single-handedly held the New Zealanders to a 3-0 final score-line.

After years of fighting an almost thankless battle for the Scottish cause, Elliot finally hung up his boots in 1954 – meaning that he was not part of the national team's revival, which began with victory over Wales at Murrayfield in 1955. The former international, John Bannerman, had by now become a leading committee member of the SRU and in his year as President he called for an overhaul of Scottish methods. Scottish clubs were experimenting with the modern 3-4-1 scrummage. Bannerman demanded a reversion to the traditional 3-2-3 methods of the 1920s sand 1930s which had served them in good stead. A new generation of forwards headed by Jim Greenwood, whose teaching commitments in out-of-the-way Glenalmond left him open to unfair criticism that he was uncommitted at club rugby level, was quietly emerging. Greenwood, after an absence of three years, was recalled to skipper the side in Paris in January 1955. Although Scotland lost and the captaincy passed to the veteran Angus Cameron for the Welsh match, Greenwood's powers of analysis, style of pack leadership and individual skill as a back-row all-rounder could not be discarded. He had able deputies in Hawick's Hughie McLeod, the Glaswegian red-head Hamish Kemp in the second-row, and a fellow teacher, Adam Robson, in the back-row. These four were the mainstay of the Scottish pack for the remainder of the decade.

Arthur Smith, a new cap on the right-wing, was Scotland's star in the win against Wales that showed the Scots had finally turned the corner of a long, straight road. He finished off a fine performance with a virtuoso solo try from a counter-attack started deep inside his own half, cementing a long overdue 14-8 victory.

That Welsh success was backed up by a 12-3 victory over Ireland, also at Murrayfield, and after such a long period of despair, it was somewhat astonishing that Angus Cameron's team should be travelling to Twickenham looking to secure the Triple Crown; however, the dream comeback was not to be and they lost 9-6, despite prop Tom Elliot's claims to have scored a try which referee Cyril Joynson disallowed.

In the context of previous disappointments this was a minor set-back. The black cloud that had hung over Murrayfield for five years had been lifted. In 1956 Scotland ended a six year run of defeats to France by beating them 12-0 at Murrayfield and they won again against a rapidly improving French side at Murrayfield in 1958. The last years of the decade saw mixed results with two more victories against Wales (9-6 in 1957 when scrum-half Arthur Dorward set Scotland on the path to victory with a towering drop-goal and 6-5 thanks to a Norman Bruce try in 1959), a win against the 1958 Wallabies and draws against England in 1958 and 1959.

After such a deep and depressing trough, these performances were building blocks for the future. As Lombardi also famously said when again paraphrasing Confucius: 'the greatest accomplishment is not in never falling, but in rising again after you fall.' Once again, he might have been talking directly about the fortunes of the Scottish rugby team during that turbulent decade.

Donald Scott: That was a great victory over Wales in 1951 – one of the best we've ever had. We played really well. Then, somehow, we were beaten in our next game, against Ireland. They lost their fullback, GW Norton, to a late tackle from Doug Elliot and that seemed to fire them up. They played with fourteen men and we just couldn't score. It was a huge disappointment because we should have beaten them.

Norman Mair: Then we lost 44-0 to South Africa. It had the same effect on Scottish rugby as an air crash might have had if it had involved the whole national team. There was no preparation for the match, it was early season, a sunny dry day in November, the players weren't fit, there was no trial, we tried to go for a heavy pack, and of course, the forwards couldn't get about the field. It was one of those awful days when everything went wrong. The Springboks played absolutely magnificently. From that day on, Scotland really did lose the way. We lost seventeen games in succession and did not win again until 1955.

Donald Scott: The reason results and performances fluctuated so dramatically from match to match was because it was all so terribly amateurish. There was no plan about what we were going to do. Probably the best captain we had was Doug Elliot, but even he said very little. He would just tell us to get out there, do our very, very best, and not make any silly bloody mistakes – because he felt that the desire to do well must just be within you.

I remember coming away from games thinking we didn't do badly but we didn't really do enough to win. I think winning was more important to some of us than others. I felt absolutely sick when we lost games we could have won, but I think some others felt that if we had put up a good show then that was okay.

A lot of rugby at that time was about getting the ball out to the wing as quickly as possible. Even if there was a great big gap in front of you, you were meant to get it straight out to the wing and give everyone a feel of the ball. Well, international players – or even district and club players – should know exactly what is happening and be able to make up their own mind about whether to kick, pass or try to make a break when the ball comes to them. Perhaps if we'd had a good coach, they'd have picked out the strength of one or two players and come up with a way of playing that suited our game. But we didn't have that – only committee guys who had played twenty-five years earlier and were a bit out of touch. Losing 44-0 to South Africa in November 1951 highlighted these shortcomings.

Norman Mair: Angus Cameron was one of those who went down with the ship when Scotland lost 44-0 to the 1951 Springboks.

Donald Scott: When I played in any match there were three things I thought the man opposite might do: they would run at me and try to beat me, they would run at me and pass the ball to change the angle of attack, or they would kick the ball.

Well, the South Africans did all that, but they also did something I had never seen before: they ran into you. They looked at you and said, 'Come and take me.'

Now, in those days back-row forwards in British rugby used to corner-flag when their team lost the ball, they would run back diagonally towards the faraway corner. So when these guys hit us in the middle of the pitch, there was a big gap between the collision point and our cover defence, and they exploited that because after they hit us they turned and popped the ball, and they had three brilliant back-row forwards – led by the great Hennie Muller – who were coming in their slipstream and taking the ball on at pace.

South Africa scored nine tries against us and seven were scored by the forwards, which was really unusual in those days. You watch rugby now and it is all about contact, and laying the ball off in different ways – and that was the first time I saw that approach. We tackled all day, but when we got our opponents down the ball just wasn't there. I remember, in the last minute of the game, I was totally knackered and found myself chasing their winger, a guy called Paul Johnstone. I got to him just as he was going over in the corner and forced him into touch.

Now I'm not a religious man, but I said at that point, 'Dear Lord, get the referee to blow his whistle.' And he did. I got up on my feet thinking I couldn't have gone on, I was absolutely bushed. There is nothing more tiring in a game than having to tackle, tackle, tackle. It was a pretty miserable experience. The only comfort I can take is that I thought I did pretty well within the context of such a heavy defeat, and I was the only back reselected for the next game.

Apart from that match, we were never really out of the frame. We lost games we should have won, because we weren't in the winning habit. I would love to have seen a team picked by the players as opposed to the selectors, because there were guys who got caps who I don't think should have been anywhere near the Scotland team, and guys who weren't capped who should have been.

Norman Mair: We panicked right through [the early 1950s]. We went for a heavy pack one minute, and then a light, mobile pack the next. We just dithered. Arthur Dorward won fifteen caps for Scotland, but for the first nine, he was in and out of the side seven times. You can argue whether A is better than B, or B is better than C, but you must have some kind of consistency in selection.

Ken Scotland: People often talk about youngsters being disheartened by Scotland not winning games, but I grew up during the era when Scotland had lost 44-0 to South Africa in 1951, in a run of seventeen defeats in a row between 1951 and 1955, and it never dimmed my ambitions. But I suppose life was simpler in those days. There were no alternatives. We didn't have computer games, we didn't even have televisions.

Jim Greenwood (Scotland 1952-1959, 20 Caps plus 4 Caps for the Lions): I played for Scotland against France in 1952 but had to wait three years before the national selectors favoured me again. I was subjected to several press attacks about not playing regular club rugby. I was teaching until 1pm on Saturdays and the Glenalmond school XV, which I coached, played in the afternoon; and, believe me, they really needed coaching, because they had not beaten an Edinburgh school for five years. I felt it was my first duty to coach them, and did so at the risk of losing my place in the Scottish XV. However, I trained particularly hard and was eventually fortunate enough to keep my place. But really it was not that I did not want to play in club football.

Donald Scott: When we went to Ireland in 1952, Doug Elliot said to me that there was going to be a meeting the next morning at which one of the selectors was going

Angus Cameron skips away from two Irish tacklers at Murrayfield in 1951.

to tell us we were being flown home, and was going to ask if anyone didn't want to go by air. He then said, 'You'll tell them that you don't like flying.'

I said, 'Why I am going to do that, Dougie? I'm quite keen to get home.'

'No, you tell them you're not going to fly.'

Now, I was a great pal of Dougie's and he was a bit older than me so I usually did what I was told. But on this occasion I thought to myself: 'I'm not going to bother too much with that.'

Sure enough, at the meeting this guy stood up and said that they were breaking with tradition and we were going to be flown home. 'Anybody not keen on flying?'

I just sat there, determined to say nothing. But then I got this bang between my shoulder blades – it was Doug.

So he and I put our hands up, along with two other guys who were staying on to play another game on the Monday.

I said to Dougie afterwards, 'What was all that about?'

'Let's face it,' he said. 'We'll all go to the dinner tonight and we'll be late to our beds and they're all going to have to be at the airport at half past eight in the morning.'

'So?'

'Well, they'll not feel great, whereas you and I don't need to get up in the morning.'

'But the ferry is pretty early, too.'

'No,' he said. 'They don't run ferries on a Sunday. We're staying at the SRU's expense until Monday.'

So we had a free day in Dublin, and he had a couple of Border pals I didn't know about who were staying over until the Monday too. We had a great party.

James 'Basher' Inglis (Scotland 1952, 1 Cap): When I started playing for Selkirk in 1945, it was first up first down when it came to scrummaging. That's where you learned your trade – if you didn't want to be hooker then you hung back. But it was all good fun because the other team were in the same situation so you hardly ever scrummed against the same opponent.

I was reserve for Scotland twice and then played against England in the last game of the 1952 Championship.

I've got a photograph of the Scottish team training on the Friday afternoon before the game and if you count how many are in the picture you'll see there is only thirteen. Jimmy Johnston and Norman Davidson were meant to be there but they didn't turn up, and I don't think anyone ever bothered about that. There were no coaches and no officials – it was just a run-around at Raeburn Place.

On the day of the match, I came out the North British Hotel [on Princess Street – now the Balmoral Hotel] and Melville College were playing Selkirk that morning so I walked to Inverleith to watch the game then walked back, and nobody asked where I had been. They weren't bothered about that either.

Then I went across to Forsyth's [department store] and spoke to the old guy behind the counter. I told him that I was in to buy a Scotland rugby tie and he asked when I had played. I said that I was playing that afternoon and he told me he wasn't supposed to sell me a tie until I had played.

I said: 'Well, when I go out that door and across to the North British, I can assure you that I'm not going to get knocked down by any bloody tram. I'll be coming down that tunnel at Murrayfield this afternoon as sure as night follows day.'

So, he gave in and sold me the tie – but he wasn't supposed to.

We had mince and tatties before the game, and some of the team weren't eating much because of the excitement. But I wasn't going to play on an empty stomach – I knew I had to keep my strength up.

I got the ball in the first line-out. I don't know if they meant to throw it to me or not. It was pot luck, really. You jumped and if you caught it then that was great. I don't remember much more about the game. I was there in the scrum and I let them know I was there, right enough.

Hugh McLeod (Scotland 1954-1962, 40 Caps plus 6 Caps for the Lions): I played for Scotland for the first time in January 1954, against France. The news that I was capped reached me whilst on a rabbit-poaching expedition and – dare I say it – on the Sabbath, too!

Ernie Michie (Scotland 1954-1957, 15 Caps): We were beaten 3-0, which was a big improvement on the previous season, when we lost all our matches fairly heavily. What shook me most about that match was not the ferocity of the game, but when I went into the first scrum the smell of the French was a mixture of garlic, aftershave and Gauloises cigarettes. It really knocked you back. Most unusual!

Having spent the night before at the Braid Hills Hotel, we all adjourned afterwards to the North British Hotel – or the Balmoral as it is now – and I remember getting into the lift with a lot of Frenchmen. Squat, swarthy chaps chatting away in French; and as a gallus youngster I thought I must be polite to these chaps, so I turned round to one of them and said: 'Comment ca va?'

And he turned to me and said: 'Whit yi think yir oan, mun? Who doi yi think you're speaking to? I'm the yin that picked yi.'

It was Bob Hogg, the chairman of selectors from Hawick. You see, I was from the frozen north, and I didn't know any of the rugby fraternity at all. Like me, he had just happened to end up in a lift with a whole lot of Frenchmen, and he was small and squat, so I had put two and two together and got five. We had a great laugh about it, but I never lived it down.

Hugh McLeod: The match that stands uppermost in my memory occurred the following month when I realised a cherished ambition by playing for my country against the world's best, New Zealand, at Murrayfield. Scotland were rated as not having a hope against the mighty All Blacks. It wasn't surprising. The Scots were in a 'trough of despond', having lost their last twelve internationals on the trot.

The Scottish team gathered for lunch on the Friday. That gave you the chance to run your eye over the blokes you didn't know. At least we weren't introduced to each other an hour before the kick-off, as in earlier days.

The run-about at Myreside in the afternoon consisted mainly of jogging, hoofing about and some forward work. There was no detailed coaching of specified tasks. It was all a bit airy-fairy, really. But three factors were in our favour – (a) We had nothing to lose; (b) the ground was soft after heavy rain and snow; (c) Douglas Elliot, who last played for Scotland two years before, came back [from a hernia operation] as national captain at the age of 29. His team talk was brief and to the point: 'No-one gives us a chance, so let's get out there and show the bastards.' Elliot played like a man inspired, and we held him in such respect that his presence acted as a spur to the rest of us.

I remember at the first line-out thinking to myself: 'Hughie, son, oo're gawn to find oot what it's aboot th' day.' Scotland were still packing 3-2-3 in the scrummage, yet we not only held our own there but got stuck into them in every phase. Ewen Fergusson, Ernie Michie and Peter Kininmonth did wonders at the line-out. Flanker Elliot, one of the great diving, long-arm tacklers, knocked them down like skittles, and we got the feet going in traditional Scottish style. The truth is that we rattled them a bit with our fire and fury, although we were still reminded that, with All Blacks, they don't come at you in single file but in ruddy great waves.

Grant Weatherstone, our wing, was just beaten to the touch after a lovely cross-kick by one of our three new caps, Graham Ross. It took a spectacular dive-tackle by that prince of fullbacks, Bob Scott, to prevent a try by our centre, Donald Cameron. The same Scott was mightily relived when Kim Elgie punted ahead with only Scott to beat and Ian Swan running clear outside. I had a lot of time for Ian. He was a nice man and a very reliable player. He was not a flying machine, but was stocky and difficult to pull down and always dealt with whatever came his way.

But Scottie had the last laugh with a 30-yards penalty goal for foot up – the only score of the match. Those All Blacks rated our pack as the best it had encountered, and although Scotland were to go another four matches before winning, that full-blooded display put new heart into the Scottish rugby game. We were on our way back.

Kim Elgie (Scotland 1954-1955, 8 Caps): When I was a student at St Andrews University, I was chosen for the North to play the South and afterwards, knowing I was South African, one of the SRU officials asked me if I had any Scottish ancestors. I admitted to a Scots grannie, but, I was told this wasn't good enough and I thought I would never play for Scotland. Then, when I moved to London and joined London Scottish, I was picked for the National Trial and when I asked: 'What about my lack of Scottish blood?' I was told, not everyone at Murrayfield felt like that, and I got my first cap against the All Blacks in 1954.

I got a letter from the SRU, which included a return rail ticket to Edinburgh, with instructions to meet up with the Scotland team at the North British Hotel in Edinburgh for lunch on the Friday, the day before the game. There, I was introduced to Donald Cameron of Glasgow HSFP, my co-centre. We had never met, so went off down to Goldenacre I think it was, and passed a ball around between us for a spell – that was our warm-up to face the All Blacks.

Jim Greenwood: At 6.20pm on one cold December evening in 1954, Jock Wemyss phoned Glenalmond School to tell me I was to captain Scotland for the first time – against France in Paris the next month. I was standing in the quad – chapel was about to start – swathed in my gown when the porter told me I was wanted on the phone. I skipped across and heard the news . . . it was my second international and I was skipper . . . I was stunned! I remember walking up the hall to my seat in the chapel feeling deadly pale and sure it must show on the surface. I felt proud later on, but not then.

Norman Mair: John Bannerman [Scotland 1921-1929] returned to the game in 1953-54 as vice-president of the SRU, and was at once struck by the subservient role of the forwards, who seemed to see themselves only as servants of the backs. Straightforward possession from the scrum or lineout did little more, in Bannerman's opinion, than put the midfield backs at the mercy of the onrushing defence – unless the half-backs kicked.

Bannerman realised that unless the cover defence – mainly in the form of the opposition forwards – could be pinned down, the backs were liable to be devoured by any worthwhile defence. He was entirely right in stressing the need for more assertive forward play and almost all Scotland's better performances, since victory over Wales in 1955 ended a run of seventeen consecutive defeats, stemmed from positive forward play, with the forwards, as their name implies, going FORWARD.

Ernie Michie: The Welsh game in 1955 was the turning point. It was the first game

Scotland had won for seventeen games. We had an extremely light pack. I was 6ft 3inches and 14½ stone soaking wet, and I was the heaviest. But we were very, very mobile.

JM Bannerman, who played for Scotland thirty-seven times himself as a second row and wasn't big, 6ft if he was lucky, came in before the match and dictated that we would change our system of playing back to 3-2-3 in the scrum (3-4-1 had been accepted for two or three years prior to that). And he said we would go back to wheeling at the scrum. He wanted us to go back to dribbling the ball and getting the shout of 'Feet, Scotland, Feet.'

This meant Hughie McLeod and I would be pushing forward, Tom Elliot and Hamish Kemp pulling back, then I had to move the ball across so Jimmy Greenwood and either Adam Robson or Bill Glen would charge at the opposing backs. I would join him, and Peter Kininmonth would come on the other side, so we would have a phalanx of three people, and we would dribble up the park. It did work for us. It got a feeling going and an *Esprit de Corps* came through.

Arthur Smith's try set the match alight. He seemed to be hemmed in when he got the ball, next thing we knew, he was away and clear and we never looked back. It really was a great win when you see the quality of the Welsh side. I was picked for the 1955 Lions tour to South Africa and eight of the Welsh team were on that tour. They had some fantastic players, which made our win all the sweeter.

We played our guts out that day. It was very emotional, too, to finally win a game after so long. There was a tear or two in the dressing room. My father and uncle came into the changing room afterwards, which was quite easy to do in those days, and I couldn't speak. I knew that if I tried I would have burst out crying.

Adam Robson (Scotland 1954-1960, 22 Caps): The reaction was hardly surprising for Scotland had just come back from the depths of a disastrous seventeen defeats. Angus Cameron was captain and had made it quite clear to us, 'We are bloody well going to win this game.' And we did.

Ernie Michie: We went on to beat the Irish well, then went to Twickenham looking to win the Triple Crown. We were robbed blind. We lost 9-6 but, Tom Elliot dropped on a loose ball over the line, right between the English posts and the referee disallowed the try. It was a clear try, I was the closest player to Tom, so I know he scored. We would surely have converted the try, had it been given, and won the Triple Crown.

It was a strange time back then with selections as Bannerman insisted that all the Scottish forwards should be playing in Scotland or for London Scottish. After I graduated from Aberdeen University, I joined the Forestry Commission and moved south. At first, posted near London, I played for London Scottish. Then, when I was relocated to the Midlands, Ian Swan [Scotland's left winger against Wales] persuaded me to join Leicester so, by joining them, I disqualified myself from Scottish selection. Then, I was posted back to Scotland, joined Langholm and, within a couple of weeks,

I was back in the Scotland set-up, although playing no better than I had been with Leicester.

Norman Mair: I used to fancy that I could have been led blindfold and still have known within minutes of the kick-off if Angus Cameron were playing merely by the sound of boot on ball. One kick in particular lingers not just in the ear but on the video-tape of memory – a monstrous, steepling up-and-under [at Murrayfield in 1955] beneath which the Ireland fullback, Bill Tector, circled unhappily in the shadow of his own posts before spilling the catch and having his chest very nearly stove in for his trouble.

His drop-kicking exploits included a towering penalty bumped over with a massive thump against England at Twickenham in 1955 when he came tantalisingly close to leading Scotland to the Triple Crown. That afternoon he scored his second Calcutta Cup try at RFU headquarters when, in the climactic match, Scotland lost 9-6 and Tom Elliot had a try controversially disallowed.

Ken Scotland: While my ambition from a very young age was to play for Scotland, as I got older and started playing for the first XV at Heriot's School it became more and more apparent that this was not a forgone conclusion. I was playing stand-off with players like Iain Laughland at Merchiston, Gregor Sharp at Daniel Stewart's College and Gordon Waddell at Fettes, all coming through at around about the same time. I knew that I was going to have my work cut out. I was still very ambitious, but it wasn't clear if it was going to be achievable.

From school I went straight into National Service, and I joined the Royal Signals specifically to play rugby because they had the best reputation for providing sporting opportunities. I continued to play for the army at stand-off, and by the time I had finished my National Service I had played six games at fullback in my whole life – it just so happens that those matches had been two National Trials and four full internationals. From then on I played almost all my first-class rugby at fullback.

After the army I went up to Cambridge and played the worst game of my life at fullback in the freshers' trial so I started my time there as third choice. I didn't play in

France versus Scotland at Colombes in 1959.

the internationals that season until Robin Chisholm was injured against Ireland and I came in for the last game of the season against England.

Jim Greenwood: My last game was against Ireland in 1959 when I was stupid enough to dislocate a shoulder! I played on. Decisions made at times like these are not always susceptible to logical analysis. The last thing I did on the field that day was to tackle Niall Brophy in full flight. I was inside him, luckily, as it kept the damaged shoulder out of the way. He checked for an instant, which let me get within striking distance, and I managed to get him down. The shoulder gave a twinge, but it was the end of the match anyway and I felt I had done something to justify my remaining on the field.

David Rollo (Scotland 1959–68, 40 Caps): I broke my nose after ten minutes in my first game, against England in 1959. Peter Jackson was on the wing for them, I went to tackle him from behind and my nose hit the back of his head. I was knocked out and when I came round they couldn't get the bleeding to stop, so I had to go off for ten minutes. Eventually they managed to get me back on the field by plugging me up with cotton wool – which I then had to spend a long and fairly agonising time pulling back out of my nose after the game.

Ken Scotland: It's pretty dire. I played four times at Twickenham and didn't win, and on the first occasion, in 1959, we lost by four tries to nil, which was a bit of a hammering in those days. That England side was the best international team I played against. It was second to none, including the All Blacks and the Springboks. But apart from that one game there was never much in it. In the 1963 game we were 8-0 up, but lost 10-8.

England regularly fielded very strong teams over my time, and the sheer weight of numbers accounts for a lot. Fifty years ago, the received wisdom was that if England got their selection right, with a good captain, they were very hard to beat. They didn't often get it right. But when they did, with a good captain . . . well, think back to Martin Johnson, Will Carling, Bill Beaumont.

Frans ten Bos (Scotland 1959-1963, 17 caps): Although my name is Dutch, whenever my mother was pregnant and about to pop, my father would send her over to Britain, which is why I and my two sisters were all born here. My father [also Frans] worked in the aviation industry in its early years, and knew war was coming because although he lived in Brussels he spent a lot of time in Holland at the family's place in Almelo, which is only twenty miles from Germany. He and his brother were very keen on shooting so they would go to Germany a great deal and couldn't understand how their friends were speaking so highly of Hitler. He had everything planned for the outbreak of war, with little nest-eggs all over the place.

One night mother woke up and said 'Frans, I'm terrified, there's a terrible thunderstorm,' and he said, 'That's not thunder, that's guns, let's go'. He had everything organised: he had a plane fuelled and ready to go, and two cars – a big one full of gear and a little one for the family – but as they got to the airport the first shell to land on Brussels airport landed right on their plane. So he filled some extra gerrycans and went down the Belgian coast, winding through the legions of refugees on the roads, stopping at every port but obviously there was no chance of getting out. So they drove down to Bordeaux, which was the last port in France, in a journey full of incident.

They spent two weeks there but couldn't get out. Eventually there were three cocoa boats from West Africa which were heading to Britain and everyone knew they would be the last boats out of France. My mother knew that the ships were only taking British subjects, but she also knew that children had precedence so she said, 'OK, well just take my children,' and handed the three of us over along with our nappies and bottles. The man was horrified and allowed my parents to go too. It was still touch and go though: of the three ships that left that night, only ours made it – the other two were torpedoed.

My father was an accomplished pilot and we were initially stationed in London, but my sister went completely doo-lally with the bombs so we moved to a tiny cottage on the banks of the Awe near my mother's best friend, who lived in Taynuilt. My father commanded a squadron of Greenock-based Swordfish fighter-bombers doing North Atlantic convoy duty from the deck of a converted oil tanker, but when he was moved to Leuchars, the family relocated to Elie.

I didn't really play rugby until I went to Fettes and even then I didn't really play properly until I went to Oxford for university and went from playing there to London Scottish when I graduated. Although I was born in London and had Dutch parents, I always felt totally Scottish.

I was 6ft 3in and almost sixteen stone in my pomp – a colossus in those days, I was a head taller than most opponents, although these days I'd be smaller than Tim Visser and about the right size to play scrum-half. I made my debut in the 1959 Calcutta Cup at Twickenham, a 3-3 draw. The rules were you couldn't meet up any earlier than twenty-four hours before kick-off. There was no time for any training, and, in any case, there was no manager or coach, so you'd maybe work out a couple of signals beforehand. First match I was with Hamish Kemp in the second row. We had a conversation along the lines of: 'Which side do you pack on?' 'The right.' 'No, you bloody well don't, I do.'

Playing for Scotland was always frightfully informal and laissez-faire and all the better for being so. The camaraderie between us in the Scotland team was terrific. Indeed it existed between all rugby players at that time. If one of your colleagues, or someone from another team, ran into trouble financially, maritally or with the police, everyone rallied round. If a chap were having a terrible time he jolly well knew there would be other chaps to help him out. It was like a big family.

I'm certainly glad I played the game when I did. We played for fun whereas now they do it for money and, as I understand it, there's a degree of thuggishness these days. You may think me a terrible snob. I'm not really, even if that's how I come across, but there was no rugger fellow from my time who I wouldn't have been pleased to bring home for dinner.

TEN

CHANGING FORTUNES
1960-1969

As the fifties gave way to the sixties, there was plenty of cause for optimism. In Arthur Smith and Ken Scotland, Scotland now had two of the most gifted backs the game has ever produced; in Gordon Waddell they had a fine tactician at stand-off; and in the pack, the likes of David Rollo, Norman Bruce, and Hugh McLeod provided an iron core. Scotland performed well during this period but despite the exquisite talents of Arthur Smith and Ken Scotland out wide and the rising quality of the pack, they rarely dominated teams as they should have. Perhaps it was the lack of a hard-edge in the team, the lack of a grizzled warrior like Douglas Elliot who had always taken the game to the opposition and who had constantly put his body on the line for the cause. In 1964 a figure reminiscent of Elliot finally appeared. He was a chemistry teacher who played for Melrose; his name was Jim Telfer.

The emergence of a new generation of ambitious and self-confident Scottish players brought fresh impetus to the team's performances. During Telfer and Peter Brown's first season, Scotland drew 0–0 with New Zealand at Murrayfield, won the Calcutta Cup, defeated France at Murrayfield and Ireland at Lansdowne Road and shared the Championship with Wales. It was Scotland's most successful season in decades.

Following a 3–3 draw with England at Twickenham in 1965 they beat South Africa 8–5 at Murrayfield. Then, in 1966, they defeated Ireland at Lansdowne Road and England and Australia at Murrayfield, while also drawing there with France.

Before the decade had ended, the team had recorded memorable wins against France, Wales, Australia and South Africa and had notable representation on the Lions tours of 1966 to New Zealand, Australia and Canada and 1968 to South Africa. Despite a relatively weak and unstructured domestic game and a run of seven straight defeats from December 1967 until November 1968, there seemed no threat of a return to the dark days of the 1950s. The team was too full of talent and, in players like Telfer, too bloody-minded to accept such poor standards. They lost matches, certainly, but then the quality of other teams operating at that time was very high. The New Zealanders were as ferocious as ever; Wales had luminaries in the shape of Alun Pask, Gareth Edwards, Barry John and Gerald Davies; Ireland had the likes of Mike Gibson, Willie John McBride, Tom Kiernan, and Ray McLoughlin; John Pullin, Bob Taylor, Keith Savage and Bob Hiller were stars for England; and across the Channel the French side was overflowing with maestros such as Pierre Villepreux, Walter Spanghero, Christian Carrere, Jean Trillo, Lilian Camberabero and Jo Maso.

But Scotland could hold its own among such dazzling company. Even when the magicians Smith and Scotland retired, in new caps Colin Telfer, Chris Rea, Sandy Hinshelwood and John Frame they were able to strike a balance between control, pace and flair, and when the backs combined with the grunt and gristle of the likes of Jim Telfer, Sandy Carmichael, Alastair McHarg, Peter 'PC' Brown and Rodger Arneil, they were truly a sight to behold.

Opposite: Captain Arthur Smith leads his team out before Scotland play Wales in 1958.

David Rollo: When I first played for Scotland I had number eight on my back. Then, against France in 1960 the selectors swapped me to tight-head and Hughie MacLeod moved to loose-head, so I played with number ten on my back. In 1961, they changed the numbering system, so against France I played number three. And in 1964, Brian Neill was captain, and he played tight-head prop, so I moved back over to loose-head, which meant I wore number one. I don't think there are many players who can say they have started international matches wearing those four different numbers on their jersey.

Frans ten Bos: After my first match at Murrayfield, against France in 1960, there was a black-tie dinner at what is now the Balmoral, at which we got absolutely stocious. I made a terrible mistake by ordering a Sunday newspaper and making one local telephone call, so I got a bill for one shilling and ten pence from the SRU – and there were 102,000 at Murrayfield that day. The SRU were formidably tight.

If you'd played previously the card would read: 'Please bring the number four jersey which is in your possession.' It was one strip for the whole season, unlike the other home nations, who could swap theirs at the end of the games. I remember ripping mine. It was in tatters. I wrote explaining this and was asked to forward it before being given a replacement. They obviously didn't trust me.

Ken Scotland: The game had been pretty stagnant from the 1930s, through the war, and into the 1950s. There had been very little, if any innovation. The forwards got the ball and gave it to the backs. The first time I can remember forwards doing moves was in 1960, when DJ Hopwood, the South African number eight, started picking the ball up at the base of the scrum, and around that time the French had started peeling round the tail of the line-out as well. Also, Oxford had a great pair of half-backs in Mike Smith, who was England's last cricket and rugby double internationalist, and Onllwyn Brace, and they started initiating moves.

So the game was evolving a bit, and I was fortunate to be a part of that because in my first year in the Cambridge team Gordon Waddell – who was a really good tactical player and with whom I had a good understanding – was at stand-off. We started developing ploys with the fullback coming into the line. We just wanted to do something the opposition wasn't expecting. In those days each player drew his man and there was no such thing as drift defence, so a fullback coming into the line automatically created a two-on-one until the opposition figured us out. We also used the blindside a lot more than was previously fashionable.

We played with a leather ball, and throughout my whole rugby career there was never any suggestion of a spin pass, and miss moves were not thought up until well after I stopped playing.

Frans ten Bos: Everyone remembers the game which I think was the worst game I ever played for Scotland, which was when we beat Wales 8-3 at Cardiff Arms Park in 1962. Scotland had never won at the Arms Park and it was a wet, muddy day. I did two things in that game – I scored my only try for Scotland and gave the scoring pass to Ronnie Glasgow for his try – but other than that I played like an absolute drain. The next day the papers kept calling me 'hero ten Bos', but it was probably the worst I ever played for Scotland.

George Stevenson (Scotland 1956-65, 24 Caps): I played in the famous match against Wales in 1963 when there were 111 lineouts. The Welsh scrum-half, Clive Rowlands, just kicked to touch every time he got the ball. I think that was one of the first times I played on the wing for Scotland and in those days the winger put the ball in at the line-out. I touched the ball more that day than I had ever touched it in any match before, but it was only to throw the ball in after Rowlands had kicked to touch again. Wales won 6–0. What a dreadful game. They changed the rules after that, making it illegal to kick direct to touch unless you were in your own 22.

Ken Scotland: I was dropped for Stuart Wilson in 1964, and he played very well that season – but, as often happens, his second season did not live up to expectations, and I got back into the side for our trip to Paris in what must have been the slowest back division Scotland has ever fielded. Unfortunately I didn't play very well in that match and I knew at the time that I hadn't played well enough to keep my place.

By that tine the injuries were taking longer and longer to get over. When that begins to happen, you know your time on the field is coming to an end. But I didn't have any regrets when I eventually retired. How could I? I had realised my childhood dream and played in some fantastic teams for Scotland and the Lions and at club and university level.

Jim Telfer (Scotland 1964-1970, 25 Caps plus 8 Caps for the Lions): My first game for Scotland was as a flanker against France in 1964. I had been a second-row forward at the school and I had never played in the back-row for Melrose or the South, so I played my first international match in a position I had never played before. I remember Leslie Allan showing me the angles to attack the stand-off at. He'd played a bit at stand-off for Scotland so he knew where the flanker should be coming from. I played two or three games at flanker with Oliver Grant at number eight. Then eventually I was moved to number eight, where I had never played before either.

Getting to the ground on match day in France was always exciting. You used to be sitting on the bus deep in your own thoughts, and then you'd spot the police outriders kicking the cars out of the way. Only a few players would be looking out the front to start with, but by the time you got into the ground everyone was watching to see what the outriders were doing to the cars in front of them. The Irish were the worst. When you were heading to Lansdowne Road, you'd be flying up these streets the wrong way and the players would be glued to the action in front. I think it was a good thing, it certainly got the adrenaline pumping.

You must remember that players at that time weren't used to going away very often.

Most people had never been to Paris, and you didn't see French club sides playing in Britain. The crowd was certainly a big factor in helping the home team – no doubt about that. They were difficult to play against. I'm not saying they did it very often, but the forwards would sometimes grab you where they shouldn't or poke their fingers in your eyes. It was mainly mythical, but it did happen sometimes. They always had big, hard forwards, who did a lot of fighting in the club games and it didn't change when they played international games. If you went down to France to play a game you were in for a hiding if you didn't take them on physically.

In those days, you would sit with your opposite number at the post-match meal, so I was beside Michel Crauste, a big North African fellow who played for Lourdes. I remember when my steak was served he just took his fork, lifted it off my plate and ate it. I was so surprised I didn't say anything. I'd never seen anything like it in my life. But he was a redoubtable character and a very good player.

David Rollo: Against France in 1964, I was reserve prop in attendance, which meant I stayed with the team right up to the morning of the match, but once the players were on the park there were no replacements. So at lunch on Saturday, I had a full three-course meal – normally I just had a mushroom omelette – and afterwards Charlie Drummond said, 'David, you're not playing, you'd be as well coming next door with the committee for a pint of beer.'

So I had one pint of beer, then I had a second, and I was halfway through my third when I happened to look up and see John Law coming through the doors looking rather flustered. After a quick word with Charlie I was told that I was wanted over in the hotel. When I got there they told me Cameron Boyle was ill and that I was playing . . . I nearly fell to the floor. But if you know you're fit then you can get through things like that. You might have a slow start but once you get going you're alright. I had a good game, we won, and I enjoyed it. But I was sorry for Cameron Boyle; I think that was his last cap.

Jim Telfer: I was a great admirer of Hughie McLeod. I think he was the best loose-head prop Scotland has ever had, better than Ian MacLauchlan, David Sole and Tom Smith. I remember playing with him for the South when I was just coming through. I'd be about twenty and he'd be about 30. We came out this scrum, charged across the park and hit the centre. I was in the back-row and I was meant to be there before anyone else, but Hughie raced past me and got to the ball first. It was an eye-opener for me. I remember just thinking, 'This boy is different.' He didn't drink, he didn't smoke – he went out training while everyone else was at home or in the pub. He was ahead of his time. I think Derrick Grant took a lot from him and he certainly inspired my attitude towards training and doing everything you can to improve your own game.

When Davie Rollo got to forty caps they dropped him, apparently because the SRU didn't want him to go past Hughie.

Peter Brown (Scotland 1964-73, 27 Caps): My first cap was against France in 1964, when David Rollo was brought in as a last minute replacement for Cameron Boyle. The interesting thing about that match was that we had a hush-hush meeting at 9am on the Friday, because the International Rugby Board rules stated that no team was to meet more than twenty-four hours before the kick-off. Now, other teams were doing it; Wales, for example, were already meeting up at Port Talbot on the Sunday before the match for scrummaging practise, but not announcing their team until after that practise so it wasn't officially a team meeting. But in Scotland, at least up until that point, we prided ourselves on not compromising when it came to following the rules.

Anyway, we all gathered at the Braid Hills Hotel in Edinburgh, met some of the team members for the first time, then got on the bus and went to Boroughmuir for a secret practise with nobody else present. We then went back to the hotel and had some lunch before getting on the bus again to go back to Boroughmuir for the official practise. It was a hoot, and the thing is, in a funny sort of way, it brought the team together. A lot of very good players got their first caps that day against France – Stuart Wilson, Jim Telfer, Billy Hunter and me – and we won 10–0.

It's fascinating now to think that back then all we did was come together, have a run-around on the Friday morning, have another run-around for the press on the Friday afternoon, a team-talk with selectors present on the Saturday, and then go out and play. There were no sophisticated line-out codes or anything like that. The big thing we practised in those days was the wheel: with the ball being struck to the feet of the left-hand second-row in the scrum and the right-hand second-row pulling with his right hand on the prop in front of him and shouting 'away', so that we wheeled the scrum and came out with our heads up, the line in front of us and the ball at our feet. Now any brave man that went down on it did well, but he also thought twice about doing it next time.

Jim Telfer: There is a tendency to think that the game was not taken that seriously back then, but the truth of it is that we took it very seriously. We used to prepare as best we could by the standards of the time. We'd meet the night before, train at Boroughmuir, we stayed at the Braids and go down on Saturday morning to practise our line-outs in the park down the road from the hotel, and the backs would bugger about doing their thing – it was pretty well organised. We were trying to be as professional about it as possible. Latterly, when I became captain, we asked for Sunday sessions at Murrayfield the week before the match. That was the first time that had ever been done.

Peter Brown: Two weeks after my debut we played New Zealand at Murrayfield. Had they beaten us they would have achieved the Grand Slam, but they could only manage a 0–0 draw. They were a wonderful team, full of greats like Don Clarke, Macfarlane Herewini, Wilson Whineray, Ken Gray, Colin Meads, Kel Tremain and Brian Lochore. I can still vividly remember Brian Neill's team-talk beforehand, he sat there and quietly went over our strengths then said it was 'absolutely essential' that they didn't get loose ball which would allow them to break free – those were his exact words 'absolutely essential' – and that's how we played the game. It wasn't rocket science, it was a clear and uncomplicated message which left us in no doubt as to what was required. We didn't plan to beat them; the whole approach to the game was about holding the All Blacks, and we were good enough. I have to say, the conditions were not good, which was great for getting in about them.

Earlier in the tour, when the All Blacks had played a combined Glasgow- Edinburgh side, and had stayed in the Marine Hotel in Troon, they asked for a physio to do the massages for the players. Well, my father was a physio in Troon so he went along and their wee stand-off needed a lot of treatment so my father brought him to his surgery, and while he was there – under the lamp – I went in and had a chat with him. We chatted rugby for a while and I told him that I had been a reserve in the game and that I could have been playing but that the selectors didn't like Glasgow players too much at the time.

My Dad must have done a good job because when the All Blacks came back to Scotland in January for the Test match they asked for him again, and at the dinner after the match my father was there, as was Kirton, who was still injured. I went over and re-introduced myself. He said, 'What you doing here?'

I said, 'Well actually I was playing number four against you today.'

He couldn't believe it.

Now, fast-forward to 1967, and New Zealand are back again and again they took Father as a physio. After the match Jim Telfer blew his top. He thought it was ridiculous that the father of one of the Scottish squad was in the New Zealand dressing-room helping them while there was nobody in the Scottish dressing-room. So pretty soon after that my Dad became Scotland's physio.

Jim Telfer: My second match was the 0–0 draw against New Zealand, which was a huge result. They were all over us. I was quite well known for putting my body on the line – not being very constructive but just killing the ball – and there was one occasion they were driving towards the line and the ball squirted out the side of the ruck and I dived on it. I just held it, held it and held it, then Meads kicked me and he nearly got sent off. That prevented the try which would have won them the game.

Peter Brown: So we had beaten France, drawn with the All Blacks and we then went to Wales. At half past two in the morning of the international the selectors returned to the hotel from the committee dinner, pissed out their brains, and they went into the players' rooms and tipped them all out of their beds saying, 'What are you boys doing sleeping? Wake up – you're playing an international today!'

But I wouldn't say that was why we lost that game. The biggest problem of my ten years in the Scottish team was the excellence of the Welsh. Do you know, in my first nine caps I played against all the top rugby nations in the world and the only ones we didn't beat were New Zealand, who we drew with, and Wales, who beat us 11–3 and probably should have won by more.

Scotland batter the All Blacks to a 0-0 draw at Murrayfield.

Jim Telfer: Beating England in 1964 was perhaps just as big a result as the draw with New Zealand. Hughie McLeod played ten times against England and never won. We hadn't beaten them since 1950, but we actually won quite comfortably that day, scoring three tries. I made the pass for two tries and scored the third – and the crowd ran onto the field to celebrate, which was the first time that had happened – and I thought I had cracked it. I was dropped the following year so I soon found out that international rugby wasn't always that easy.

Peter Brown: We only discovered afterwards that it was the first time in thirteen years that Scotland had beaten England. I didn't appreciate that Hughie MacLeod and Kenny Scotland never played in a victory over England – the coverage in the press wasn't the same in those days.

At the end of the 1965 game against England at Twickenham we were leading 3–0 and all over them. Then David Whyte, on the right wing, got the ball, came infield and kicked; they picked it up and fed it to their left winger, Andy Hancock, who nobody had ever heard of before. He starts running – down the touchline, infield, back out to the touchline – is he in touch, is he not? – Iain Laughland misses him and he collapses over the line in the corner; they miss the conversion and it finishes 3–3.

Jim Telfer: We toured Canada that summer and although there were no official capped Test matches, we won all five of our matches which was a great way to finish the season. I thought that it would set us up perfectly for the following year, but 1965 didn't quite go according to plan.

We had four internationals out of the Melrose club that season – David Chisholm, Eck Hastie, Frank Laidlaw and myself; we played ten internationals together and were never beaten – and I am the only player to have played against all three of the big southern hemisphere sides for Scotland and never been beaten, so I'm pretty proud of that. But we lost the first three games of the Five Nations to France, Wales and Ireland and on the back of those results I was then dropped.

Mike Campbell-Lamerton was the captain during that tough 1965 season and he was a wonderful guy, a real genuine bloke who put his heart and soul into everything he did. He was a great hulking man who was very effective at using his size. He was named captain of the 1966 Lions but was torn to pieces by the media and was replaced as captain half way through the tour, which was a terrible thing to happen to such a good man.

David Rollo: I remember playing England on a very hot day in 1965. Norman Suddon and I were the props and it was a great game to play in – with a lot of running rugby. There were scales in the dressing room, and I weighed myself before and after the match – I had gone from 14st 7lb to just under 14st. After we had finished we discovered we were both playing with number one on our jersey, so whichever one of us was meant to be at loose-head must have got a rave review – it would have looked like we were doing the job of two men.

Jim Telfer: It became known as 'Hancock's Game' because we were leading 3–0 when Andy Hancock, the English wing, took a pass from their stand-off, Mike Weston, and charged seventy-five yards up field dodging tackles from all over the place to score. Luckily the cover defence forced him in at the corner and they missed the kick, so it ended 3–3. I was sitting up in the stands because I was a reserve and just had to watch the whole game, which was pretty tough – although not as tough as having to do it a month later when we beat the Springboks 8–5 and I was still out of favour.

But I was back in the team for the 1966 Five Nations and we opened our Championship by drawing 3–3 with France at Murrayfield. We then lost 11–5 to Wales in Cardiff but we turned things around by beating Ireland and England. I was selected to tour with the Lions that summer to Australia, New Zealand and Canada, which was a fantastic honour, but when I came back I was injured for the autumn win against the Wallabies at Murrayfield as well as the opening game of the 1967 Five Nations, which Scotland won in France – so it was disappointing to miss out on all those famous wins.

Sandy Carmichael (Scotland 1967-1978, 50 Caps): I made my debut against Ireland at Murrayfield in 1967. I could hardly tie my boot-laces I was so excited. I think I played okay. Well, I must have done because one of the Irish props took a chunk out of my lug-hole. Have you ever been bitten on the ear? Bloody sore. There was a bit of an inquiry and the chap never played for his country again.

John Frame (Scotland 1967-1973, 23 Caps): They used to say in the seventies that it was harder to get out of the Scottish team than get in. When I was first selected in 1967 I was a fresh-faced twenty-one year old student at Edinburgh University and I was about to face New Zealand, the best team on the planet. I was up against the great Ian MacRae and Bill Davis in the centre. We played fly-half and left and right centre, while they played first five-eighths, second five-eighths and centre, so half the time I was marking one and half the time I was marking the other. Earlier in the tour, Danny Hearn had broken his neck on Ian MacRae's hip bone whilst playing for London and the Home Counties against the All Blacks. It had been a horrible accident, nobody's fault, but I suppose it would have added to the trepidation at the back of my mind that I was going up against this great powerful New Zealander. We lost 14–3; they scored two tries and Colin Meads was sent off for almost taking Davie Chisholm's head off with a wild kick – I remember it all vividly.

Sandy Carmichael: I was partly to blame for Meads getting sent off. I kneed him in the gut because he'd been punching one of our guys. He lashed out with a foot and caught Davie Chisholm. At the dinner later Meads was upset. That was the only time I saw the big man cry.

Colin Meads heads to the changing rooms after being sent off at Murrayfield.

John Frame: It was obviously pretty exciting. The New Zealand team came with this terrifying reputation, especially Meads, and they all looked like they had been hewn out of granite. My mother sat in the stand and panicked every time the ball came near me because she knew all about the All Blacks.

I remember having dinner in the McRobert Pavilion after the game and I was sitting opposite David Rollo, having probably had a drop too much to drink. I was musing about the whole experience: as a twenty-one year old from Inverness, to be winning my first cap against the mighty All Blacks in front of however many thousand people, it was kind of emotional. Davie had this lovely manner about him. He said, 'Aye, it's a great thing to play for your country.' That was me, I collapsed in a well of emotion.

Alastair McHarg (Scotland 1968-1979, 44 Caps): In 1968 I went from nowhere, just junior rugby to a district game against the All Blacks and a Scotland debut in Dublin. I remember looking along the line at Peter Stagg, Pringle Fisher and David Rollo, guys who'd been my heroes. Was I daunted? No, I couldn't wait to play.

John Frame: The Scottish and Irish teams used to stay in the same hotel in Dublin when they played in the Five Nations, and I remember Tom Kiernan saying in his after-dinner speech in 1968 that he really thought it was time that the two teams had separate hotels. 'The reason I say this,' he explained. 'Is that doing my rounds last night as a good captain should always do, I came through the reception at about 11.30pm and saw that man Syd Millar there, and his pal Davie Rollo, in their green and blue blazers, walking through the reception with their arms around each others' shoulders, singing: *Take me back to the old Transvaal.*'

That was them having had a couple of pints of Guinness together on the Friday night before the international, and then singing a song they had learned together on the 1962 Lions tour.

Ian McLauchlan (Scotland 1969-79, 43 Caps plus 8 Caps for the Lions): I won my first cap against England in 1969. You never know how you are going to cope with becoming an international player until you have lived through it. I've seen people freeze up, I've seen others who couldn't stop talking as they tried to overcome their nerves, but for me the feeling was of complete exhilaration. I couldn't wait to get into the dressing room and get my hands on the blue jersey, and when we got in there I grabbed it off the peg and pulled it down over my shoulders as quickly as possible, just in case the selectors changed their minds. I was twenty-six years old and had waited a long time to get hold of that strip, and it would have taken a brave man to try and prise it away from me then.

Much of that day is a haze, but I remember sitting in the changing room at 2.50pm. Jim Telfer, the captain, was giving his pep talk, with a few special words of encouragement for myself and fellow debutant Billy Steele. 'Open the doors,' I thought. 'Let me get out there and at them.' I had waited all my life for that moment. I loved the adrenalin rush of a ruthlessly physical contest and the deep sense of satisfaction which came from knowing that you have gone toe-to-toe with a worthy adversary and not let your teammates down. It was dream to run out at Murrayfield in that dark blue jersey with the thistle on my chest, the adrenalin pumping through my veins, a wall of sound in front of me, and a nation at my back.

Jim Telfer: I was fit again after the win in France and came back into the team for our game at Murrayfield against Wales. They were a great side with guys like Barry John, Gerald Davies, John Taylor and Alun Pask but we played some super stuff and I scored a try in our 11–5 win. The rest of the Championship was a little disappointing after such a good start: we lost to Ireland at Murrayfield 3–5 and then fell 27–14 to England at Twickenham.

I injured my knee playing against Kelso for Melrose and was ruled out until the final game of the 1968 Championship against England. Fortunately I did enough in that game to be selected for the Lions tour to South Africa, which was fairly remarkable considering how long I had been out for and the fact that Scotland had endured a terrible Championship when they didn't win a game.

The 1968–69 season started very well for us. I was selected as captain to face Australia at Murrayfield in November and we won 9–3. It was our first victory in eight Tests and set us up well for our opening match of the 1969 Five Nations against France.

I can't remember much about the matches I played in because it was such a long time ago, but that is one of the games about which I do still have a vivid memory. I was captain of the team and it was at Colombes, which is the stadium where Eric Liddell won his 400 metres gold medal, and to get to the pitch you had to come through this wet tunnel with water dripping down on you, and then you came up right into the middle of the stadium. It was like being a lion being released into the Coliseum. You looked around and realised you were suddenly the focus of this huge hostile crowd.

They completely outplayed us but it was significant that Gordon Connell got injured halfway through the first-half and Ian McRae came on as the first ever replacement in international rugby. He was our saviour because he was a far more nuggety type of player. The French got a scrum about twenty meters out and McRae hassled his opposite number, snatched the ball out the side of the scrum and fed me, and all I had to do was run over Pierre Villepreux to score the try. That took us 6–3 ahead.

For the next hour the French played some beautiful open rugby without ever scoring a try. They were twice over the line but didn't get the ball down and we managed to survive a late onslaught to record a special victory.

Norman Suddon (Scotland 1965-1970, 13 Caps): We got a licking that day but still managed to come away with a 6–3 win. The French had plenty of flair but they just couldn't get over the line. They did everything but score. Having said that, we defended well – we stopped them dead in their tracks. They kept coming at us and coming at us, but we had the bit between our teeth. It was a great victory. Larry Lamb from England was the referee and he got escorted off the pitch after that game to save him from the wrath of the crowd – but it was a fair result. The French might have dominated the game but we stopped them scoring, and that's what rugby is all about – doing the business when your back is up against the wall.

Jim Telfer: Norman Mair wrote in his article on the Monday morning that the Scottish team wouldn't need to fly home, because they could walk over the Channel. You can imagine how the referee was hassled. He had a police escort from the field. As years go by people start to assume that we played very well that day, but we actually held on for sixty minutes.

Alastair McHarg: My abiding memory of that game is lying on the turf around halfway and peering through blades of grass as four Frenchmen bore down on our line with no Scots in sight. 'Oh no,' I thought, 'they're bound to score.' But France were overelaborate and wasteful. Chris Rea congratulated me on putting one of their guys into touch right at the death. I'd no memory of that so can only assume I was so dazed from the onslaught.

Chris Rea (Scotland 1968-1971, 13 Caps): Having beaten Australia 9–3 at Murrayfield in November in my first cap and then beating France away in my first Five Nations match, I felt as if I was on a roll – but reality soon caught up with me. We were stuffed by Wales 17–3 at Murrayfield and I got a very bad dislocated shoulder against Ireland, which put me out for the rest of the season. It was very frosty at Murrayfield and the pitch was fine but immediately off the turf it was rock hard. I smother tackled Mike Gibson on the far side of the field, opposite the main stand, and as I hit the ground my shoulder came out. It was excruciating. Their hooker was a guy called Ken Kennedy, who was a surgeon, and he came across and said he would put it straight back in, there and then. Sandy Carmichael, thinking Kennedy was up to some skulduggery, charged across and shouted, 'No, leave him alone.'

And that was catastrophic for me, because by the time they got the stretcher out and got me into the changing room, I was frozen, and the medic on duty was Sir John Bruce, who was the Queen's physician, who probably hadn't put a shoulder in since his university days. There were three people standing on my chest as they tried to get it back in. I've never known pain like it, and I still have problems with it today. But dear old Sandy thought he was doing me a favour.

Jim Telfer: I picked up the most bizarre injury in that Ireland game. I was standing out in the backs as a lineout was taking place and was next to the referee, Merion Joseph. As the ball went into play he raised his arm and caught me in the eye with his elbow. I was concussed and had to go off and then spent the night in hospital. I was replaced by Peter Stagg who was this big lump at 6' 10' and as he was getting ready to go on he sat on me – which was just what I needed.

That summer we went on tour to Argentina. When people ask me what was the hardest tour I ever went on, I always tell them it was that trip to Argentina, without any question of a doubt. We went with twenty-one players and I was captain and coach as well. I was left with terrible memories of all the bullet marks along the side of the hotel that we stayed in. It was just after Juan Peron had promised the poor people everything, and they all flocked to the cities. I have never been in a country that was so wasted by capitalism, as far as I could see. There were the very, very rich and the very, very poor; and huge slums on the road in from the airport in places like Rosario and Buenos Aires. The poverty there just stuck with me. The difference between rich and poor was so stark. All the people we met were rich, of course. The club rugby was very, very strong, and it was centred around the school system.

On the field we were on our own. There was no communication between us and

Britain. Ken Oliver twisted his ankle at the first training session, so we asked for Tom Elliot to come out – he'd trained with the squad because Ken had been a doubt before we lef – but they wouldn't allow it. I thought at the time that it was the IRB but I found out many years later that it was the SRU who had decided we should just get on with it. So Rodger Arneil and I played in all six games. We won all the provincial matches but in the first game against the national side we lost Ian Murchie in the opening minutes when he was short-armed by a guy called Alessandro Travaglini. Ian's feet were off the ground – and he was never the same player again.

We then went to Rosario and there was these national strikes going on. We had to walk to the game in twos and threes because the buses had been commandeered by the strikers and they were burning them. Before we left for the match, we went up onto the hotel roof in Rosario and we were looking around pointing out fires to each other – it was the buses being burned. The atmosphere was very hostile.

Our fullback, Colin Blaikie, would take all our place-kicks and he had to try and do it while the crowd threw coins at him – they were bouncing all around him and ricocheting off his head and arms and legs. It was unbelievable, a real bear pit. It was brutal stuff. But we never gave an inch, and that to me was the best performance by a Scottish team in my time as a player.

Sandy Carmichael: Being in Argentina was closest I've ever been to a war. Things were crazy out on the streets – and pretty crazy out on the field as well. One game had to be postponed for two days due to snipers, which was a first. The Argentines had a guy called Raul Loyola who was basically the contract man. Their team would point to you and he'd come in for a whack.

Jim Telfer: Ian McLauchlan was the toughest guy I saw on a rugby field. He brought a hardness to the Scottish forward game which started about 1968–69 and went through the seventies. I'm sure that tour to Argentina gave him a valuable insight into what was needed in international rugby. It taught a lot of our forwards about how to look after themselves on a rugby field and about the kind of aggression you need to win international matches – and it was no surprise to me that so many of them went on to be great players for both Scotland and the Lions.

Ian McLauchlan: That tour to Argentina was absolutely brutal. But the thing I liked about the Argentineans was that you could hit them as hard as you liked and they would never bother. They would dish it out, but they'd take it as well – and they'd never complain because as far as they were concerned it was all part of the game. For a lot of guys on that tour they went out as boys and came back as men.

On tours you usually come up against an international or two during the midweek games, so you can get an idea of what they are like. But the Argentineans took all their internationalists away and to get around the amateur laws their whole squad happened to go on holiday to a place called Mar del Plata – a couple of hundred miles south of Buenos Aires – together for six weeks.

So we were playing these sides and beating them fairly easily – albeit at a physical cost – but when the Pumas came out the tunnel for that first match you would have thought someone had tied a bit of elastic to their backs and then let it go. They came out of the tunnel with their legs and arms pumping and their eyes bulging. Our guys weren't small, but these guys were built like brick shit-houses. The Argentinean guy I was playing against was an Olympic rower: he was a strong, strong boy. And there was a bit of jiggery-pokery going on early doors, so I smacked the hooker then turned to him and said, 'You're next.'

This guy spoke pretty good English, and he said, 'No, no, I don't play like that.'

I said, 'Great – I do.'

We came back from Argentina and in our next match beat South Africa 6–3, which was pretty special. They were a very good side, with a great back-row, where they had Jan Ellis, Tommy Bedford and Piet Greyling, who was a brilliant player – a real dog, his face was never more than two inches off the turf.

But because of the apartheid thing they were never able to relax and enjoy being here. The management wouldn't let them put on a pair of jeans and go to a party, they had to get the blazers on and as soon as they did that they became a target.

I took a couple of their players to a party in Edinburgh and because they had their blazers on a guy who had obviously had a few beers started giving them a bit of a stick as soon as we got there. Straight away they said they had to leave, they couldn't stay there in case there was trouble.

So it definitely wasn't a happy tour for them, but for Scotland it was still a big, big result. We played very well that day.

John Frame: I remember a stand-up shouting match at the Braid Hills Hotel before the South Africa match. Peter Stagg, one of our second-rows, was a huge man who was a delightfully erudite and well-educated chap who had a very English accent, and he had submitted his expenses to the secretary, including in it a copy of *Playboy*, which at that time was ten-and-sixpence. Peter had received his cheque from the SRU for his air flight, but with a red line through the copy of *Playboy* on his expenses form. To the great amusement of the Scottish team, and to the embarrassment of the dowager ladies who used to live as permanent residents at the Braid Hills Hotel, Staggy and John Law had it out in the main reception area of the hotel. Staggy was launching forth, using a number of thoroughly unrepeatable expletives to describe John Law's approach to frugality, and explaining that while John Law may have a preconceived idea of what *Playboy* was all about he clearly had never taken the trouble to look at it, otherwise he would know that it was full of sophisticated and educational articles. Staggy pronounced vociferously that if Law was not going to entertain his ten-and-sixpence then he would never play in the blue jersey again. I think the management eventually managed to sort that one out, but from then on Staggy was regarded as a folk hero because he had the temerity to stand up to the great, ever-forceful secretary John Law.

Jim Telfer: The last game that I played in a Scotland shirt came in the autumn of 1969, not long after our return from Argentina. It was a controversial fixture against the Springboks right at the height of the anti-apartheid demonstrations and I think the players were a bit spooked. It got really hostile towards them in Scotland and I remember in Galashiels we were even told by the police that we, the home South team, had to walk the mile or so down to Netherdale because if we got on our bus it might be stoned.

Their players were under a huge amount of pressure off the pitch and it was reflected in their performances on it. They had some of the all-time greats in their team, guys like their captain Tommy Bedford, Frik du Preez, Piet Greyling, Hannes Maria and Henry de Villiers, but the outside influences were clearly getting to them.

Police were everywhere at the ground. There were thousands of protestors and we were even spat on as we ran down the steps and on to the pitch. The South Africans were quite a young team and were taken aback by the intensity of the hatred and it must have been tough to focus on rugby. The atmosphere at the ground was very aggressive, bordering on evil.

Gordon Brown (Scotland 1969-1976, plus 30 Caps plus 8 caps for the Lions): I made my debut against the Springboks in December 1969. The dressing-room atmosphere was very emotional. When I pulled the Scotland jersey over my head I caught a glimpse of myself in the far corner mirror. I was nearly in tears.

Bang! Bang! on the door. 'Let's go, lads,' and we were away down the corridor to the top of the tunnel. By this time I had an unbelievable lump in my throat and tears in my eyes. If anyone had asked me something I would have been unable to reply.

When I took up position to field the kick-off. I could hardly see it because of the tears in my eyes, such was the emotion of the moment. I caught the ball and whole Springbok pack caught me – and the emotion evaporated.

Jim Telfer: We recorded a famous victory, but the day really belonged to Ian Smith. He scored a penalty but then gathered the ball deep in our half and went on this sweeping run that arced along the pitch and then just sliced right through the defence to score out wide – it was a moment of pure magic.

Gordon Brown: The champagne flowed at the North British Hotel that night. During the match I ran faster, jumped higher, and scrummaged harder than I'd ever done before – and at eleven o'clock that night, I felt as fresh as a daisy, it was amazing. But then I tried to get out of bed the next morning and I couldn't move an inch. It took me two weeks to recover physically from that match.

Jim Telfer: Although it was heart-wrenching never to play for Scotland again, looking back it was as good a result to finish your career with as you could ask for. Not many Scotsmen have captained their side to victory over South Africa; it was very special.

ELEVEN

FRUSTRATED GENIUS
1970-1980

The 1970s much like the 1950s, was a decade of two extremes. Between 3 February 1973 and 10 January 1976, Scotland went unbeaten at Murrayfield for eight matches, collecting the scalps of Australia and of all their Five Nations opponents, including, on two occasions, the celebrated masters of the game from Wales; the closing years of the decade, however, saw consistently poor performances and between 1977 and 1979 Scotland could only manage two draws and a solitary win.

But, despite these latter woes, the 1970s was a decade scattered with star-dust. Mention the names Leslie, Lawson, Morgan, Hay and McHarg to Scottish fans of a certain age and you will invariably see a smile break across their faces. Add the names Irvine, Renwick, McGeechan, Brown, McLauchlan and Carmichael and you'll have them purring like Cheshire Cats. Even in defeat, even during the long period when Scotland went thirteen games without a win, those players could light up any match with moments of genius. While the decade may belong to Wales's 'Golden Generation' and the historic achievements of the '71 Lions in New Zealand and the '74 Lions in South Africa, the seventies will always be looked upon with genuine affection by Scottish rugby supporters. Results could have been a lot better, but statistics only tell a small part of the story of this decade.

Made up of players with a vast assortment of differing skill sets, on their day Scotland were a match for anyone. In Ian McGeechan they had a gliding tactician operating outside the calm control of Colin Telfer; in the athletic Alastair McHarg and the colossal Gordon 'Broon frae Troon' Brown they had the exuberant engine and powerhouse of the team; in David Leslie they had the ferocious and uncompromising spirit of the ultimate competitor, balanced by the serene goal-kicking PC Brown at number eight; in Sandy Carmichael and Ian 'the Mighty Mouse' McLauchlan they had granite hard power and technical supremacy at the coalface where, more often than not, the fate of a game is decided. Around this core were an array of other players who gave their all for the Scottish cause. Scrum-halves Alan Lawson and Dougie Morgan pushed the forwards on, darted and probed, and were the driving spark for the rest of the backs; Nairn McEwan was a foraging force in the back-row; Chris Rae, John Frame and later Alastair Cranston were imposing presences in midfield; and out wide the electric pace of Billy Steele was complemented beautifully on the other wing by the barrel-chested power of Bruce Hay.

Peter Brown: I missed the start of the 1970 Championship against France, but I was fit again for the Wales game. When the letter arrived telling me I was back in the team, I thought I better phone my brother Gordon – who we had all assumed would keep his place in the second-row – to commiserate. He always knew the team first, but when he answered the phone on this occasion I could tell immediately that he

Opposite: Two of Scotland's all-time greats, Andy Irvine and Jim Renwick.

didn't know, so I said, 'Great news, I'm back in.'

He said, 'Terrific, who's dropped?'

I said, 'You are.'

Then, in the game, I tweaked my thigh chasing the kick-off at the start of the second-half, and of all the great things Gordon did, that is what he ended up in the *Guinness Book of Records* for: being the first brother to replace a brother in an international match.

Gordon Brown: One wag suggested afterwards that if Peter and I worked it properly, we ought to be able to give each other about twenty caps apiece.

John Frame: We were going to Wales for the second match of the 1970 Championship, and we used to gather at the North British Hotel on the Thursday at lunchtime, where a bus would collect us and take us to the airport so we could fly down to Cardiff. I had been at a lecture in the morning and had to arrive slightly late. When I got to the NB I saw George Thomson, a Watsonian who was one of the selectors, and explained the situation. I must have looked sufficiently pitiful to prompt George to say that he was sure that nobody would mind if I went into the restaurant and had some lunch with the out-of-town players.

George got it badly wrong because the secretary minded, and I remember George being rubbished in the corner by John Law, the SRU secretary, and being told that he was completely out of order for giving a player permission to have lunch. I suppose in those days it was better that we starved.

Peter Brown: The only game Scotland won in the Championship that season was the last match at home against England, 14–5. By then I was the recognised goal-kicker and in those days you weren't allowed on the pitch at Murrayfield before an international, so I asked Frank Laidlaw, the captain, if I could take the kick-off to get a practise shot at goal. The idea was that I would kick it dead, they would drop-out and always at the first line-out the referee would penalise one team or the other and it was a toss-up as to which one. So I converted the kick-off, Bob Hiller dropped out, ball into touch, line-out to

Peter and Gordon Brown relax at the Braid Hills Hotel in March 1970.

Scotland, penalty to Scotland, and I kicked the goal. So everything went to plan and straight away we were thinking: this is going to be our day.

We introduced the tap penalty move to world rugby in that game. Nobody remembers that except us. We wanted to do something different and Ian McLauchlan came up with this idea at the team meeting. I'll always remember the stir it caused when Scotland were awarded a penalty just outside their own 22, and the Mouse walked to the ball and then turned his back on the opposition. The crowd were aghast as Alastair McHarg, my brother and I all ran forward in different directions, and the ball was passed to Gordon at the beginning of a move, I think, which ended with John Frame being tackled into touch close to the English line. Up until that point, when awarded a penalty you either kicked for touch, or you kicked for goal, or you sent a Garryowen up in the air.

Gordon Brown: Peter and I were at long last selected together to play for Scotland in that England match. We all played out of our skins. It was fire and fury all the way, the forwards produced possession and, with Ian Robertson at his silky best at stand-off, the backs produced the exciting thrusts for the tries – a forty-yarder from Alastair Biggar and the second from Jock Turner after a sizzling scissors with Ian Robertson. We won 14-5. Peter and I played alongside each other in the Scottish team on ten further occasions, though never once as second-row partners.

John Frame: We toured Australia at the end of the 1970 season, and that wasn't a particularly enjoyable tour. Frank Laidlaw was captain and he was a nice enough guy but a very, very intense character. Creamy was there as a coach. It was the first tour when there was a frowning approach towards alcohol, and we used to have these illicit drinking sessions which would end with guys hiding under beds and in wardrobes for fear of being caught drinking. Frank was terrified that we would be let down by not being fit, so we trained for three hours in the blazing sunshine the day before the Test. We took the field absolutely knackered and lost the Test match fairly heavily. We fielded Jock Turner at fullback, which was a suicidal waste of talent, and we had never played together as a back division in that shape before. It just didn't work. We lost 23–3, and you might say we were lucky to get away with that.

The decade was one of mixed fortunes for the Scotland team, but it also saw the most consistently excellent years of British rugby and oversaw subtle but fundamental changes in the game itself. In 1971 Bill Dickinson came in as 'advisor to the captain', the first move towards a legitimate coach at international level, and Scotland led the way in the British domestic game by establishing competitive leagues around the country.

Chris Rea: We went to France at the beginning of the 1971 season, led 8–3 at half-time, and were playing really well. Jock Turner was at fly-half and was causing all sorts of problems with his size and strength, running at their fly-half. Then Ian Smith, at fullback, was injured, and they brought Brian Simmers on as a replacement, and instead of making a straight swap, for some extraordinary reason they put him at fly-half and moved Jock to fullback. Brian was lightweight, and he had played a lot of games for Glasgow Accies at fullback, so it was crazy – making two changes when one would have been more than enough. We ended up losing 13–8.

Gordon Brown: That was my first trip to Paris and I was eager to explore the nightlife. Peter took me aside and said, 'Keep your eyes on the French team at the end of the dinner and when they move out, follow them onto their team bus – I'll see you on it.' I duly obeyed his instructions and found myself at the back of their bus, attempting to converse with them in my school French, which was of course failing miserably. The bus was just about to move off when Peter came on with their skipper, Benoit Dauga, and we set off on a trip to remember. The journey took us to (and through) numerous nightclubs at which we were given free champagne and front-row seats if the club had a cabaret. What amazed me was the lack of objections from any of the patrons about having to vacate prized, and probably prebooked, seats. It was an exhilarating way of forgetting about our defeat in the match – even if only for a few hours.

Chris Rea: Our next game, against Wales at Murrayfield, was considered at the time to be one of the great matches of that decade. It was so fast and the lead changed hands eight times. I scored a try in the last ten minutes to make it 18–14 and Peter Brown missed the conversion from in front of the posts. That was crucial, because if he had kicked it they would have had to score twice and they wouldn't have come back.

I've never known noise like it. I was in the centre with John Frame, while Jock Turner was at stand-off, and we had to shout right into each others' ears but you still couldn't pick up what each other was saying. That was one of the reasons why we lost that last try. It was our throw-in at a line-out in our own twenty-five and Billy Steele got the wrong call, he couldn't hear in that incredible noise level. They wanted the ball to the front, but he threw to Delme Thomas at the back.

Then we immediately made another costly mistake when the Welsh sent the ball right. We had agreed that in defence the wings would stay out no matter what, so when I saw JPR Williams coming into the line I started moving over from John Dawes to cover him, when, to my horror, Alistair Biggar came in off his wing to make the tackle, leaving Ian Smith scrambling across to get to Gerald Davies.

Gerald scored, and then, of course, John Taylor added two points from the touchline, with what was described as 'the greatest conversion since St Paul's.' I've never been so heartbroken. We were all just devastated.

John Frame: There always was an issue of slight inferiority. The Welsh were the first to kit their guys out in tracksuits, while we used to turn up in this selection of weird and wonderful alternative outfits. I'm not sure how much difference these things made when we got on the pitch, but there is no question that if you make a team feel like a team by treating them with a degree of respect, then it is beneficial. Some of the guys involved with the Scottish team at the time really did take the ultimate amateur view. The Irish, by all accounts, were pretty much the same.

Peter Brown: At the end of that season came our famous win at Twickenham. Because it was the centenary season since the first international between Scotland and England at Raeburn Place in Edinburgh, we were scheduled to play two matches against England, at Twickenham and then Murrayfield, to celebrate.

Chris Rea: Broonie [Gordon Brown] dined out for years on his brother's team-talk before that Twickenham match. PC was going completely over the top, listing all the great Scottish victories over England, at Bannockburn and so on. Then at the climax of his speech he looked up at us and said, 'Remember Culloden.'

There was a pause before Gordon piped up, 'Peter, I don't think we did very well in that one.'

And not to be outdone, PC responded immediately, 'I said remember Culloden, and that's what I effin' well meant – because after Culloden they didn't have to get changed and have dinner with the bastards.'

We hadn't won at Twickenham since Wilson Shaw's match in 1938, but we had a feeling of real confidence before that match. We probably should have beaten both France and Wales that year, and although we had lost fairly heavily against Ireland we knew we had a really strong side.

It wasn't a great match but there were some exceptional moments of play. The English three-quarter line was huge, with Janion, Wardlow, Spencer and Duckham all close to the fourteen stone mark, which was very big in those days, and they scored a fantastic try with the ball sweeping across the field and back again before Hiller eventually touched down, and they led for most of the match.

We were 15–8 down when Duncy Paterson scored a try to make it 15–11, then with time running out we won a ruck and the ball went to PC, who was in the stand-off position for some reason. He lobbed this pass which I just managed to catch above my head. With John Spencer, the English captain, coming across I ordinarily would have

The teams pose together for the Centenary Match photograph.

passed to Steven Turk, who was on the left wing after replacing John Frame, and we would almost certainly have scored. But it would have been out on the touchline and I knew three points was no use to us – so I just went for it, as straight as I could. I was clattered by Spencer and a couple of others on the line, but managed to get the ball over.

It left PC with a hell of a difficult kick, halfway out to the touchline, and given that he had missed one in front of the posts against Wales earlier that season I wasn't overly confident. He just did his usual routine: turned his back on the ball, walked away, blew his nose, swung round and ran at it. I turned away, I couldn't watch.

Gordon Brown: I remember standing there just thinking, 'Come on, Peter! I've seen you kick that kind of goal hundreds of time. On the beach at Troon. At Marr College. At West. At Murrayfield. Just do it once more! Never mind the usual act of turning your back and walking away from the ball and blowing your nose all over the place. Just kick the goal. Please! Oh, no . . . He's turned his back on it. He's blowing his nose. Doesn't he know time's nearly up? He's blowing his nose again! God, he's actually enjoying it! *Bang*. It's over. I love him!' I sprinted toward him to kiss him but he just pushed me away, screaming, 'We've still got a few more minutes to get through!'

But we did get through it and then I gave him his kiss! The pitch was swarming with Scottish fans. A marvellous mayhem – I loved it.

Chris Rea: I saw the conversion later on TV and the ball never looked as if it was going anywhere near the posts until the very last moment when it veered in . . . it was just totally bizarre. I always say I feel a bit like Stan Mortensen, who scored a hat-trick for Blackpool in that magnificent FA Cup final against Bolton Wanderers in 1953, and it became known as Stanley Matthews' Final. Nobody ever remembers Mortensen; and Scots will always remember who kicked that winning conversion but not who got the try. It was a terrific moment but you don't really appreciate what you have achieved until long after the event. There have only been four winning Scottish sides at Twickenham to date – in 1926, 1938, 1971 and 1983. So we were part of something really special that afternoon.

John Frame: After we won that first centenary match at Twickenham, John Spencer stood up at the dinner and said that there was one thing the RFU forgot to mention to the SRU and that was that the game the following week was actually the centenary game and we were playing for the Calcutta Cup then and that they intended to win. And there was a collective rumble around the room.

That first game at Twickenham saw Fran Cotton win his first cap, and he said afterwards to Ian McLauchlan that the way McLauchlan had played was not the way he thought rugby should be played, and McLauchlan's great reply was that Cotton had seven days to get used to it.

Chris Rea: We were treated to another fantastic team talk the following week. Bill

Dickinson had been brought in earlier that season as adviser to the captain – we were not allowed to call him a coach – and he was a real character. And because it was the centenary match we got new shirts with a rose and a thistle side-by-side on the left breast. Well, Dickinson came into the changing room, marched up to PC, and poked his finger into his chest. He said, 'Right lads, see that badge? The thistle intertwined with a rose. You know what happens when a thistle gets intertwined with a rose? I'll tell you, the thistle effin' strangles the rose. Now we want you to go out and do exactly that to those bastards today.' That was our team-talk – fantastic.

We were presented to the Prince of Wales and that was done early so we actually started the game at five minutes to three, with people still coming into the ground. We kicked off, they tried to run the ball but it was dropped in the centre, and John Frame pounced on it to score which was the quickest ever international try at that time, PC kicked the conversion, they kicked off, we kicked back, they were penalised, PC kicked the goal, so we were 8–0 up and it still wasn't three o'clock.

The forwards were superb against a huge English pack that day and we ended up winning comfortably, 26–6.

John Frame: When England came up to Murrayfield this guy John Reason – who was regarded as being the doyen of the English rugby writers – said that England had lost the first game because they hadn't used their superior back division, which obviously didn't please us too much because we didn't think they were superior to us at all. I scored two tries in that match; the first came about because Jock Turner banged the kick-off deep into the corner and Jeremy Janion, their winger, tried to run it back, then panicked when he realised that the whole Scotland team were closing in on him and he chucked the ball inside. John Spencer dropped it under the posts and I capitalised . . . and that all came about because they were intent on believing that they had this superior back division.

Police hold back the crowd after Scotland defeat England
in the Centenary match at Murrayfield.

Everyone is always very admiring of the fact that I scored after just ten seconds, and I have to explain to them that all I did was run fifty yards, and there is no great achievement in running fifty yards in ten seconds.

In 1972 two players emerged onto the international stage to begin Test careers that would carve their names in Scottish rugby history forever. Jim Renwick and Andy Irvine were players of true, unadulterated, genius. The finest two players ever to play for Scotland? Few who saw them would argue otherwise.

Irvine's style was characterised by an almost recalcitrant attitude to anything approaching preordained tactics, by his unstinting flair and luminous brilliance, and his instinct to run, to always run, to attack from anywhere – and the deeper the better. He had a few weaknesses, particularly in defence or under a swirling high-ball, but with a broken field before him he was one of the stars of his generation; collecting the ball in space, he would open up his long stride and as the defence pushed up to meet him there would be a subtle change of direction, a swerve, a shift in balance. . . and he would be gone. The defence, beguiled by his nimble feints, would be left floundering in his wake, left to raise their heads from the turf and stare, breathless, at his brilliance.

Some would argue that Irvine lost more games for Scotland than he won, but the manner in which he could change the face of a game, the excitement that would grip the crowd when his hands touched the ball and which would rise to fever pitch as he fizzed and flickered, darted and weaved his way to the try line with an almost otherworldly grace, etched his place in the hearts of rugby fans forever.

If Telfer and McGeechan were the calm and controlling midfield generals, Renwick was the impish artisan outside them, a purveyor of bold adventure in attack and heroic defiance in defence. A mischievous Puck with ball in hand he could conjure space from nowhere with a shimmy, a step, a lacerating angle or a sleight of hand and then he would put on the afterburners, accelerating into the line, through it and beyond. There was artistry in every moment of his play and a desire, like Irvine, to attack and to enjoy the game he was playing at all times. Small in stature, he looked – with his thick moustache and balding crown wreathed by dark curls – like a swashbuckling character from a Dumas classic.

Jim Renwick (Scotland 1972–1984, 52 Caps plus 1 Cap for the Lions): We used to stay up at the Braid Hills Hotel in Edinburgh from the Thursday before the game. What a place that was – you needed an o-grade in map reading to find your room – it was like a rabbit warren. It was a rickety old place with all these long winding corridors and it seemed compulsory that every room had squeaky beds and floorboards and windows that rattled in the wind. It wasn't flash but they really looked after us well and the food was good.

Things have really changed over the years. My first cap was against France at Murrayfield for our opening game of the 1972 Five Nations. On the Thursday night before the game there was none of this sports psychology and analysis of the opposition, or even sessions to go over our moves or discuss our tactics – we used to go to the pantomime! All these big lads shouting, 'Oh no, he isn't!' and, 'Look behind you!' as part of their preparation to take on the French. Changed days.

John Frame: Yes, going to the pantomime really was a bit odd, now you look back at it. Well, we all thought it was a bit odd even then, but you just went along with it.

Jim Renwick: On the Friday we would go up to the stadium but we mainly just hung around having our photos taken and talking to the press – we weren't allowed on the pitch. A few years later they let the goal-kickers on to do some practice, but that was it, no one else was allowed to set foot on the grass. It was a tough day on the Friday because there was very little else on – you would just be kicking your heels and getting all worked up before the match. We'd have one or two team meetings, go into town for a walk around or go and catch a game down at one of the clubs who were playing a touring team from France or Wales or Ireland, whoever was playing Scotland that weekend. Sometimes we'd play snooker or go bowling, but it was tough trying to find something meaningful to do to keep your mind off the game.

On the Friday night the hotel would be full of all these committee men as there was always a big dinner on the night before the game – and a lot of them would be looking really rough on the Saturday. We would be sitting in our rooms, unable to sleep, hearing every creak of the bed or the rattle of the window and just thinking about the game the next day. A lot of us couldn't sleep on those nights, so we would head down to the bar and have a few pints – just to settle the nerves and to help you sleep, nothing major.

I used to enjoy the bus trip to the ground on the Saturday. You packed your bag just before leaving the hotel and Bill McLaren would be on the TV doing the build-up for the match, so you were really getting a feel for the occasion by that stage, and when you went through Edinburgh you would see all these folk in their kilts heading to ground, waving to you as you passed and you hoped they couldn't see how green you were. I used to be sick before games – not always, but mostly. The nervous tension always got to me, but in a good way – it made me sharp.

We used to do most of our warm-ups in the changing room because there wasn't really anywhere else. Now and again you'd need a bit more space and there was one year that I had a bit of a dodgy leg that needed a proper warm up, so I went out into the car park on the back pitches and was dodging around between all the cars.

PC Brown was captain for my first game. He was quiet and wasn't all about fire and brimstone in his talk before we took the field, but I liked his approach – he was completely confident in his own ability and that helped you feel confident too.

I don't remember much about that first game – you're just living on your wits and although you know the game is going to be fast you can't prepare yourself for what it is actually like. It hits you and the whole thing seems to pass in a blur. There are a few things I remember though – Colin Telfer gathered a loose ball near our line and started a counter-attack, passing the ball to Arthur Brown who hared off up field. He managed to get the ball to Alastair Biggar who stood up the last of the defence and passed inside to me for a clear run to the line from twenty-five yards out. If ever there was a way to settle the nerves in your first cap, it was that!

Alan Lawson (Scotland 1972-1980, 15 Caps): I was a sub in the first ever Scotland B game, which was against France in Oyonnax. I remember them calling a five-man lineout and their scrum-half, Jean-Michel Aguirre – who went on to win a number of caps at fullback as well as scrum-half – wandered up to the lineout looking kind of disinterested. The hooker threw the ball over the back of the lineout and Aguirre suddenly came alive and burst onto it. He set off into midfield and fed the back-row who had shuffled into the centres and they created absolute havoc.

So it got to the Five Nations match against France at Murrayfield and Aguirre was picked at scrum-half. I was on the bench and Spivey [Ian] McCrae was at nine for us. Half an hour to go and France call a short line out. Aguirre comes up, looks disinterested, takes the high ball and bursts into the midfield. But because of Oyonnax we were wise to this tactic and Sandy Carmichael had been told to stand by Colin Telfer and told to poleax Aguirre if this happened. But no one had told Spivey that this was the plan. Spivey tackled Aguirre around the ankles – and Sandy charged right over the top of Spivey and broke three of his ribs. And so I then won my first cap!

John Frame: I scored against France in that game, and it involved a set move from a scrum near the West Stand heading towards the old clock end. The idea was that Colin Telfer would flip me the ball, I would pull in the backrow and then pop it back to Colin to go through the gap and score under the posts. So we started the move and everything was going to plan, but these were the days when balls had laces and I had a snagged nail which caught on the lace, so I couldn't deliver it and I had to pull it back. I just carried on with the French pack trying to figure out who had the ball. Everyone was talking about how brilliant it was, but it was all down to that snagged nail.

Sandy Carmichael: I always had this fear of being sent off. When we came back from the Lions tour in '71 [from which Carmichael was sent home early with a smashed cheekbone suffered during a brutal encounter against Canterbury the week before the first Test], we had France in our first game and Ian MacLauchlan came over to me in the changing room and said: 'Look Sandy, they've got you down as a wet nurse, so if you see anything then just hit their guy because the referee won't believe it was you.'

So we're well into the game and Bonoit Dauga was in an offside position so I whacked him. The whistle went and Meirion Joseph, the Welsh referee said, 'Penalty. Punching.'

And MacLauchlan said, 'Who?'

Meirion pointed at me, and Ian said, 'He doesn't punch.'

'Well I saw it with my eyes. He punched him.'

And Ian just turned to me and said, 'Well done big yin – let's go.'

I never punched again – I got caught! I would take anything on: scrum-wise, tackle-wise, you name it … but not the knuckle. I didn't think that way. Dickie [Bill Dickinson] used to get so disappointed in me because I wasn't a brawler. But when I came off the pitch after that game, he shook my hand and said, 'Well done, son. Well done. You're in my pack now.'

Ian Barnes (Scotland 1972-1977, 7 Caps): When I was called into the Scotland side for my first cap in February 1972 as a replacement for Alistair McHarg I was doing my CA apprenticeship in Edinburgh being paid £52 per month. I got the call at work on the Wednesday morning so I went down to see the senior partner. I said, 'I am in the Scotland team for Saturday.' He jumped out of his seat. 'That's great news, Ian! Great for you! Great for the firm! Have a seat! Have a sherry!' Halfway through the sherry I told him that I would need Thursday and Friday off to go down to Wales.

'That's no problem, Ian. No problem at all – just take a couple of days holiday!'

We trained at Murrayfield on the Thursday morning and flew down to Cardiff in the afternoon. We were staying in the Angel Hotel directly opposite the Arms Park. The place was jumping – mobbed with supporters – and the Welsh team were there as well so you kept bumping into them in the foyer and in the dining room. On the Saturday we just walked across to the ground for the game mingling with the early crowd – not particularly professional but it fairly got the goosebumps going.

I don't remember much about the game. It was that great Welsh side of the early seventies with JPR Williams, Gerald Davies, Barry John, Gareth Edwards and these guys but we did reasonably well in the first half and were actually leading with twenty minutes to go but we got humped in the last quarter. Gareth Edwards scored a great try – the BBC kept showing it every week for years at the start of *Sportscene*. He came round the back of a lineout in our half and kicked ahead, the ball stuck in the mud and he beat Jim Renwick to the touch in the corner. He handed me off as he came round the corner – and it felt as though a horse had kicked me.

Jim Renwick: I still marvel at the distances that Gareth Edwards could pass the ball – it was like a torpedo – which gave Barry John the space and time he needed to work his magic. It wasn't a great game from our point of view, but I was happy that I made it on the score sheet again with a penalty when PC was injured.

Two weeks later, on 30 January 1972, British Army paratroopers shot dead thirteen civilians on the streets of Derry in Northern Ireland. The incident came to be known as Bloody Sunday. Three days, later, over 20,000 protestors gathered in Dublin's Merrion Square to march against the atrocities; they were joined by an IRA march and soon violent clashes broke out between the protestors and the police. The British Embassy was petrol bombed and several buildings with British connections were razed to the ground. The Troubles were raging.

Scotland were due to travel to Dublin to play Ireland, but with wing Billy Steele and hooker Bobby Clark actively serving in the armed forces at the time, and with general fears about potential terrorist reprisals, the SRU made it clear that they were uncomfortable with the prospect of honouring the fixture. The IRFU sent a party of delegates to Edinburgh to try and offer some comfort, citing two occasions when Scotland had played in Dublin during the heights of the Wars of Independence and emphasising that no paramilitary group had ever targeted the Republic. Dublin, they said, would be safe for any incoming rugby team.

The IRA then issued a statement in February that declared that there was no threat to the Scottish team, its officials, or any who travelled with them: 'The rugby match should go ahead. No true Irish Republican will offer an opposition to them.' Despite all these assurances, the SRU stood firm. The Scottish team would not travel to Dublin.

The outcry in both Ireland and Scotland was vociferous. It was felt that the SRU were cowering to terrorism – despite the assurances from the IRA themselves – and that the future of the Five Nations was being placed in jeopardy.

And indeed it was, as Wales also refused to visit Ireland that year. If it weren't for the actions of the French, who played an extra fixture in Dublin in 1972, and the England team of 1973, who travelled to Dublin to fulfil their fixture despite being in far greater potential danger than any Welsh or Scottish side, the Five Nations might never have recovered. England were hammered 18-9 by a superb Ireland, but their presence at Lansdowne Road and the post-match words of their captain, John Pullin, were infinitely more memorable than any action that took place during the match. 'We may not be any good,' said Pullin. 'But at least we turn up.' It was, regrettably, something that the Scots and Welsh could not say.

There were chilling footnotes to 1972, however. On 21 July the IRA exploded twenty six car, van and parcel bombs at various locations in Belfast. Nine people died and 130 others were injured. Between 26 November 1972 and 20 January 1973, there were four paramilitary bombings in the centre of Dublin. Three civilians were killed and 185 people were injured. With these December and January attacks, bombings had come to the Republic, just as the SRU and WRU had feared. Not that it would have changed the minds of the 1972 Scotland team, members of which remain convinced to this day that their safety was not an issue and still feel regret over the way the incident was handled.

Peter Brown: We wanted to play in Dublin to make up for the loss in Wales [a fortnight before] and the famous try in the mud by Gareth Edwards. The players were not consulted or in any way involved in the decision. The interminable wait for a decision to be taken led to me being completely misquoted by the Reuters news agency. As instructed by the SRU, I stonewalled questions but, unfortunately, I closed the phone call with the Reuters journalist with the words that came back to haunt me. I said I was 'delighted that a decision had at last been reached'. The headline the next day was 'Scotland captain pleased with decision'. My name was mud in Ireland. I never forgave Reuters for that.

Ian McLauchlan: If they'd asked me, then I would have said I was going. Rugby is no place for politics. We made a terrible mistake. I don't know who was the driving force but there wasn't a chance I would have stayed away from Ireland had I a say in the matter. Were we in danger? No way. Christ almighty, we're a rugby team and Ireland is a united rugby nation. Nothing was ever likely to happen. Never in a million years did I see danger.

John Frame: I don't remember being involved in a decision about whether we should go or not. I certainly don't recall being asked. You'll probably find someone who says the players were all asked but I don't have any memory of it.

Alan Lawson: I was picked for the game and I said that I was happy to go. I don't know how many others felt that, but I wanted to play. Obviously the powers that be decided otherwise, but I would have loved to have gone. I understood their worries, but I would have played and would just have hoped that everything would be OK.

Bobby Clarke was in the Navy, but he was keen to go, too. At first, when the decision was still up in the air, he was told that he could grow his hair a bit longer so it didn't have quite such a military look to it. Master of disguise!

I remember when we eventually went back to Ireland in '74, we had armed bodyguards with us. We went to the cinema on the Friday night and there were people sitting in the front row of the upstairs, who got up and left their bags behind. And so there was a bit of a ruckus about that. But it turned out that they had just left their ordinary bags behind and they came back to collect them. But there was definitely an air to the place at the time.

I'd been to Northern Ireland to play in a sevens tournament not long before and there had been a bomb in the docks that day, and we had been told to stay together and not go out in the town that night. So all this was going on, but I thought – rightly or wrongly – that sport was kind of above all of that, so I wanted to go.

Jim Renwick: I was only a young player at the time, but nobody asked me anything. Aye, I'd have went. I'm not a political animal.

Ian Barnes: It never entered my head that we shouldn't go. Were we under threat from the IRA? Total shite.

Sean Lynch (Irish hooker): I wasn't angry that they didn't come. It was their prerogative. But then Wales refused to come as well a few weeks later and it became a serious problem.

Ray McLoughlin (Irish prop): I had no difficulty in understanding the decision that was taken. They felt it was risky coming over because of what was going on. I can't judge whether they were justified in feeling concern about it. I didn't think that there was much risk but I could understand them thinking that there was.

Wallace McMaster (Irish wing): It was my first season on the team. I used to travel down to Dublin from Ballymena in the car with Willie John McBride and Stewart McKinney because the feeling was that if you were on the train and there was a bomb on the line then that was you stuck. In the car, if there was a bomb on the road ahead, you could put the thing into reverse and go down another road and away you went.

We lived through that. We understood it. And we just got on with it. But the Scots and the Welsh were understandably shaken. On television they would have seen stories about bombs going off and it would have looked a lot worse than it actually was. So I totally got why the union guys in Edinburgh and Cardiff did what they did.

Willie John McBride (Irish second-row): I was angry about it. The unions in Edinburgh and Cardiff made the decision and didn't consult the players. It's the players who go on the field, not the bloody administrators. It was always my belief that rugby people stood by each other. Throughout the murder and mayhem in Northern Ireland there wasn't a single game of rugby ever cancelled between a team from the north and a team from the south. We crossed over the border all the time to play against each other and the game was a great unifier in tough times. It kept people together. It preached tolerance. So for the Scots and the Welsh to stay away, that was disappointing.

Jim Renwick: There was over a month between the game in Cardiff the Calcutta Cup game that year because we didn't go to Ireland. We had wanted to get the showback on the road after losing the Wales by playing Ireland, but obviously that didn't happen. Luckily we were able to do it against England at Murrayfield and thumped them 23–9.

In December the All Blacks came to town and we were unlucky not to win, to be honest. We lost 14–9, but it was 10–9 going into extra time and a score from either side would have nicked it – unfortunately Sid Going intercepted an inside ball from Alistair McHarg and ran the length to score. It was disappointing to lose but they had a great side. I was up against Bruce Robertson and that was some education – he was a big lad who had great hands but he knew how to run and kick too. They had great balance across the park – size and skill in Bryan Williams on one wing, electricity in Grant Batty on the other; Sid Going was always busy at scrum-half; they had a huge pack and in the back-row they had some of the all-time greats in Grizz Wylie and Ian Kirkpatrick. They were bigger and fitter than us, but the key thing was that they just didn't make mistakes – their basic skills were flawless. It was in that game that I realised that I needed to work on my pace more if I was ever going to live with these boys. That's the one truth in any sport, but especially in rugby – you can never have too much pace.

That game also saw first caps awarded to Ian McGeechan at fly-half and Andy Irvine at fullback. Geech was pretty small like me, but we linked well together and stood up strong in defence against the All Blacks, and I liked his approach to the game; I think he enjoyed playing alongside me, too. Andy wasn't even fully fit because he'd knackered his knee during the National Trial the week before, but he had been an unused replacement during the Five Nations and was desperate to play – and despite his knee being dodgy he still managed to kick six of our nine points and he made some fantastic breaks. He was great to have at fullback and it was a position that suited him well as it gave him licence to attack from anywhere and to hit the line wherever he saw some space opening up. He wasn't the best defensive fullback I ever played with, but he had the attitude of: if you score three, I'll score four. Some people criticised him for being too flash, but he had steel in him too.

Andy Irvine (Scotland 1972-1982, 51 Caps plus 9 Caps for the Lions): Jim Renwick is about as close as Scottish rugby has ever got to producing a genius. He had a tremendous side-step, he had a lot of pace, he was very quick off the mark, and he had great balance, he did actually have everything. He could dummy, he could swerve, he was a tremendous tackler, he was a tough boy with a very strong and powerful upper body from the swimming he did in his youth, he could kick goals, he could drop goals, he could control the game, and to be honest he could have played anywhere on the park if he put his mind to it. He was only 5' 9', but even today, although the boys are a lot bigger and more physical, he would have been a great stand-off. He could have easily coped with the big hits and the power because he was tough and he was awfully strong.

Alan Lawson: Jim Renwick was just exceptional at reading the game and seeing space; and he had a jink to die for.

Andy Irvine: It was great having someone like Jim playing in front of me in that first match – he was so comfortable out there and so confident, it just gave me the confidence to try things too. I think Geech really appreciated having someone like that playing outside him too – a steady influence in tricky situations, but also someone who was really enthusiastic about attacking when it was on, or who was able to make something out of nothing. That was especially the case towards the end of the seventies when John Rutherford came into the side – Jim and John together were a tremendous combination.

Ian McGeechan (Scotland 1972-1979, 32 Caps plus 8 Caps for the Lions): I played in the National Trial as a stand-off and I remember being chased all day by Jim Telfer and Rodger Arneil as they tried to take my head off. It was some introduction to what would be a long career with Jim.

I was first capped against the All Blacks and it was the third time I had played them in four weeks because I had faced them playing for the Rest of the Scotland and the North of England. The Mouse took over the captaincy in that first season and he was a real inspiration – a great leader who always led by example and always said the right thing.

Ian Barnes: They used to hold trial matches in December each year – purgatory – miserable freezing Saturday afternoons in a bleak empty Murrayfield, a couple of hundred spectators in the old West Stand and miles of empty terracing; there was no shape, no structure, no chance if you were in the Whites, you were cannon fodder for the Blues; it was eighty minutes of watching the clock on the south terracing dragging its way towards 3.20pm and a warm bath – and then being told that the selectors wanted another half hour. I must have played against McHarg in a dozen trials and I honestly cannot remember winning a single lineout. And Gordon Brown wasn't bad either! So I more or less spent the next five years sitting on the bench and in those days before tactical substitutions the only way you got on was if somebody was hurt.

I would have liked to have been playing but I was happy enough just to be there. Home international weekends were tremendous. A heavy session at Murrayfield on the Sunday – four, maybe five hours – and it was tough because we had all played league games on the Saturday. We'd meet again at Murrayfield on the Thursday for a full session – three, maybe four hours – and then up to the Braid Hills Hotel. Evening meal – prawn cocktail starter, scampi fish course, fillet steak fully garnished, toffee pudding, cheese and biscuits – down to the Canny Man for three or four pints. A run through at Murrayfield on the Friday morning. Back to the Braids for lunch – prawn cocktail starter, scampi fish course, fillet steak fully garnished, toffee pudding, cheese and biscuits. A walk along Princes Street on Friday afternoon then dinner at the Braids – prawn cocktail starter, scampi fish course, fillet steak fully garnished, toffee pudding, cheese and biscuits. Cinema at night – always a western, preferably John Wayne – and a couple of pints on the way home.

Alan Lawson: The pre-match meal was extraordinary, you'd have all the guys eating scampi and whatnot, and Broon would be eating chips and honey. We had none of the science that they have now. I tended to eat Fisherman's Friends because they were so disgusting they put you off eating anything, which is what I preferred to do before a game. I look back and wish I knew about diet and weight training, speed training and so. But you can only play in the era you were born in and no one did weights or anything like that. You might get the odd prop who lifted weights, but that was probably about it – and even then it was pretty primitive stuff.

Ian Barnes: The replacements tended to be a bit peripheral on the Saturday in the build up and during the game but the Saturday nights were glorious. Bus from Murrayfield to the NB, a couple of pints with the punters in the downstairs bar, change into your DJ, champagne reception, then the Match Dinner in the NB ballroom with its spectacular view along Princes Street to the floodlit Scott Monument and the castle. Everybody that was anybody in Scottish rugby was there and it was cigars, white wine, red wine, vintage port, the works – and after the formalities we were joined by wives and girlfriends for a real shindig fraternising with the opposition.

Andy Irvine: My first game in the Five Nations was Scotland's opening match against France in 1973 – which was also the first game to be played at the new Parc de Princes. There was a hell of an atmosphere at that game, the crowd were just crazy – 50,000 mad Frenchmen with a sprinkling of Scottish supporters, bands that played throughout the game along with drums and firecrackers and trumpets all over the place. The crowd would build themselves up into a frenzy as kick-off approached and as you came out of the tunnel you could actually feel the air beating with the noise. The passion on show was just incredible – it was a brand new ground but instantly it was a fortress. I had never experienced anything like it in my life.

Alan Lawson: It was a cauldron, the Parc. You drove in under the stadium and there was a big moat around the pitch. There was a camber on the pitch and while I'm not saying that I was great kicker, it was a bloody hard place to kick along the touchline as a result because you couldn't always see the lines on the far side.

The first twenty minutes of that match, I don't think we needed a ball, it was just so physical. Geech [Ian McGeechan] got a bit of doing and there were fights kicking off all over the place. There were games when the French came to play rugby and other times when they came with one objective and that was to smash you off the park. That game was one of the latter.

Sandy Carmichael: I played opposite Armand Vaquerin. He blew his brains out playing Russian Roulette a few years later. A mental case. Can you imagine what he was like in a Test match?

Ian McLauchlan: They had a guy in the second-row called Alain Esteve. He was known as the Beast of Beziers. Interesting guy; liked a wee scrap, which was fine by me.

Sandy Carmichael: Yeah, the Beast of Beziers. Bloody enormous. Mental. A scary bastard.

Ian McLauchlan: No he wasn't.

Andy Irvine: We started the game quite brightly while the French team seemed a little overawed by the occasion. At one point their centre, Jean Trillo, was clattered in a tackle and the crowd started a huge chant of 'Maso, Maso' – calling for Jo Maso, their star centre who had been omitted from the squad. For periods of the game we actually seemed more popular with the crowd than the home team because of the style we were playing – we ran the ball from our own line at one stage and swept all the way up field and the crowd went mad, loving it – hooters were sounding and firecrackers were exploding, it was something else.

France scored a neat try through their outside centre Claude Dourthe and although we scored a try through Alan Lawson, PC Brown kicked a couple of penalties and Geech struck a drop-goal their fly-half Jean-Pierre Romeu kicked three penalties and a drop-goal and that was the difference.

Alan Lawson: We got six penalties but PC missed four of them, which was a killer.

Then I remember we launched a high up-and-under and Jim Renwick got his hands on the ball and fed me for a try. We missed the conversion and although Geech also got a drop-goal, we lost 16-13 and it really came down to those missed kicks. Given we only won away from home twice throughout the entire 1970s, that was a tough one to lose.

Andy Irvine: Weekends in Paris were fantastic and the post-match dinner was always superb – six courses and unlimited amounts of the finest wine, port, brandy and liqueurs – and the crowds were always so welcoming when you went out after the match.

Ian McLauchlan's first game as captain was against Wales in the second match that year. He took over from PC Brown, even though Peter was still in the team. I liked Peter as captain, but the Mouse had this aura about him that just gave you confidence – he was so aggressive and he always led from the front. As we prepared to run out of the tunnel and onto that famous Murrayfield pitch, he pulled us all in tight and gave one of the most inspirational team-talks I have ever heard. It was real power and passion and it still sends a shiver up my spine to think about it.

We were heading out to play on our home ground against a team that Scotland hadn't beaten since 1967 and contained nine British Lions, all of who were true greats of the game. Before you go out into battle, those are the kind of words you need to hear – they burn away the apprehension and the fear and ignite a fire in your soul. With a guy like the Mouse leading you in the battle, you were ready to take on the world. We fizzed down that tunnel and we unleashed hell on them.

Ian McLauchlan: That Welsh side was filled with guys like JPR Williams, Gerald Davies, Phil Bennett, Gareth Edwards in the backs, Mervyn Davies, John Taylor and Derek Quinnell in the pack, so we weren't expected to win.

We played them at Murrayfield and the tradition at that time was for the president and all the selectors to sit in on the team talk, and I went to the president beforehand and asked him if he would mind leaving the room at that point so that I didn't have to speak to anyone except the players. He agreed but didn't brief his other selectors, and after he had wished us all the best he said they would now leave the room and you could see that the rest of them were pretty reluctant to go.

Alistair McHarg turned to me and said, 'You do realise that if we lose today, you'll never play for Scotland again.'

Fortunately we won 10–9. I just thought that you should be able to say certain things to players, and they were inhibiting that.

Ian McGeechan: Gerald Davies always used to say that he wished he had been a fly on the wall during the Mouse's team talk before that game. He said the way we came down the tunnel and the ferocity of our performance was incredible and you could see the Mouse's influence over the way we played and took the game to Wales.

Ian McLauchlan: In our next match, against Ireland, I came off the field with a suspected broken leg and got put in a taxi on my own to the Royal Infirmary, because nobody wanted to miss the game. It didn't bother me, because being part of the international set-up was fabulous, and the fact that we were ten years behind everyone else was all part of it.

If you tore your shorts during a game and got given a new pair, then they were waiting for you coming off the field so that they could get them back. You had to go home and get your mother to darn yours.

It turned out my leg wasn't broken, although the bone was cracked. We played England at Twickenham two weeks later for the Triple Crown, and the doctor said I was fit to play so I played. I played before and after that injury, so I didn't miss any games because of it. There were a lot of guys carrying knocks that day, but basically we underperformed and that is why we lost.

Gordon Brown: The truth is that Ian should never have been in London, let alone leading Scotland, but his determination to play was fierce. His stubborn, burning fanaticism eventually warded off the committee's feeble efforts to make him stand down. I believe that Ian honestly felt he could do the job he was selected for and not let anybody down, least of all himself, in the process. Nevertheless he was only a shadow of his normal self on the day and the team definitely suffered because of it. It would be totally belittling ever other performance for Scotland that Ian played to say otherwise. He was undoubtedly the best scrummager I ever played behind, his work rate in the line-outs as a blocker and in the loose was immense, but at Twickenham he demanded too much from his body.

Andy Irvine: In retrospect, although we were happy to see that the Mouse was in the team, there was no way he should have played. They said that it was a cracked fibula – but no matter how you dress it up, it was a broken leg, and who can play rugby with a broken leg? I suppose it's a testament to the kind of guy he was – how hard he was – that he was able to make it through the match at all and I can't even begin to imagine the pain he was in when he was scrummaging. But the Mouse wasn't the only player in the pack injured – there were a whole raft of them carrying heavy knocks. We might have been a good enough team to take on England at Twickenham and win with one or two guys carrying slight knocks, but we weren't good enough – and I don't think there would ever be a team good enough – to win with a pack of forwards who only had two or three guys who were one hundred per cent fit. In the changing room before we went out there were guys getting pain-killing injections and others that were literally being held together with tape and bandages. It was crazy. But caps weren't as readily available in those days as they are now – and nobody really knew when their last chance might be, so you played no matter what. If they picked you, you played. But looking back it was no surprise that we lost – going into the game with players in that kind of condition was only going to have one result. It's still enormously disappointing that we didn't win the Triple Crown that year because, fully fit, we were more than good enough to do it.

Jim Renwick: The following year we lost narrowly down in Cardiff in the opening game of the '74 Five Nations. It was 6–0 to them in the end and their try was little bit dodgy – Terry Cobner scored after some great play from Gareth Edwards, Phil Bennett and Gerald Davis, but Cobner's grounding was suspect – in those days you had to release the ball when you were tackled to the ground, but Cobner didn't and then managed to get the ball down over the line and the ref gave it. It would have been a tough call either way, but in the end it swung theirs. It was pretty hard to take at the time because we had competed well throughout the game, but they had class all over the park and probably deserved to shade it in the end.

The following week we played a real ding-dong match against the English at Murrayfield where the lead changed hands four times in the last twenty minutes. Andy Irvine scored an incredible try in the last five minutes or so when he took the ball at pace down the blind-side and stepped past four defenders to score in the corner. I thought we had it sealed then.

Andy Irvine races down the wing to score against England at Murrayfield in 1974.

Andy Irvine: I was convinced that my try had won the game as there were only a few minutes left and then Colin Telfer gathered a loose ball on our twenty-five and kicked it clear – it went dead straight and landed right in Peter Rossborough's arms and he slotted a perfect drop-goal. I was standing under the posts as it sailed over and I was devastated – to lose a game like that was just agony.

But we still had time. The Mouse said to us as we ran back to half-way that we just needed to get into range to kick a drop-goal or win a penalty, anything. The way the game had gone I didn't think it was likely that the lead would swing back in our favour again, but you never knew. It had been a crazy eighty minutes. We kicked off and launched a last-ditch offensive. In a moment of pure madness from a player of pure genius, David Duckham played the ball from a blatantly offside position and we were awarded a penalty.

The kick was tricky – it was on the wrong side for me and around forty yards out near the touchline, but I felt incredibly confident as I teed up the ball and as I readied myself to kick it I just had this sense that it was going to go over.

Jim Renwick: Some of the boys hoisted Andy on their shoulders and carried him off the pitch, which was a bit much I thought at the time, but sometimes when you've worked so hard in a game, you've won it and you've lost it and you've won it again emotions run high.

Alan Lawson: If you were to put your money on anyone to kick a goal like that to win a game, you'd put your money on Andy. Gordon Brown and I got in trouble after lifting him up after the game. You didn't do that in rugby.

Ian McLauchlan: You know, we never won in France while I was playing. The French were always trying to bully you, so we tried to give as good as we got – but that didn't always work. We played them at the Parc des Princes in 1975, and at the first line-out all hell broke loose. Everyone was in, giving it plenty, except Sandy Carmichael standing at the front and Victor Boffelli at the back, who wasn't a fighter either. Eventually the referee gets control back and he pulls Sandy and Boffelli aside. He says, 'Any more of that and you're off,' then writes their numbers down.

Sandy was pretty upset because in those days you just didn't get sent off in internationals, so he says to me, 'That's it. I can't do my share of the fighting now.'

I thought, 'Thank God for that.' He would probably have hit me. Sandy is the bravest guy I know, he would do anything that needed done on the rugby field, except he wasn't interested in punching. And you couldn't say to him, 'Punch that guy,' because he didn't want to do it and he didn't know how to do it. It was against his nature, totally outwith his normal pattern of behaviour. He would scrummage hard, he would tackle hard, he would go down on the ball, he would get trampled all over – but that side of it was totally alien to him. And that is where the French were maybe used to a tougher rugby culture than us. We were distracted by the fighting, whereas it fired them up. We never seemed to settle into our game in France.

Alan Lawson: For a guy who smoked heavily, Sandy Carmichael was a freak of nature. His pace around the park, his tackling ability was just phenomenal, and he had this tremendous engine that meant he could just run and scrum and tackle all day – and he only had about a tenth of a lung to work with. You'd almost expect to see him running around with a cigarette in his mouth.

Andy Irvine: We lost in France but we had beaten Ireland the match before that, and then two weeks later played Wales at Murrayfield. In those days we didn't warm up on the pitch but we would go and have a wander around as soon as we arrived at the ground, to see how firm the playing surface was so that we could decide the best length of stud to wear. I remember walking out of the tunnel with the old east terracing facing us and it was crammed full. It was so busy that for a moment we thought we'd got the wrong kick-off time – that it was two o'clock instead of three o'clock.

When you turned round the main stand was nearly empty, because that was all ticketed – but because everyone wanted to see the game they had packed themselves into the rest of the ground more than an hour before kick-off. By the time the game started there were 104,000 people in the ground altogether. And if you listen to some rumours there were plenty more on top of that who weren't officially counted. They changed the rules after that: from then on it was all ticketed.

That was a great Welsh team, with fourteen of their starting XV being Lions at some point in their career. They went on to win the Championship that year, but not the Grand Slam because we beat them 12–10 that day.

1975 was very similar to 1973. We defeated Wales and Ireland and had to travel to Twickenham to try and win the Triple Crown. Most of Britain and Ireland felt that we had blown it in 1973 because we were a much better team than England and had beaten them in each of our four previous encounters. After the success at Murrayfield in 1974 things looked to have got back on track and as we headed down to London, England looked even less of a threat than they had two years before.

We had a superior backline that day as England were missing guys like Duckham, Preece and Evans and we hoped for fine weather so that we could really take our running game to them but the heavens were well and truly open and the pitch was a quagmire.

It was 3–3 at half-time but England stole the lead shortly after the game resumed. Peter Warfield punted the ball from our ten-yard line and it sailed over my head. I ran back expecting it to die on the sodden earth, but it bounced high and over my head again and skidded over our line. It was a foot race between me and Alan Morley and I swear to this day that I touched it down first, but the referee awarded Morley the try.

We were only 7–6 down and should have manufactured a way to score, but Dougie missed two penalty attempts and Geech was wide with a drop-goal attempt. The win would have given us the Calcutta Cup, the Triple Crown and the share of the Championship title. But we went home with nothing.

Ian Barnes: I got on again at Twickenham in 1975. I must have been on the bench about twenty times by then and I suppose I was getting a bit blasé about it because as I was going up to my seat in the stand an English boy, Peter Yarrington, who I knew from the Penguins, offered me a pandrop and I just stuck it in my mouth and sat down. England kicked off – Dave Rollitt hit Nairn McEwan with a straight arm right from the kick-off and broke his jaw – so I was on. I got such a fright that I swallowed the pandrop down the wrong way and choked. Colin Telfer who was sitting next to me started banging me on the back. Bill Dickinson, the coach, was going spare but eventually we got down the stairs and out of the stand. You had to go out the back to get into the dressing rooms but when we got there the corridor door was locked. Bill Dick lost the plot. There was a policeman hanging about so Bill borrowed his truncheon and broke a glass panel in the door – but he cut an artery in his wrist doing it and there was blood spurting everywhere. The policeman put a tourniquet on it and told me to hold it. We got into the dressing room just as they were bringing Splash [McEwan] in and he was in a hell of a state – blood coming out of every orifice. By this time, I was shot to bits. I needed a ticket from the English doctor to give to the touch judge to get onto the pitch but everybody was ignoring me, running around fussing over Splash and Bill Dick. The team manager, Dod Burrell, came in – and he went mental because I was still there. He grabbed the doctor, got the ticket and pushed me out the door. I sprinted down the corridor my studs scraping on the concrete floor . . . I turned right . . . and right again . . . then left and right again . . . I could hear the crowd roaring but I had missed the tunnel. It was like a rabbit warren. I came to some steps up into the stand, so I went up them to try to see where I was. People were sitting there wondering who was going to come on – and I was peeping over the top wondering how I was going to get there. I managed to get hold of a steward who showed me the way.

Allan Morley scored a pretty dodgy try for England – Andy Irvine definitely touched the ball first. Minutes to go and they were leading 7–6 when we were given a penalty thirty-five metres out slap in front. I remember standing there thinking to myself, 'This is the big time – the first Triple Crown since 1938 – and I am playing!' But Dougie Morgan missed the kick. Full time – back into the dressing room – the heads were down. Dougie's was about his ankles, absolutely inconsolable. Then Renwick looked up and said, 'Hell, Dougie, I could have backheeled a chest of drawers over from there.'

Alan Lawson: The Calcutta Cup in 1976 was a pretty memorable one for me. I always had a mentality that I would always contribute something to a game, no matter what, even if I wasn't playing well; and to honest, I didn't get off to a great start in that game. Ronnie Wilson was at fly-half and he saved my bacon a few times after I threw him a couple of horrendous passes. I was really struggling to get into the game. Then all of a sudden I had twenty minutes when things just started to click. I had a fly-hack that went forty yards down field and then bounced into touch which it had no right to do, and I had one or two other things that just worked out as I started to find myself at the right place at the right time. Both the tries that I scored were really just cases of me running hard to get in support and I was lucky enough to get on the end of both moves and to be the one that crossed the line. I always preferred creating tries to scoring tries, but having said that, scoring those two against England as we won the Calcutta Cup at a packed Murrayfield was pretty special.

John Frame: We went on tour to New Zealand in the summer of 1975 and I had a wonderful time. It was a peculiar tour for me to go on because, as my wife says, she

Alan Lawson dives over to score one the all time great
Scotland tries during the 1976 Calcutta Cup.

thought I had given up by that point. I don't know why I was picked – but I had the interesting distinction of playing in every one of Scotland's winning games and never experienced defeat on that tour. New Zealand is an incredible place to tour.

Andy Irvine: We always had a great time after international matches, but the best times were always had on tour. We were at a civic reception during the 1975 Scotland tour of New Zealand and I remember Ian Barnes putting his false teeth in Billy Steele's cup of tea. Billy didn't notice at first but as he got to the bottom of his drink he spotted something lurking. He went to fish whatever it was out and when he realised that it was something pretty unpleasant he instinctively threw them in the air. They flew across the room and just missed the British High Commissioner to New Zealand's wife by a few inches.

Alan Tomes (Scotland 1976-1987, 48 Caps): We had started really well on the tour, beating Nelson Bay in the first match, scoring eight tries to win 51–6, but then we lost to Otago at the House of Pain in Dunedin, which was my first game for Scotland. We then went to Christchurch and lost to Canterbury and were completely outplayed by their forwards. We managed to get things back on track by beating Hawke's Bay 30–0 and followed that up by beating Wellington at Athletic Park, 36–25. We then went to Gisborne to play Poverty Bay and although we had won the last two matches, we had been getting a bit of a doing up front all tour, so Bill Dickinson gave the forwards a real roasting, and Duncan Madsen was on the receiving end of some really harsh words. In the changing room he was bouncing around trying to look as angry as he could when he kicked the door leading into the showers. Well, his foot went right through it and it was like a fish hook – the studs got caught and he couldn't get his boot back out. Just then the referee came in to give us the usual chat about behaving ourselves and not getting too rough – and Madsen was hopping around with his foot stuck in the door.

Ian Barnes: We trained hard, we played well and we had a great time socially. We threw it away against Otago and had no luck whatsoever against Canterbury but we were in good shape and genuinely fancied our chances against a transitional New Zealand side in the Test match. Then the rains came – an inch an hour for four hours. The pitch in Auckland was under water – two inches in places – there is no way the game should have been played – but we were booked in to fly home the next day so we took a vote and decided to get on with it. We played into a gale of torrential rain in the first half and held them to 6–0 at half time. I remember saying to Jim, 'We can win this!' Then when we lined up for the second half the wind had turned 180 degrees straight back into our faces.

Jim Renwick: It was a joke. Grant Batty tried to drop a goal, and the ball just died in the water. The game should never have been played, but we were flying home the next day and 50,000 folk had turned up to watch – so I suppose they didn't have a choice. We were playing into a gale in the first-half and we were only 6–0 down at half-time, which wasn't bad considering. But the wind changed at half-time and we got beat 24–0. If the wind had stayed we might have done better, but that's rugby for you.

Ian Barnes: International rugby can be a fairly intimidating place and there was nowhere more intimidating than the Parc des Princes. It started with the bus journey to the ground, hitting 100mph along the Périphérique with the police motor cyclists kicking the cars out of the way to let the bus through. The stadium itself was just a mass of concrete swinging out over the pitch so the crowd seemed to be right on top of you. The dressing rooms were like a luxury hotel – thick carpets, televisions, trouser presses, coffee machines, refrigerators, the works. Then when you hit the pitch, the noise was unbelievable – Basque bands, cockerels running about, jumping jacks going off. The place erupted when the French came out – and they seemed to be doped up to their eyebrows, all lathered up with a glazed look about them.

When I played there in 1977 France had a boy called Gerard Cholley playing tight head prop and he was a real scary guy. He looked like Moby Dick in a goldfish bowl. He was the French Army heavy weight boxing champion. If he had gone down a dark alley with King Kong, only one of them would have come out the other end – and it wouldn't have been the monkey! I was rooming with Jim Aitken. He said to me, 'I don't think this guy Cholley is as hard as everybody makes out – first scrum we will both hit him.' Now I was not too keen on this idea but I was not going to let Jim know that, so I just kept quiet.

Ron Wilson kicked off – not ten – scrum back. Aitken slipped his binding . . . I hit Cholley . . . Jim didn't . . . Cholley exploded . . . fists flying everywhere. I was trying to keep him away with little pokes. Eventually Merion Joseph, the referee, got things settled down. Fouroux put the ball into the scrum, Romeau stuck in a diagonal kick and the ball went into touch just outside our 22. As we were running across to the line-out Cholley was kicking at my heels. When we got there I was at four, Cholley was at three and he was right in my face, and it did not take Einstein to figure out what was coming next. Mike Biggar was leading the forwards and I was praying that he would not shout my number and at least give me a chance to cover up. At the time we were doing this tag from six to four where I stepped out of the line and the big South African, Donald MacDonald, jumped into my space. Biggar shouted it, I stepped out, big Donald jumped into my space and got it right on the chin – and disappeared off on a stretcher not to be seen again.

I spent the next hour and a half avoiding Cholley – and that is a fair old trick in front of 70,000 people without anybody noticing.

Jim Renwick: In 1977, while the Lions were on tour in New Zealand, the SRU took what you would now call a development tour to the Far East. I don't know who it was at Murrayfield who decided it was a good idea to go on a rugby trip to Hong Kong, Thailand and Japan – but good on them, whoever it was.

We took a lot of young guys like Colin Deans, Bill Gammell, John Rutherford and Roy Laidlaw, who were all just beginning to make their names as big time players. There were a few older heads as well, like Mike Biggar, who was the captain, Ian McLauchlan, Lewis Dick, Ian Barnes and myself. Nairn McEwan was the player-coach, and with a good squad of boys and a good committee the tour went really well. Everybody had little jobs to do – Gordon Dixon was the team photographer, and he kept that job right through the trip even though he didn't have a camera. We played five games and won them all fairly easily, but it was tough because of the temperature and the humidity.

Euan Kennedy (Scotland 1983-84, 4 Caps): Andy Irvine and Bruce Hay were both tied up with Lions duty, so I was selected to go on that tour. The games themselves were fairly easy going but the humidity was just a killer. I remember that we were all instructed to take salt tablets on a regular basis because the medical thinking at the time was that we were losing salts through our sweat. But of course, it's not the salts that you're really sweating, it's fluids and we all overdosed on these tablets because we were taking between four and eight of them a day. I remember after the game in Thailand, which was against the full Thai international team who we beat by about eighty points to nil, Ian Barnes came back into the changing room and pulled off his shirt which he then rung out into a bucket; we used to get weighed after the games to try and judge how much water we had to take back on board to keep hydrated, and they realised that Barney had lost around 14lbs in that one game. He had a couple of glasses of water and then just moved onto the beers with the rest of us.

After we played Japan we went to this great closing dinner which was hosted by Princess Chichibu and at the end of the dinner she said that she would like each of the Scottish players to come up individually to receive a gift. So we all started to go up one by one to receive a little box which we opened when we got back to our tables – and they contained these beautiful silver Seiko digital watches that had been engraved on the back with our names and 'from the Japanese Rugby Football Union'. Now, these watches were still several years away from being available in the UK and we were just delighted with them, but the members of our management started getting incredibly tense when they realised what we were being given because they were worried that we would be contravening our amateur status. In the end we all just kept quiet about it and nothing ever came of it.

John Rutherford (Scotland 1979-1987, 42 Caps plus 1 Cap for the Lions): My first involvement with Scotland was on that Far East tour. It was a great balance between experienced players and up-and-coming youngsters, and although Roy and I had played together a few times for the South under-21s, that tour was really the beginning of our playing career together.

Ian Barnes: The Scotland tour of the Far East in 1977 was my swansong. We played pretty well beating Japan 74–0 in Tokyo with Colin Mair getting into the *Guinness Book of Records* for scoring thirty odd points in an international – albeit a non cap one. Japan was interesting but for me the highlight of the trip came in Bangkok when Jim Renwick and I went for a walk in the red light area. We ended up in this club just as the floorshow was starting. A girl got up on the stage and started slicing a banana with, what the compere euphemistically referred to, as her 'lady garden' . . . then she put a candle out with it . . . and as a grand finale she got herself up in this harness thing and started shooting ping pong balls out of her 'lady garden' into a jam jar on the other side of the stage. Six out of six and Jim turned to me and said, 'Hell, Barney, just think how many goldfish she could win at the shows.'

And that was my international career. It was not much but I enjoyed it. Rugby was, of course, a simple game then. It had a heart and it had a soul. And it had a tremendous community of spirit. It was run by the people for the people.

Jim Renwick: We were guests of honour at a banquet at the Hilton Hotel in Hong Kong. Everyone was in dinner jackets and bow-ties while we were in our number ones – again. No expense had been spared, they had The Young Generation dance troupe on the stage and everything was going well until they brought the starter out, which was sliced pineapple with a lotus leaf as decoration.

I was sitting next to Gerry McGuinness and before I'd even started he was coughing and spluttering with an empty plate in front of him. He's saying, 'My throat's on fire – I need water.'

'What's wrong with you?' I asked. I thought he was mucking about.

'It's that leaf, there's something wrong with it.'

I said, 'Gerry, you greedy bastard, you're not supposed to eat the leaf, it's part of the decoration – it's like eating the skewer as well as the kebab.'

By now you could see that his throat has swollen up and he was frothing at the mouth. We were shovelling ice-cream down his neck and the head waiter was running round in a panic because nobody had eaten the leaf before so he didn't know what was going to happen. Gerry was alright the next day but he was in quite a lot of distress at the time. At the next court session we had him up on a charge of gluttony. Toomba [Alan Tomes] was judge and his punishment was that Gerry had to eat this big cake we had bought. We were just going to let him start then shove his face in it, but he ate the whole thing – no bother to Gerry!

We played Ireland in Dublin in our first game of the 1978 Championship and were losing 12-9 near the end when Brian Hegarty ended up being bundled into touch just before scoring in the corner. Then we got a penalty and our captain, Dougie Morgan, opted to run the ball and go for the win rather than kick it and go for the draw – but Mike Biggar knocked-on. So, that was one that got away. I remember Mike Gibson [the great Irish centre] saying years later that Dougie was the first Scotsman to be elected as Ireland's Sports Personality of the Year after that.

Then, against France, Andy Irvine got injured just before half-time and rather than replace him we decided to wait until the break and see how he was doing. So we shifted Bruce Hay to fullback and Heg [Hegarty] was moved from flanker to the wing. France kicked off into the corner, got a line-out, and Jerome Gallion stuck up a box kick. Heg dropped it behind his own line and Gallion scored. I remember looking at Heg and he just shrugged. What else could he do? He normally had good hands but he was playing out of position and everyone makes mistakes. I felt sorry for him, but that didn't stop me asking him every Christmas from then on whether Gallion had sent him a card that year. We ended up losing that game 19-16, so that was two defeats by less than a score.

We lost 22-14 in Wales on a horrible day, but felt we had given them a run for their money – at least in the first half – and Cardiff was always a pretty tough place to go, especially against a Wales side which won the Grand Slam that year.

We played England at Murrayfield at the end of the Five Nations. Neither of us had won a game so it was a big match because nobody wants to end up whitewashed. But we didn't play very well on the day and we lost 15–0. I nearly scored in the corner but got pulled down just short. But I've no complaints about the result – we got what we deserved. I think we knew deep down we were the poorest team in the Championship that year. We had a few injuries and a few guys coming to the end of their careers. We used three different stand-offs – Ron Wilson, Geech and Richard Breakey – which is an indication that things weren't quite right. It also meant we lacked continuity. But we weren't that far away from getting results, and although we didn't win anything the next season either, we got two draws against England and Ireland, so I think we were moving in the right direction. And with John Rutherford coming in at stand-off we were beginning to get a bit more consistency. Another guy who made a difference was Keith Robertson, who gave us a bit more spark in the backs.

Keith Robertson (Scotland 1978-89, 44 Caps): My first game for Scotland was against New Zealand in 1978. I'd only played once on the wing before, for the South against the Anglos, when I had a good game against Lewis Dick, who was in the Scotland team at that time, so two weeks later I was selected to play against Bryan Williams. He was fifteen stone – four stone heavier than me – and probably the best winger in the world at that time. I was shitting myself.

It was a horrible, wet day so inevitably the first thing they did was send a high ball up. I was standing there waiting to be flattened, and I'll always remember gathering that kick and Mike Biggar coming in and blocking off Williams before he could get to me, and I've remained eternally grateful to Mike ever since. It was one of those sorts of moments in your life when you look back and think, 'If I'd made an arse of that then would that have been the end of my international career before it had even started?'

But I still had eighty more minutes to get through. Fortunately, Williams didn't cope very well with the conditions, he dropped three balls when he was one-on-one with me, and I know that if he had held onto any of those passes he could have just wiped me away because he had that capacity to simply run over the top of people.

I actually came off the field thinking I hadn't done very much. Everyone was saying congratulations, but I was just relieved that I had got through it. I was never going to back down, but I was playing out of position and at a completely different level to anything I had experienced before – and until you have done it you never know if you are going to be able to handle it.

We could have drawn that game against New Zealand in 1978. Geech went for a drop-goal, Bruce Robertson charged it down and hacked it the length of the field to score between the posts. The final score was Scotland 9, New Zealand 18.

Jim Renwick: We really weren't playing that badly and we weren't getting beaten by a lot. Nairn McEwan had taken over as coach from Bill Dickinson, and I felt sorry for him because he put a lot of work in and he didn't always get the breaks. We were maybe just a few players short of being able to win these games that we were losing by one or two points.

Andy Irvine: We had a really good pack for a long time during the seventies, built around Ian McLauchlan, Sandy Carmichael, Alistair McHarg and Gordon Brown. But by 1978 these guys were either finished or coming to the end of their careers and there was a bit of a gap before the next generation were ready to take their place. So, while we had a lot of very dangerous backs – with Jim Renwick, David Johnston, Bruce Hay and myself, plus John Rutherford and Roy Laidlaw coming through – we were always living off scraps. We went thirteen games without a win between beating Ireland in 1977 and beating France in 1980, but it wasn't all doom and gloom, we were always competitive, and we had a couple of draws in there too – we drew 7–7 with England at Twickenham in 1979 which would be a huge result for Scotland today – so I don't think the public or the team really felt like we were completely detached from the rest.

John Rutherford: We had great players at the end of the seventies, but not much success. But then Jim Telfer came in as head coach and took us to New Zealand where he ran us into the ground – and it was on that tour that we really started to have a change of attitude to everything we did; there was a real mental shift within the squad. He instilled a mental toughness in us, but we were also fit – we were as fit as any team we played against, if not fitter, and we trained really, really hard. In the pre-professional years, we could gain a real edge over our opposition if we were fitter than them. Of course, since the game went open, every player in every country is as fit as possible and so we lost that edge – and it was then that the differences in resources and so on really began to tell. But we were lucky in those days; we had the players and we were a pretty settled side – and every team needs to be settled to develop continuity between the players, and it's on those foundations that you can build success.

Jim Telfer: When I became a coach I wrote a paper about how Scotland should play the game. I thought we were suited to the New Zealand rucking style. People seemed to accept that's the road we should go down because we were never going to be bigger than the opposition, but we could be smarter.

Jim Renwick: That was certainly the style in the borders. We were used to playing that way. We always wanted to ruck.

Jim Telfer: It began when I was in New Zealand in 1966 and I watched how they played the game. I was underneath most of the rucks and they were kicking hell out of me.

As the 1970s came to a close and the careers of Renwick and Irvine began to enter the twilight years, France rode into town for the 1980 Five Nations fixture. If ever there was a game that summed up the rolling fortunes of these two players and of the national team during the previous decade, it was this one. During a wretched afternoon, Irvine missed seven kicks at goal, one of which was directly in front of the posts. For over an hour it seemed that the great hero was at last fallen, the magic having finally deserted him. But then, as the clock ticked around into the final quarter, everything changed. Just as Mohammad Ali had gone to the ropes in Kinshasa, pounded mercilessly by George Foreman for eight rounds, battered and bested until the crowds feared for his life, Irvine, like Ali, pulled himself up and out and began to dance. Mustering from who knew where a masterclass of running, passing and kicking, Irvine dragged Scotland back into the game. In the final twenty minutes of the match he scored two tries, a conversion and two penalties to turn a 4–14 deficit into a 22–14 victory and brought to an end the run of thirteen matches without a win.

Jim Renwick: When we beat France in 1980, for our first win in three years, it was typical Andy Irvine. He didn't play that badly in the first-half, but his kicking at goal was terrible – he missed everything and the crowd were beginning to boo him, which was really unusual in those days. If you had been allowed subs he'd have been off.

I remember saying to him at half-time, 'Have you got your boots on the right feet?' And he looked down to check.

He said, 'You know Jim, if I could get a taxi home right now then I would.'

I said, 'Good idea, I'll pay for it.'

But then in the second-half he turned it around. He scored a try in the corner, kicked the conversion from the touchline, scored another try which I converted, and then he kicked two penalties. We were losing 14–4 at one point and ended up winning 22–14. He was unbelievable and it was a hell of a turnaround. But if anyone could play like that, it was him. When he turned it on he was something else. By the end of the game the crowd were all chanting, 'Irvine, Irvine, Irvine.'

That was Andy's style – he wouldn't let the fact everything was going wrong effect him. His attitude, as I've said, was always: you score three and I'll score four.

They were great days, the seventies and into the eighties. The game wasn't as predicable as it is nowadays, boys used to play off the cuff the whole time and we knew how to react to the game, how to adapt to situations and counter. We were good enough to win some cracking matches, but we fell away in others. Wanting to attack too much maybe . . . and mistakes, little mistakes cost us. But the will to win was always there. It never leaves you. Above all, you wanted to win.

Jim Renwick in the 1980 Calcutta Cup match, while being watched by the respective captains, Scotland's Mike Biggar and England's Bill Beaumont.

TWELVE

IN SEARCH OF GREATNESS
1980-1983

By the end of the 1970s a new generation of players were coming to the fore, establishing themselves in the Scotland team and creating a hard core that would remain together for a number of years. Jim Aitken was a robust prop capped in 1977, Colin Deans a dynamic hooker who made his debut against France in 1978 and by 1979 there was a new rock to replace Sandy Carmichael as the cornerstone of the scrum at tight-head prop in the shape of Iain 'the Bear' Milne. Alan Tomes, David Gray and Bill Cuthbertson shared the work in the engine room. Competition for the back-row was as fierce as ever, with John Beattie, Jim and Finlay Calder, David Leslie, Iain Paxton, Derek White and John Jeffrey all vying for the three starting jerseys throughout the eighties, while in the backs Roy Laidlaw and John Rutherford were about to establish themselves as Scotland's greatest ever half back partnership, and the axis from which Keith Robertson, David Johnston and Roger Baird alongside the old heads of Renwick, Irvine and Hay could be unleashed outside.

In the summer of 1980, Jim Telfer replaced Nairn McEwan as the national coach. Ruthless, hard and uncompromising as a player, Telfer employed identical attributes in his coaching. No team under his stewardship would finish second because of a lack of effort; every ounce would be squeezed from every man. He was determined that Scotland should not just be entertainers; the result at the end of each match was the thing that mattered to him and he set about instilling a hardness in the squad, offering a coaching and playing structure like never before and selecting tours that would push his players to the limit.

In his first Championship in charge, Scotland beat Wales and Ireland at home and were seven and six points adrift in Paris and London respectively. Nearly-men still, but things were beginning to change.

John Beattie (Scotland 1980-1987, 25 Caps plus 1 Cap for the Lions): I grew up in Malaysia and I spent my childhood running around barefoot in Borneo and Penang for twelve years. My father used to tell me about Scotland – what a great place it was and which Scot invented what. He would play pipe band music on his wee gramophone and we would march up and down to its beat, pretending to be in this far away place. It was sentimentalised over there with big St Andrew's nights and Burns suppers, all these expats coming together to celebrate their roots. You don't find a prouder Scotsman than one who lives abroad.

I didn't start to play rugby until we moved back to Scotland and I went to school in Ayr. It was a game I loved immediately; it was rough and fast and the lifestyle I had enjoyed outside had toughened me. I was the misfit boy from Borneo and the only thing I could do was sport, so inevitably sport became a huge part of my life.

I won my first cap against Ireland in Dublin in 1980. As a student you were plucked

Opposite: David Leslie.

from anonymity to suddenly being in the eye of this storm. I was rooming with David Leslie and he used to talk me through how I should sleep, lying in what he called 'The King Position': flat on my back with my arms outside the covers. Then in the middle of the night he was jumping out his bed and tackling things. I couldn't sleep a wink – I had to take a sleeping pill. Then it was up early in the morning, massive breakfast followed by a huge lunch with prawn cocktail, steak and chips – it's crazy when you think about it now.

Now I wasn't scared of Ireland because I had been there with the B team and beaten them. But it was a bizarre feeling – one minute you are watching these games on TV, the next you are in the middle of it. I still think there are times when I played international games and didn't do as well as I should have because I wasn't really in the moment, I couldn't quite believe I was there. I remember a hush in one game, when someone shouted, 'Beattie, for fuck's sake, do something!'

Norrie Rowan (Scotland 1980-88, 13 Caps): We went on a short tour to France in the summer of 1980 when the Lions were away in South Africa. It was Jim Telfer's introduction to coaching the national team and we were his guinea pigs – so you can imagine what that was like. I've got a scar on my face from a punch-up in the first match in Côte Basque. I was new to all that. I was waiting for the ref to blow his whistle, but in France they wait until everyone has finished knocking the living daylights out of each other and then they scrum down and off they go again.

Playing out there was a bit like being a gladiator in reverse. Instead of it being: 'Eat, drink and be merry, for tomorrow you die,' in France they kill you first and then afterwards they treat you like a superstar. All the restaurants and bars were free, free, free!

Keith Robertson: That trip to France was exactly what Jim Telfer wanted. He was determined to toughen us up – the French were knocking hell out of us on the pitch, and we were knocking hell out of each other in every session. Before the French Barbarians match in Agen he focused in on this chap, George Mackie. Jim was saying, 'Stand up for yourself. You're too nice – stop being so bloody nice,' and he shoved him against the wall. But Mackie came back at him like a raging bull and drove him back against the opposite wall. He knocked the wind out of Jim, but he was delighted. 'That's what I want to see. Now get out there and show these Frenchmen what you're made of!'

Jim Calder (Scotland 1981–85, 27 Caps plus 1 Cap for the Lions): The first time I played England, at Twickenham in 1981, I scored a try with only a few minutes to go when Steve Munro flipped the ball back inside and I dived over. That made it 17–16 to Scotland, so we just had to get through the next two or three minutes and we would have beaten them down there for the first time in ten years. As you would expect, England had one last go. They sent the ball along the backline, but it was very scrappy and the final pass ended up behind Mike Slemen. However, he recovered the ball and did this loop right round all the backs and the forwards to the opposite

John Rutherford dashes past the last of the French cover
to score at the Parc des Princes in 1981.

touchline, before passing to Huw Davies. Suddenly, out of nowhere, Norrie Rowan, our prop, was chasing their fastest player and there was just no other defence. That would have been a big result for us. Full marks to Slemen, he was a lovely rugby player and he danced his way out of trouble, but it was really tough to swallow at the time.

Andy Irvine: Bruce Hay was one of the toughest guys I ever played with or against, but he used to get some stick about his pace. He scored this interception try against Ireland in 1981 and was chased all the way to the line by Tony Ward, who wasn't the fastest thing on two legs either. As Bruce ran back over the halfway line, Renwick said to him, 'Aye, that's the first time I've seen a try in slow motion and live at the same time. It's lucky it was only Tony that was chasing you.'

In the summer of 1981 Scotland toured New Zealand. Although the injury-ravaged tourists were blown away 40–15 in the second Test, they had run the All Blacks close the week before at Carisbrook, the notorious House of Pain in Dunedin, before eventually losing 11–4. This tour had a resounding impact on the squad and on Telfer. They trained incredibly hard, won five of the six provincial games they played, including a 23–12 victory over the mighty Canterbury, and grew together as a group.

Norrie Rowan: We arrived in New Zealand after a horrendous flight and stayed in this wee town called Taumarunui for this week-long training camp before playing King Country. We were staying in a travel lodge type hotel and every morning we would walk down to the local park carrying our boots, go through two or three hours of hell with Jim Telfer, walk back up, shower, change and when you came out the hotel after lunch there would be a row of cars waiting for you, with a liaison officer saying, 'Right, who's fishing? You're in that car. Who's shooting? You're in that car. Who's golfing? You're in that car.' They were all local farmers, and they'd take you off to do whatever you wanted, and invariably you'd end up back at the farmhouse having dinner, drinking beer and enjoying the chat, back to the hotel at night, straight to bed, up in the morning and off to training again.

Jim Renwick: I thought we had a real chance in the Test series because the All Blacks maybe weren't as strong as they had been in the past. If we had taken a few chances earlier in the match then we might have done it. We had a good scrum and we kicked well. The difference was that when we had them under the cosh they held on, then at the start of the second-half they were putting a bit of pressure on us and we gave away an easy try when the ball came out the side of a scrum and Dave Loveridge pounced on it. That wrapped it up for them and that was maybe the difference between them and us – they did the damage when they got the chance.

Iain Paxton (Scotland 1981-1988, 36 Caps plus 4 Caps for the Lions): My first cap was on tour in New Zealand. Carisbrook was an old stadium shared with cricket, wood-panelled, holes in the floor from all the studs that had tramped over it, and before the kick-off I was beside myself. Tears were streaming down my face. Playing for Scotland meant everything to me that day and every day after. When I had to stop, when I wasn't getting picked anymore, that really hurt. Rugby had been such a huge part of my life and I really loved it.

Jim Renwick: We trained hard for the second Test right up to the day before the match and I felt we were just a wee bit burned out by the time we got there. If I'm being honest, I think we trained too hard on that trip. Jim wanted to put up a good show – there's nothing wrong with that – and to be fair we didn't play too badly. We only just lost the first Test in Carisbrook, which was a good effort, so maybe he was right in some ways. But they put forty points on us in the second Test, and I thought we did too much work in the week before that match. We were in the game right up until halftime, and it was only in the last twenty minutes that they ran away with it, and I think a lot of that was down to boys being dead on their feet.

Andy Irvine: We created enough chances to win that first Test. John Rutherford was fantastic, he took the ball to the line whenever he could and had their defence at sixes and sevens; he made some great breaks, but we just weren't able to finish them off. That try by Loveridge was infuriating.

The second Test saw us lose 40–15, but it was much, much closer than that. They pushed into a 22–6 lead but then we came back at them with some fantastic play and Bruce Hay scored a scorcher of a try. I converted and then added a penalty and we were back in contention at 22–15. We were denied another score under their posts and then Steve Munro broke clear. If he hadn't been in bed with flu during the two days leading up to the Test he would have cruised in, but he was struggling and was caught by Bernie Fraser. Shortly after that Jim Calder touched down for a perfectly good try but we were brought back for a very dubious forward pass. The frustration at all these missed opportunities was growing too much and we imploded slightly towards the end. The All Blacks ran in three tries, all of which were converted, and scoreboard took on a lop-sided look that in no way reflected the quality of our play.

Norrie Rowan: I thought that that tour was fantastic, despite the Test results and the slogging that Jim Telfer gave us – the combination of hard work and such good times off the field bonded us and created a real team ethic while lacing the whole thing together with fun. Everything that followed stemmed from that tour.

In November that year Scotland welcomed Romania and Australia to Murrayfield. Both were defeated and the 24–15 result against the Wallabies really made the rugby world sit up and take notice. Telfer was shaping a unit of dogged fighters who were developing a will to win to go with the intermittent flashes of dazzle and spark for which they had grown famous.

Jim Renwick: Australia toured Britain in the late autumn of 1981 on the back of series victories over both the All Blacks and France and we played them at Murrayfield in December. The conditions were fairly horrendous that day so it was mainly all kicking. Andy Irvine kicked five penalties to give us an 18–15 lead and shortly afterwards their fullback, Roger Gould, caught me with his boot as he took a mark and I had to go off to get some stitches. I was just back on the park when Rudd [John Rutherford] put a high kick up which David Johnston chased. I should have done the same, but I was still a wee bit groggy. Anyway, Gould and Johnston both missed it and the ball bounced over everyone's head into my hands and I scored under the posts. That's what they call good vision. I call it being lucky. But after all those years of disappointment I began to wonder if we might be on the brink of something special.

The Five Nations of 1982 did not begin with the bang that Telfer had hoped for. Scotland drew 9–9 in the Calcutta Cup match at Murrayfield and lost 21–12 to Ireland in Dublin. These were not the standards that Telfer had either set or was willing to accept from his charges. The training sessions grew longer and their intensity increased to boiling point. He flogged and abused the players, ripped them apart, tore them to nothing; and then, as only he could, he built them up again.

France flew into Edinburgh for their 6 March meeting. They were Grand Slam champions and although they had lost their opening two matches against Wales in Cardiff and, shockingly, against Les Rosbifs in Paris, they were determined to make amends against Scotland. They knew how Scotland would play – with no little courage or gusto, but with a shaky defence that would crumble when the pressure was applied. What they encountered out on the Murrayfield pitch that spring day was quite a different beast. Hard, disciplined and ruthless in everything they did. Scotland won 16–7.

And so the team turned its attention to Wales. Cardiff had been the graveyard of so many Scottish hopes in the past. For twenty years the thistle had confronted the dragon in Cardiff without success; but Telfer was not prepared to have his team lowered into the grave to just wait for the sound of the shovels. Colin Telfer had come in as assistant coach for the start of the Championship and he instilled an understanding in the players that in Test match rugby, players have to make their own luck, create their own chances, and when openings appeared, they had to make them count. Andy Irvine's men did not disappoint. In a moment to be replayed time and time again in montages of the greatest ever Five Nations tries, Roger Baird, with the impudence of youth, gathered a loose kick from Gareth Davies deep inside the Scottish half just before it went out of play. The Welsh line had chased well and there was virtually no space for Baird to move. From the stands it looked as if the ball would have to be carried or kicked out and Wales would have an attacking lineout in a prime area of the field. But then Baird stepped. He pivoted and like a hare out of the traps he accelerated. As the covering defence met him on the half-way line, he slipped the ball to Iain Paxton who opened up his long lolloping stride. Paxton was felled at the Welsh twenty-five but he got the ball to Alan Tomes who in turn passed out of a final despairing tackle to Jim Calder who skidded over the try line.

Not only was it a fabulous try conjured from nothing, it was also a catalyst. The Welsh, stung by a try the like of which their Golden Generation would have been proud, fought back with all they had, thundering into rucks and mauls and hitting as hard as they could in the tackle. But it was to no avail. The shackles were off. Attack, counter-attack, furious rucking, booming defence. It was all Scotland. They scored five tries in a 34–16 demolition of their old foes and it marked a special occasion for Jim Renwick for this, his 47th cap, was the first time he had tasted victory in a Test match away from home and he celebrated with a searing run which took him from deep within his own half to score under the posts.

Telfer's hand was beginning to show and it was a line in the sand from which this team never looked back. Scotland finished the Championship one point behind the winners, France.

Roger Baird (Scotland 1981–88, 27 Caps plus 4 Caps for the Lions): We stayed down at the St Pierre Hotel just outside Bristol before the Wales game in 1982 and did all our preparation there. Jim Telfer's team-talks were legendary, even at that stage. It was worth getting picked just to hear what he was going to say. On this occasion it was just after the SAS had swung in through the windows at Whitehall to end the Iranian siege – so that was the theme. We were going to be like the SAS. We were coming from Bristol, going into Cardiff, going to kick the shit out of them, and get the hell out of there – and it all went to plan.

It wasn't a bad Welsh side, they were coming to the end of their great spell, but there were still some fantastic players there – Gareth Davies, Ray Gravell, Elgan Rees. Fortunately, we got the bounce of the ball, and things just clicked for us that day.

Jim Renwick: You've got to have a culture in the team where guys aren't scared to take a chance, and everyone is expecting the good runners to have a go. It's a self-fulfilling prophecy. If the team believes that they can run at the opposition and cause some problems then they are geared towards doing that, and even if it goes wrong then they are ready to tidy up, and when it works it's worth it. But if the team as a collective isn't thinking that way then you have no chance. Our game plan was based on a strong defence and patience, waiting for our moment to counter-attack. We knew it would come. In every game there are one or two chances that come your way and if you take them you can swing the match in your favour. So we knew we just had to bide our time and when the moment came, no matter when it was or where we were on the pitch, we would go for it. All-out.

Jim Calder: I knew I wasn't the quickest thing on two legs so I had to be thinking two steps ahead the whole time. I remember glancing across when Roger Baird fielded that ball from Gareth Davies and half expecting him to kick the ball into touch but I was also thinking that I might start edging my way up field, just in case. So I gave myself a head start. Colin Deans was on the other side of Alan Tomes – he was a sprinter and actually got there before me, but the way Toomba turned after he took the ball from Iain Paxton meant that I got the pass.

It's funny, I was in the Roseburn Bar recently with an old friend. He was chatting away and he said, 'The best try Scotland ever scored was when Roger Baird collected that kick at the Arms Park in 1982 and broke up the left touchline.' He talked his way through the whole build up, 'Roger passed inside to Packie who opened his legs and what a sight that was. Packie was tackled but managed to get the ball away to Alan Tomes.'

I was just sitting there enjoying the moment.

'It looked as if Toomba was going to score, but the Welsh had come blazing across the pitch and he was pulled down just short, so he threw the ball out to . . .' And then his brow began to furrow, and he said, 'Who got the try?' At first I thought he was joking, but he was being serious. I suppose because he was a winger he remembered all that open running rather than the wee guy who flopped over the line at the end.

John Beattie: I broke my knee cap on the back pitch at Murrayfield just before the 1981 tour of New Zealand. It was the last ruck of the practise and I was given the ball by Jim Telfer. I ran into Iain Milne and my left knee-cap just exploded. It came halfway up my thigh. I was rushed into hospital, operated on, and I was there for three weeks. It got badly infected so I was told that if the drugs didn't work I'd get my leg taken off. I remember lying in my hospital bed and Andy Irvine came in to see me with his tour blazer on; Iain Paxton had been given my blazer, and I just burst into tears.

After that I had a year watching, and I remember watching the 1982 Wales game on television at Glasgow Accies' clubhouse, thinking it was brilliant. But when Paxton ran up the wing . . . I died . . . every step he took . . . I died.

Roger Baird: People say I was brave to run it back, but it was a percentage thing. I was right next to the touchline so the worst that was going to happen was that I was going to be put into touch. I think that score released the pressure on us a bit. It gave us a bit of confidence that we could compete with these guys and take it to them. The hard work ethic that Telfer had instilled was beginning to show dividends, not just in our ability to win ball up-front but in our belief that we were capable of dictating how the game was going to pan out.

It went on from there with fantastic scores from Jim Renwick, David Leslie, David Johnston, Lucky Jim Pollock and Derek White. I remember, we were walking back to the halfway line after the last of those scores and the young guns were getting pretty full of it – Renwick turned to us and for once he wasn't joking around. 'Just watch what's going on here boys. This ain't over yet.' That was Jim's 47th cap and he still hadn't won away from home, so it meant a lot to him. When Jim gets serious you take notice.

Of course, we held on for one of the great wins in Scottish rugby history, 34–18. It really was a brilliant day. That match was a big watershed. Winning away from home was a big thing, and we weren't used to winning as emphatically as that.

Jim Pollock (Scotland 1982-85, 8 Caps): When I got called into the Scotland team for that Wales game, I thought it was a wind-up. I had played quite well for the Anglo-Scots two weeks before, but I had only been involved in one training session, and it never occurred to me that I might be involved in the Five Nations until the Thursday before the match I got the call. I naturally thought it was a friend of mine taking the piss – but I rang the number and this very somber voice said Keith Robertson had tonsillitis and I was taking his place. I rolled up on the Friday not really knowing anyone's first name, never mind anything else. We went through the moves on the 17th fairway at St Pierre Hotel golf course, then pitched up against Wales and beat them quite convincingly and I scored a try. International rugby? A piece of cake!

The season after that I got my second cap when we went down to Twickenham and won there. So I had two victories out of two and those were Jim Renwick's first away wins after more than a decade in the Scotland squad. My next match was the draw against New Zealand, and then I played against England, Ireland and France during the Grand Slam season. So, in my first six games we won five and drew one against the All Blacks – I think I deserved the nickname Lucky Jim.

John Rutherford: It was a terrific advert for Scottish rugby at the time. There were a lot of wee guys in the team, but we were quick and jinky and skilful. At the dinner afterwards Gareth Davis, the captain, stood up to make his speech. 'From a Welsh perspective,' he said. 'There's not much we can say about today. We took a real hammering.' Then he paused and said, 'Can I ask all the Welsh players to please stand up.' So up they stood and then, on his lead, they began to sing *Flower of Scotland*. It was an incredible moment. It spoke volumes about them as men and about the values of rugby in those days. Unfortunately, I can't see something like that happening nowadays. It was just the most fantastic thing for them to do.

In the summer of that year, Scotland toured Australia. There was no let up in the training regime; indeed, if anything, it was harder than ever. Telfer drove his men to the edge, beyond the edge. And on a hot and humid day in Brisbane, he drove them into the history books as the team recorded their first Test victory against one of the southern hemisphere's big three away from home. It was testament to the progress the team was making under Telfer. The building blocks were falling into place.

Norrie Rowan: We went to Australia and it was a similar sort of trip to the New Zealand tour the year before. We had a training camp up the Gold Coast and then we played a game in a place called Mount Isa. They put on a barbeque for us, which we got taken to on this old school bus along a really bumpy road. Eventually we arrived in this valley which was packed with the whole town. There were bands singing and it was just fantastic. Jim Telfer says, 'Everyone back on the bus at ten o'clock.' This was at about seven o'clock, and by eight o'clock Jim Pollock is on the stage singing *King of the Road*. Creamy is going mad, 'Everyone back on the bus, now!' But it took him ages to track down all the players. Back at the team room, Jim is going mad. 'You're here to play rugby, you're no here to sing and dance. You're here to represent your country.' That was at nine o'clock.

Jim Calder: Looking back, you realise all the things that that Scottish side achieved – we won in Cardiff for the first time in twenty years, beat Australia in Brisbane, drew with New Zealand in 1983, we won the Grand Slam in 1984, eight of us toured with the Lions in 1983 – and I'm not sure we appreciated at the time just how special those successes were. Of course, there were no world rankings in those days and Scotland and Australia were much of a muchness in those days, so while we were obviously delighted to win over there we didn't feel as if we had turned the world on its head.

Keith Robertson: It was a strange one because Bob Dwyer had been appointed as the new Australia coach. He was a New South Wales man and had based the team on players from that state. The Queenslanders gave Dwyer a bit of stick and we had a lot of support that day, even from the Australians.

Andy Irvine was coming to the end of his career and said it was the kind of moment that doesn't come along too often in a career and you have to savour it. I scored a try in the game which was a great moment. It squirted out from the base of a scrum and John Rutherford decided to come right instead of left, which is what the original call was, due to the way the ball came out. It caught the Australians by surprise and I went over nice and easy in the corner. All I had to do was catch it and run. A simple try but one of huge significance for us in terms of a team that was starting to build. Scotland hadn't won in the southern hemisphere before and haven't too often since. It is a tough thing to do.

Keith Robertson: We had beaten Australia before at home, but no Scottish team had ever won in the southern hemisphere, so that was something new. Strangely, the match we won was in near perfect conditions, but the second game, when they got their own back on us, was played in a gale, which you would have thought would have suited Scotland better. But it was the end of a long, hard tour; a few players were carrying knocks, and we perhaps didn't have quite enough strength in depth to back up that first result.

Andy Irvine: Australia were not the side in those days that they are now because out of five times I played them I think we only lost once. But that one in 1982 was a very good Australian team and they were beginning to come up in the world, going on to win a UK Grand Slam two years later.

But we were also a good side and just on the verge of becoming a great team, and it suited the type of game we played in those days, the hard grounds, fast track and the ball moving around a lot. They had a very good back division with guys like Glenn and Mark Ella, Andrew Slack, Michael Hawker and Michael O'Connor, but we had a tremendous amount of pace and flair. Of our back division almost every one ended up playing for the Lions and in Test matches, guys like Roger Baird, Keith Robertson, John Rutherford, Roy Laidlaw and myself. We made a tactical change that was crucial in that first Test. The Wallaby attack was tremendous and they seemed to have an extra man all the time, but our scrummage was really strong, so we decided to take Jim Calder out of the scrum and use him as an extra back in defence, and that nullified them.

We had played New South Wales the week before and it worked there and so we took it into the Test. NSW were really strong in those days and we gave them a good doing in Sydney which not many teams did. We came back from that tour pretty pleased with ourselves and confident that we knew each other on and off the field better, and that I believe was one of the reasons why we were so good in 1984.

Roger Baird: There was outrage in Australia after we beat them because they had dropped Roger Gould and Paul McLean, who had been two stalwarts of their team for a long time, to bring in the Ella brothers – Glen and Mark – at stand-off and fullback respectively. They brought those old-stagers back for the second Test in Sydney a week later and absolutely stuffed us. Gould scored two tries and McLean kicked five penalties and three conversions and Michael O'Conner scored their third try.

That defeat to us in Brisbane was perhaps a bit of a turning point for Australia because it forced them to have a long hard look at themselves. Certainly, when they came to Britain in 1984 and achieved the Grand Slam, they were magical. I was lucky enough to be in the South side which beat them at Mansfield Park the week before the Scotland Test and they clearly didn't fancy it in the mud that day – but when they got up to Murrayfield they were on a whole different level. Mark Ella was back at stand-off, Michael Lynagh was at inside centre, Andrew Slack at outside centre, David Campese on the wing, and Gould still at fullback.

Keith Robertson: The 1983 Five Nations was very disappointing by and large – having had a good season the year before, we lost to Ireland, France and Wales in the first three games and only really put in a good performance against England at Twickenham.

That was obviously a famous victory and it remains the last time we won there. We played tremendously well throughout the whole match and Roy Laidlaw scored a great try off the back of a scrum which Peter Dods converted to add to his two penalties. I dropped a goal and then big Tom Smith scored in the last minute to take the match out of England's reach at 22–12.

Jim Aitken (Scotland 1977-1984, 24 Caps): We went down to Twickenham as complete no-hopers; we had no chance. The only people who thought we had a chance were the twenty-one players in the squad and Colin Telfer and Derrick Grant, who were our coaches. You don't go out there expecting the game to go in any particular way, but the one thing we did know was that these guys would come at us hard for the first fifteen minutes and blow up. And what happened? They came at us hard for fifteen minutes and then blew up.

Roger Baird: We were very lucky that we played in an era with some good Scottish players coming together at the same time and who were blessed with some very good coaches, when you look at Jim Telfer, Colin Telfer, Derrick Grant and then Ian McGeechan. We went down to Twickenham with belief when few others had it in 1983. We'd won in Wales the year before and that had provided some confidence, and we had some very good players, Renwick, Rutherford, Laidlaw, and you go into the pack and we had great players dotted all over the place. England had a big pack, and a good pack, but we scrummaged well against them, Jim Aitken, Deano [Colin Deans] and the Bear [Iain Milne], and as long as we could get a platform for the backs, we were sure that we could do something.

And that was the way it turned out. We had a fast gameplan. That was the way we played. We have five back row forwards in the pack and so that was what suited us. And it was a gameplan that we took into the following season – with significant results, as it transpired.

Jim Calder celebrates after a Scotland try by Roy Laidlaw during
their last win at Twickenham, in 1983

THIRTEEN

THE SECOND SLAMMERS
1984

1925. An historic year in Scottish rugby. The year of the first game at Murrayfield. The year that Herbert Waddell struck a match-winning drop-goal against England to deliver the first – and only – Grand Slam north of the Border. 1925. . . A millstone. An albatross.

Every January hopes would rekindle anew that a Five Nations title might come Scotland's way; that, perhaps, even the mythical Grand Slam might be achievable. And every year since 1925 those hopes were scattered to the four winds. But something had been building under Jim Telfer's watchful eye, and an eight-strong core of the team had their class confirmed when they were selected for the 1983 Lions tour to New Zealand. Telfer was head coach of that tour and Scottish rugby was very much on the rise. But the 1983 Lions tour proved to be something of a double-edged sword. The Scotland players who travelled to New Zealand had their eyes opened to the difference between them and the very best the Home Unions. The Scots players were, in John Rutherford's words, 'fitter, better and mentally stronger than the best players from England, Wales and Ireland.' However, for all this this discovery boosted confidence among the Scottish contingent, it was a devastating experience for British and Irish rugby in general, with the tourists going down to a 4–0 whitewash for only the second time in their history. And it nearly broke Telfer. For a while he considered giving up coaching altogether. Asked by a journalist what his future coaching plans were, he answered, 'Is there life after death?'

But something special had been building in the Scotland camp. After the team had toured Australia and New Zealand in 1981 and 1982, there was an understanding of what it took to perform and win at the highest level. The victory in the first Test in Brisbane in 1982 built a confidence that the team took into its 25–25 draw with the All Blacks at Murrayfield in the autumn of 1983. And then the spring of 1984 rolled in. Scotland had a strong and competitive squad filled with battle-hardened players. Jim Telfer continued to be assisted by Colin Telfer and had the inspirational prop Jim Aitken installed as his captain. Although injury had robbed the squad of two of their most celebrated players in Jim Renwick and Andy Irvine, there was still plenty of firepower elsewhere in the Scottish line-up. Roy Laidlaw and John Rutherford, who had both come through the Scotland B ranks under Jim Telfer, were forging a commanding partnership at half-back; the back-row of David Leslie, Iain Paxton and Jim Calder were ferocious, dogged and devastating; the front-row of Aitken, Colin Deans and Iain Milne were full of power and guile, while in the engine room behind them Alan Tomes and Bill Cuthbertson were the heartbeat of the team; in the midfield Euan Kennedy and David Johnston combined power and lightning acceleration to release wingers Keith Robertson and Roger Baird, while Peter Dods proved to be a points machine at fullback. Complementing these fifteen were John Beattie, Alastair Campbell, Gordon Hunter and Jim Pollock, who each came into the

Opposite: Peter Dods kicks Scotland's first conversion of the Ireland match, 1984.

team as injuries and form dictated and were as tenacious, ambitious and excellent as any other player in the squad. But there was pressure too; great pressure. Fifty-nine years of it.

Jim Telfer: That Lions tour really took a lot out of me. I was very disillusioned when we got back and I felt that maybe I wasn't cut out for coaching at that high a level. I seriously considered quitting rugby altogether. I also expected someone else to have come in to replace me, but they left the door open for my return and once I was back in a tracksuit again and back in the Scotland environment I felt reinvigorated. That was down to the players – the enthusiasm that was going around that squad was infectious and you couldn't help but be drawn into it. Jim Aitken was the new captain, having taken over from Roy Laidlaw at the end of the 1983 season, and I thought he was very good – he was excellent at looking after the other players, encouraging them and so on and he led from the front in everything he did. And although the Lions tour had been tough on me, the players who went gained a lot from it and, ironically, David Leslie, who didn't tour, seemed to gain even more.

Iain Paxton: There was a lot that was grim on that '83 Lions tour. The Bear should have played the Tests and, of course, Deano [Colin Deans] should have played – he was the best hooker. The All Blacks couldn't believe those two weren't picked.

But despite everything that went wrong, the Scottish guys on the tour got a wee important something out of it. At that time, I think Scots felt a bit inferior to the English and the Welsh. Personally speaking, I definitely thought I was going to be a second-class citizen out there. And then we got a look at our fellow Lions at training. We were like, 'He's not that fit. He's just dropped it again. Maybe we're actually all right.' New Zealand was a step along the road to '84, to the Grand Slam – and it was big for Jim Telfer, too. He came back from that disappointment with the Lions and got us playing rugby that was ahead of its time.

John Rutherford: We all came back from the Lions with a lot of confidence about how we measured against the other players. Most of us pushed our way into the Test team during that tour, while guys like Colin Deans should have been in, but he was contesting the hooker berth with the captain, Ciaran Fitzgerald.

There was a feeling of a point to prove when we got back as well, though, because in many cases we felt that we were as good as – if not better – than guys in our positions from the other countries. Colin Deans really felt that he had a point to prove having been clearly the best hooker on the tour, and I was stuck out in the centre when I really felt that I could have been doing the job at ten. I felt sorry for Ciaran because he was a really, really good guy but he was under tremendous pressure every week. And it maybe proves that picking a specialist position as captain for the Lions is a tricky thing to do because they really have to put all their effort into the technical aspects of their job and to have the pressure of captaincy added to that can be too much.

When we faced the All Blacks at Murrayfield we all went into that game believing we could win. And although we drew the match, we really felt we should have won – and I don't think there can be any more than a handful of Scottish sides who could say that they felt that when playing New Zealand. You could see that the team was getting better all the time, the belief was growing and we all felt that we were part of something special. At that stage we really felt that we could beat anyone we played against and if you keep your feet on the ground and prepare as well as you can, it is great thing to have that confidence in your ability and that of the team. It's what sets champions apart – and is something that is so often lacking in Scottish sides.

Keith Robertson: I remember John Rutherford at the first session saying after the Lions tour, 'We know these guys and we have absolutely nothing to fear. We should be looking to win the Championship this season.' And I think that was the beginning of the belief developing which led to the Grand Slam in 1984.

Euan Kennedy: I captained Edinburgh against the All Blacks in the Wednesday game about ten days before they played Scotland. We lost but despite the fact they had a pretty much full-strength team with guys like Stu Wilson, Wayne Smith, Bernie Fraser, Robbie Deans and Murray Mexted playing we pushed them pretty close and if we had kicked more of our goals we could have put them under some serious pressure.

On the Sunday the Scotland squad all met up for training. It emerged that Keith Robertson had been injured playing for his club the previous day and there were all these whispers going around that I would definitely be in as his replacement – but you can never tell what the coaches and selectors are thinking, so I had to just get on with things as normal. Before we headed out Jim Telfer sat us all down in the changing room and told us that Keith had indeed been injured and that I would be starting. It was a wonderful way to find out I was going to win my first cap – normally you get a letter through the post and you don't have anyone around to tell, but I was there with my peers, with guys who I had been playing club, district and B rugby with for years, and there were some lovely words said by them at the time.

John Beattie: There was a TV strike so the game wasn't being televised in the UK. Jim Telfer had been on the Lions tour that summer and it hadn't gone well, a lot of the English players hadn't believed in what he was doing so hadn't carried out his instructions on the pitch, and he was determined to make amends for that disappointment. We were determined to help him out.

This was him moulding the team that would win the Grand Slam the next year. I remember being in a team meeting and it was decided that anything went. The basic plan was to stand on them as much as we could. I remember being in one ruck when it felt like you had fallen off your horse coming over Beechers Brook in the Grand National. It has never left me: that image of white jerseys going right over the top of me. There were a couple of rucks where we blew the All Blacks' pack apart.

Euan Kennedy: Because of the TV technicians strike the game wasn't televised in the UK at all – but I was able to get a copy of the New Zealand broadcast, which is a great memento although it's a shame that it was commentated on by the Kiwi pundits rather than Bill McLaren.

Players always warn you that the step up, in terms of pace, physicality and intensity – as well as a reduction in the time you have to think and make decisions – goes up significantly from club to district level and again from district level to B level, which it does. But the step up from B to Test rugby is just incredible.

We wore white jerseys and shorts and blue socks for that match and within about a minute of the kick off I had my hands on the ball and took it into contact and Bill Cuthbertson thought he would help me out and bound onto me as I took the tackle – but in doing so he completely unbalanced me and I ended up on the other side of the ruck . . . which is the last place you want to be against the All Blacks, especially in the first few minutes when everyone's really fired up. Their entire pack danced all over me, raking me out the back. I was absolutely covered in welts and stud marks and as I got up I noticed this red patch just below the thistle on my shirt – and because we were playing in white it really stood out. But by the time we went in at half-time the entire left side of my shirt and the leg of my shorts were covered in blood, just saturated. There were no blood replacements in those days so I had to ask the ref if I could go and see the doctor at half-time. Donald Macleod, the SRU surgeon, pulled off my shirt to reveal one particularly bad stud mark that ran from my collarbone and down my chest . . . and we both looked in horror at my left nipple, which had been severed and was literally hanging on by a couple of threads. Fortunately because of all the adrenaline pumping around my system I couldn't really feel it, so he put in two or three stitches to put things back into place, bandaged me up and got me a new shirt before sending me out for the second-half. As I left the medical room to go down the tunnel, Donald called after me, 'Welcome to international rugby!'

That first cap was an incredibly emotional moment – especially as it was at home. But as time went on and I began to think more and more about the game I realised how frustratingly close we had come to beating the All Blacks, something that Scotland have still never managed to do. Our forwards that day were just incredible; it was one of the finest rucking performances Scotland have ever had, they completely out-rucked the All Blacks pack and every time they went into contact you could have thrown a blanket over them.

Jim Pollock: We trained as usual on the back pitches at Murrayfield the day before that match, and tried to get this set move to work. Jim and Colin Telfer, the coaches, had done their homework on the All Blacks and knew they came up flat in defence, so they devised this move where we took the lineout – I think Bill Cuthbertson won it – and moved it out to David Johnston, and he kicked it over them for me to race up the touchline and score. But there was a gale force wind and David Johnston was kicking it here, there, everywhere, and I was running around like a blue arsed fly for two or three hours chasing this ball. I was absolutely knackered. Jim Telfer was losing the plot – he wanted to scrap the whole thing because if it didn't work in training then it wasn't going to work in the game – but David was adamant that he could pull it off, and things were getting a bit heated between the pair of them. Fortunately, on the day, it all went to plan. That try pulled us level but the conversion was from wide on the right and unfortunately Peter Dods couldn't kick the points, so we had to settle for an honourable draw – which I think we more than deserved.

Euan Kennedy: That game was really the foundation to the Grand Slam season a few months later and I can only say how fortunate I realise I am that I got to experience it when someone like Jim Renwick missed out on it all because he was injured. I felt hugely humbled by

John Beattie reaches the ball under pressure from New Zealand's Murray Mexted, as Jim Calder follows up in support.

the whole thing and so proud to have been there; it meant so much to me, but I can only imagine how much it would have meant to Jim to have been part of it after all his caps and his years of playing for Scotland.

Jim Telfer: We'd gone to Australia in 1981 and New Zealand the year after that. Eight went with the Lions to New Zealand. Scotland's results had not been great, but we were building up a strong, solid, stable core to the team. We also had a very good selection panel. The convenor Ian MacGregor and the president of the Union, Adam Robson, had both played for Scotland. They were down-to-earth people whom the players liked and respected – and that always helps. Colin Telfer hasn't ever really received the credit he deserved. He was an excellent player and an extremely good coach of our backs.

One of the cornerstones of 1984 was that the players were able to accept constructive criticism from me and from each other and then acted upon it. That was the key and it was the same in 1990. Both squads were full of characters and strong-minded individuals who made sure that they lifted the efforts of all those around them. They demanded the best out of each other and that fitted well with my approach to coaching – it was the same with the Lions in 1997 and the Scotland team in 1999. I'm the first to hold my hands up and say that my style didn't fit every player, but every now and then you would get a squad of like-minded individuals that would all be on the same wavelength and you knew that you could achieve something special with them.

Jim Calder: Going into the Five Nations, you would look around the team and see class everywhere. John Rutherford and Roy Laidlaw were the best halfbacks in the Championship, we were solid and strong in the midfield and in players like Colin Deans and the Bear you had grit and awesome power.

Then you would look at guys like David Leslie; he was a real eccentric off the pitch – he used to wear gloves in bed and sit in the changing room until the last minute before training reading a book, looking as if the last thing he wanted to do was play rugby. But when it came to the build-up to an international he was a different animal altogether, absolutely ferocious. He was eccentric in every way but he was also the ultimate warrior that you would want beside you in the trenches – he would do everything he could, push his body to the very limit, to get a win.

David Leslie (Scotland 1975-1985, 32 Caps): I was brought up on Commando comics. Because my dad worked for the publisher [DC Thomson in Dundee] I got them free. And I like to visit war memorials. When I've gone to these places I've thought: 'I didn't do what these boys did, I wasn't in the trenches. These are the brave ones.' Next to what they sacrificed, playing rugby was nothing. But I have to say that there were times in games when I did think: 'I could quite happily die out here. If those boys could give up their lives for the sake of future generations, then I should be prepared to die.'

I knew I wasn't going to die on the pitch but using rationale wasn't what was required. I needed to get it on to this other plain where I thought I could accept death. The approach worked and it made me think: 'I can do anything'.

But I look back now and think, 'Was that me?' I could only play what was in front of me. I just did it. And, hey, there were times when I could be fairly languorous! People called me suicidal sometimes, the way I'd go after the ball, but I don't think I was suicidal; I was simply going after the ball when it had to be won. I was very aware, in big rugby games, that you had to make the most of yourself, really push it. I did what had to be done. Someone like Mike Biggar was just as selfless, but maybe not everyone played the way we did – which is why I'm remembered, I suppose.

I always understood that if I hesitated, I was as good as dead. That's not original but it counts for so much. It was also about anticipation, which is always better than reaction. I didn't really care about my well-being. You accept the consequences – this is what you can do, and you do it. No more than that.

Jim Telfer: All really good sides need a nutter in their pack and when your nutter is also a Scottish public schoolboy you really are quids in because let me tell you they are the maddest of the mad, the bravest of the brave.

David Leslie: It wasn't automatic. You had to get yourself to that level mentally, but that was easy to do playing for your country. But it's a team game, and most importantly you had to spin off people about you and elevate them as well. I see the guys these days wearing their headphones on the bus or in the dressing room. I don't like that at all. I'd have pulled them off any team-mate of mine. You have to be a team all the time.

Jim Telfer: Pound for pound David Leslie was possibly the best Scotland player, certainly the best Scotland forward, I ever coached. When he had the ball you could relax because technically he was superb but he could be too brave for his own good sometimes. It could be frightening to watch him put his body on the line – the batterings he took – but what a man to have in your team. He was as hard as nails but we had other very tough guys. The thing about David though is that he also had this Kamikaze thing going on.

It was Glenalmond College he came from and they have produced a couple of others of the same ilk up there. Rob Wainwright was mad as well – and ended up as a doctor would you believe – and although David Sole used to disguise it pretty well the signs were there for all those who cared to look. They all spoke so beautifully as well. It's a mystery but there you go, they were all mighty players and men for Scotland. If you could find fifteen of that sort and put them in the same team. . .

John Beattie: David was such an eccentric, but Christ, you loved having him on your team. What a player he was. Such intensity. I think what was really key for us, though, was Jim Telfer. He was so far ahead of the rest of the world in terms of coaching that he was this strange combination of visionary and hard task master. He was undoubtedly technically the best coach in the world at the time, and he knew that his players had to be rougher and much fitter than everyone else. The fitness programme he put in place was way ahead of the rest of the Five Nations countries at the time.

Iain Paxton: One of the revolutionary things Jim did was to play with five No. 8s. There were a few of us around 6ft 4ins who were quite quick around the paddock. It was clever. But we couldn't field that combination for every game and it came down to a big rivalry between me and John Beattie for the number eight shirt. It was intense. I remember always thinking, 'What if he's doing extra training?' I remember one Christmas morning thinking, 'I'd better go for a run.' Burntisland to Kinghorn, back along the beach through the water, and then I got my mum to sit on my feet for proper sit-ups. 'Beat that, ya bastard!' But we were good friends through it all, John and me, and years later he confessed to doing something pretty similar. And then Derek White replaced both of us. He must have been running Christmas morning *and* afternoon!

Jim Telfer: Scotland always have the best chance of winning a Grand Slam or a Championship when we play France and England at home and Wales and Ireland – and now Italy – on the road. It was the same in '84. We went down to Cardiff for the first game and they had picked Richard Moriarty, a great big fella, at the back of the lineout to try and dominate David Leslie. But because of his size, he was slow and David just had the run of the game over him. Colin Deans would throw long at the lineout and David would just drop back to gather it, his pace taking him away from Moriarty at the tail.

We scored two great forwards' tries in that game – the first off a set move from a free kick when David Leslie charged onto the ball at pace then offloaded to Iain Paxton to score, and the second from a series of drives from a lineout that saw Jim Aitken dive over.

John Beattie: Jim Aitken was a hugely under-rated prop. In some senses he had to battle against a thought process that pigeon-holed him as merely a rough customer whereas he was a gym goer before it became fashionable. Every team needs a captain and Aitken was a Gala player when there were huge tensions between players from the Borders and he both played on that and overcame it too.

Jim Telfer: Jim was pushing thirty-seven. We'd left him out a couple of years earlier, but he forced his way back in. He listened to his coach, was a disciplinarian and played in a very successful team at Gala. It was like having a version of myself on the field.

Jim Aitken: We had some great players, guys like John Rutherford and Roy Laidlaw at half-back, what class they had, and David Leslie who, to my mind, is the best back-row forward to come out of Britain. You couldn't win back then without someone like Iain Milne; the guy just wouldn't budge. Bill Cuthbertson must have been a nightmare to play against, Sally [Alastair] Campbell did a similar job, Alan Tomes just kept plugging away. We were still being written off, though. The hierarchy at the SRU didn't reckon we were going to do anything. The players? That was the difference. We genuinely believed. As captain I didn't have time to think about the jersey, the crowd or anything. But I will say this: I never went on to the field and not thinking: 'We're going to take this lot today.' I was absolutely convinced that whoever we were playing they were in for a gubbing.

Euan Kennedy: Playing my first Five Nations game at the Arms Park was wonderful. The whole experience was just amazing, playing in front of that passionate Welsh crowd and then to get the win away from home in our opening game was a great way to start the Championship.

I played against Robert Ackerman, who ended up going to rugby league shortly afterwards and had played for the Lions, and I just remember him sledging me through the entire match. Because I was thirty at the time and it was only my second cap he kept calling me granddad all game; we would line up against each other and he would ask how my old, tired legs were feeling, or we would tackle one another and he would push me into the ground as he got up and say, 'Oh, you're doing well granddad, keep it up.' I just gave him a wink when the game was over; granddad did alright.

Iain Paxton: The first half against Wales just flew past without anything major happening, then I scored just coming up to the interval. It was my first try for Scotland, so it did feel good. The pass from David Leslie to put me through was like a baton pass, it was right on the line.

John Rutherford: It was almost certainly a forward pass but we got away with it. Jim Aitken's try was from exactly his distance. I think it was one metre from the line from a line-out but it was probably the most important try he ever scored.

Roy Laidlaw (Scotland 1980-1988, 47 Caps plus 4 Caps for the Lions): Jim Aitken was good at motivating the troops and after that try he pulled us together and told us in no uncertain terms that we had to keep focused and concentrate to make sure of winning the game.

Jim Calder: Winning in Wales was a great feeling. I remember Wales captain Eddie Butler crying in the toilets when the evening meal was on the go and it was quite a nice feeling being witness to Eddie's state of mind at the time.

John Bevan (Wales coach): They had a superb middle five, by this I mean the back-row of David Leslie, Jim Calder and Iain Paxton and the half-backs, Roy Laidlaw and John Rutherford. They outplayed us in the lineouts and the rucks and although there was a great deal of illegal play on the ground, they certainly got to broken play far faster and got the ball away. It was the fact that they handled so well off the ground that there were so few rucks, which was a disadvantage to us as we expected to beat them in that phase of play.

I was also impressed by Iain Milne who proved so destructive in the scrums and the way in which Tomes, Cuthbertson and Leslie disrupted our lineouts. Colin Dean was splendid not only for his throwing but for his all-round ability. I was baffled why

Iain Milne carries the ball up against Wales at the Arms Park.

he never played a Test in New Zealand for the Lions. Another player who surprised us was Peter Dods; he played so much better than we thought he could play and our kicking to him proved fruitless and counterproductive.

Jim Telfer: A tremendous amount of confidence comes from that away victory. Away wins in Test rugby are like hen's teeth, you don't get them very often.

The Calcutta Cup up at Murrayfield was the hundredth game between Scotland and England and they came into the match on the back of a great win over New Zealand in the autumn. It was the classic clash of the English maul versus the Scottish ruck and on the day it was the ruck that won out. I had managed to assess the strengths and weaknesses of the English, Welsh and Irish players during the Lions tour. Maurice Colclough had hardly played in a couple of months and Peter Wheeler wasn't fit.Our players – especially our forwards – were faster and fitter and in the end that was the big difference.

John Beattie: As a squad of players we felt very honoured to be involved in the hundredth game against England, but we never needed any additional motivation for games against the auld enemy.

John Rutherford: We had drawn with the All Blacks in November but England had beaten them. They were a good team and were fancied, not least by themselves. But we caught them cold. They had not played together since the New Zealand game, having been the odd country out during the first weekend of the Five Nations. And, of course, poor old Dusty Hare had a nightmare.

Jim Telfer: We concentrated on putting a lot of pressure on Dusty Hare, their fullback, because it was a pretty filthy day and Roy and John were punting kicks to him all day while our outside backs chased him down. It obviously rattled him because he ended up missing six kicks out of eight at goal.

We scored a super harum-scarum try in the first-half with a long ball over the lineout that Iain Paxton hacked on and then David Johnston dribbled it a bit further, controlled it and scored. The second was one of the all time great Scottish scores – Jim Calder wrestled the ball from Dusty Hare, set up a quick ruck and the ball was fed to John Rutherford who picked it off his bootstraps, drew Clive Woodward and dropped a lovely ball out to Euan Kennedy who shot home to score. We ended up winning 18–6.

Euan Kennedy: I experienced all the highs and lows of rugby in one game in the Calcutta Cup by scoring a try and then ripping all my knee ligaments to pieces. The try was a wonderful moment, although if David Johnston had been playing outside John Rutherford when he gave that pass it would never have happened. John did a great job of taking the ball off his boots, but he then compensated with his pass and it

Euan Kennedy charges over to score against England.

flew about eight feet in the air. Luckily I'm 6'5' so I was able to take it and go through, but even then it was close.

There's a photo of me just after I scored and my fists are clenched in celebration and I'm just roaring with delight – that moment typified everything that it meant for me to play for Scotland because in that moment everything I had dreamt about for that day had come true. I had scored the winning try against England in front of a packed Murrayfield crowd. David Leslie talked about that same photo in the book that came out after that season and he said that, for him, that photo typified what it meant to all of the team and to Scotland when we won the Slam.

Dick Greenwood (England head coach): There was nothing wrong with our thinking or planning, the England players were just inadequate. The Scots performed our battle-plan far better than we could have hoped to. For years Scotland won no ball and were brilliant counter-attackers. Then they had a spell of winning the ball and not having a clue what to do with it. This time they decided that if they didn't think too hard and simply kicked, what ball they won could be useful. Is that not therefore the most efficient way to set about winning a Grand Slam?

Jim Telfer: There was a month between that game and our next fixture over in Dublin and I flew down to see Ireland play England at Twickenham. It wasn't a great game and the Irish lost 12–9. They changed quite a few players in time for our match after that.

To be honest, I had no benchmark to go on for how to prepare a team for a Triple Crown match because it hadn't happened in my time. Christ, it hadn't happened since 1938. The night before the game I decided to use some reverse psychology on the players. I showed them a video – not of us beating Wales or England, but of the South losing to the All Blacks. Ten of our team had played that match and it had been refereed by Fred Howard, who was taking charge of our match with the Irish. I wanted to keep their feet on the ground by showing them that defeat and I wanted them to get a sense of the kind of interpretations that Howard had of the rules. It's the kind of thing that only works with honest players. In '84, that was what we had.

Keith Robertson: Ireland had shared the Championship with France the previous year, and gave us a real fight. Their captain, Willie Duggan, won the toss and let us play with the wind – a real swirler – which was what we had been hoping for.

The first-half was an absolute dream. Roy Laidlaw scored two tries in the same corner – one from a lineout peel down the blindside and one that was just raw pace off the back of a scrum. For years Scottish supporters took a banner and put it up in that part of the ground that read: 'Laidlaw's Corner'.

Jim Telfer: He was a dangerous runner, Roy. Scoring two tries, and kicking the goals as well, we were over twenty points up at half-time. It was just a dream come true.

John Rutherford: I remember speaking to Willie John [McBride, the Ireland coach] afterwards and he said they had talked about defending the blind side against Roy but it just didn't work and Roy scored two tries in the first half and then he got himself concussed and he went off at half-time.

Roy Laidlaw: Just as well for the Irish, eh? If I'd have stayed on I'd have got four.

Willie John McBride (Ireland head-coach): I honestly believed that we had devised tactics to contain Laidlaw, but when the match got going there was simply no way he could be stopped. Had we managed to put the shackles on him, I'm convinced the outcome would have been a lot different.

The players erupt as the fulltime whistle goes in Dublin.

Keith Robertson: We also won a penalty try from a scrum when it was wheeled and the ref said that Duggan had illegally prevented us from scoring. We went in at half-time 22–0 up and the second-half was much of the same. Gordon Hunter came on at scrum-half for Roy and made a fantastic break – I ran a scissors angle off him and he gave me a great pass in space that put me in under the posts. And then we scored another cracking try as Roger Baird made a break up the touchline and fed Peter Dods on his outside to score in the corner. We won 32–9.

The Irish boys came over and said they had a party arranged for us back at the hotel. There was a big banner proclaiming us as Triple Crown champions and we didn't put our hands in our pocket all night.

John Rutherford: To win a Triple Crown for Scotland was really special. There was a massive visiting support in Dublin. There were hundreds of them at our hotel to cheer us. They were in the foyer, they were on the stairs clapping the team and patting our backs. It was just fantastic for Scottish rugby.

Keith Robertson: It was strange because we hadn't even thought about the Grand Slam at that stage, it had been so long since we had won anything that all we were thinking about was the Triple Crown, and it wasn't until the next day that we started thinking about the France game.

I think a lot of players would agree that the Grand Slam was almost an anticlimax after the Triple Crown, which seems a strange thing to say given the magnitude of what we achieved and the atmosphere in the ground that day. It was just that until that stage, winning the Triple Crown had been our entire focus.

Jim Aitken: Most of the alickadoos at Murrayfield thought that was it after the Irish victory. I knew that a couple of them were saying that it wouldn't matter if we didn't beat France, because we'd already had a great season. I replied that it would be a disaster if we lost the last match. We had to finish the job.

Jim Calder: The French had looked strong all season and there was a big doubt about Roy Laidlaw playing because of his concussion, and his replacement, Gordon Hunter, had got his cheekbone depressed when he knocked heads with a supporter as he ran off the pitch at the end of the Ireland match. So they were talking about bringing back Dougie Morgan or Alan Lawson. In the end Roy was fit.

In the build-up to the game France had been wracking up the points at will and Peter Wheeler, the English hooker, had called them 'unbeatable'.

Jim Telfer: The only changes we had during the tournament were because of injuries, so we had good continuity. But before the last match, France lost Dominique Erbani, one of their back row, and instead of simply replacing him they made about five changes, moving people around.

John Rutherford: I remember Jim Telfer getting it across to the team that the first three games had been tough but this was going to be a different level altogether. The French team were outstanding – Didier Codorniou and Philippe Sella in the centre were world-class.

Jim Aitken: France were a rare team but I knew we were going to do it, all the more so when they hammered us for the first fifteen minutes and couldn't score.

Jim Telfer: We were completely outplayed by the French in the first half. The second half was different, we came out realising that we were lucky not to be too far behind them on the score board, and we had a bit of luck in a lineout where they had shortened the line and they threw the ball over the line for Gallion, their scrum-half, to run onto. Now we knew that they would do that.

Jim Calder: David Leslie did two things that really had a huge impact in that game. First, he took out Gallion, who was the heart of that French team, with a phenomenal tackle off the tail of a line-out which was only just on the legal side – and Gallion had to be taken off.

Then, with the French leading 12–9 midway through the second-half and really putting pressure on us, I remember lying on the deck in a ruck and seeing the blond hair of Jean-Pierre Rives being scraped back by Leslie's boot. He wasn't kicking but he was scraping away. Of course, the French were incensed; and all that the referee saw was Phillipe Dintrans, their hooker, come charging in and taking out Leslie, so we got the penalty.

John Beattie: Basically, what happened was that Leslie's knee delivered a glancing blow to the head of Jerome Gallion, the wee French scrum half. Gallion was a very good player and after that and the French were all at sea. Leslie once said that the key to winning rugby matches was 'Self-sacrifice of the body'. Some allege he was sacrificing Gallion's.

Euan Kennedy: David Leslie was not someone you wanted to get in the way of 48 hours before a game, let alone two hours before. He was so focussed . . . furiously focused . . . the most focussed individual I have ever come across, and he would be the first guy that any player in that team would put on the team-sheet to go into battle with.

David Leslie: It was totally accidental. That wasn't my style of play. And anyway, Pierre Berbizier wasn't a bad replacement, was he?

Jim Telfer: It changed the game completely. Jean-Pierre Rives started mouthing off to the referee and got on the wrong side of him, and in all games of rugby you should always try and keep on the right side of the referee because he can be your friend. And after that the French started to be penalised a lot.

Jean-Luc Joinel (Fance flanker): We had thought of all possibilities, we really thought of everything. Except one thing – a one-eyed referee.

Jim Aitken: They didn't lose the game because of Gallion or the referee. They were already beaten by then. David just ran into him.

Jacques Fouroux (France head coach): We didn't lose because of the loss of Gallion. We let victory go begging while Gallion was still there.

Jim Calder: The French were up in arms – everyone talks about French indiscipline but on that occasion they lost the rag for a good reason – and the referee marched them another ten yards back, to put Peter Dods within range for a penalty. All of a sudden we were back in it. We should have been penalised and back on our own line defending, instead we were kicking a penalty and the French had worked themselves into a state of agitation which festered for the rest of the game.

The whole match was brutal, but particularly in the scrums. The French have always prided themselves on their scrummaging and if they don't dominate you there it gets under their skin. Well, our front-row were strong, really strong, and loved to scrum. The Bear was one of the greatest tight-heads the game has ever seen. He was the cornerstone of that whole pack and the French couldn't shift him; he was a block of concrete.

Iain Milne (Scotland 1979-1990, 44 Caps): Some saw Gallion going off injured as a turning point but we were already doing well in the scrummage. I remember one scrum on the halfway line where we marched them right back. We started to dominate and normally when I got on top I was quite relentless. I would not give up.

Jim Calder: Eventually they knew that the only way to have any chance of getting into the ascendency was to start throwing cheap shots. From the back of the scrum you could hear these punches coming in from the French, you could hear them connecting with the Bear's face and around his head . . . but he didn't retaliate, didn't throw one punch back. He just took the hits and then took revenge by scrummaging them into the ground. It was frightening. I had never seen anything like it.

Jim Telfer: It was sealed by Jim Calder's try, of course. John Rutherford had put a high ball up on Serge Blanco, their superstar fullback, just a few minutes before and as he took it he was caught by our forwards and driven back downfield. The French cleared the ball and gave us a line-out just a few yards from their line. Colin Deans threw the ball in to Paxton who was going to tap it down to Jim Calder, but Jean-Luc Joinel got to the ball first and deflected it – and it fell straight into Jim's hands just as he had been expecting it to! Everyone says that that try was a fluke, but with the exception of the wrong hand getting to the ball to begin with it worked like a dream.

Jim Calder: Suddenly I had the ball in my hands and I was over the line. I thought I was offside but there was the referee signalling a try and I thought, 'Magic, we've got away with it.'

Jim Calder scores the Grand Slam clinching try.

Jim Telfer: Peter Dods kicked the conversion and then added a penalty, his fifth of the day, to extend our lead – that last kick was particularly impressive as he could only see out of one eye, the other was swollen shut after a bash.

When the final whistle went it was a strange feeling – I experienced more elation the week before when we claimed the Triple Crown. It wasn't until much later that our achievement sunk in. It had been fifty-nine years since our last Grand Slam and this was only the second one to ever be recorded by Scotland.

Jacques Fouroux: When all is said and done, maybe Scotland wanted victory even more than we did.

Jean-Pierre Rives (France flanker): Scotland were a very good side that year. That is all that needs to be said; forget the referee, the injuries, whatever. They deserved their Grand Slam.

David Leslie: After the match everyone was terribly pleased but I was sat on the bench, my usual spot near the shower-door, and Alan Tomes was sat opposite. We were too knackered to do anything more than nod to each other and share a look that said, 'I was there, and you were there.'

John Rutherford: When I look back now on that whole era, I realise now how lucky I am to have been a part of something so special. And as a group we were incredibly lucky that all the various strands came together as they did because that team was made up of combinations that worked well together rather than being a team of superstars.

When I was first capped in 1979 it was as much to do with luck as anything else. I was probably third in line but there were a few injuries so I got in. Again luck had played a part a couple of years earlier when the SRU had taken a bit of a punt and selected me for the tour to the Far East; not only was it a great trip to be a part of, but it was also when my partnership with Roy Laidlaw really started.

If you split Roy and I up I don't think either of us were anywhere as near as effective. He got to know my play well – he knew what I would be looking to do in any situation; and I got to know his play – how far he could pass it, what side he was stronger on, that sort of stuff. It is one of those things, just as it was with the entire team throughout the early eighties – the whole was better than the sum of the parts.

Jim Telfer: It remains perhaps my greatest achievement as a coach – greater even than the triumphs of 1990 or even those of the '97 Lions.

I always say Grand Slams are funny creatures because they confer on you a status and kudos that others equally deserve yet are denied. Some of the greatest Scotland players in history have not played in a Grand Slam – you think of Andy Irvine and Jim Renwick both of whom just missed out in 1984 – and some of the best coaches in Championship history have not coached a Grand Slam.

I'd argue, though, that the 1984 squad was an exceptional group by any criteria. If you were picking an all-time Scotland XV I fancy five or six would come from that team. They established, or possibly re-established, a very definite style of play and set the benchmark for some fine Scotland teams that followed in the next decade, including the 1990 group.

We were fitter than anybody else but that was an advantage you could always gain in the amateur game. If you wanted it more, trained harder, made more sacrifices you could always get fitter than the others. Professionalism has taken that away a bit, but call me biased, I still think that style is fit for purpose at the very top level. Scotland in 1984 were a team for the ages, their rugby would never date.

FOURTEEN

THE NEW BREED
1984-1989

Norrie Rowan: In the summer of 1984, we went to Romania – what a reward that was for the boys who had just won Scotland's first Grand Slam in 59 years!

A pal of mine from school, Rob Cunningham, who had toured there with Bath the previous year, told me to take over stockings, perfume, soap, cigarettes and what have you, to barter with. Well, they confiscated my bag at the airport and I had to kick up a real fuss to get it back. They just wanted the stuff for themselves, and it took some serious diplomacy from Brian Meek, the journalist, to persuade them to give it back to me.

The only decent meal we got was the lunch before the Test match. We'd been starved for three weeks then all of a sudden there were Chateaubriand steaks and all the food we wanted – which was obviously the last thing we needed before a game.

We lost the Test match 28–22 and there must have been a thousand people at the reception that night, all going bananas. We went back in 1986, and we beat them and there were barely fifty folk at the function that night. It was all politics. They saw rugby as a way of promoting their politics and if they got beat nobody wanted to be associated with it.

Euan Kennedy: I made it back from my knee injury in time for the Romania tour, which was Jim Renwick's last tour and the Test match where he equalled Scotland's record number of caps. But it was a tough place to go, the poverty was just awful.

People had jobs but often the jobs they had were so menial. You would be travelling down a dual carriageway and you would see gangs of twenty people trimming the grass verges with hand sheers.

Deodorant was unheard of and soap was a luxury item out there and we would give the hotel chambermaids bars of soap and it was like we had given them a bar of gold. It was a real eye-opening tour and history has obviously shown what a terrible regime they had in power there at the time.

I remember we went down to Constanta on the Black Sea to play a game. I was sharing with Tom Smith, who was about 6'8'; I was 6'5' and we were in this tiny wee room like a rabbit hutch. We were about fourteen floors up, so I went out on to the balcony to get a bit more space and to look out over the seafront and I suddenly saw a pair of feet bobbing up and down from above me – it was Sean McGaughey doing pull-ups on his balcony on the outside of the hotel.

John Beattie: We had our own food and I remember leaving used chocolate wrappers lying around and when we walked away the waitresses would be licking the foil – and

Opposite: Gavin Hastings.

I remember thinking, 'This is real poverty.'

It was baking hot. We had been given one of the earliest versions of Gatorade, but they had mixed up the wrong concentration so it was almost all salt with a bit of liquid. You took a quick gulp and suddenly your whole mouth stuck together. You couldn't separate your tongue from the roof of your mouth so you couldn't breathe.

Euan Kennedy: I was involved in four pretty momentous games; unfortunately my fourth and last Test match was momentous for the wrong reason because it saw us come up against one of the all time great sides in the 1984 touring Australian team. They had some of the very best players ever to emerge from that country – guys like their captain Andrew Slack and Michael Lynagh in the centre, Mark Ella and Nick Farr-Jones at half-back and obviously Campese out wide . . . they were an outstanding team. With Ella leading the attacking line and really revolutionizing it with that flat, flat alignment they used and with runners changing direction at the last minute and hitting the line straight, it was so hard to defend against and in the end they just embarrassed us. The Home Union backlines in those days all used to get the ball in their hands and then arc out so that they were almost running at a forty-five degree angle. This meant that the defending stand-off would call the drift and the entire backline would drift across the field, tracking the attack and usually giving the defensive line a man overlap so that they had cover for the attacking fullback or blindside winger coming into the line. But the Australians took the ball straight, cutting against the defence, making it difficult to defend against using a drift system, but then they combined it by passing the ball late and right on the gain-line . . . it was like nothing any of us had encountered before and they just cut us to ribbons.

I didn't have a long international career but every moment was wonderful. It is good to look back and talk about the good times but it was even better experiencing them. How would I describe my rugby career? Sixteen seasons, brilliant memories, great laughs and lots and lots of friends . . . lifelong friends. What a game.

In 1985, in a campaign that proved to be a polar opposite to the previous season, Scotland went through the Five Nations without registering a single victory. There was a realisation throughout Scottish rugby that the time had come for a new broom to sweep through the squad. In 1985, Derek Grant was made head coach, with Ian McGeechan appointed as his assistant.

Roger Baird: In 1985 it was a crying shame because we went down to Twickenham and should have won. Peter Steven and I had a huge chance on a bouncing ball to hack on and score down the right-hand side, but we recycled it, and we went left. John Rud [Rutherford] will always hold his head here because all he had to do was give the pass and Iain Paxton was in, and that was us winning two years in a row down at Twickenham, but he went himself and got tackled.

Jim Pollock: The last game I played for Scotland was in Paris in 1985, when I was called up as a late replacement for Roger Baird. It wasn't a great game, it was quite a dour affair which we lost 11–3, and as you can imagine the changing room was a pretty depressing place afterwards.

Then this chap came in and said he owned a nightclub in Paris and if anyone wanted to go he had some tickets available. So the tickets were snatched out of his hands and thrown on the floor, and I casually picked them up. We went to the after-match function and afterwards I said to a few of the boys that I had these tickets, so off we tootled.

We found this place and I couldn't believe it, there was these really expensive cars parked outside and everyone was dressed in fur coats. Of course, we're all in our dinner jackets. So I went to the front of the queue and said something like, 'Ecosse – tickets.' And we were immediately ushered through the door. I went to the bar and ordered two whiskies, a vodka and a gin and tonic. Bang, bang, bang, bang, the drinks were laid down: two bottles of whisky, a bottle of vodka and a bottle of gin. I tried to pay but the barman managed to explain that the first drinks were all free, so I decided to throw a bottle of champagne in as well.

About two hours later, after we had played all sorts of drinking games, and Serge Blanco had come in – with a white dinner suit on and all the women in the nightclub falling all over him – I decided it was time to leave. God knows what happened to everyone else.

So, I'm outside lying on top of a Porsche when this blue van with a flashing light on top of it comes round the corner and these four guys in blue suits jump out, pick me up and throw me in the back. It was one of those sobering moments when you think: I'm in big trouble here. I couldn't explain where the hotel was or anything like that, but I happened to have the invitation for the dinner in my pocket so I showed them that – they just seemed to ignore me. The van was tootling along at about ten miles an hour when suddenly the backdoor opened and one of the policemen kicked me in the backside, propelling me out of the van.

So I'm rolling along the street, my dinner suit is wrecked all the way down the left side, and as I turn around to call them all the names under the sun I notice my hotel to the right. Somehow I made it through the foyer and to my room. I opened the door, and walk in – and there is absolutely nothing there. No wardrobe, no TV, no bed, no chair . . . absolutely nothing. I ended up sleeping on the carpet floor in my ruined dinner suit. When I woke up the next morning my suitcase was outside the door – but the furniture was still gone. Who took it? Well, nobody was coughing up to that the next day.

Six new caps were selected for the opening 1986 Five Nations fixture with France at Murrayfield. And what a selection of players it was. In the history of Scottish rugby, could there ever have been a higher standard of debutants winning their first caps in one game? Of the six, three would go on to captain their country with distinction, four would play Test rugby for the Lions and two of those would captain Lions tours. Those six new caps were

Jeremy Campbell-Lamerton, Matt Duncan, Scott Hastings, Gavin Hastings, David Sole and Finlay Calder – who came into the team as a direct replacement for his twin brother, Jim. A new broom and new breed of player. Physically powerful, dynamic, charismatic, tenacious and ferociously ambitious.

After the whitewash of 1985, 1986 was quite a different campaign. In a thrilling opening encounter, the new players made an immediate impact. Despite the French scoring from a quick throw-in after Gavin Hastings' kick-off went directly into touch, the fullback more than made amends by steering his side to victory and his name into the record books by kicking six penalties to edge Scotland home 18–17, his efforts in front of goal eclipsing the previous Scottish record of seventeen points in a single match which had been jointly held by Andy Irvine and Peter Dods.

Scott Hastings (Scotland 1986-1997, 65 Caps plus 2 Caps for the Lions): There was a trial in January 1986 at Murrayfield, a Probables vs Possibles – and the most amazing thing happened. The Possibles absolutely smashed the Probables, 41–10. The trial was just incredible with Soley [David Sole] driving over the gainline and Finlay – who was twenty-seven, so maybe that was his last attempt – thundering around. Gavin kicked all his goals and I scored a try and had another disallowed. But every one of us played outstandingly well. Gary Callander did brilliantly against Colin Deans, the Scotland captain, and Stuart Johnston – David's brother – outshone Roy Laidlaw. The guys in possession of the jerseys were, I think, in a state of total shock. There were obviously going to be changes. The question for the selectors must have been: 'How many do we stop at?'

Pals were telling me, 'You're in, you're in' but I had a couple of pints in Stockbridge and then sloped off home. Then three days later I got the envelope – the manila one, none of your white rubbish, and embossed 'SRU' with a tick in the 'player' box in the late secretary Bill Hogg's scrawl. Gavin, who was home from Cambridge University, got his and there followed the kind of really basic conversation that only two brothers can have: 'You in?' 'Yeah. You?' 'Yeah.' 'See you later, I'm off to work.'

The chairman of the selectors, Ian MacGregor, came up to me the weekend before the game and said, 'Remember son, you didn't get my effing vote.' That gave me bags of confidence!

The excitement before the game was incredible. The rap on the dressing-room door, the dimly-lit corridor, the smell of the rubber mats, ten paces right, another ten left, the mouth of the tunnel, the cacophony . . . but the game itself passed in a complete blur.

Gavin Hastings (Scotland 1986-95, 61 Caps plus 6 Caps for the Lions): I left school at eighteen and wasn't capped until I was 24, so that was a reasonably long apprenticeship – maybe that was why I hit the ground running. Mind you, that first match against France couldn't have got off to a worse start.

I tried to land my kick-off on a sixpence but I went a bit too far and landed it just in touch. I thought, 'Oh God, that's not a great start, the boys aren't going to be too happy with me putting the kick out.' I turned and started jogging back towards the posts, ready for them to scrum down on the halfway line, then all of a sudden I heard this big roar, so I turned round and I saw half a dozen Frenchmen running towards me. It was a case of: eeny, meeny, miny, moe; and I picked one of them but he didn't have the ball and Pierre Berbizier scored. At that point I thought, 'Oh-oh, the rest of Scotland are not going to be very happy with me.'

You can't see the try on TV. They out-foxed the camera men as well.

I don't remember what was said behind the posts, Colin Deans was the captain and he was probably wondering why they had picked this silly bugger at fullback, but at least I had plenty of time to redeem myself. If you're going to lose a golf hole it might as well be the first one, because you've then got seventeen more opportunities to win it back.

Scott Hastings: I was under the posts saying, 'What happened? What happened?' I looked at John Beattie, and he said, 'I don't have the foggiest idea,' or something a little a bit more colourful than that. It was a rude awakening to international rugby.

Maybe a few of the new boys were wondering if the faith shown in us had been justified. Then John Rutherford shouted, 'Right Scotty, you're putting this next one up on Blanco!' And that kick brought me into the match.

Gavin Hastings: Fortunately things got a wee bit better, and in a funny sort of way it probably did me quite a lot of good. That's what international rugby is all about – expect the unexpected. I have never watched that game again, so I have no idea how many kicks at goal I had, but I would wager that I had at least ten opportunities – and I missed two or three that I was really cross about – so it wasn't my best kicking performance of all time.

I remember lining up my first penalty opportunity and thinking, 'This is the biggest kick of my life.' And I was really chuffed to get that one over – because you never know if you are going to be able to do it until you are in that position. There are a lot of people who have been put in that position and not managed to live with the pressure.

I have no idea if it was any good as a game of rugby or not, but looking at the statistics I would expect it was a really boring match. I don't suppose it really matters.

Two weeks later, we went down to Wales. In those days Cardiff, with that old horse-shoe of a stadium, was an amazing place to play. It was a brilliant atmosphere – fantastic singing – and perhaps we were a bit over-awed by suddenly playing in somebody else's backyard. It was a game we probably should have won, but Scott had a try disallowed early on and Paul Thorburn had his kicking boots on that day.

It was wet and horrible, and we were playing with these Mitre balls which were crap – you couldn't kick for toffee. But with them leading 16–15, Thorburn lined up this penalty from about ten metres inside his own half. I thought there was no chance – that he was just wasting a bit of time. Then this ball came through the posts like a torpedo. I think it bounced off my chest because it was going so fast and I wasn't actually sure if it was going to duck under the bar or scrape just over. I've never seen a bigger kick. I could hardly see him – he was miles away. The ball just sneaked in through the corner of the post and the crossbar – it could not have been closer. He kicked another penalty after that, and that took the game beyond us, 22–15.

John Beattie: A key game in my life was in 1986 when we beat England by a record score. I'd read a book – New Zealand half-back Dave Loveridge's autobiography – and he talked about how the All Blacks had thought the 1983 Lions weren't very fit so had decided to speed the game up. Now, the only way to do that was at the line-out, so they had extra ballboys making sure that they were always able to get the ball back into play as quickly as possible.

Well, we were very fit because there had been a really deep frost that winter which meant lots of club games were called off and we were training through at Murrayfield together every weekend. Meanwhile England had this huge pack, which didn't move around the park very well at all. So we got the SRU to supply a lot of extra ball boys. Colin Deans was very fit and very fast, so every time the ball went out he ran to the spot and the ballboys got the ball to him straight away, he did this code which was designed so that rather than standing there shouting numbers and letters it depended on the way he was holding the ball, and he would throw it in. You could see the English struggling – it was just faster than anything they were used to.

Also, on the Thursday, during a team meeting, the phone went and it was Jim Calder for Finlay. He said that he knew I didn't get on very well with Maurice Colclough so at the first line-out I should start punching him – and those genuinely were our tactics: speed the game up, start a fight, and shout abuse at them the whole time. Now with tactics like that it was never going to be very precise, but the mayhem suited us because we were very fit and everything was happening at a hundred miles an hour.

John Jeffrey (Scotland 1984-1991, 40 Caps): Jim Calder phoned up to remind us that Maurice Colclough had been shit scared of John Beattie on the previous Lions tour – which you can understand, because John was crazy.

That night we went to see *The Terminator* and we all loved it when Arnie came out with that immortal line, 'Fuck you, asshole'.

So we were talking about it all after the film and we thought it would be a brilliant idea for us to turn to the English boys at the first lineout, make pistols with our hands and say, 'Fuck you, asshole' . . . and John Beattie would deck Maurice Colclough.

So we got to the first lineout and that was exactly what we did; but instead of decking Colclough, John decked Wade Dooley. It was the most ridiculous case of mistaken identity I'd ever seen. And unfortunate too, because it was never a good idea to upset big Wade and a massive scrap broke out. But it worked in a way because all through the rest of the game Wade was on the lookout for John trying to hit him again and Colclough was scuttling around with one eye over his shoulder waiting for John to get him too – and the rest of us just got on with things.

John Beattie: People always talk about the physical aspect I brought to the game, but that's not something I really focussed on. I always thought of rugby as a game of chess, and that's what really fascinated me about it as a sport. When I played I came up with different back-row moves, some of which led to tries – those were the most satisfying parts for me, thinking my way through a game, plotting strategies to beat the opposition; it certainly wasn't all physical.

I've always found the whole Scottish-English thing a bit funny because I always think a border is just something someone drew when they stole a bit of land. It doesn't mean you hate the people on the other side. As an international player, you kind of pretend to – but you never do.

That game in 1986 was particularly special for me because there is a bit in Bill McLaren's commentary when he says, 'What a game John Beattie is having,' and that will stick with me for the rest of my life. People talk about luck in those wins, but that was the start of players like the Hastings coming through, Fin Calder and JJ – dynamic and powerful, a whole new mindset and style of Scottish player.

Gavin Hastings: We finished joint top of the table with France that year, having scraped past Ireland 10–9 in our last game. That match probably should have finished as a 12–12 draw, but I missed a conversion after Roy Laidlaw scored yet another try at Lansdowne Road, then we conceded a penalty in the dying moments, but Michael Kiernan missed a fairly straight-forward kick. So we scraped through but were pretty lucky because we hadn't played all that well.

All in all, it was a pretty good season. We had a really good team spirit in that squad, and the fact that some of us were younger and were only just breaking into the team I think helped. It was a breath of fresh air for some of the more established guys, like Roy Laidlaw and Colin Deans.

At the end of March, the squad returned to Bucharest to make amends for the previous summer's disappointment and saw away their hosts with ease to record a 33–18 win.

Roger Baird: I have this unfortunate record of having played twenty-seven times on the wing for Scotland and never scored a try . . . but I actually scored a try against Romania when we went there in the summer of 1986, believe it or not. It was one of the most bizarre things ever. Laurie Prideaux was the touch judge and Roger Quittenton was the referee – a couple of Englishmen – and I got the ball on the left-hand side, beat my man, ran in, touched down and thought, 'Great, that's that bogey put to bed.'

I looked round and there was Prideaux with his flag up. I couldn't understand it, because I wasn't anywhere near being out of play. I think he must have had an episode because we got photographs the next day and I was miles away from touch. I suppose that was the moment that best illustrates that it just wasn't meant to be.

I suppose it did play on my mind a bit. As a winger, not scoring in twenty-seven

Test matches . . . well . . . it's not great. I should point out that I did score for the Lions, and I was top all time try scorer for the South, and since the old districts have now been disbanded I probably still hold that record. But for Scotland, the longer it went on the more of a burden it probably became. It certainly didn't do your confidence much good.

Norrie Rowan: Because Romania had lost, the dinner after our game there in 1986 was pretty low key and didn't last long, but afterwards we were invited down to the British Embassy for drinks. And when the guys got back to the hotel, everyone was blootered. That was the season when Scottish & Newcastle brewers started to move into sponsoring Scottish rugby, and I always remember Iain Milne had the chairman of S&N round the neck, leaning practically all his weight on him, completely pissed, and waving round this ceramic beer stein full of wine and singing songs. The look of terror on this wee guy's face was classic.

Roger Baird: There had been a bit of trouble at the dinner after the last home international in 1986 Five Nations. Somebody had thrown a tomato and it had hit the head of the Royal Bank of Scotland on the head. They were SRU's chief sponsor so the committee were pretty unhappy, so Dod Burrell, the president of the SRU, told us that there would be big trouble if there was anything less than exemplary behaviour at the dinner after the Romania game.

Well, we went to the dinner and you have to remember that this was Romania in the time of Ceauşescu. There was no food and no drink. It was just a hellish, awful affair. But afterwards things got a bit out of control and there was some wrecking done at the hotel that night. The next morning we're all sitting on this bus looking into this hotel which had a big glass façade and we can see Dod Burrell and Bill Hogg negotiating with the hotel staff. When Dod got on the bus he was shaking with rage, and you could hear a pin drop. He said, 'You've let yourselves down, you've let your clubs down, but most of all you've let your country down.' Nobody dared look up . . . except Roy Laidlaw, who still hadn't sobered up. He put his hand up and said, 'Aye Dod, but at least we behaved at the dinner.'

It was not a nice place to visit. We had folk trying to jump on the bus to claim asylum, there was queues for food everywhere. It was serious depression.

In 1987, the Calcutta Cup match at Twickenham was postponed until the end of the tournament because of bad weather, and by the time the team travelled to London, they had beaten Ireland and Wales at Murrayfield and fallen just six points shy of France at the Parc des Princes. Arriving in London at the beginning of April, Scotland's preparations were marred by Scott Hastings' withdrawal with a fractured cheekbone. In an effort to increase the speed of the pack, Grant selected five players who, at the time, were all playing number eight for their respective clubs: Iain Paxton, Derek White, John Beattie, John Jeffrey and Finlay Calder. On paper it was a wonderfully aggressive and athletic back-five behind Sole, Deans and Milne, but it proved, in reality, to contain one major flaw: there were no players of any notable height to operate and control the middle of the lineout. The 1987 battle for the Calcutta Cup was effectively settled along Twickenham's tramlines, with Nigel Redman and Steve Bainbridge absolutely massacring the Scottish lineout and laying a perfect platform for their own backline to attack. England went on to win 21–12, reclaiming the Calcutta Cup and burying Scotland's Triple Crown hopes.

Gavin Hastings: In 1987 we were due to play England first up at Twickenham, but there was snow and the game was postponed, and if we had played them then I'm sure we would have smashed them – probably by as much as we did the year before – but we then played them in the last game of the season. So we won our two home games against Ireland and Wales, and went down there with a chance of the Triple Crown, but we played appallingly and lost.

Marcus Rose was their fullback. He used to catch the ball and dribble it five yards into touch, and the whole of Twickenham would roar. It was just the most negative brand of rugby you have ever seen. I don't quite know how we contrived to lose that game. I remember the following day we went to the FA Cup final. Charlie Nicholas was playing for Arsenal and he scored two goals on the most beautiful day you could imagine. It had pissed it down at Twickenham the day before, so I suppose the gods had conspired against us.

To compound matters, the game saw a devastating knee injury suffered by John Beattie. Tackled by Gary Pearce after taking a quick tap-penalty, Beattie's knee ligaments buckled under the impact from the Northampton prop's shoulder. Carried from the field of play he was never to wear the blue of Scotland again. It was a bitter and tragic blow for both Beattie and the team, especially as it meant he would miss the inaugural Rugby World Cup later that year, held in New Zealand and Australia. Sixteen nations would contest for the coveted title of world champions between 22 May and 20 June.

Despite the loss of Beattie, Scotland looked like a formidable force as they flew to the Antipodes for this landmark tournament. But their prospects were undermined by an injury to Scott Hastings that kept him out of the first match, and by another career-ending knee injury. In the week following the conclusion of the 1987 Five Nations, John Rutherford, Iwan Tukalo, Matt Duncan and Iain Paxton were invited to play in an exhibition game in Bermuda, despite an SRU decree that all players should rest before the start of the tournament. Rutherford, one of the most senior players in the team, its tactical controller and one of the most talented players ever to pull on the number ten shirt for Scotland, injured his knee during this North Atlantic soujorn. He had an operation to try and repair the damage when he returned home and hoped that it would hold up throughout the tournament. It didn't. The first game of Scotland's World Cup was against France and less than fifteen minutes were played before Rutherford was forced off, with his knee in pieces. Like Beattie, he was never to return.

John Rutherford.

David Sole (Scotland 1986-1992, 44 Caps plus 3 Caps for the Lions): The first World Cup was a huge success. It was very much uncharted territory, but the New Zealanders were so passionate about it, and their team swept everyone aside, so there was a real buzz the length and breadth of the country.

John Jeffrey: Not everyone thought Scotland should go to New Zealand. There was a view that this was an amateur sport and that a World Cup would hasten commercialism. The players, though, were dead keen.

David Sole: For Scotland, it was really tough. We had a nightmare journey out there, which didn't help. We flew from London to LA in blazers and ties, where we picked up the US and Canadian teams then flew to Hawaii to refuel, then from Hawaii down to Auckland. But as we were about to land in Auckland the captain came on the tannoy and explained that we would have to take another loop and hope that visibility had improved. We did this twice before the decision was made to divert to Christchurch. We landed there but weren't allowed off the plane. Then the captain announced that the fog had cleared in Auckland so we could go back there, but unfortunately the flight engineer's tachograph was up so we had to wait for a relief crew. We were on the ground in Christchurch for five hours before we flew back up to Auckland. When we landed we were all pretty tired after thirty-six hours in transit, and it was decided that it would be a good idea if we went out for a jog.

Everyone was worn-out and pissed-off, the last thing they wanted to do was go out jogging. We headed up to this local park and we had a game of touch, which turned into a game of what you might call 'Samoan touch'. There were t-shirts getting ripped off as tempers flared, and if nobody came to blows then quite a few came damn close. Eventually we stumbled back to the hotel with bleeding noses and ripped t-shirts to get ready for dinner.

The next morning the Irish, who were staying in the same hotel as us but playing in a different group, asked if we were interested in getting together with them for some live scrummaging. That sounded fine, so after we had done our own training, we met up. It was all pretty gentle to start off with, it was still less than twenty-four hours since we had got off the plane and we eased our way into it – and then, all of a sudden, the Irish decided that they wanted to really go for it, but they didn't tell us beforehand.

The next scrum . . . BANG . . . they piled into us. Of course, it all kicked off. From that moment onwards it was like an international: the Scottish pack and the Irish pack were kicking lumps out of each other on some back pitch in Auckland. You think about how the players are wrapped in cotton wool now, and you shake your head in disbelief at the way it was.

Gavin Hastings: Those first few sessions we had of the tour were ridiculous. We had just come off a killer journey and boys were firing into each other playing touch and again when we had the session against Ireland. The World Cup was a whole new concept for everyone and no-one wanted to feel that they were under-prepared, so they went into the training sessions hammer and tongs – an approach that would be unthinkable these days. The session we had with the Irish

Roy Laidlaw.

lasted three hours and in the last few minutes my brother pulled his hamstring. That was effectively his World Cup over after that – he missed the France game, ran around for a few minutes against Romania which aggravated the injury, and he missed the rest of the tournament. Compared with how players are looked after – and look after themselves – these days, we were in the dark ages.

Rugby was pretty low key in those days. Apart from a few weeks during the Five Nations, it was always relegated to deep inside the sports pages. We all had full-time jobs and enjoyed our rugby at the weekend before getting a few beers down our necks, and if you were lucky then four or five times a year you played in front of a big crowd at an international match – so, arriving in New Zealand was amazing because the streets were awash with bunting. Andy Dalton, the All Blacks captain, seemed to be on the television every half hour appearing in commercials, and I remember we composed this letter which was sent to a guy called Russ Thomas, who was the chairman of the World Cup, pointing out that this seemed to be a contravention of the amateur regulations. The way they got round it was that they would have a slogan on the bottom of the screen saying: 'Andy Dalton – Farmer'. They just overlooked the fact that he was the All Blacks captain as well. You could see professionalism beginning to sneak in through the back door.

Finlay Calder (Scotland 1986-1991, 34 Caps plus 3 Caps for the Lions): I remember when we got the plane to fly from Auckland down to Christchurch for the first match against France, the Scots were in the number ones – white shirts, blue blazers, ties – and we're thinking we look pretty smart. Then on came the French and they sat down beside us and they're all in Gucci suits, listening to Walkmans, and I remember just thinking to myself, 'Who pays for all this?'

John Jeffrey: There was no opening ceremony like they have now, just a welcome dinner. We went out for some beers afterwards and we arrived at this one place and the bouncers wouldn't let us in. 'Bugger,' I thought, 'I'm going to have to use the "Do you know who I am?" line.' I pointed out we were all here for the first-ever World Cup. 'We know, John,' they said, 'but this a gay nightclub.'

Gavin Hastings: Walking out onto Lancaster Park for the opening match with France was awe-inspiring. We really knew that we were part of something special with this first World Cup and we were there in this great bear pit that was ringing with noise – bagpipes trilling on the air and it was wonderful to see and hear such a lot of support so far away from home. That match saw come classic gamesmanship from France – a couple of players were down injured in the field of play and while they were being attended to, Blanco took a quick tap-kick and snuck up the touchline and ended up scoring under the posts.

You could argue that the French were just cannier than we were – they had shown that when they had played us at Murrayfield the season before and scored from that quick lineout after my kick-off went out on the full and all our boys were trooping back for the scrum on halfway. But that try at Lancaster Park got our blood boiling and we fairly roared back at them after that.

John Jeffrey: John Rutherford got injuried early on, then Derek White pulled a hamstring scoring a try.

John Rutherford: At that time, because the game was strictly amateur, one of the few perks that you got was the chance of little trips abroad to play now and then. And at the end of '87 season I got the chance to go out and play this game in Bermuda with Tukes [Iwan Tukalo], Matt Duncan and Packy [Iain Paxton]; it was a nothing game, just a bit of fun, but of course I did my cruciate ligament which I regret massively now because going into the World Cup we had a great team and had a chance to do really well.

I came back from Bermuda and I had an operation and I thought I was OK to go. In the build-up to the tournament, we played a lot of games against one another as a squad and I was put through a whole series of tests to make sure my knee was OK and I genuinely thought that I was back to normal . . . but it obviously wasn't. If you had the same operation now, you would spend a year or so recovering and working back to full strength with a carefully monitored recovery programme, but that kind of sports science didn't exist then. And then in the opening game I took the first hard tackle and the ligament just snapped and that was it – I never played again.

But I can't be bitter about it; I had nine great years. Amazing years. Sometimes it's easier for a player to pick up an injury that forces them into retirement – it makes the decision for you. It's very hard for most players to know when the time is right to step down, so it was something of a silver lining, I suppose, that I didn't have to go through that process.

Gavin Hastings: In the end it came down to my kick to convert Matt Duncan's try, which went just wide. That was disappointing, but it happens. What it meant was that unless one of the other teams in our pool caused a major upset against France, we were heading for a quarter-final with New Zealand, which was ominous.

Finlay Calder: We then travelled to Wellington to play Zimbabwe at Athletic Park. We put a full-strength team out and ran them ragged, winning 60–21, and scored eleven tries. Gav picked up another record – he seemed to collect them for fun – by kicking eight conversions to add to the try he scored. We went down to Dunedin to play Romania eight days later and put out much the same team as the previous two Tests. We won 55–28 but we were in pieces by then. Squad rotation was unheard of, but we really should have been smarter about how we used our players. Zimbabwe were never going to be a threat to our chances, but I think after the France game the coaches didn't want to take anything for granted. We secured qualification through to the quarters, but the team was being held together with sticking tape at that stage.

John Jeffrey: I scored a hat-trick of tries against Romania, not that I remember because I was concussed. Eventually the boys got me off. They could see I was gone.

David Sole: We were in a killer group and we picked up a lot of injuries; I remember on the Thursday training session before the quarter-final there were only three fit forwards training: myself, Fin Calder and Colin Deans. So how we managed to put a competitive team on the park was a miracle. Obviously we knew the lay-out of the games before we arrived in New Zealand, but we didn't manage it very well. We should have rested a few players for the Zimbabwe game, but they chose not to take a risk and we ended up beating them by fifty-odd points. We basically tried to play the same team in four matches within the space of fourteen days. Roger Baird and Jeremy Richardson were in the 25-man squad but didn't get a game, which was senseless.

Colin Deans: It's difficult because it had never been staged before and you didn't know what you were getting into. No-one really had played in pool games; it was all just straight out internationals, one against one. Recovery at that time wasn't as important as it is now and hydration, nutrition. If you wanted to video a game and go through the video yourself, that was the analysis.

   We went on tour with a manager, a coach or two, a doctor, a couple of physios and that was about it. No one actually told you what to do, when to do it, when to rest, when to train, what to eat. There was no ice baths – sometimes you couldn't get into the hot bath quick enough!

Keith Robertson: By the time we got to the quarter-finals, we were just patching guys up to get them out on the park, which is always going to end in disaster against a team like New Zealand. I had a broken finger, Iain Paxton was struggling with a shoulder

John Jeffrey races away from the Zimbabwe defence in Wellington.

injury, Alan Tait had a dead leg. Meanwhile, New Zealand had been pretty smart in their team selections during the group stage so they were fighting fit and ready to go, and we were just holding onto their coat-tails.

Keith Robertson: We all believed beforehand that we had a chance if we played to the best of our ability and took what opportunities might come our way, but once we got on the park we were just trying to fight off wave after wave.

Gavin Hastings: That All Black team was something else. They had cruised through their pool, beating Italy, Fiji and Argentina and scoring 190 points in those three games; no-one was going to stop them getting their hands on that cup. They were physically bigger, faster and more skilled than any other team in the world, everything about them was already professional in anything but name. They were awesome. It was then that I decided that I would stay on and play a season in Auckland – I wanted to learn all I could from those types of players; and the lessons that I learned playing with guys like Grant Fox and Sean Fitzpatrick changed the way I played and approached the game forever afterwards.

It was disappointing to be going home at the quarter-final stage but it had been a wonderful experience to be part of that first World Cup. We could all see how it was going to change the game and open it to audiences around the world. It was a special time to be involved.

David Sole: Derrick Grant spoke avidly about what we had just experienced – humbling though it may have been to be defeated like that by the All Blacks, he said that this was now the standard that we had to aspire to achieve; this was our Everest, our mountain to climb – words that stayed with me throughout my playing days.

Ian McGeechan was promoted to the role of head coach in 1988, replacing Derek Grant. Roy Laidlaw's career was coming to an end and he was soon succeeded by another young scrum-half from his home town club, Jed-Forest. Gary Armstrong, a stocky farmer's son blessed with a sharp snipe and the strength of a number eight cultivated on his father's farm, was some replacement indeed. Over the next decade he would fight fierce duels with the likes of Melrose's Bryan Redpath and Dundee High School's Andy Nicol for the Scotland number nine shirt, but when fit and on form he was always considered vital to any Scotland success. Outside Armstrong, Rutherford's successor had emerged in Melrose's Craig Chalmers, who was first capped in 1989 when he was just twenty years old, making him the youngest-ever Scotland cap at the time. And out wide another youngster had pushed himself into contention for international recognition. Tony Stanger was a gangly centre from Hawick who had only recently converted himself into a winger. Another new face – quite literally – was that of centre Sean Lineen, son of All Black great Terry, who arrived to play for Boroughmuir in October of 1988 and who, thanks to his Scottish grandfather, was eligible to play for Scotland – a feat that he realised in January 1989 against Wales at Murrayfield.

John Jeffrey: We had a good win against the French in '88, but the rest of the campaign was a wash-out and not particularly memorable – except for one incident. After the Calcutta Cup match, which was an awful, drab affair that we lost 9–6 at Murrayfield, we had a fairly massive night out – as you always did in those days. I remember all the tables had a load of booze on them that was virtually all gone by the time they even said grace. Four of our players were in bed before the end of the dinner. In retrospect, I wish I had been one of them.

After the dinner the captain used to take the cup out with them and you'd fill it with drinks all night and offer it around to punters to drink from. You'd get some pretty nasty mixes of drinks in there so it's not surprising that my memory of the whole night is fairly hazy. But I do remember bits and pieces. Dean Richards and I decided to fill the cup with whisky and then poured it over Brian Moore's head. He started chasing us and we ran out of the pub and into a taxi, still with the cup. We went to another two or three pubs and then came back. I don't remember an awful lot after that.

Norrie Rowan: Deano and JJ were throwing it around and it got smashed off the floor. There was nothing malicious, they were just passing it around like a rugby ball, but they kept on dropping it. The last time I saw it the doorman at Buster Browns had a broom handle through the lugs of the cup and was trying to wedge it back into shape.

John Jeffrey: After a while I sobered up a bit and I remember looking at the cup and thinking: this is a bit of a mess. We headed back to our hotel eventually and handed it in at reception. When I woke up the next day all I could remember was the thing lying there behind the reception, battered to pieces.

Both Deano and I were banned by the RFU and SRU – although he got away with it more than I did. He was banned for a week while I was banned for five months! It's a chapter of my life that I am not terribly proud about, but I'm still annoyed about how long my ban was compared to his.

Dean Richards (England Number Eight): All I can remember about it is that I was incredibly drunk, and that John Jeffrey and I took the Calcutta Cup outside and it came back in a worse state. The SRU were having huge problems with their players at that time – and the RFU weren't – and the handling of it showed a stark contrast in attitude. My view is that I should have had a longer ban and JJ a shorter ban for what happened. However, I had no impact on what his union said and did. After my RFU hearing I expected the same ban as John got, if not worse, and was quite surprised to get only one match. I felt embarrassed about the incident.

Sean Lineen (Scotland 1989-1992, 29 Caps): I arrived in Edinburgh in October 1988, just to play a bit of rugby for Boroughmuir and have a bit of fun, and by February 1989 I was playing for Scotland. My first taste of it was for Edinburgh against Australia that November. They asked me to play in that match and of course no Kiwi is ever going to turn down a chance to play against the Aussies, and from there I made it into the Probables team at the National Trial. I played really badly in that game but for some reason the selectors decided to go with me anyway.

I remember getting the letter from SRU secretary Bill Hogg saying I had been selected to play for Scotland against Wales. I was so excited I ran down the road to tell my mate, it was pouring with rain and I slipped on a big pile of dog shit and nearly wiped myself out – that would have been a novel way of getting in the record books for the shortest international career in the history of rugby!

I qualified because my grandfather had been born in Stornoway. A few years after I was capped I went up there to present the rugby club with a jersey and meet my grandfather's brother. Finlay Calder and David Sole had told me that they only spoke Gaelic up there, and being a thick Kiwi I believed them. So they gave me a couple of phrases to use. I remember getting off the plane and they had the whole entourage out to meet me – radio, TV, everything – it was a big story in the Outer Hebrides. So I hopped off the plane and greeted them all by saying some sort of friendly salutation but apparently in Gaelic really meant 'Up your arse.' They got me a good one there.

Chris Gray and Kenny Milne were also making their debuts that day, so that was the final pieces in the jigsaw for the 1990 Grand Slam being put in place. Only Gavin Hastings, who was injured, was missing.

The thing that got me most playing in that first game was the crowd – the noise was unbelievable. I'd never heard anything like it before. We won that game fairly easily, 23–7. Then we drew with England at Twickenham.

I'll always remember Finlay giving Andy Robinson such a hard time that day. He patted him on the head and gave him abuse at every line-out. 'You're too small, what are you doing here, you're too small. Oh, here comes the ball, I'll get that. You can't reach it. You've lost it again. You're too small.' Then JJ got in on the act, and it was a real torrent of verbal abuse. Robinson just lost it. He was chasing them instead of the game. JJ and Finlay were pretty clever at that sort of stuff.

The Ireland game in 1989 was a cracker. We beat them convincingly in the end, 37–21, and played really well, with Iwan Tukalo scoring a hat-trick in that game – the little bugger never passed the ball.

So we went over to France looking to win the Championship – but we got absolutely slaughtered 19–3. I remember Gary Armstrong saying that he learned a big lesson about scrum-half play that day against Pierre Berbizier, who stood on his toes and got in his way all afternoon. He just didn't let him play. I suppose that was a wake-up call, that we still had a lot to learn.

I remember there was a fight at one point and I came flying in and smacked Laurent Rodriguez, their number eight, on the back of the head, and only succeeding in hurting myself. It was like a fly glancing him on his head; he turned round and looked but I was on the other side so he saw Derek White and planted him instead.

Tony Stanger (Scotland 1989-1998, 52 Caps): I won my first cap against Fiji in 1989, which was obviously a very memorable game for me as it was my first game and I scored two tries, but it was also momentous because it was the first time that *Flower of Scotland* was played as our national anthem before a game. It used to be *God Save the Queen*, but it was changed that year and *Flower of Scotland* has been our anthem ever since.

Ian McGeechan: Billy Steele brought *Flower of Scotland* to rugby. It became the tour song on the '74 Lions tour. We sung it before every game and every Test match and it was the last thing we would sing before we got off the bus – and we wouldn't get off the bus until we'd finished it. And we then sang it live on television after the tour and gradually the players in Scotland began to sing it until it became the thing that we sung before the matches. I can still remember the first time it was sung before an international and I realised how far it had come. I remember it being sung and thinking about Billy and how he had started all that – and it was a very powerful, emotional song that a lot of people had shared, not just Scots.

FIFTEEN

MARCH INTO HISTORY
1990

After leading the Lions to a Test series victory over Australia in 1989, Ian McGeechan returned to the Scotland squad with his mind spinning into overdrive. The key personnel in the series victory had, by and large, been English. Despite early clashes of culture between players from England and Scotland, the two dominant countries that had made up the Lions squad, McGeechan and his assistant coach, Roger Uttley, had managed to create a successful amalgam between the Scottish quick-ruck play and the thundering juggernaut of the English maul, which had allowed the Lions to take the game to the Australian forwards before unleashing the wit and guile of their fast and powerful backs.

Lessons about his charges had been learnt and McGeechan would, in due course, rack his brain for a game plan to take on the English superstars; but first there were three other games to be played, and each, as ever in the long history of the Championship, presented as difficult an assignment to overcome as any other.

Towards the end of 1988, a group of senior players had travelled down to Selkirk for a meeting with Jim Telfer to see if they could encourage him out of retirement. Iain Milne, Iain Paxton and Finlay Calder had taken it upon themselves to stir the passionate rugby flames that still burned so brightly in Telfer. They knew that if the team was to follow in the footsteps of the '84 Grand Slammers and savour the sweet taste of Championship success, then the silver haired task master, who had been there and done it all before, was the final piece of the jigsaw that they needed.

Jim Calder: I got all my caps between 1981 and 1985, whereas my twin brother, Finlay, was twenty-seven-years-old when he made his international debut against France in 1986. I think I blossomed as a player earlier than Fin because I had it in my mind from a young age that that was what I wanted to do. I remember going to watch a Scotland trial – Blues v Whites – when I was about eight-years-old and just sitting there spellbound by the whole thing. It just got into my blood and into my system at an early age that this was what I wanted to do with my life.

But it didn't hit Fin like that. He was just a different character. We had a field alongside our house and I would spend hours there kicking a ball about, while Fin would be off at my cousins' farm driving tractors and so on. That drive to succeed in rugby didn't kick in until a wee bit later. I probably didn't help because as a youngster I was always trying to keep him in his cage. I remember when we were in primary seven, we beat Leith Academy six tries to nothing. Fin had scored four and I had scored two. I was captain so I had to write down on this wee team-sheet who had scored the points to hand over to the head of rugby the next day, and on the bus home to Haddington I persuaded Fin that he had only got three tries and I had got

Opposite: David Sole marches his team into battle.

the other three. I can still see the look of confusion on his face, but he took my word for it. Even at that age I didn't want anyone to think Fin was a better player than I was, so I was gently undermining him without him realising it.

It really started to happen for Fin when he went to Melrose just after leaving school and Jim Telfer started to coach him. But he got married young and he was working while I was at university, so he had other things going on when I was making my way into the Scotland team. When he came back to Stew-Mel he was about 24 and we played him at number eight and sometimes even in the second-row because we were a closed club with limited options. He might have come through sooner if he'd decided he was going to be a seven earlier. It was Creamy [Jim Telfer], who was now involved with Scotland, who changed his thinking and said, 'You are a seven.'

A defining moment in Finlay's career was this horrible, wet, windy November evening in the mid-eighties, when we had gone out to train together. We were running round the perimeter of Riccarton campus in Edinburgh and no matter what direction we were going the wind seemed to be in our faces. About halfway round I'm thinking, 'This is really hard work but I have to keep plugging away,' so I push on a bit and get into the changing room.

Eventually Fin stumbled in and I said to him, 'You're fucking useless. It was hard for me as well, but you just gave up.' It was like a light-bulb came on above his head. He said: 'Was it? Was it really tough for you?'

We did the same run a week later, and at about the same spot he just took off, and he never looked back. It goes back to him having less confidence but it eventually dawned on him that he could do it, and Telfer gave him a bit more confidence, and all of a sudden he was captain of the Lions and this incredibly important player in a great Scotland team. Because he had pace and that in-built hardness on the pitch, he found it remarkably easy to step up once he had switched on to what he was capable of.

Finlay Calder: We had a great team coming together towards the end of the eighties and there was a steely determination throughout the squad that we wanted to be the very best that we could possibly be. But we also knew our limitations. We knew that at our best we could compete with any team in the world, but we were also aware that we lacked depth – should we lose players in certain positions to injury, we would probably begin to struggle. So we had to maximise our potential with the resources that we had. To do that, we needed to have the best drilled pack around. That meant that we needed Jim Telfer back in harness.

I asked Jim to meet with me at the Philipburn Hotel just outside Selkirk and I brought Iain Milne and Iain Paxton with me. They knew him better than anyone else in the squad and I knew that they all respected and trusted each other. It was quite a tricky meeting and I didn't actually think that Jim would come back because he was so involved with his job as the headmaster of Hawick High School. It had also been his life's work putting the '84 squad together and I wasn't sure if he wanted to commit himself to trying to do that again.

Jim Telfer: Fin and I had a very strong bond that went back many years and when he phoned and asked that I meet him and a few other players in Selkirk, there was no way that I felt that I could say no. Bob Munro, the convener of selectors, had also telephoned me and warned me about what they were coming to talk to me about, but even though I knew that they were going to ask me to come back to coach the Scotland forwards, I still hadn't made up my mind by the time I met them. I was fully committed to Hawick High School and I wasn't sure if I was willing to make any compromises with my job. But I had a very positive meeting with the director of education at the Borders Regional Council, and I eventually decided that I would give it another go – the lure of being involved again was too strong to resist.

Scotland played Australia at Murrayfield in my first game back and David Campese took us to pieces. But we were able to blood Gary Armstrong in that game and over the next few matches we also gave caps to Craig Chalmers, Chris Gray, Kenny Milne, Tony Stanger and Sean Lineen. The 1989 Five Nations was positive for us and we beat Wales and Ireland – scoring a record thirty-seven points against the Irish – and drew with England, and on the back of those performances more Scots were selected for the Lions tour to Australia than for any other tour before or since. Fin was named as captain and he was joined by David Sole, Gavin and Scott Hastings, JJ, Derek White, Craig Chalmers, Gary Armstrong and Peter Dods – and only Gary, JJ and Peter failed to play a Test match. That's a major core and they came back much improved as players.

Finlay Calder: Jim always had a fascination – some would say an obsession – with the way the All Blacks played. Scotland have not always had the personnel to emulate that style, but in 1990, just as in 1984, we had the players to do it – a big man at tight-head and seven quick and hard-working forwards. The Lions tour was seminal for all of us – training and playing with our rivals we realised, as the '83 Scottish Lions did, that the Scottish players were fitter and trained harder than anyone else.

Derek White (Scotland 1982-1992, 41 Caps plus 1 Cap for the Lions): I think the time spent on the Lions tour made a huge difference to our psyche. The six weeks we spent with the English boys dispelled some of the mystique about them. For one thing, the Scottish guys soon learned that we had by far the superior fitness and a better work ethic, too. Dean Richards used to tell Roger Uttley when the forwards had done enough training, not the other way around. There wasn't a cat's chance in hell that any of the Scottish boys would have turned around and suggested anything like that to Jim Telfer! Jim and I never saw eye to eye, but there is no doubting the discipline that he instilled in us or the improvement he made in our technical ability.

John Jeffrey: We boys in the back-row used to take a hell of a lot of stick from Jim Telfer. It was his dominion. There was no hiding from him. Luckily for Fin and me, he used to give the most flak to Derek White, but when he turned on you it wasn't a good place to be. There was one game against Ireland in 1989 when Brendan Mullan came back on a switch and cut right through the three of us. You should have heard Jim afterwards. He said that we were an embarrassment and that if we didn't sort ourselves out he could take three guys off the street and could train them to be an international back-row. If any other coach said that you would roll your eyes and say, 'whatever', but it is a mark of the man that I believe he could actually have done it.

Kenny Milne (Scotland 1989-1995, 39 Caps plus 1 Cap for the Lions): Jim Telfer's bollockings were something else. He gave Derek White a hard time, there's no doubt about that, but he used to destroy me. I'm not convinced that it was necessarily the right psychological approach to have taken with me. I might have been a better player had I been encouraged more than barracked the whole time. But Telfer's approach did work in one respect – I was determined to do everything I could to avoid giving him an excuse to bollock me, so I was focussed on perfecting every facet of my game.

Sean Lineen: The back-row used to have this whisky club and I remember one night before a fitness test up at Glenalmond when the three of them drank this bottle of whisky. The next morning we were set this shuttle running test and, as far as I'm aware, Derek White still holds the record for the lowest number of lengths. You were meant to sprint the hundred metres, have a twenty second rest and do it again. He did one, was halfway back and had to charge off into the trees to be sick.

   But they were three fantastic rugby players, and I think the whole team had a great team spirit. There were so many strong personalities in that group, and we had a hell of a lot of fun.

Jim Telfer: I was keen for Fin to continue as Scotland captain after the Lions tour, but he didn't want the job. He recommended that we give the captaincy to David Sole – which we eventually did, but not before a lot of debate as many of us wondered whether it should instead go to Gavin Hastings. David and Gavin are very different, and not just in the obvious difference between their positions on the field, but in personality. Gavin is brash and confident while David is more thoughtful and reserved. But they were both strong personalities and when David retired in 1992 it was a natural move to hand the captaincy to Gavin – which he was also given for the Lions tour to New Zealand in 1993. David led the team very well. He was quiet but strong and led from the front.

Ian McGeechan: As captain David Sole was no tub-thumper but he carried so much respect among the players that he had no need to be.

Finlay Calder: I always felt that my role as captain was just a caretaker one. I strongly believe that the man to captain any side should be the best player in the team – and for me, in 1989, it was David Sole. There was a hardness to him, an edge, and that is what you needed in the team for Scotland to compete. It was an attitude that Derek

Helped by his desperation to avoid the ire of Jim Telfer, Kenny Milne
worked tirelessly on his lineout throwing.

White, Damien Cronin, JJ and myself also had and I think that's why we did so well
despite not being as big as guys playing for teams like England and France. That edge
we brought to things definitely helped the Lions in Australia – when you combined
our attitude to fitness and the aggression we brought to the game with the skills of
guys like Guscott and the power of guys like Dean Richards and Mike Teague, it was
a potent recipe.

*Having sat out the first round of matches of the 1990 Championship, Scotland started
their campaign by scraping past Ireland 13–10 at Lansdowne Road, having been 7–0
down at half-time and 10–6 down before Derek White stole the show and the result for
the visiting team with the second of his two tries.*

Finlay Calder: We watched all the games in the Championship, but obviously it was
hard to ignore England. I remember us all sitting in the bar at Gleneagles watching
them play Ireland at Twickenham the first weekend. They started off pretty slowly in
that game but they came to life in the second half. I remember Brian Moore took a
tap penalty at one stage and went off on a big run and that seemed to spark things for
them. They went on to win 23-0. They smashed them.

It was always the same, though. You'd watch the other teams but you were always
focused on the job in hand. It was important not to get distracted, or to look too far
ahead. But a lot was being made in the media that England's fixtures mirrored those

of 1980 and that there was every chance that they would be coming north at the end of the tournament to play us in a Grand Slam game. Their Grand Slam game mind, not ours. We weren't thought of as Grand Slam contenders. Not by anybody.

Ian McGeechan: I spent a lot of time of analysis that year, probably for the first time. I'd bought a VHS player that had four heads – serious technology at the time – that allowed you to pause and get a pretty decent picture. All very basic when you look back at it now, but at the time it was revolutionary.

I was teaching full time and had a young family. Rob was eleven, Heather was six. We spent a big sum of money on that video and we didn't have a lot. I was driving an old Ford Capri that had about 120,000 miles on it. We didn't have luxuries. Judy, my wife, was studying for a degree during the day and in evening time she'd go out and serve food in the university halls of residence. I'd come home from school and she'd head out to work. And that was the difference between us being able to pay the mortgage and not. I'd put the kids to bed and then get my clipboard out and watch videos. I'd be there until one a.m. usually, studying other teams, taking notes, soaking in anything and everything.

Jim Telfer: Our first game of the Five Nations was against Ireland in Dublin. We had to go there without Ian McGeechan because he had flu, which wasn't ideal – especially as I was suddenly in charge of the team, which was not something I had prepared for at all. It wasn't a great game, but Derek White scored two tries – although one was a bit dodgy as it came from a forward pass. It's interesting that we scored from a forward pass in Ireland in '84 and that Roy Laidlaw scored a brace then too. The main difference was Sean Lineen, though. He brought a different element to our attack that had been missing before – he used to hit the line short off Craig Chalmers and run straight. Very simple, but what a difference it makes to opening up space and catching out defenders on the inside. It's just something that New Zealand-reared players do so well and so naturally – it was the same with John Leslie when he came on the scene in 1998. It was Sean's pass to Derek White that was fractionally forward and we were lucky that the referee missed it, but we deserved to score off the move purely because of the angle Sean took – a flat, tight ball off the back of the lineout that got us in behind the Irish defence and then the offload to Derek.

Tony Stanger: I grew up watching Hawick win championship after championship, and we won it again in my first year in the Hawick side; then I came into a settled Scotland side which was having an unusual amount of success; so I always had this expectation that we would win games.

I scored two tries against Fiji in my first game then three tries against Romania in my second, which was a great start – but with no disrespect to those countries you knew that at that time they were ranked much lower than Scotland in the pecking order. It was a really good way to settle into the team and get used to the pressure of international rugby, but my first game in the Five Nations was against Ireland away and it was a huge wake-up call. I was against Keith Crossan, who I have always had a huge amount of respect for as a player, his technical abilities and understanding of his job as a winger really did open my eyes. It was a different type of game as well, a lot of pressure and not so much ball. You were getting hit harder in the tackle than anything I had experienced before, you had no time to make decisions. I learned a lot in that game.

Kenny Milne: Sean Lineen and Derek White played really well out in Dublin and Chic [Craig] Chalmers' kicking saw us home, but people tend to forget the shift that Paul Burnell put in in that game. We were in real trouble at one stage in Dublin, 7–0 down and the home crowd going mad, but Paul's play – something that most people would totally miss – was instrumental to us edging past them to win.

Derek White and I had formulated a tactic to give him an edge on our attacking scrum ball. As Gary Armstrong fed the ball in, I would hook it as hard as I could so that it would fire straight through the second-row and into Derek's hands. As I say, we were struggling badly at one stage, but we held in there and managed to win a scrum close to their line. Paul Burnell got his side up just as I struck the ball hard into Derek's hands. Those fractional seconds and the angle of the scrum made all the difference. Derek was gone before the Irish back-row even knew that the ball had left Gary's hands, and Derek's acceleration took him to the line.

Derek scored, but it was really all down to Paul. The effort he put in to get his side of the scrum up was huge and without it Derek would never have made it.

Finlay Calder: I remember coming off the pitch after the game and just feeling relieved that we had managed to win – to get a result on the road is as good a start to a Championship as you can get and we had won without playing particularly well, so we knew there was more to come.

We were getting showered and changed and I remember overhearing bits and pieces of conversation about the England game in Paris. Both games were on the same day, so we'd obviously not seen any of it. But news was filtering in that something pretty special had happened out there. By the sounds of it, England had blown France out of the water. At the Parc des Princes, that didn't happen very often. To anybody.

I remember thinking that the French game the following week was going to be huge for us – even bigger than it would have already been. The French would be hurting after losing like that in Paris. They would come out all guns blazing – either to run us off the park or to batter the hell out of us. But I also knew that they would either bounce back in sensational fashion, or they would be damaged mentally. If we could keep in the game, or even dominate it, then they could crumble.

Kenny Milne: I could have ruined that season for myself after the Ireland game. I went a bit mad at the post-match meal and was downing glasses of wine. Loads of them. I ended up being sick at the table. I was in a terrible state and then Willie

Finlay Calder races away with the ball against Ireland.

Anderson, the Irish captain, got up to make his speech and he started by saying, 'Isn't it nice to see Kenny looking so well,' and everybody turned around to look at me. I could feel Creamy's eyes burning a hole through me. So I went up to him afterwards and I said, 'Jim, honestly, it's not my fault, the lads know I'm allergic to wine and they're making me drink it.'

Later on, one of the boys heard him saying, 'Kenny's not drunk, he's got an allergy to wine.' I still don't know how I fooled him. It was the first and last time it ever happened. If he'd known the truth he would have dropped me – and I don't think I would have ever got over that.

I hated Creamy at times. The way he belittled you, I didn't think it was necessary. He destroyed my confidence. Don't get me wrong, he was a fantastic coach and I have absolute respect for him, but he could have got more out of me had he handled me differently. We had a strange relationship. He could destroy me, but we also always had a bit of banter as well. I remember we had a move called 'JJ Watsonian' which worked off the back of a scrum and involved JJ, Gary and Gavin. In the week before the France game Jim said that we had to rename the move because it came out clearly on the TV during the Ireland game. I said, 'Simple: we're playing France so we'll just rename it *Jé Jé Watsonian*.' I got a good clout over the head from Jim for that one.

Gavin Hastings: We knew the French would come at us hammer and tongs. They had been humiliated by England in Paris and they then had to endure two weeks of flak from the press and, no doubt, every man, woman and child on the streets. They would have been given an ear-full by their coach, Jacques Fouroux, and beasted in training. They made something like ten changes to the team, including dropping their captain, Pierre Berbizier. They made Laurent Rodriguez captain – and that was intention enough for us; he was known as the Dax Bull and he was a madman. They filled the pack with monstrous specimens, and they picked Alain Carminati on the openside flank. He was only twenty-three and didn't have that many caps, but he played like a veteran in that team. He was a huge man – six foot five, around sixteen or seventeen stone. In the amateur era, that was like a lorry. And he was hard.

Derek White: We played against him on the summer tour to France in 1986 when he was only nineteen, but even then he was a headcase. Not many players are regarded as hard men in the French league when they're only nineteen, but Alain Carminati was. So when we saw that he'd been picked, we knew what kind of gameplan the French were coming with. I remember saying to JJ, 'You watch, he's going to do somebody, he's dangerous.' And that's exactly what happened.

John Jeffrey: We had a poor first half. We had a strong wind at our backs but we didn't make proper use of it. We went in 3-0 up at half-time, but it was at least a ten-point wind. It was disappointing to say the least. But then we came out for the second half and they kicked off to us. Gavin punted the ball back – and it went about sixty metres. The wind had changed. Unbelievable. You could see the French players thinking, 'Oh, for fuck's sake.'

So they were pretty pissed off at that stage. There was a ruck shortly afterwards and, as often happened, I found myself tangled up at the bottom. Just to be a bit of nuisance, as I liked to do, I grabbed hold of a French leg, to hold whoever it was in. In retrospect, that was an error. I looked up and saw that it was Carminati. Oops.

Finlay Calder: Carminati did what we all longed to do and kicked JJ in the head. It happened a few minutes into the second-half and we were only three points to the good at the time. It was a decisive moment. We had been dominating much of the game but hadn't converted that dominance into points but when Carminati was sent off by Fred Howard you could see their heads dropping and that was when we stepped up a gear. It was exactly as I had thought – they were fragile and it just needed something to crack them. Carminati getting sent off was the trigger. They were ghosts after that.

We peppered Blanco with kicks all afternoon and he had a fairly torrid time of it. When they went down to fourteen men they really began to be stretched and we started to run them ragged. Our defence was strong and we controlled the ball well in the elements and I felt that we were comfortable all the way through. It ended 21-0. Good, next.

Kenny Milne: We headed down to Cardiff for our third game and I remember thinking that we were going to be on the receiving end of a serious backlash. Wales had been thumped 34–6 at Twickenham and in the aftermath of that game their coach, John Ryan, had quit. He was replaced by Ron Waldron who was the head coach at Neath, who were a super side. Neath were quite like us – they played a fast, loose game with athletic forwards, so it was set up to be a really fast-paced game.

Finlay Calder: But they left out the key ingredient. As Jim Telfer knew from his studies of the All Blacks, to be able to get away with a fairly light forward pack, you need to have one or two immovable cornerstones. We had Paul Burnell at tight-head and Damien Cronin at lock. Waldron went light-weight all the way through his pack and Brian Williams, his loose-head, was only a shade under fourteen stone and he was completely gobbled up by Paul. We destroyed them in the scrums and it was a bit disappointing that we didn't translate that dominance on the scoreboard. Del Boy [Cronin] scored a try and Chic kicked three penalties – it was tight, but Cardiff has always been a hard place for Scotland to go and win so there were no complaints.

Gavin Hastings: It was a strange year. We went over to Dublin first up and sneaked a win, then came back to Scotland and beat a fourteen man France fairly handsomely, then went to Wales and won. So we weren't playing particularly great rugby, but we were winning our games and all of a sudden we were going into the last weekend with three wins and a real chance of a Grand Slam. It just kind of crept up on us.

And so it came down to one game. Winner takes all. Now McGeechan and Telfer, with their assistants Dougie Morgan and Derrick Grant, had to find a way to stop the English players that McGeechan had cherished so dearly in Australia just a few months before; they had to find a way to counter the awesome power of Mike Teague, Wade Dooley and Paul Ackford, the ferocious competitiveness of Brian Moore, the calm control of Rob Andrew, the sublime genius of Jeremy Guscott, and the scorching speed of Rory Underwood.

The back-row of Teague, Peter Winterbottom and Mick 'the Munch' Skinner growled with muscle and menace. In the front-row, Moore packed down with two of the most powerful scrummagers ever to wear the red rose – Jeff Probyn and Paul 'the Judge' Rendall. Behind them Dooley and Ackford had been imperious in the lineout, freeing the electric English backs to tear through the opposition ranks at will. The power, control and relentless attacking play of the 1990 England team had swept all before them in the Championship. Guscott and Will Carling had been at the epicentre, Underwood the arch-finisher with four touchdowns. The team had scored eleven tries and conceded only two. Scotland had scored five and also only conceded two but in none of their victories had they displayed the dominance that England had shown in the previous rounds. Carling's men had had Irish eyes weeping with a 23–0 demolition at Twickenham; they had sacked the proud bastion of the Parc des Princes, hammering the French 26–7; and had doused the fire of the Welsh dragon 34–6 at Twickenham. All that was left were the Scots. Bloody-minded, certainly, and with a back-row that could bend the letters of the law to breaking point, but ultimately lucky to have found themselves in a Grand Slam play-off. The Championship, the Triple Crown, the Calcutta Cup and the Grand Slam were England's for the taking. Surely nothing could stand in the way of their destiny.

Ian McGeechan: In the lead-up we deliberately kept things low key – it was important that we didn't give the English players anything to feed off; instead we let them talk up their Grand Slam hopes and used that ourselves to fire up our players. For Jim, Derrick, Dougie and me, the game really lasted two weeks. I spent a lot of time on video analysis before the game. From that I was able to get a feel for the way England played and I studied the patterns of their game. I could see that they blew teams away early on. They dominated physically and their lineout was superb – from that dominance they were able to get the ball out to Carling and Guscott in the midfield, backed up by the back-row. I would stay up until one or two in the morning trying to work out a way to beat them. In the end it was a cold, calculated strategy mapped out on A4 paper then filed in plastic folders and labelled, then boxed and labelled again.

Craig Chalmers: England were a fantastic team and had sailed through the previous games in the Championship, scoring lots of tries, and we had struggled through our games to get the wins, so we were massive underdogs. But we still believed we could win. That squad of players was the most competitive group I was ever involved in. They'd fight for anything, whether it was pool, tiddlywinks, snooker, whatever, these guys wanted to win. I always remember we would play Hawick Ball the Friday before each game, backs v forwards, and it was a battle. The guys were ready to knock each other out just to win those games. And I think that competitiveness showed up in all our games, from '89, '90, all the way through to '92. It was a real good side.

Gavin Hastings: I think a big thing that helped was that in the old Five Nations, there was always one country that had to sit out a round of matches and the way it worked out, England had sat out the penultimate round and so hadn't played for a month. They had had to sit around waiting to come up to play for the Grand Slam. And it was only after we had scraped past Wales in Cardiff that we realised we were in the same position. Jim Telfer took us aside and said, 'Right, I don't want any of you saying a word to the press about this.' We just sat back and let Will [Carling] and the rest of their team soak up the attention.

Jim Telfer: The fact that England were coming up as overwhelming favourites really didn't bother us too much because we had an inner strength, we had a lot of leaders – men who you would go to war with and expect to do well. History showed that England were right to be favourites – they usually won, whether it was at Twickenham or at Murrayfield. And they had been absolutely superb that season, so we knew all the plaudits would be going their way and the talk would all be about them coming up to take a sensational Grand Slam, as they had done in 1980.

Gavin Hastings: Yeah, that sums it up perfectly. It was a conscious decision not to speak to the press and to let the English guys do all the talking. Let them take the focus and attention, we'll just get ready quietly, under the radar, then let them see if they can handle us. It never crossed my mind that we were going to lose that game. I was totally comfortable with our ability. We hadn't played particularly well up to that point so we were due a big performance.

It was a massive rugby occasion for both countries, but the atmosphere was ramped up to near incendiary levels by the national press, fueled in a large part by the furious resentment and opposition across Scotland to Margaret Thatcher's Poll Tax experiment.

England's rugby team, and their captain Will Carling in particular, were portrayed as Thatcher's representatives on the sporting field. Which was a ridiculous thing to tarnish them with, especially as members of the England team, such as hooker Brian Moore, were as vocally opposed to the poll tax as the Scots themselves. But the press and the public lapped up the ill-feeling as the match approached and everything from Bannockburn to Flodden was trotted out as the home team prepared to welcome the English to Murrayfield.

Brian Moore (England hooker): Half of England hated Thatcher and most of Scotland despised her. I understood why we were hated. I got it. There's always an anti-Englishness in Scotland but this was of a more virulent strain. Thatcher was desperately unpopular for a variety of reasons, not least because of the poll tax. She used the Scots like they were experimental rats. That's how it looked anyway. That's how it felt to the people and they hated her for it and we were English and so came along with that. And you could feel all of that in the atmosphere. You could. They saw us as Thatcher's team. We drove straight into something powerful.

If you're faced with the barrage of abuse we got, what are you going to do? You're going to bridle, aren't you? What sort of person is going to say, 'I'm an English bastard, am I? Oh right, thanks for that'. No, you say, 'Well, fuck you, pal'. That sort of atmosphere wasn't in Ireland or France and it wasn't even in Wales – and it was hardly pleasant down there. Because of all the things going on at the time in Scotland, the atmosphere was nasty. It was nasty and hard. Fair play, if I was a Scot in that climate I'd have been the same. Hatred is not the wrong word. Not on that day. It wouldn't have gone into physical violence, but it was total enmity.

Tony Stanger: From a personal point of view, that game was about rugby, it was about beating the fifteen men out there on the pitch, not the whole nation or avenging something that happened hundreds of years ago or about the poll tax – it wasn't a grudge match. The downside of the media sometimes is looking for the sensational angle and reading something into a situation which quite simply doesn't exist.

Will Carling (England centre): Up until then we were really only getting a taste of the anti-English feeling through the media. Now it was in our faces. If you'd told me a week before that I'd have Margaret Thatcher, the poll tax, Butcher Cumberland and Bannockburn thrown at me, I'd have told you that you were on drugs. Butcher Cumberland? I'm not sure I'd even heard of him. They said I was Thatcher's captain.

The Scottish media stuck that label on me and everybody bought it. People just assumed things about me that were wrong. Most of my teammates didn't really know what was going on in my head so I don't know how the Scots thought they did. Thatcher's blue-eyed boy? Bloody stupid.

John Jeffrey: From a players' point of view, I don't think the poll tax question or the political disruptions in Scotland as a result had a big bearing on the match itself because none of us in the team were that politically aware. The press used it as another mechanism to wind up the English and to get the crowds going. I felt that there was more pressure coming from the cancelation of the annual England-Scotland football match, which was the one time every year that Scotland got to go down and do a Bannockburn again and send England backwards. And I used to love that. And then that was cancelled and all of a sudden there was a vacuum, there was a void for all the Scots people to have a go at England. And because we had a fairly successful rugby team at the time, everyone basically just jumped on the bandwagon of the rugby. So I think there was a wee bit more of that than the political hype.

Tony Stanger: The beauty of it was that it was a winner-takes-all situation, and the way England were playing made them the overwhelming favourites. While we naturally didn't like that because they were coming up to our patch, we also acknowledged they had played great rugby that season and scored some fantastic tries. So we knew we were going to have to go some to beat them – but we felt we were capable of causing an upset.

There was a lot of hype in the media about the match being nothing more than a formality for England, and we heard stories about them ordering t-shirts with 'Grand Slam Champions' printed on the front, but you never know if that was true.

Kenny Milne: We were sitting in the changing room after training one afternoon and Jim Telfer sat us all down. He said that we had to prepare ourselves as best we could before the England game, that there would be no drinking and that we had to do all we could to ready ourselves for the challenge that lay ahead. 'This is a once in a lifetime opportunity,' he said. 'We're playing for the Calcutta Cup, the Triple Crown, the Championship and the Grand Slam.'

'Well,' I said, 'we're bound to win one of them.' I thought Creamy was going to take my head off for that one, but he saw the funny side. I think.

Jim Telfer: The media attention was incredible in those final few days before the match – there were headlines everywhere, even in the tabloids, which was a rare thing for rugby coverage at the time, and the build-up was all over the radio and on the TV. It was a huge moment for Scotland to be in that position again and there was a level of expectation higher than ever before because of what had happened in 1984. And the English media were all over it as well, although in a slightly more arrogant way. They had played some incredible rugby that year and when they had won their last

Grand Slam in 1980, Bill Beaumont had led them up to Edinburgh and skelped us with five tries to seal the Championship. The English newspapers had a carbon copy of the scenario all mapped out. And the key that day was that their players believed the same thing. They thought that all they had to do was show up, bully us off the park and let their backs run riot.

Kenny Milne: The forward sessions were brutal all season and there was no let up the week of the game, either. Creamy absolutely beasted us. I remember one scrum and rucking session on the Wednesday before, in driving rain and a howling gale. It was horrendous. But it made you tough. And we were pretty used to it by then, we'd been training like that ever since Jim had come back.

Sean Lineen: There was a brilliant team talk by Geech on the morning of the game, but I think the guys knew all week that we were going to win it.

Ian McGeechan: Yeah, that was emotional. I talked about how they would be playing not just for the fans who were in the stadium and not just for those who were watching the game around the country; they were also playing for all those Scots throughout the world whose lives had taken them away from the land of their birth and for whom the blue jersey still meant so much – because the jersey was a symbol of their home and their roots and who they were and to win would make them prouder than anyone else in Scotland. I was thinking about my dad when I said that because his heart had always been in Scotland.

David Sole: Creamy had spoken and so had Geech and now, as the time was closing in, it was my turn. I couldn't match Geech's emotion from the hotel, but I said we were about to experience something out there on the field that would never happen again. 'Boys, no matter what happens in the next eighty minutes, life will still go on, but this afternoon we have a chance to make history. Let's go out and grab it. Let's enjoy it, but let's go and win this game.'

Jim Telfer: I could hardly hear him. I felt like saying, 'David, speak up!' But it wasn't my place. The time comes when you just have to retreat, when you have to accept that there is nothing more you can do. That was the time. The players were on their own. It was up to them now.

David Sole: From the moment England beat Wales all the build-up had been about the fact that they were going to pick up their first Grand Slam in ten years. It become a bit irritating that it was apparently a foregone conclusion. Nobody was writing or talking about us, it was all about England, so I was determined that we would make a statement early on that if they wanted their Grand Slam then they were going to have to get past us first, and during the build-up to the game I put quite a bit of thought into what we could do to show that we were playing for the big prize as well.

We had a training session on the Wednesday before the match, which went incredibly well . . . everyone was so fired up. Afterwards I got a few of the guys together and said I had this idea about making a statement of intent, and Fin said he was against it because he remembered walking out at Sydney Football Stadium for the first Test against Australia on the 1989 Lions tour and getting absolutely stuffed. Big Gav piped up that he thought it was a great idea, and that we should have a piper leading us out, and all wear kilts which we'd whip off Bucks Fizz style.

And Fin said, 'Where are we going to put our claymores?'

To which Gavin replied, 'Now you're just being stupid.'

So I bounced it around some more of the guys and the general consensus was that it wasn't a bad idea, and then, in the last few minutes before the game when I was making my final pitch to the players, I basically said, 'We're walking out there and we're not going to hold back: this is our time.' It was something a bit different.

A lot of us knew the English players very, very well, because we had been on the Lions tour the previous summer. That had been a squad which had fought its way through some pretty tough moments – we were stuffed in the first Test, we were 18–4 down in the midweek game against ACT, and we had to dig really deep to turn things around. It had brought us together as a group and when you go through those sorts of things with those sorts of players there is a huge amount of respect and affinity there. But, on the other hand you hit your friends the hardest. Sure we respected them, but we wanted to get one over on them because if we didn't they would get one over on us.

Bill McLaren (in commentary): *And welcome to the commentary box at Murrayfield. You'll have already have sensed the quite unique atmosphere here in the heart of Edinburgh, on what is a quite unique occasion – the first time in the history of rugby union that two Home Countries have met head-on for the Grand Slam. They've played internationals here at Murrayfield since 1925, but in all the intervening time, I don't think Murrayfield has ever buzzed with the same air of feverish anticipation as at this very moment, as one of the great sporting occasions is about to unfold.*

The ground, as you can see, is simply packed with its capacity crowd of 54,000 – that includes fifty from Glenbuchat up in Aberdeenshire, where David Sole's family home is, fifty of them down to cheer on the Scottish captain today in this crucial match; graced by the presence of her Royal Highness the Princess Royal, and blessed – well, almost – with right royal weather. I say almost because there is a stiff wind blowing and the sun has disappeared, but the ground is in great condition.

And here, Will Carling leads on the England side, with their tremendous record of having scored eleven tries to two in the Championship so far in their three matches.

And some great cheering, and some good natured booing as well, as England take the field.

And now the Scottish team, led there by David Sole, with Ken Milne just behind him. You notice how tense they all are. They've waited for this moment a long time.

Gavin Hastings: In the years that followed, I spoke often to the England players – and they all said that as they watched us marching out that they had a sudden sense of foreboding, that we had stolen an advantage on them before the match had started.

Will Carling: I had brought the guys into a huddle and I was talking to them, so we didn't see their famous walk. I heard the reaction to it, though. Jesus, did I hear it.

David Sole: For us, it was the equivalent of doing the Haka. It was a message of intent.

Will Carling: It was something we had to learn, how much other teams like Wales and Scotland wanted to beat us – and how much it meant to them to do so, and to then have the right kind of emotion back at them. But there's no doubt it took us by surprise when they marched out like that. I just remember thinking, 'Bloody hell, they look up for this.'

Scott Hastings: The reaction of the crowd was just unbelievable. I don't think there had been an atmosphere like it before at Murrayfield. To be in the middle of it was so stirring. Just talking about it now, you realise the emotion that was wrapped up in it and that it meant so much to so many people.

Jeremy Guscott (England centre): Scott Hastings was like a zombie. He wasn't there. He was away at the races, gone from the emotion and the history of it all. After they came out I was looking for the players that I'd toured with eight months earlier with the Lions – and there was no recognition from any of them.

Bill McLaren (in commentary): *Listen to the acclaim for them! Well, I've never known support quite like that for the Scottish team. They're still clapping and cheering.*

Gavin Hastings: It was an amazing thing to walk down the tunnel. You came out and suddenly you could see the vast terrace of East Stand and the noise was startling, just this huge, huge noise. And you still had another thirty or forty yards to go, and all these thoughts go through your head as to what the next eighty minutes are going to hold. Were we going to do it? Were we going to be good enough to win the Grand Slam?

Ian McGeechan: The famous walk out was done so the home support would understand we were there for real; that it was our Grand Slam as well. And when the team walked out, that was exactly the message that was delivered. The noise of the crowd shook the whole ground.

Tony Stanger: I think everyone was pretty honest with themselves, saying we could win the game, but it wasn't until that walk onto the pitch that we realised just how big an opportunity it was. I didn't know we were going to walk out until just before it happened. It had obviously been discussed at some level, but it wasn't something that I needed to know about until it was happening. Normally everyone fired out of the tunnel at a hundred miles an hour because they were bursting to get going – so this was completely different and it could have gone either way. And fortunately for us it just set the whole thing up, it hooked into the mood of the crowd: hopeful rather than expectant. But the reaction of the crowd did catch me out, then we had the anthems which calmed us down but there was the same sort euphoria for the kick-off – and then we were into it. Everything remotely positive, be it a Scottish tackle or an English knock-on, was met with this huge surge from the crowd. I think every player would agree that a crucial component of the success we achieved that day was the passion of the crowd.

Sean Lineen: When we walked out the noise was unbelievable. It was real lump in the throat stuff. And when the crowd sang *Flower of Scotland* – well, that was just frightening. Crowds are not that great in modern day rugby. There are moments, but I think people expect more from professionals and there isn't that same blind devotion. The crowd can be the sixteenth man, and in Scotland, in games like that, we really need to have that sixteenth man on our side all the time.

Bill McLaren (in commentary): *England have given a vote of confidence to the fifteen that beat Wales 34-6, and only Simon Halliday and Mike Teague haven't played in all the Championship games. Those three-quarters [in the England backline] have claimed thirty-two international tries; Rob Andrew and Richard Hill have gelled into a singularly effective hinge; and that mighty pack will be hoping to lay the foundations for Will Carling to become England's third post-War Grand Slam captain.*

Finlay Calder: I knew so many of the English boys so well after the Lions tour and they were just a fantastic bunch of players. Jerry Guscott was just effortlessly brilliant, Underwood had speed that defied belief and the pack were all enormous – except for Brian Moore. But what Brian lacked physically, he made up for mentally. I'm so glad that people now see in Brian Moore the man which I have known all this time. He's an extraordinary human being. I've never seen a man as driven about anything and everything in my life. He's just a compulsive winner. We're a funny nation because if he was Scottish we would have been so proud of him, but because he wore an English jersey he became this figure of hate. He had a lot of Scottish traits – not particularly big, thrawn, bad tempered and with this phenomenal desire to win. With the Lions I quickly recognised that this guy knew a lot more about rugby than me, so I put him in charge of the forwards and he revelled in the role, because it was recognition for him, and he had the respect of his peers.

The contact in international rugby is unbelievable. It's like a cartoon, you see stars, and to think clearly through all that muddle takes some doing – but a few guys have the ability to do that, and Brian is one of them. And England didn't need Brian to be big because, as I say, every other player in their pack was a monster. They had cruised through the Championship, dominating everyone physically and then whipping the ball out to those electric and clever backs. What a team.

Brian Moore: Their pack, right. David Sole: great ball carrier, not a great scrummager, was going to be targeted in the scrum. Kenny Milne: different story. Strong, good technician; I knew I was gonna have a battle there. Paul Burnell: journeyman, made the most of what he had, which wasn't a lot. Chris Gray: tremendous competitor, but not the biggest. Damian Cronin: great bloke, but not the fittest. JJ: a fucking nuisance. Finlay Calder: a mate and an icon, but actually a very limited openside, not the greatest of hands, not that quick, but for fearlessness and sheer bloody-mindedness, there's nobody like him. And Derek White: ball-player. It was a good pack, but we were better.

Kenny Milne: Some of the boys didn't like Mooro. I thought he was okay. A bit gobby, but fine. It was all an act with him.

John Jeffrey: Me and Mooro, we were quite similar. If you're going to be the bad guy you may as well be the real villain, there's a certain honour in that. Brian took it as a compliment, and so did I. What would you call him? An aggravating little bastard. First boy you'd want in your team, though.

Bill McLaren (in commentary): *For the first time ever, Scotland field the same fifteen for all four games in a Five Nations Championship, which means the back division are together for the fifth time, the entire pack for the eighth time. They face a searching examination in set-piece play. Behind them the key figures will be Craig Chalmers and Gavin Hastings. The eight British Lions include that experienced loose-forward trio [of Jeffrey, Calder and White] with seventeen international tries between them, and David Sole is the captain for the sixth time.*

John Jeffrey: 1990 was the first season that we had *Flower of Scotland* as our official anthem. For years we'd been asking to have our own national anthem. Not that we were against singing *God Save the Queen* as such, we're British and I have no problem at all with it, but when you're playing England and their anthem is *God Save the Queen*, you wanted something of your own, something that could give you a bit of an edge.

Jim Telfer: I know there's debate as to whether we should sing it or not, but it made the hairs on the back of my neck stand up when I heard it. It still does.

Bill McLaren (in commentary): *Well I've never heard such an emotional rendering of* Flower of Scotland *as we've just heard.*

Ian McGeechan: I knew that if we could keep the ball away from England and keep it in play that we could nullify their efforts to establish those early patterns of play; and we did it – in the first fifteen minutes of the game, England didn't touch the ball. The video analysis meant that we knew how England would play and we just had to be there first, knocking them backwards at every phase of play. There was a system but they never assumed we might have thought things out and planned how we were going to play, so they all claimed that it was just chaos – but it was organised, planned out meticulously and then executed by the players.

Derek White: Mike Teague tells a story about Mick Skinner in the build-up to that game. He had been swanning around all week telling everyone in the team, in the management, in the press, just how easy it was going to be – they were going to stroll to the Grand Slam. They were the best English team yet.

The game was only minutes old when Fin took a quick tap and launched himself into the heart of the English pack. He was met by a big hit from Skinner, but Fin kept his feet, kept pumping his legs and moments later the rest of our pack were in behind him, powering on through Skinner and the rest of the English forwards. We won a penalty and as Skinner was getting to his feet, his shirt covered in stud marks, Teague turned to him and said, 'Still think this is going to be easy?'

Jim Telfer: Finlay, what a bloke, that was the moment for me. Our boys had worked like beasts on the training ground and me screaming at them all the while, 'Get lower, get tighter!' When they did it on the day it was precision, it was textbook. England were driven back and the crowd went wilder than I had ever heard them before. And I felt a shiver. All these years later I can close my eyes and still see it. A piece of perfection you dream about.

Tony Stanger: The game plan at that time did not involve a huge amount of rugby being played, it was about kicking and putting them under pressure, and I suppose that febrile atmosphere suited our style of game.

John Jeffrey: There was – and has been ever since – a lot made about how Fin and I used to spend our lives offside on a rugby pitch. The English boys made a lot of noise about it during the build-up to the game and Carling was moaning about it throughout the match. Maybe they were right, but the way I see it, the laws of the game are fairly flexible. You push it to the limit until you're caught – and the ref can only penalise you if he sees you. In many ways I think it was a more honest time – you put your body on the line to slow up the ball or to try and pinch or disrupt it and in turn you go your dues for doing so from the boots of the opposition pack. But I knew what I was doing out there and I deserved the shoeing. It was all part and parcel of the game.

Gavin Hastings: The whole crowd erupted when Fin took the ball in and the forwards crashed in behind him to win that penalty, and it set the tone that we weren't going to lie down to the English. And every single decision that went Scotland's way was cheered to the rafters. That's what I remember most about it – we were cheered with every positive passage of play. We got two early penalties that Chic kicked to put us 6-0 up, but then England struck back with the kind of attack they'd been showing all season.

Assisted by Gavin Hastings, Craig Chalmers lines up a kick for goal.

Bill McLaren (in commentary): *Teague holding it in [at the back of the scrum] for England on halfway. Teague picks and goes. Tackled by Calder. Hill . . . lovely break, Carling is away, there's a marvellous overlap here . . . out to Guscott . . . Guscott has dummied and is going . . . and Guscott has scored! That is a magnificent English try. Jeremy Guscott's seventh try for England in just six internationals – and it was a beauty.*

Scott Hastings: I've often said that enthusiasm can win matches but it can also lose you games, and I was completely sucked in for that try. I was completely pumped up with adrenalin and looking for a big hit, but in doing so I got pulled out of position that allowed Will Carling to slide off Richard Hill's pass and step around me and into space. Sean Lineen screamed at me; he couldn't believe I'd made such a basic error. And it was Jeremy Guscott who took the ball in and scored – it was a superbly worked try, but it was my mistake and I knew it was. But nobody pointed the finger at me because they didn't need to; I knew I'd done wrong. All we talked about under the posts was what we had to do next to get ourselves back into position in their half. But soon enough we were under pressure on our own line again.

Bill McLaren (in commentary): *It's a penalty for offside. And England have opted for a scrummage. Now there's an interesting development. They could have taken the penalty, but they've gone for the scrummage.*

But Scotland have got a bit of a shove on there! And Craig Chalmers has hoofed it clear.

Tony Stanger: People made the connection afterwards between them not kicking penalties and that being a sign of over-confidence, but I don't buy that. They made the call on the pitch and there is nothing wrong with being confident in your own ability.

Kenny Milne: The English forwards were massive; I mean real man-mountains. And they loved to scrummage. The pressure and weight that came on in every scrum was just phenomenal, it felt as if your eyes were going to burst from the sockets, that you were going to rupture every vein in your body. Every time we went in Jeff Probyn would be boring in on me so that I couldn't hook, or piling so much pressure down on Soley that I couldn't see the ball coming in. Every scrum was a fight for survival and Soley was really struggling. I was quite big for a hooker in those days, so Paul Burnell and I worked to take as much pressure as we could off Soley. I would focus on scrummaging against Probyn with Soley, leaving Paul to take on the Judge and Mooro. But for all our efforts we were starting to give away one free kick or penalty per scrum and this was still only in the first quarter of the match, when we were at our freshest. We knew that if we crumbled up front, that would be it. Every set-piece was a challenge both physically and psychologically. If one broke, so would the other, and the game would be gone.

David held in there. Just. Everyone remembers Stanger's try, Gavin and Chic Chalmers kicking, the back-row, Scotty Hastings' tackle on Underwood. No one remembers the shift that the front-row put in, but for me, that was the key.

Will Carling: People talk about not going for goal being the turning point. The abuse I got for that. Fucking hell. Not being funny, but bollocks. We should have had a penalty try but, okay, we never got it. My view is, it's far out on the right hand side, it's a hard kick, so keep ploughing on in the scrum. That was a lesson for me because I asked the wrong guys. I asked Mooro, who loses all rational thought from about Thursday. 'Can we shove them back, Mooro?'

'Course I fucking can, course I fucking can'.

Wade Dooley (England second-row): People say we were cheated. No. You do what you have to do. If Sole collapses the scrum two yards out on six occasions and gets away with it, all credit to Sole. It's up to me and Probyn to keep him up. Sole survived. That's what you do. You try and survive, by any means necessary.

Craig Chalmers: Surviving those scums was a massive confidence booster for us. We had to do all we could to keep them out at that stage and we did that. All these little things helped to build up our confidence that this was going to be our day. We won a scrum from that hack on, up around the half-way mark, and then we were back in business. We got a penalty a minute or two later and I was able to knock it over from about forty-five yards, on the angle.

Bill McLaren (in commentary): *Chalmers then. . .. Oh, he's done it once more! I mean it looked so inebriated as it went over, you would have thought it would have keeled over. But he's done it. Three penalty goals for Craig Chalmers, Scotland 9-4 ahead and the crowd are delighted.*

Finlay Calder: The crucial error England made was that Dean Richards was fit bit not selected. At that point we began to think we had a chance. People don't realise how strong he was. He had calves like I had never seen in either a professional or an amateur. If he'd had a bad temper then he would have been a real bad man, but he didn't have that edge to him. I used to always reckon that if Dean Richards was playing and Rob Andrew was playing then we had no chance. If it was one or the other we had a half chance, but both of them could strangle the game in their own way – Dean with his strength, Rob with his right boot.

But they didn't pick Dean, they went for Mike Teague at number eight instead. Mike was a wonderful player, as hard as they come and had been voted man of the series for the Lions, but he wasn't a number eight. We knew that. But more importantly, Mike knew that too. The technical aspect of playing number eight detracted from what he was so very good at – which was pulverising the opposition in the tackle and taking the ball at pace from a playmaker, not picking from the back of a scrum and implementing play himself.

Dean would have been a different story at eight. He would have strangled the life out of us, as he did several times over the following years.

When we scored our try it was from an error at the back of the England scrum by Teague. I don't think Dean would have made that mistake. The ball was turned over and we were handed a golden opportunity to attack off the resultant scrum.

Tony Stanger: I didn't play well against Wales and I went through serious hell thinking that I would be dropped for the Grand Slam game. I wanted to try and get myself back on track, so I made myself available for Hawick for a big game against Stewart's Melville. It seemed a good idea at the time to get back up on the horse, but Alex Brewster landed on me during the match and my collar bone shot out. I had been selected again for the Scotland team, but now there was a chance that I might miss the game because of the injury rather than my form during the Wales match. They called in Roger Baird as cover – so he nearly got two Grand Slams to his name – and put me through the mill with some contact work to see if the shoulder was OK. It was pretty painful but I tried to hide how sore it was when I was hitting rucking shields and tackle bags – and then Ian McGeechan made me do some live tackling on Dougie Morgan. It was painful but it didn't restrict me too much, so I was cleared to play. The next day, of course, I woke up and my shoulder was agony. It was OK so long as I didn't have to put my hands above my head. And I just figured, what are the chances that I'm going to have to do that . . .

Gary Armstrong (Scotland 1988-1999, 51 Caps): That turnover from Mike Teague's knock-on set us up in a cracking part of the field to launch an attack from first phase – slightly to the right of the posts, around forty yards out from the try line. A position like that gives you plenty of room to attack on either side of the scrum and as a result it puts doubt in the mind of the defending players – they don't know if you're going to whip around one side or the other, flood the blindside or move the ball open.

We had called a move earlier in the game when I would get the ball from the back of the scrum, carry it forward to commit the English back-row and then release Gav as he came into the line from fullback. When we ran it, I passed the ball to Gav too early and didn't commit the back-row at all so they just smashed him. One of the things I remember most about that match is the bollocking I got from Gav for that.

When we got that turnover ball and the scrum was ours, we called the move again. I took the pass from JJ, who was playing at number eight after Derek White had gone off injured, and took off. I could sense Gav coming up on my outside and could see Mike Teague and Rob Andrew covering across. I knew that I had to hold on, hold on, hold on . . . and just as they had to check to tackle me I passed. It wasn't the best pass I've ever given and Gav did well to catch it. That piece of skill he showed to juggle the ball, fix Rory Underwood and then put in a chip kick as he was ushered into touch was class.

Tony Stanger: Without it ever being discussed, I think everyone appreciated that the next score was going to be crucial. It was absolutely on a knife edge. And the timing could not have been better for us, or worse for England. We started the second-half but our kick-off didn't go ten which gave England a scrum on the halfway – but they knocked on at the base which gave us the chance to have a go – and the rest, as they say, is history.

It was a planned moved which we had worked on a lot which we called 'Fiji', and the kick at the end was always an option. It just so happened that Gav came across in front of me towards the touchline and his chip forward was inch perfect.

Once the play is in motion you act instinctively, then you jump around a bit excitedly, then you realise you have thirty-five minutes to knuckle down and hold onto the game. It can't have been much of a spectacle as a rugby match, with us hanging in there, tackling and tackling, but when there is that much at stake the excitement can be all consuming.

Gavin Hastings: You only ever see Tony Stanger's famous try in that match from the movement of the scrum, so people forget that it came about right at the start of the second-half after I kicked off and the ball went straight into touch – just like it had on my debut against France. We came back, scrummed at halfway and Mike Teague knocked it on at the base, so we were given the put-in and we scored from that.

It was a set move called 'Fiji' which we had worked on for years in practise, and there it was – it just worked. I was bundled into touch after putting in the kick ahead, so I didn't ever see Tony touch it down – and of course some people still argue that he didn't touch it down at all. You wonder in these days of television replays whether it would have been given, but it would have taken a brave man to disallow that score.

Tony Stanger celebrates his try with Chris Gray.

Tony Stanger: It was definitely a try. I remember being given a try against Australia in 1996 when I was tackled over the touchline and didn't get the ball down but the referee gave the score. I was very aware at the time that it shouldn't have been a score, so you instinctively know when a try should be given and when it shouldn't – and I instinctively knew at the time that it was definitely a try.

I'll never complain about people wanting to talk to me about that moment. I remember Brian Hegarty dropped a ball in 1978 and Gallion scored the try which gave France victory at Murrayfield. He was playing out of position on the wing, but nobody at Mansfield Park ever let him forget it. It was a shame, because he was a great player for Hawick, he worked hard and played four times for Scotland that year, but that is the incident which will always be attached to him. So I'm not going to complain about scoring the try which won the Grand Slam always being attached to me. It is a very positive thing to be associated with. I still get people coming up to speak to me about that match now – and it is amazing the number of people who tell me they were at the game, I'd never have thought Murrayfield could hold that sort of capacity. I think almost every rugby supporter in Scotland was there, and a few more. As a player, nothing else has come close to that sort of atmosphere.

Finlay Calder: We had the element of surprise, we had the home advantage and that gave us inner belief. It was a good side full of good people. There wasn't a position where we were carrying a passenger – everybody was there on merit.

Right from the off Ian McGeechan recognised that if we got involved in a roly-poly match we were in trouble, so he said we had to raise the pace of the game and not allow them to settle. So we took quick line-outs, took two man line-outs and did all those sorts of things. Our performance that day was a classic example of the whole being worth more than the sum of the parts. The day just surged its way through and took everything with it.

Micky Skinner and Mike Teague battle for the ball with Finlay Calder and Derek Turnbull.

Sean Lineen: It was typical of England – they decided early not to kick their penalties and to go for tries – they just thought they were going to turn up and win. They made it so easy, they gave us all the ammunition we needed – and the guys were well up for it.

Finlay Calder: I can't recall a shred of nastiness in that game; maybe there was the odd slightly late incident, but there was an enormous respect between the two groups which had toured together with the Lions the previous year.

I remember one point, when Will Carling stepped inside and came back at the forwards, and about five of us got him. He was inside our twenty-two and we just picked him up and took him about twenty metres back. That was a big psychological moment, as was Scott's tackle on Rory Underwood. Rory was lightening quick and he went searing through the middle, but out of nowhere Scott caught him up.

People don't realise how good a tackler Scott was, he was absolutely fearless. I once saw him in Hong Kong, when he tackled three guys in quick succession then ran the length of the field to score, and then got straight back on his feet ready to go again. That was in 1989, when he was at the height of his fitness. He was a phenomenal specimen for an amateur. The two of them – Gavin and Scott – were away ahead of their time in terms of physique. They were also supremely confident people, and rightly so. I got my first cap on the same day as them in 1986, and while everyone was psyching themselves up that pair were flicking the ball off their biceps to each other. An awful lot of people are driven on by the fear of failure, but I don't think the prospect of failure ever entered their heads. They just believed they were as good as or better than anyone else on the park and that's a great thing to have as long as you have the ability to back it up – which they did.

Scott Hastings: I knew then that I'd sort of settled a score in some ways. Having given away a try, I'd then saved one. Those moments never leave you.

Will Carling: You prepare yourself for Test matches mentally, as much as you can. You know it's going to be tough and therefore you know you have to stay calm because it's not all going to go your way. There's no point in panicking, you just have to be confident in the things that you're doing and if plan A isn't working, then you switch to plan B and so on. But we had none of that because we had plan A and plan A had worked all season, and we thought plan A would again. And when it didn't you could feel a tension spreading through the whole team. 'Why isn't this working? What the hell are we going to do now? Um . . . well, I don't know.'

Bill McLaren (in commentary): *The referee's whistle goes for the end of the game and Scotland have won a famous victory. One of the unique occasions in rugby union football – and Scotland have won by thirteen points to seven. And the scenes of euphoria here . . . well just look at them. It has been a remarkable triumph.*

Ian Robertson (in commentary): *It was too much for England, and every man Jack is a hero as Scotland, for only the third time in one hundred and twenty years, complete the Grand Slam.*

Finlay Calder: When the final whistle went the whole place went crazy – the crowd swarmed the pitch and we were just hugging each other. From a personal point of view I was delighted that I had matched my twin in winning a Grand Slam.

John Jeffrey: When the whistle went? I just ran. Total headless chicken stuff. The elation was uncontrollable.

Kenny Milne: Everyone was running around, but I wanted to just soak up the moment. The crowd swarmed the pitch and I just let them surround me. I made my way slowly back through them towards the tunnel, just enjoying in every second, taking everything in. The most incredible few minutes ever.

Chris Gray (Scotland 1989-91, 22 Caps): We were knackered. Totally spent. I sat down in the changing room and didn't get up for ages. I looked over at Creamy and he was happy, but his emotions were in check, as ever. I looked at him and thought to myself: 'I owe that man my career'. But you wouldn't tell him. Oh, Christ, no. But it's true.

Jim Telfer: I can't remember saying much after the game. We'd beaten England and that kind of thing didn't happen very often. We'd beaten them to the Grand Slam and that was a first. If I was quiet in the dressing room it was probably just me letting the players get on with it. Because it was their victory, their day. They were a fantastic group. Especially the forwards. Hard as nails. Honest. Hungry. All the things you look for. I was proud of them, every last one of them.

Finlay Calder: Mike Teague is a very close friend of mine, and he said to me afterwards that he knew we were going to win after the first ruck, when he was caught on the ground and studded to bits by eight snarling Scotsmen. He also said that, in a funny sort of way, he was glad that we had won, which was a fine compliment. And, in fact, that game also did the most extraordinary amount of good for English rugby because they went away after that and regrouped, and they came back stronger and more determined to succeed than they ever would have otherwise.

Will Carling: Murrayfield 1990 was easily the most painful defeat of my life and that includes a World Cup final of 1991 and semi-final of 1995. It was entirely down to us and our own personal failings. We were arrogant and it came back to bite us. From a captaincy point of view I totally misread things and failed to notice an unhealthy vibe in the squad. There was still a huge hangover from the Lions tour in '89, which I had missed through injury. On that tour the Scots, bar Gavin Hastings and Finlay Calder, pretty much gave second best to all the England players in Test selection issues and there was undoubtedly an unhealthy feeling of superiority among England's Lions over the Scots.

We badly underestimated them, from me the captain downwards, which is ridiculous, that's a great team they had. From very early on I didn't think like we were ever really in that game.

Tony Stanger: Winning in 1990 was so special not because it was England that we beat but because it was a great England team. They proved that by winning back-to-back Grand Slams over the next two seasons. It was a great achievement for us because it was such a big challenge.

Brian Moore: That Grand Slam game was a big staging post for the England team and the immediate consequence was it made us tighten up and go into our shells, which meant we stopped playing the extremely good brand of rugby we had been playing that season. We ground out the 1991 Grand Slam and to a certain extent did the same in 1992 although we played a bit more rugby then. The short term result was

Grand Slam champions. David Sole is enveloped by Chris Gray and Finlay Calder.

that I experienced an excruciating Sunday lunchtime in Edinburgh after the Scots had clinched the Grand Slam. I never forgot that.

Gavin Hastings: I'd arranged for Brian to come to lunch at Watsonian's the next day. Fair play, he turned up. He even made a speech, although you could tell it was the last bloody thing he wanted to do. An amazing guy.

Iwan Tukalo: I always stick up for Mooro. I talk to Scots and they all say what an absolute arsehole he is: 'He's just a biased, arrogant little man'. So I say, 'You don't understand the guy'. Would I have had as much dignity as him if the roles had been reversed and I was down in England having just lost a Grand Slam? I'm not sure I'd have been as gracious as he was. That's the side of him people never saw.

Scott Hastings: Brian stood and spoke to a silent crowd. And he spoke brilliantly. You had to say fair play to the guy. That took some amount of balls.

Paul Burnell: I didn't particularly like him, but I was at Myreside that day as well and I thought, 'Maybe I'm going to have to reassess you, Mooro'. Because it was a classy thing to do.

Chris Gray: I was really embarrassed at the way some of the guys in the audience were shooting their mouths off. They'd had too much to drink and were coming out with a load of anti-English rubbish. People thought, 'Ah, this won't bother Mooro, he's a

The crowd flood the field as David Sole is carried shoulder-high to the tunnel.

tough old boy'. But it did bother him. Christ, it did.

Paul Ackford (England second-row): Bill McLaren came to one of the sessions at Peebles before the game. We were so well-prepared, everything was picture-perfect. As we were coming off, Bill told me that he had rarely seen a team look so good and train as well as that. That's the way we went into the match but in the game itself everything felt difficult, everything you tried to do felt laboured.

In the changing room afterwards there was just silence at first, then some began to talk about it. I was already thinking that we had to move on and confront what had happened. So after the dinner, the wives and girlfriends were there, Wade Dooley and I went up Princes Street wearing our blazers, just to show our faces, show that we weren't cowed and we weren't going back into our box. The reception was just fantastic – completely counter to what I thought it would be.

Sean Lineen: That Scotland side was definitely the best team I ever played in and continuity was a key factor. During the Grand Slam season the only change to the side was against England when Derek White got injured and Derek Turnbull came on.

But that team and that success wasn't because of the system – it was despite the system. It was luck that brought that group of players together at that time. We had half a dozen genuine world class players – the three back-row boys, David Sole, Gary Armstrong and Gavin Hastings, while Scott Hastings wasn't far away – and the rest of the side was made up of very good players, and the coaching team was pretty useful as well.

SIXTEEN

INCHES FROM GREATNESS
1990-1991

With the Grand Slam sealed for the second time in six years, Scotland returned to the Antipodes in the summer of 1990 for a tour that included six matches against New Zealand's top provincial sides and two Test matches against the All Blacks.

There is little doubt that this Scotland squad was one of the finest ever to come together. Their legacy had been secured by their success in the Five Nations, but if they wanted to truly stamp their mark on the record books, a victory over New Zealand away from home would seal their place in history as Scotland's greatest-ever side. The players and the management knew that winning in New Zealand would boost confidence to a level previously unknown to a Scotland team. From there they could carry their progress into the autumn Test against Australia at Murrayfield, the 1991 Five Nations, the one-off Test in August against Romania in Bucharest and then into the World Cup, hosted by England but where the majority of their games would be held at Murrayfield. Rugby, like all contact sports, is a game of the finest margins, a game where the team that wins the small battles and rides their luck can tip the balance of power in their favour, no matter how narrowly, to emerge victorious. It is a game of inches. And in the end, that's exactly what it came down to.

Jim Telfer: It was hard not going on the tour to New Zealand, but I had too many commitments to fulfil with Hawick High School. I was confident that there would be little or no interruption in the coaching set-up caused by my absence – with Ian, Dougie and Derrick we had a super four man coaching panel who were all on the same wavelength and they kept me up-to-date with how things were progressing throughout the tour. New Zealand is a wonderful place to tour – the hardest of rugby playgrounds – and it was a real testament to the quality of our team that they went unbeaten in the provincial matches and came so close to winning in the Test matches. But the players learnt valuable lessons out there that we would take into the World Cup the following year.

Doddie Weir (Scotland 1990-2000, 61 Caps): I was selected for the senior Scotland tour to New Zealand in 1990 and was part of Brewster's Breezers midweek team. Alex Brewster led by example both on and off the field and the whole tour was a hell of an experience. I was this nineteen year old skinny lad and suddenly I was on tour with these guys who had just won the Grand Slam, travelling first class and staying in five star hotels; it was amazing.

John Allan (Scotland 1990-1991, 9 Caps plus 13 Caps for South Africa): My family emigrated to South Africa when I was seven, but my father was always keen to ensure

Opposite: David Sole.

I never forgot my Scottish heritage and he used to get me to read *The Broons* and *Oor Wullie*, which he had posted over every week. We used to watch Five Nations rugby together and listen to Bill McLaren, and I would imagine fulfilling my father's dream of one day running out in that blue Scotland strip.

I decided to come back to Scotland the day I was selected for a South Africa XV to play an international XV and the game was called off because of the anti-Apartheid sanctions. I knew that if I was to achieve my goal of playing international rugby, I would have to follow my roots back home to Scotland. I wanted to play the best teams in the world at the 1991 World Cup and I figured that I would need to play at least two years of domestic rugby in Scotland before I would have a chance of being selected, so I arrived in Edinburgh in time for the 1989–90 season.

The first game I played in was down at Hawick where Edinburgh Accies hadn't won for twenty-five years. The Scottish selectors were present to watch Jim Hay, the Hawick hooker, and a few others. I knew they were present but I was more interested in impressing Bill McLaren, my boyhood hero, who was also there. We won the game and we did very well in the scrums and lineouts and before I had even really settled in Edinburgh I was called up to the Scottish squad sessions. Thinking back, every athlete has to be ready for that moment – right time, right place – and I know how fortunate I was that it worked out so well.

To this day I talk about the first time I heard *Flower of Scotland* sung at Murrayfield as a player – on the Grand Slam day in 1990. On that day, even as a reserve, I felt that I came of age and really inherited the Scottish passion which is still with me today. I was so proud to have been born in Scotland and to be there representing them on the international stage. My first cap was against New Zealand on the summer tour and it was daunting not because I was playing the All Blacks; I had no fear of them thanks to my South African upbringing. It was daunting because I was replacing the Grand Slam hooker, Kenny Milne, and would be scrumming with his brother, the Bear. I had no doubt that the brothers were upset that I had come into the team, and that was natural, but they treated me with respect and we all recognised that as a small nation we had to stay united if we were to be victorious.

The night before the game there was protestors outside my room chanting, 'Allan hooks for apartheid' – fortunately I'm a heavy sleeper but I was told that some of the boys chased them away.

Sean Lineen: We played really well in the provincial games on that 1990 tour and beat West Coast, Nelson Bays/Marlborough, Southland, Manawatu and Canterbury, which was massive, and drew with Wellington. That Canterbury game was really vicious. We just didn't lie down and the forwards were outstanding.

We shouldn't have been as far away from winning the first Test as we were. Iwan Tukalo had a shocker. It wasn't necessarily his fault, but every try they scored was on his wing, and he was dropped for the second Test. He just had a bad day, with bounces of the ball and that sort of stuff, and we lost some silly tries there. I scored a try from a move that we had worked on a hell of a lot, so that was a high for me and we scored another two through Chris Gray and Soley.

Scott Hastings: Sean Lineen and I had very quickly struck a great rapport with each other. In and around Edinburgh the teams used to meet up in the bars and socialise with each other, so it was always great fun – and here was this guy, Lineen, who wanted to play and party as well. There was this common understanding there that we were playing this game for fun, but we would take it very, very seriously when it came to the big games. We understood each other, we knew each other's angles and we loved to test each other. We were probably regarded more as a defensive pairing than an attacking unit, but when we were out in New Zealand in 1990 we decided that the back-row of Finlay Calder, Derek White and John Jeffrey were getting too much of the ball. And we decided that not enough teams were having a real go at the All Black midfield – we particularly wanted to have a run at Smokin' Joe Stanley. That was a turning point because we played some good rugby on that tour and we scored some damn good tries. I put Lineen in for a score under the posts down in Dunedin, and as he ran back into position I high-fived him, and my hand is still stinging now – we were both so pumped up. I also remember the line from the stadium announcer was: 'And the New Zealander scores against New Zealand.'

We didn't quite get the scalp in the end, but we came pretty close, and that second Test still irks me because it was there for the taking.

David Sole: The rugby that we played in the Test series was, without doubt, the finest that I ever experienced with a Scotland team. We really pushed on from the Grand Slam, which was rare for a Scottish side to do – to follow success up with continued improvement. The fact that we played so well made it all the harder that we fell short when a famous result was almost within our grasp.

Sean Lineen: After the first Test, it began to dawn on us that we were actually capable of beating the All Blacks. So for the second Test in Auckland, the guys were ready for it, and we should have beaten them, there is no doubt in my mind about that. We scored two tries to their one, and I think most people would agree that Mike Brewer was offside when he tackled Gav and won the penalty that Grant Fox kicked to make it 18–18. Fox then added another penalty to scrape a 21–18 victory for New Zealand. But we're not the only team that will feel they have let a golden opportunity slip against the All Blacks in New Zealand. They have this handy knack of getting away with things.

John Allan: After I returned to South Africa and was picked for the Springboks in 1993, one of the major differences that I noticed between playing for Scotland and playing for the Boks was the belief against the world's best. I remember when Scotland were beating Buck Shelford's legendary All Blacks team by ten points in the first Test in 1990, one of our players said he couldn't believe that we were winning.

I told him that that's what we were supposed to be doing; of course, we eventually lost that game. When I played for South Africa and we got into a similar situation, my teammates would be saying: let's beat them by twenty points or more. Losing for Scotland was bad but not life threatening; losing for South Africa was – and still is – a national disaster.

Gavin Hastings: The two most frustrating parts of that game were the try that David Sole scored which was disallowed because the referee couldn't see him grounding it under a pile of bodies, and the penalty that Mike Brewer won from an offside position was a shocker. We were that close to making history and it still hurts. It was inches. If they had a video referee back then, Soley would have been awarded the try. And then Brewer won that penalty that should never have been given and they drew level. Foxy held his nerve and that was us. Defeated by the All Blacks yet again. But we had played well and deserved so much more.

Tony Stanger: The good thing was that we had this expectation that we were going to win. It wasn't arrogance, it was just recognising that we were all surrounded by good players and that we were beating some good teams. We took that self-belief to New Zealand. As a young man you didn't appreciate just how special it was to be part of a Scotland team capable of going to places like Auckland believing that if you played well you could beat the best team in the world in their own backyard. There had been some pretty dark days for Scottish rugby before that, and I was part of a few pretty harrowing defeats later in my career, but those few years around the start of the nineties were a real pinnacle in our hist-ory.

Doddie Weir: I was selected to play against Argentina for my first cap in the autumn of 1990. They were not the team they are now but it was still a great achievement when we ended up winning 49–3. I was very tall and skinny – I was 6'6' and only thirteen stone when I was first capped which would be unthinkable these days, but fortunately I was scrummaging behind the great Iain Milne, who more than made up for my lack of weight – I think each of his legs were probably about thirteen stone. I'm not one to remember all the matches I played in or all the details, and although I know the date – 10 November 1990 – I can't remember very much about the match itself. With all the adrenaline pumping and playing at a speed that I'd never known before, the whole thing went by in a flash.

There was always a big thing made of you in the squad after you'd won your first cap and there was a lot of major drinking which doesn't happen so much nowadays I'm sure, but it's a pity if it doesn't because it was a huge thing to win your first cap and it should be celebrated – and it makes you feel more at ease within the squad if you go and have a big drinking session with all your teammates, it makes you really feel like you belong.

Gavin Hastings: There was a lot of expectation on the team as we went into the 1991 Five Nations. We had started the season with a resounding win against Argentina at Murrayfield in November, winning 49–3. But the odd years are always harder for Scotland in the tournament as we have to travel to Paris and London. We lost the opening match against France 15–9, then won well against Wales at Murrayfield before heading to England where we were overpowered 21–12 as they marched to the Grand Slam. We finished on a high by beating Ireland at home, but it was tough to see our old rivals assuming our Grand Slam crown and beginning to look ominously strong for the World Cup.

Sean Lineen: Coming back from New Zealand, we were obviously incredibly disappointed not to have won a Test, but we had gone unbeaten in the provincial games and had continued to bond after the highs of the Grand Slam. The World Cup was fast approaching, so we had to concentrate on the positives that we gained in New Zealand and switch our focus to 1991 Five Nations and the World Cup.

We didn't do very well on the road that season, but the Parc des Princes and Twickenham are tough, tough places to go and win, no matter who you are, and we won our home matches comfortably.

As part of our build-up to the World Cup we then travelled out to Bucharest to play Romania . . . and got cuffed. Romania was a difficult place to go at the best of times and keep spirits high, but to lose there made it doubly tough. At the dinner David Sole, as captain, was up at the top table and you could see he was not enjoying himself. At our table there was Finlay Calder, Derek White, JJ, Damian Cronin, young Graham Shiel and myself, plus six Romanian guys. So each of us took it in turn to go up and down a drink with Soley, and by the time he had to make his speech he had skulled six glasses of red wine and was pretty pissed.

He got through it, but when he sat back down Damian Cronin said, 'I've never liked these blazers.' And he grabbed the breast pocket and ripped it clean off. Derek White burst out laughing, so I grabbed his pocket and ripped it off. The next fifteen minutes were spent ripping clothes off each other. You could see Bob Munro, the convenor of selectors, and the other committee guys looking at us then shaking their heads in disgust. We ended up walking out of the dinner, looking like refugees from some Monty Python comedy sketch, and getting a taxi back to the hotel where we had a great night.

Gavin Hastngs: Despite the hiccup in Romania, as a squad, we were nicely settled for the World Cup. The main core of players had been together for a number of years and we had been through some real highs and lows together – which added experience and steel to the group. All our pool games were to be played at Murrayfield and we knew that we were better than the other teams in our pool – Ireland, Japan and Zimbabwe – so we had every chance to do well.

Jim Telfer: We based ourselves in St Andrews in the build up to the tournament. As we had all of our games at home we decided that St Andrews would be a good spot to get away from all the hype building up in Edinburgh. It worked really well. We had great facilities at Madras College to train at and the players were able to get away from rugby by playing golf or walking along the West Sands, and they were able to go out for drinks in the evening in the knowledge that it wouldn't get out of hand.

Finlay Calder: The management of our squad was a world away from '87. We played a strong team for our opening game against Japan and won 47–9 and then rotated things for the Zimbabwe game, which we won 51–12. That rotation was the key to our success in that tournament because everyone got a chance to play and everyone wanted to perform when they got a chance. We were ruthless whenever we took to the field, no matter who was wearing the jersey.

Sean Lineen: The pool came down to a Scotland versus Ireland play-off at Murrayfield. There was a real Irish invasion in Edinburgh for the match and the atmosphere was incredible. It was a pretty tight game, but the turning point came when Chic Chalmers put up a high ball on Jim Staples and as he caught it Fin Calder almost knocked him out of the stadium. Fair play to Staples, he took the hit pretty well and played on, but we could see he was shaken and a few minutes later we put another ball up. We put another great chase on and the volume of the crowd just rose up and up as the ball started to come down on Staples. We were right in his face as he took it – or tried to take it – and the ball ricocheted off his shoulder and straight into Graham Shiel's arms, who scored under the sticks. We also scored a couple of tidy tries through Gary Armstrong and Scotty Hastings and Gav and Chic kicked solidly. We went on to win 24–15. We finished undefeated in the pool stages and were through to the quarter-finals to play one of the real surprise packages of the World Cup, Western Samoa, who had shocked Wales and Argentina and had given Australia a real scare before losing 9–3.

Jim Telfer: Nobody expected us to face Western Samoa in the quarter-final before the tournament – everyone thought it would be Wales. The Samoans had played some fantastic rugby throughout the tournament and their victory against Wales had been well deserved. We didn't know an awful lot about them, but Ian McGeechan was meticulous with his video analysis and we soon concocted a game plan for taking them on. They were very powerful physically and were confident in their own abilities, but we knew that if we could match their physicality, absorb their hits and look to nullify that area of their game, then they would be there for the taking.

Gavin Hastings: The best we played during the 1991 World Cup was against Western Samoa. I think we would have beaten anyone in the world that day. They were a good side, they had already beaten Wales, and if you look at all the guys who were playing for them that day, they were a wonderful side. Frank Bunce, Steve Bachop, Pat Lam, Peter Fatialofa – these guys were all playing provincial rugby in New Zealand, so they were playing a far higher standard of rugby week-in and week out than anyone in the Scotland set-up was. So we knew that we had to be at our very best if we were to have any chance and in the end we gave them an absolute doing, 28–6. Jim Telfer got his tactics spot on that day, he suggested I take the ball up short during the first ten minutes and because they were all looking out wide for the big hits, we were able to gain the yardage through the middle.

So, that was a very positive performance leading into the semi-final against England, which I still say to this day was the toughest game of rugby I was ever involved in – both physically and mentally. I got an absolute shoeing all game. The first time England got the ball, Rob Andrew sent it up in the air and when I caught it the English forwards just trampled right over the top of me.

Finlay Calder: The semi-final was a pretty dour affair as a spectacle, but it was tense and tight, just as knock-out games tend to be. We had won the Grand Slam game the year before by playing fast and loose and taking our opportunities when they arose, but the writing for England's performance was on the wall when we played them at Twickenham in the 1991 Five Nations. They had learned lessons for 1991 and tightened their whole game up, controlling everything through their forwards and Rob Andrew. It may not have been pretty, but it was a masterclass in power play and employing the necessary tactics to win in a tournament like the World Cup.

John Jeffrey: Unlike the Grand Slam game, we weren't going to be able to talk England up beforehand or do the slow march. First scrum, we went left instead of our usual right and they were all waiting for us. We were like: 'How the fuck are they there?' The little edges we had managed to find ourselves in 1990 weren't there in 1991.

Scotland look on dejectedly as the English players celebrate their passage
through to the World Cup final.

Gavin Hastings: If I could change one thing about my rugby career it would be that infamous missed kick from in front of the posts when the scores were level at 6–6 – but it's just one of those things that I can't do anything about. There was a penalty awarded and Micky Skinner hit me bloody hard, I was down and the physio was on giving me treatment just before the kick was taken, so I suppose if one of us had thought about it a bit more, it might have been sensible to step aside and let Chic have a go – but it is easy to say that with the benefit of hindsight.

At the end of the day, I'm glad it's me rather than anyone else – because I know I can live with it. It's an annoyance in my life in that it gets brought up every now and then – nothing more, nothing less. It missed by a couple of inches. The slightest change in the angle of my boot when I struck the ball and it would have gone over. But when you're a goal-kicker, that is sometimes all the difference there is.

After the game it was an important hour in the changing room, and I was able to put things in perspective. Yes, our World Cup dream was over – but I didn't mean to miss it, I didn't want to miss it and I played a pretty good game apart from that. It allowed me to put the whole rugby thing into perspective – no one had died, no one had been seriously injured and no one had lost a job, so I was able to move on, and I think I had moved on by the time I left the changing room. Basically, there was hee-haw I could do about it.

I don't think anyone in our squad felt we weren't going to win. We hadn't necessarily played all that well in the three previous games. But then we had this huge opportunity against England and games against them had always been close affairs. Because of the Murrayfield factor, I always felt we were going to be good enough. It was an utter belief and conviction that we were going to win the game.

John Jeffrey: It was a dreadful match but that wouldn't have mattered if we'd got to the final. None of us wanted to go out that night but we forced ourselves. Folk came up and said 'Hard lines, big man – you did us proud,' which made losing worse. I remember my defeats more than my victories because I always – always – wanted to win.

I'd already made up my mind that the World Cup was going to be my swansong. Only the team knew, which was why I got to lead them out for the England game. Thanking the crowd at the end was pretty emotional.

Tony Stanger: Scotland will probably never have a better chance to go all the way. We played all our pool games, the quarter-final and the semi-final at Murrayfield, with a team that had shown over the previous eighteen months or so that they could beat teams like England and hold their own against the All Blacks.

It was a high pressure environment. Because of 1990, England knew what could happen and they played a very smart tactical game. People talk about Gavin's kick, but I honestly can't remember much about it – what I do recall is that at the time we didn't feel like it was a kick to win the game. It wasn't in the dying minutes, and if he had kicked it the whole contest of the game would have changed and who knows what would have happened.

It was two good teams nullifying each other. Because of what was at stake there wasn't much risk taking going on. It was a game of chess.

It was a good opportunity, but let's not take anything away from England – the reason why 1990 was special for Scots was because England had so many fantastic players in their squad and we didn't beat them for the next ten games. We deserved to win the game in 1990 but I'm not sure you could say that about the semi-final in 1991.

Sean Lineen: After we lost to England in the semi-final, we went down to Cardiff to play the All Blacks in the third/fourth place play-off. Three nights before the game we all decided to have a night out, but Jim Telfer got wind of it, so after dinner he stayed down in the foyer waiting to nab us on the way out. John Allan was the first ready, and he came strolling down the big stairs into the foyer with a Hawaiian shirt and pair of loud trousers on. Telfer let rip. We all sneaked down the fire escape, but John was too scared to go out after that.

The night after that we went out to a show which wasn't very good. So most of us left and we ended up going to a bar and getting absolutely wasted. That was two days before we played the All Blacks – there is no way we should have been out. But the guys worked really hard, which meant we felt we were allowed to play hard sometimes too. I would say the Scottish guys were among the fittest in the world at that time, because we had to be given the style of rugby we played.

Jim Telfer: It was hard for the players to pick themselves up mentally and physically after the semi-final defeat to play the All Blacks in Cardiff. It felt as if the tournament was already over and that it was just a dead rubber – which it was. Both teams were hurting, but as defending champions, the All Blacks were hurting all the more and there was no way that they were going to suffer further ignominy by being beaten by us. In the end it was quite a tight game – Walter Little scored the only try of the match near the end to give them the win, but I was very proud of the manner in which the players performed.

Doddie Weir: There was a bit of a fuss made after the final because a few the Scotland players turned up at Twickenham wearing Australia shirts. It was just a bit of fun and it got blown out of all proportion.

Jim Telfer: The squad started to break up after the World Cup – JJ and Fin retired and Chris Gray was never selected again. John Allan returned to South Africa, Derek White retired after the 1992 Five Nations and then following the summer tour to Australia that year Sean Lineen and David Sole hung up their boots. It is always sad when a great era comes to end, but these things are part of life and although you are sad to see them pass, the next chapter is always an exciting prospect.

SEVENTEEN

THE ROAD TO THE RAINBOW WORLD CUP
1992-1995

Following Australia's triumph in the 1991 World Cup, Scotland turned their attentions to rebuilding – both figuratively and literally. After claiming a powerful win over Scotland on the opening weekend of the 1992 Five Nations, England marched irresistibly through the rest of the tournament to claim a back-to-back Grand Slam. Although they lost to Wales in Cardiff, Scotland posted wins against Ireland at Lansdowne Road and France at Murrayfield and then travelled Down Under in June for two Tests against the world champions in Sydney and Brisbane, which were lost 27–12 and 37–13 respectively.

New players such as Andy Nicol, Rob Wainwright, Peter Wright and Kenny Logan were blooded that season and construction began on the redevelopment of Murrayfield Stadium, converting it into an all-seated amphitheatre to match any sports arena in the world. The new North and South stands were opened for Ireland's visit in the 1993 Five Nations, which Scotland won 15–3, but it was a mixed tournament for Scotland that year as they lost to France and England away from home, but backed up the Ireland victory by defeating Wales comfortably 20–0 at Murrayfield.

At the conclusion of the tournament, Ian McGeechan stepped down as head coach. Jim Telfer took up a new role as director of rugby and Richie Dixon and David Johnston were appointed as Scotland coaches. Their first season in charge was a baptism of fire. It began with a 51–15 humbling by the All Blacks at Murrayfield and continued through the Five Nations, where the best result was a 6–6 draw with Ireland, and into the summer tour to Argentina when the two Test matches in Buenos Aires were lost 16–15 and 19–17.

Rob Wainwright (Scotland 1992-1998, 37 Caps plus 1 Cap for the Lions): I was at Cambridge University for six years and I think I probably started to get noticed after playing well in the Varsity matches. I played for the B team against Italy in 1989 and then dropped off the radar for a couple of years before playing in the Trial in January 1992. In those interim years it had basically been a case of waiting for JJ and Finlay to retire, but I have to say that I felt very sorry for Graham Marshall, who was a bloody good player, but had been very much the understudy for both JJ and Finlay for several years. When they retired it looked as if it was Graham's time, but he suffered a career-ending injury early in 1992 and so I rose one vital notch in the pecking order.

I had a good game in the Trial match at number eight and was capped later in the season off the bench against Ireland in the Five Nations. In those days you didn't have substitutions, only replacements, and Neil Edwards very kindly left the pitch with about three minutes to go so that I could get on. I was moved into the second-row and I don't think I actually did anything in those couple of minutes but run around a bit, but it was still a great thing to win that first cap and to be a part of a victory at Lansdowne Road.

Opposite: The 'Toony Flip'.

We played France in the third game of the tournament and Ian Smith was injured, so I started at open-side flanker. I don't remember an awful lot about the game except that it rained a lot and the ball was like a bar of soap – although again I hardly touched it – I just ran around like a blue-arsed fly.

The summer tour to Australia in 1992 was the first time that I consolidated my place in the team. I was still pretty new to the whole set-up and just tried to keep my head down and work hard. It was an amazing experience, though there was a bit of tension on the tour between the captain and the coach which could be a little uncomfortable for the rest of the party. David Sole and Richie Dixon publicly clashed with one another now and again throughout the tour – on the training pitch, in meetings – and it wasn't good at all. I remember thinking that all that sort of stuff should have been handled privately between them backstage, but it all came back to haunt me six years later when I was captain and had a very similar experience. David was annoyed about the changes made in the coaching style with Richie replacing Jim Telfer, while conversely in Australia in 1998, I was annoyed about Jim coming in to replace Richie – and we had one or two public spats which I wish had never happened.

As I came into the Scotland set-up, a lot of the elder statesmen in the team were either gone or were coming to the end of their careers. Derek White, Derek Turnbull and David Sole were still there, but everyone else was pretty young. We went out to Australia on tour in 1992 and it was one of those tours with a lot of young guys trying to make their mark – although I never had the feeling that any of us really believed that we would win a Test match. It is the perennial problem in Scottish rugby and I suppose that much of that belief stems from the raw fact that historically we very rarely win against the southern hemisphere teams, and had only once done it away from home against one of the big three, in 1982. Even when we went ahead against Australia on that tour I don't think that many of us felt that we would be able to hold on to secure the win – and it was a self-fulfilling prophecy.

Peter Wright (Scotland 1992-1996, 21 Caps): My first cap was against Australia in Sydney in 1992. They had big screens at either end of the stadium and it was the only time that I played in a Test with them showing replays of the action during the game.

We kicked off and obviously I was pretty pumped up for my first Test match – playing against the world champions in their own back yard. Tim Gavin collected the ball, made a couple of yards and was tackled. Now, nobody believes me, but it was purely an accident when I kicked him in the head as he went down.

At the time, I was thinking to myself, I'm going to get sent off here in the first minute of my first cap. But fortunately the referee didn't see it and gave a scrum to Australia. I was looking from side to side to see if the touch judges were flagging, and they weren't – which was fantastic. I was thinking, Got away with that one!

Then, as their physio ran on, I looked up and spotted the big screen showing the replay, with my foot clipping Tim Gavin's head. The crowd were howling. The referee sauntered up to me and said, 'Lucky I can't penalise for something being shown as a replay.'

Later in the match, I had given away a penalty and was standing there holding the ball. Nick Farr-Jones – who had just been voted Australia's most eligible bachelor and was a national hero after leading Australia to World Cup glory in 1991 – came up to get the ball and just as he went to take it I dropped it in front of him. They showed that on the replay about five times, and the crowd were going nuts. I wasn't a popular guy at all that day. It was like pantomime – with me as the villain.

Before the second Test, Bob Dwyer, the Australian coach, said the only way Scotland could win the ball in contact was illegally, and Colin Hawke, the New Zealand referee, penalised us off the park. That was David Sole's last game and he scored a try which was the last ever four-pointer in international rugby; he got up at the after match function and absolutely destroyed the referee. Usually it is all platitudes and votes of thanks, but he said he couldn't believe the referee had been taken in by the comments Australia had made and called it pathetic. I thought it was quite refreshing to see someone stand up and say what they really thought.

I was the first Scottish player to be yellow carded in an international. It was the Scotland versus England game at Twickenham in 1993, the referee was a wee red haired Irishman called Brian Stirling, and basically Will Carling had come right over the top of a pile of bodies so I went in and rucked him out the back. The referee blew the whistle and pulled Gavin, the captain, and myself aside. He said to Gavin, 'Look, I'm going to yellow card number three for dangerous use of the boot on number twelve.'

And Gav, tongue in cheek, replied, 'A yellow card? He should get a medal for stamping on that bastard!'

I came off after that game and Jim Telfer just shrugged his shoulders and said, 'Unlucky.' It was one of the few times when it was actually just good rucking, with my shoulders in front of my hips. To his credit, Will came and spoke to me at the dinner after the game and said he was on the wrong side and deserved what he got – but at that time referees were beginning to get strict about putting your feet on players. The good thing was that in those days it was just a warning and you didn't get ten minutes in the sin bin.

Sean Lineen: After games at Murrayfield we used to get changed and head to the Carlton Highland Hotel where we met the wives and girlfriends, who wanted to talk about anything but rugby while all you wanted to do was talk about rugby. You love your wife but with the best will in the world you want to have a beer with the guys you have just done battle with – so you would be champing at the bit to get down to the President's Reception and have a drink and a bit of chat with your mates.

Then they did away with the President's Reception because everyone was sick and tired of having to go through all the boring formalities – but we didn't tell the women that; we still had the President's Reception, but it was around at the Mitre Bar in the

Royal Mile. The whole team would be there. It ended up with the wives saying, 'It's getting earlier and earlier this President's Reception.'

The guys would be getting into the hotel, dumping their bags and saying, 'Right, I'm off to the President's Reception. It's a big one today – mustn't be late.'

Gavin Hastings: When the All Blacks came to Edinburgh in November 1993, they really showed the world that they had taken the game forward, yet again, to a level previously unknown. They were all pace and power and intricate moves done at speed and with perfect precision. They had an incredible pack with Zinzan Brooke, Jamie Joseph, Ian Jones, Olo Brown, Craig Dowd and Sean Fitzpatrick and in the backs they had Va'aiga Tuigamala, Frank Bunce and Jeff Wilson. Wilson made his debut against us and scored a hat-trick of tries. The way they played was just frightening – they blew us off the park at every stage and all we could manage were a few penalties between me and Craig Chalmers and they hammered us 51–15.

Rob Wainwright: Jeff Wilson and the other three-quarters were just unbelievable. Even when they were thirty or forty points up, those guys were still grinding, looking for more. It was the sort of game you try to block out of your memory.

Mercurial. It is an oft-expressed term in sporting parlance, used to describe a player capable of match-winning genius one moment, of catastrophe the next. The Oxford English Dictionary defines the term as 'volatile, lively and unpredictable; likely to do the unexpected'. In the lexicon of Scottish rugby that term would simply have a name inscribed in its entry: Gregor Townsend.

Townsend was never a steady controller at stand-off in the mould of Colin Telfer, John Rutherford or even his teammate in the Scotland squad, Craig Chalmers. His game was one of adventure. There are a handful of Scottish internationalists who will forever hold a place in the hearts of the Murrayfield faithful for their acts of bravery or creative daring, for their sparks of genius, for their ability to turn a game on its head with a moment of sublime inspiration that no one else could have imagined, let alone realised, in the heat of a Test match battle. David Bedell-Sivright, Bill Maclagan, GPS MacPherson, Herbert Waddell, Douglas Elliot, Ken Scotland, Arthur Smith, Andy Irvine, Jim Renwick, Roy Laidlaw, John Rutherford and Gregor Townsend. Geniuses all. But like any genius, not without their flaws. For to conjure space or to throw a match-winning pass, to shimmy and break, to commit to an interception or to kick for glory, one must take risks. And risks, by their very nature, sometimes lead to disaster.

But if Townsend was the maverick genius in the Scotland three-quarter line of the mid-1990s, he had a steady anchor backing him all the way. Gavin Hastings was recognised the world over as one of the finest fullbacks ever to play the game. Physically intimidating, powerful, fast and as canny as a fox, he possessed great courage, tactical awareness, classic skills and a siege-gun boot. His place kicking for goal was exceptional, even if the miss against England in the 1991 World Cup will haunt the rest of his days, and as he entered his swansong years he was still Scotland's number one place-kicker. But even if the legs were tiring and his body less able to absolutely consume an opponent in the tackle as it had before, his brain was as sharp as ever.

If ever there was a match in which these two greats of the Scottish game combined, it was in Paris during the 1995 Five Nations. From the outside, that season was looking bleak for Scotland. But for all their trials, Dixon and Johnston had been able to continue the blooding of new players. Between 1993 and the autumn Test against South Africa in 1994, Townsend, Derek Stark, Bryan Redpath, Peter Walton and Craig Joiner had all gained Test match experience. In the January match against Canada at Murrayfield and the Five Nations of 1995, Stewart Campbell, David Hilton and Eric Peters would also gain Test recognition as the squad began to take its shape in preparation for the third World Cup, which was to be held in South Africa that summer.

With the World Cup looming, it was vital that Scotland generated some momentum during the 1995 Five Nations. They started strongly by defeating Ireland and then travelled to France, where Scotland had failed to record a win for twenty-six years. Despite their progress against Canada and Ireland, Scotland were written-off before the first kick of the game had even been struck. France were formidable and were looking to stamp their authority on Scotland, who would also contest Pool D with them in South Africa. But in Paris in the springtime, the most wonderful things can happen. It was during this game that Gregor Townsend truly made his mark on Scottish rugby with a display of daring and accomplished skill and for a moment that he will be forever remembered – his famous 'Toony Flip' – a delicate pass out the back of his hand to Gavin Hastings as he was being tackled, releasing the ageing warhorse at fullback for a clear sprint to the posts for what would prove to be the clinching score. The whole performance from the team had been outstanding that day but in that one phase of play Townsend had displayed the type of weapon that he had at his disposal; it was a phenomenal piece of supreme rugby skill that left Scotland delirious and sent shockwaves through the rugby world. In that moment, Townsend had announced himself on the international stage; although he was playing outside centre at the time, he was widely regarded as the heir apparent to the great John Rutherford and a figure who bore all the enigmatic traits and creative majesty of Andy Irvine.

As a team, Scotland were incomparable to the one that had been playing during the previous two seasons. As French Federation president Bernard Lapasset stated in the aftermath of the Paris match, 'Rugby is not for the country that is stronger and richer. It is for the country that shows the greater courage, discipline and teamwork for eighty minutes.'

Two weeks later, Wales were blown away in Edinburgh 26–13 and on 18 March the team flew south to Twickenham for the final match of the Five Nations and another winner-takes-all play-off. But with England as powerful and claustrophobic as ever, Scotland's Grand Slam dream came unstuck against the metronomic boot of Rob Andrew, who scored seven penalties and a drop-goal to secure a 24–12 victory and a third unbeaten English campaign since 1991.

Devastatingly, a few weeks later Townsend ruptured the posterior cruciate ligament in his knee playing for Gala against Hawick and was ruled out of the World Cup. But despite this set-back, the rest of the squad was in positive shape as they prepared for South Africa – which would prove to be the most extraordinary World Cup yet.

Gregor Townsend (Scotland 1993-2003, 82 Caps plus 2 Caps for the Lions): The 1994 Five Nations was my first full year in the international set-up and we were going through a bit of a tough time. I was injured during the autumn internationals when we lost heavily to New Zealand, then I came in at centre against Wales and we were badly beaten again, so it hadn't been a good six months and we were getting heavily criticised.

I was moved to stand-off for the England game at Murrayfield, which was great because that is where I wanted to play, but I wasn't happy with my performance. We kicked a lot, which worked I suppose because we scored from a high ball, but I was playing well below my potential in terms of going through with breaks and making the sorts of decisions I would normally make.

We were losing by two points with not long to go so the call was that I was to kick a drop-goal whenever we got within range. I missed one but then got another chance and slotted it with less than a minute left on the clock, which looked like it had won the game for us. But then we lost the ball from the kickoff and England were set up for a drop-goal of their own, with Rob Andrew in the pocket. Two years previously I had been sitting in the crowd behind the posts when Gav missed that kick to go ahead and then Rob Andrew had kicked the drop-goal to win the World Cup semi-final, and now he was ready to do it again.

Well, I was determined to stop history repeating itself, so I sprinted out – I was onside – and I charged it down. And I felt far more elation then than when I kicked the drop-goal a few minutes earlier, especially when I saw Ian Jardine diving on the loose ball, because I knew in my heart we had won the game then – naively so, as it turns out.

Possession ended up coming out on the English side, which was strange, and then the referee gave them the penalty – which was doubly strange because surely if we had cheated on the ground the ball would have come out on our side.

The penalty was between the halfway line and the ten-metre line, John Callard kicked the goal and that was the last action of the game.

We were incredulous at the time, but we didn't have enough video evidence. Then two days later, Reporting Scotland came out with this story that England had blue sleeves on their jerseys and they had a tape of Rob Andrew's hands on the ball, trying to win it back after his kick was charged down.

At the time I was upset with the defeat, I wasn't too happy with my own performance, but I didn't have the history with Scotland versus England games that some of the senior players had, and I didn't realise it would be another six years before we would beat England again.

Gavin Hastings: The rest of that season was pretty hard going. We drew with Ireland 6–all in a pretty dreadful match at Lansdowne Road and then lost to France at Murrayfield. We then went on tour to Argentina, which is a tough, tough place to go and we ended up losing both Test matches. The results were poor but we were able to give game-time to Craig Joiner, Kevin McKenzie and Andy Nicol, who all won their first caps, as well as to players like Gregor Townsend, Bryan Redpath and Kenny Logan who were still pretty new to the set-up, which was important for the continuing development of the team as you always need fresh impetus as well as building experience in your squad before a tournament like the World Cup.

The following season the Springboks came to Edinburgh and much like the All Blacks the previous year, you could see them trying to develop their game as the World Cup approached – which was a huge occasion for them because it was the first time they had been allowed to enter and it was being staged in their country. We were battered in that game and lost 34–10 and they scored some cracking tries through Japie Mulder, Joost van der Westhuizen, Rudi Straeuli and Chester Williams, although again it was a useful exercise for us because you need to test yourself against the very best and players like Iain Morrison, Graham Shiel and Kenny Logan were able to get further Test experience, which was vital. Their team was full of guys who would go on to be the core of the 1995 World Cup team and become household names around the world – guys like Andre Joubert, Pieter Hendriks, Pieter Muller, Hennie le Roux, Os du Randt, Mark Andrews, Ruben Kruger and, of course, Francois Pienaar.

1995 started much more positively with a good win over Canada at the end of January which was followed by another positive performance against Ireland at Murrayfield, which we won 26–13. Our second match of the Championship was against France in Paris, which had been a bit of a graveyard for Scottish teams for over a quarter of a century. Although we had played well against Ireland, no one really gave us much of a chance as we headed into that second fixture.

Gregor Townsend: I can remember virtually every minute of that day in Paris in 1995: the walk we took in our hotel grounds during the morning, which happened to be the beautiful Versailles Palace; the police motorcycle outriders taking us to the game, banging their fists on the cars in front as we bombed right into the stadium; and the Parc des Princes atmosphere which was something different to anything I had ever experienced before, with the bands inside these enclosed concrete stands almost deafening you.

Going to Paris, you just knew it was going to be a game that tests everything: your mental strength in that atmosphere, your focus and concentration because they are constantly going to be asking you questions, and your fitness because they are going to be running at you all day and you have to play better rugby and more rugby if you are to have a chance.

They scored in the opening minute and in a funny sort of the way that was the best thing that could have happened to us. It was the shock to the system we needed, we needed to start playing and we did, and managed to get ourselves into a 13–5 lead at half-time.

Then with a few minutes to go, and the scores tied 16–all, I was involved with a wayward kick which led to a French try which we didn't defend very well. So, from being in a position to get a draw or even a win, we were now looking at a defeat.

But we got possession back, got up to their halfway line, and then Chic sent the ball to me on a miss-one. I could feel the defence drifting over towards me and I knew I had to cut back inside. Gavin had been on my shoulder the whole game, running great lines. I knew if I could suck in both the centres – Philippe Sella and Thierry Lacroix – and get an offload away on my outside then there was a slight chance of putting Gavin into space. So my first job was to get my elbow free, I did that and managed to hold the contact for that half-second I required, but Gavin wasn't calling for it outside, he wanted it inside, and as I went down I managed to turn the ball under my arm to get the pass away.

I'd never done that in a game situation before. I don't think that's because I'd not been able to do it, it's just that no one had called for it. It's just a small adjustment, the skill itself is nothing special. It was all about Gavin grasping the opportunity. If he had gone outside he would have been closed down by their fullback, Jean-Luc Sadourny, but the angle beat everyone.

I think any try would have been great – we hadn't won there in twenty-six years – but scoring in the last minute with the captain – and not just any captain, but Gavin Hastings – scoring it. Well, you couldn't have written it any better.

Rob Wainwright: That '95 game in Paris was incredibly exciting to be involved in because the lead changed hand so many times and then Gregor pulled off his Toony Flip and sent Gavin in and we were all jumping all over the place in celebration. But I remember that Gavin wouldn't look at any of us after he touched down because he knew he still had to take the kick to win the game – and he had some demons to quell there after 1991.

Gavin Hastings: Most people will hopefully remember that about my career – rather than the missed penalty four years earlier. It was a source of huge personal pride and pleasure. People often talk about a moment when everything happens in slow motion. For me, that was the moment. I got this ball and the space just opened up, then suddenly these posts appeared as if by magic in front of me. It was silent all around me and I just remember running towards the posts – it was easy. I felt in complete control.

If I look back at any game in which I was captain then that was the one which gives me the most satisfaction, because I firmly believe that the attitude I took into that match as captain was fundamental to us believing that we could win it.

It was my thirteenth game as captain and it was Scotland's thirteenth attempt to win there since 1969, and I quite like these little statistics, which give you a reason why you are going to win the match.

Gregor Townsend: We sang *Flower of Scotland* in the changing rooms straight after the match, then we went back out to the pitch and sang it to all the Scots who were still in the stadium, throwing our socks and shorts into the crowd. And then the dinner that night – well, it was one of the great amateur nights.

Peter Wright: We were all sitting at the same table, which is the way the French always did it. As you can imagine, we were having a great time, when Gavin turned to Stewart Campbell and said, 'The first time I played over here one of the boys showed me a trick.' Then he picked up the knife which was really, really heavy and tapped the middle of this huge plate, which smashed into a hundred pieces. There was a silence for about three or four seconds, as we all looked at each other, then all at the same time it dawned on us that this was a good game and we all picked up our knives and started tapping plates which all shattered. We just scooped the plates up and threw them under the table. When the waiters turned up to serve the steaks there was nothing there to put the meat on. Things degenerated from there.

Rob Wainwright: That game and the night out afterwards really drew a line, in my opinion, under the amateur era. It was one of the all-time great amateur nights out; we drank the most incredible amount of champagne after the match and just had this amazing evening. All the police escorts we had were drinking away and were then giving the wives and girlfriends rides up and down the street on their bikes.

The SRU's coffers were much healthier in those days because they weren't paying any players, so they would always pick up the bar tab afterwards. I remember going to the team hotel after the win in '99 and because all the money was going to the players and into the running of the professional teams, there was nothing like the same money going around for the post-match entertainment and the whole atmosphere was completely different.

The amateur era was a great, great time. It was a chance for us to escape from the mundanity of life and spend some time in the limelight. The team spirit was fantastic and we would always stay together after the matches, and the wives and girlfriends always got involved after our official dinners were over; everything just felt incredibly tight knit – which all started to change when professionalism came in.

Gavin Hastings: It took a while to come down from cloud nine after that match, but once we were home we knew we had to turn our attention to Wales, who were coming to Murrayfield two weeks later. Wales weren't at their strongest in those days, but they still had great players with guys like Ieuan Evans, Nigel Davies, Neil Jenkins and Robert Jones. Robert, who I knew very well from the Lions, scored a good try in that match and Neil Jenkins was metronomic with his kicking, as he always was, but we played some scintillating stuff and David Hilton and Eric Peters both scored tries which I converted and I kicked four penalties and we won 26–13.

That obviously set us up for a Grand Slam showdown with England. It was very similar to the 1991 showdown which had also been played at Twickenham. It was a game for the purists, as they say – not particularly exciting and although we tried to play a running game, they had learned their lesson against us in 1990 and made sure that they strangled the life out of proceedings whenever we met. As ever, they had a huge pack, absolutely monstrous, and with Dean Richards at the heart of it, they kept the game very tight and Rob Andrew's boot did the rest. It was disappointing to lose such an important game that way, but England were clever and did what needed to be done – they kept the ball with guys like Deano, Ben Clarke, Tim Rodber, Martin Johnson and Martin Bayfield, even though they had a fantastic set of backs – and they ground out the win. It wasn't very inspiring, but it was a demonstration of how to win crucial games clinically.

Rob Wainwright: We came unstuck against England in that last match, but we had been playing some fantastic rugby and been involved in some truly great games that season. When we went down to Twickenham I genuinely think that only three or four of us actually thought that we stood a chance of winning – because Scotland's record there is so appalling. Conversely, when you look back to that Paris game, it's interesting to note that some of the best games Scotland have ever played have been against France in the Parc des Princes or the Stade de France – the 1995 and 1999 games in particular – but often the return fixture is a pretty terrible affair. The latter point has much to do with the approach that the French have when they travel, but with the former, for whatever reason, Scottish teams tend to look to play an expansive, attacking game in France. Strangely though, they can't seem to replicate that same attacking intent when they go to Twickenham.

Peter Wright: The first game of our 1995 World Cup campaign was against the Ivory Coast, up in Rustenberg near Sun City in the North West Province of South Africa. We won at a canter, 89–0, and afterwards we went out for a beer. So we went into this bar and the guy behind the counter said that we had to hand over our guns, which would be put in the gun room. We said we didn't have any guns and he thought we were mad because we had gone out in Rustenberg without a gun. I was speaking to a girl in a nightclub later that night and I'd bought her a couple of drinks, she offered to buy me one back and when she opened up her purse there was a gun in it.

We got accused of wrecking a restaurant. I think the story had come from the French. We were training in Pretoria the day the story broke and afterwards we were all sitting at the front of a stand recovering from a particularly tough session. The press were behind us, and Dunc Paterson was behind them speaking to the *Pretoria Star* newspaper asking for a retraction and apology. He obviously wasn't getting very far, and all of a sudden he came out with immortal words, 'Well, if you don't put a retraction in I'm going to send my four biggest guys up there and then you'll find out what wrecking is all about.' You could see all the press guys' ears pricking up.

Scott Hastings: When we were staying in Rustenberg we made trips out into the townships and it was one of the most incredible experiences of my life – we were all struck quite profoundly by the whole thing.

As we travelled around the country you could see the impact that the tournament was making – in terms of support for the team, from money coming in from around the world with the fans touring around the place and from government incentives as they pumped money in for the tournament. The legacy that the World Cup would leave on South Africa was plain to see and it was wonderful to know that the tournament could make a real difference to people's lives.

Kenny Milne: South Africa was a very interesting place to go for the World Cup, but it was also fairly dodgy. We had armed guards with us all the time and we were told in no uncertain terms that there were areas that we were just not to go to. I thought that when the football World Cup was played in 2010 that there would be more incidents of people getting into trouble in the rough areas than there were, but the fact that there weren't was fantastic and you could see the good that tournaments like that can do.

Doddie Weir: South Africa was a great place to travel to, but there was still a risk of trouble so we always travelled everywhere with armed guards. But we still got out and about, did some safaris, went to Sun City, played a lot of golf and generally took both our rugby and our play seriously. It was a great tour.

Peter Wright: The French pool match was our big one. The referee in that game was a guy called Wayne Erickson, who was an Australian and an ex-prop. He set up a scrum and put his foot in to mark the distance apart he wanted between the two front-rows. Well, he stood on my toe, and for some reason he had running spikes on, so it was absolutely agony. So he got a volley of abuse for that, and it was the one time I got away with it. He did apologise to be fair.

In that same game I remember rucking Thierry Lacroix and managing to take the strip off his back, which I thought was quite impressive. But as I was standing there admiring my handy-work, Marc Cecillon came right across the ruck and smacked me in the side of the jaw. I spent the rest of the game trying to get him back. If I'd known then what I know now – he's in prison for killing his wife – I maybe wouldn't have been quite so keen to make an enemy of him.

We had to win that game to play Ireland in the quarter-finals, whereas if we lost we were going to play New Zealand, so we knew what was at stake. We got ahead and were playing well, but then we let them back into it, and Lacroix, who had been struggling with his kicking in the tournament up to that point, couldn't miss. We lost a try in the second minute of injury time from a free-kick scrum. We had been pushing their scrum all over the park and this time we wheeled them and shoved them into touch. It collapsed and the referee gave them the free-kick, which they took quickly and Emile Ntamack scored in the corner.

I remember asking the referee after the game why he had given the free-kick, and he said, 'Because I did.' That was all he would say. And then they wonder why players have a massive dislike of referees. Why would we give away a free-kick when we were that much on top? It was ludicrous. And if he'd put his hand up and admitted he made a mistake you could have accepted that – everyone has a job to do and we all make mistakes, but the bigger person is the one who puts his hand up and takes responsibility.

Gavin Hastings: If ever there was a game we contrived to lose, which we should have won at a canter, then that was it. There was a defining moment with about fifteen minutes to go, when we were attacking near their 22, and one of our boys put in a late tackle after the clearance kick had been made. The ball landed on the halfway line and then we got marched back another ten yards because one of the forwards argued. Thierry Lacroix kicked the goal, so all of a sudden we had gone from really piling the pressure on them to conceding three points ten seconds later. The French might not have won the game until injury time, when Emile Ntamack scored that try and Lacroix kicked the conversion which made it 22–19 – but to me, that was the moment when we lost it.

Bryan Redpath (Scotland 1993-2003, 60 Caps): We were confident because we had won in Paris for the first time in years, and we were facing them again only a couple of months down the line. We had had two good wins in our opening games against the Ivory Coast and Tonga and had been playing some nice rugby. We knew that if

Rob Wainwright breaks through against the French in a thrilling first-half where Scotland dominated proceedings but could not, ultimately, hold of for victory.

we performed then we knew we could get a result – with the team we had and the style we were playing we felt that we were capable of beating anybody. But we killed ourselves in that game. We gave three consecutive penalties away in the second half, two of them for late tackles, which was just stupid.

I remember the stadium clock reading 84 minutes as the scrum packed down – and we were still in there. Then the scrum dropped and we were penalised; Ian Jardine went to tackle Abdel Benazzi and took a bang to his eye so he couldn't get up again. They cleared the ball and their backs threw out a miss pass, and Ntamack scored out wide and that was it – they created a simple overlap and their wing scored.

Scott Hastings: I remember tackling Ntamack in the last play. I went from becoming a hero to zero when he checked my stride as I tackled him. If I had hit him full on then I could have stopped the try. The fact that I didn't make the tackle resulted in us being pitted against the All Blacks in the quarter-finals and not Ireland. Every World Cup since then, this frame by frame memory creeps into my psyche. It was me who did not have control in that tackle, at that precise moment, on that precise day. I was also part of a team that lost a World Cup semi-final to England in 1991; these things never leave you.

Kenny Milne: The France match was a real heartbreaker. We hadn't played very well against them in Paris earlier in the year and won; in the World Cup we played much better than them and lost. It is one of the cruel ironies of sport that these things happen. Right at the death it was never a free-kick to them after that scrum – we had the shunt on them and should have been rewarded for it. It was hard to stomach because we felt that we had deserved to win that match which would have taken us into a quarter-final with Ireland, and we hadn't lost to Ireland in years, so we would have been pretty comfortable with facing them and would have expected to progress through to the semi-final. As it was we got New Zealand in the quarters and they were a phenomenal side.

Peter Wright: On the same day as we lost to France, Max Brito – who had played against us a few days earlier – broke his neck playing for the Ivory Coast against Tonga. It was a couple of hours before our game and I remember watching it. He went into a ruck and didn't get up again – but we didn't know how serious it was at that stage. When we came off after our game we were pretty down and disappointed about the whole thing, then Duncy Paterson came in and told us how serious Brito's injury was. And it was a really strange thing because in a macabre sort of way it perked us up. We had lost a game of rugby which meant we were going to have to play the All Blacks instead of Ireland next, who we would really have fancied our chances against, but Max Brito wasn't going to walk again. It put everything into perspective. We had no right to feel sorry for ourselves when you thought about what that guy and his family and friends were going though.

Kenny Milne: In the build up to the quarter-final because all the focus was on Jonah Lomu. Gavin, being the man that he is, was going around all week saying that Lomu would be easy to tackle – all you had to do was tackle him low and the momentum of his run and his size would just fell him. Well, within a couple of minutes of the kick-off the ball went out to Lomu and he sets off on this run. Craig Joiner reckoned that it would be easier to tackle him from the side or from behind, so he gave Lomu his outside shoulder, which the big man duly took. What Craig hadn't accounted for was how fast Lomu was and as soon as he had made the break on the outside he was gone – Craig didn't get near him. So all that was left of our defence was Gavin. One on one. Gav ran up to meet Lomu, dipped his shoulder for the tackle . . . and was completely trampled over. Behind the posts Gav pulled us all into a circle and started saying, 'Don't worry lads, it's just a minor setback,' and so on, but all I could think was: 'I thought Lomu was supposed to be easy to tackle!'

Gavin Hastings: New Zealand had already established themselves as the team of the tournament by the time we met them. They had demolished Ireland, Japan and Wales in their pool and had clocked up over 220 points in just three games, which was just unbelievable. Having played them in 1993, we had seen a glimpse of what was to come, but even that didn't really prepare us. We were a good side but their play was just from a different planet – the speed and the strength and the skill across every position. And in Jonah Lomu they really had something that no one had ever seen on a rugby pitch before – and he had only just turned twenty at the time.

We scored some good tries that day. My brother got one and Doddie Weir got two, and I pretty much kicked everything that I could to try and keep us in it, but they ran away with it in the end. I had decided to retire after the World Cup, so as they began to really rack up the scoreline, I knew that the final minutes of my international career were drawing to a close. It was an emotional time, but what a fabulous tournament it was to bow out from. We didn't recognise the impact that the World Cup would have on South Africa at the time, nor did we really appreciate until later the symbolism of Mandela wearing the Springbok jersey to the final, which had for so many

Jonah Lomu rampages through the Scotland defence

decades been the ultimate image of apartheid to much of the country. But looking back on it all, it really was an incredible thing to have been involved with and I am so proud that I was there to play a little part in it – even if it was just as a very peripheral figure amongst so many others at the tournament.

Kenny Milne: That New Zealand game was Gavin's last match, but it was also mine and Iain Morrison's. Gav and I came onto the scene together on tour to Canada in 1985, so it was nice to go out together in 1995.

Scott Hastings: The emotion that swept across the country when South Africa won their first World Cup match was extraordinary – and you suddenly realised what it meant to the country to be back from their international ban and to be playing, finally, in a World Cup. You could see the awareness of what the Springboks were achieving growing and growing throughout the tournament in every facet of society, not just the white communities, and by the end it was just unbelievable. And when Nelson Mandela appeared wearing the Springbok shirt, it was incredible. The way they won it – against the All Blacks, who had been far-and-away the best team in the tournament – showed the courage of their players, but it also showed how sporting performances can be carried on an emotional wave of support, and you could really see for the first time how rugby could change the face of a country. It really was amazing to be part of the whole thing.

Doddie Word and Rob Wainwright carry Gavin Hastings from the field as Scotland's captain says farewell to the international arena.

EIGHTEEN

CROSSING THE RUBICON
1995-1998

There is an ancient Chinese curse: 'May you live in interesting times'. In Scotland in particular, 1995 will be remembered with both delight and poignancy. The Toony Flip, the wonders of the Rainbow World Cup. . . and Vernon Pugh's announcement in Paris on 27 August that the game was now 'open'.

Some would say that rugby union had, in one way or another, been professional for years. There is the apocryphal story of Barry John declaring that he had no interest in playing for a professional rugby league team because he 'couldn't afford to'. Others would argue that the advent of the World Cup in 1987 was the first true step to professionalism, for an event that generated so much revenue could not continue indefinitely without the entertainers on show eventually demanding their share of the spoils. Indeed, one of the defences that the IRB cited when declaring the game open was to dispel the culture of shamateurism that was already prevalent in a number of the leading rugby nations.

The various levels of professionalism in different countries before the game went officially open can be discussed and debated at length. In Scotland, however, it is generally accepted that the players prided themselves on adhering to their staunch amateur roots. The SRU itself was draconian in enforcing its dogmatic stance on professionalism and clamped down severely on any hint of money being earned by a player as a result of his rugby status. Roy Laidlaw and John Rutherford were banned from rugby for three years following the publication of their co-authored memoir, Rugby Partnership, *as was Colin Deans for publishing his autobiography,* You're a Hooker, Then.

But while the SRU's defiance was, in many ways, a noble defence of the game's amateur traditions, it also meant that the union was catastrophically under-prepared for the professional era when it at last arrived.

In 2007, Gill and Macmillan published Brendan Fanning's From There to Here: Irish Rugby in the Professional Era, *a fascinating study of the transformation of a disorganised Irish Rugby Union – which was once brutally derided by its own president Noel Henderson, who observed that 'while the state of British sport may be mostly serious but never hopeless, the state of Irish sport, though mostly hopeless, is never serious' – into one of the most successful unions on the domestic, European and international stage. Ulster, Munster and Leinster have dominated in Europe for over a decade, each having lifted the Heineken Cup (twice in Munster's case, three times in Leinster's) and featured almost perennially in the knock-out stages of the competition. Leinster won the Magners League (later the RaboDirect Pro12, then the Guinness Pro12) in 2002, 2008, 2013 and 2014, Munster in 2003, 2009 and 2011, and Ulster in 2006. Meanwhile, the Irish international team won the Triple Crown in 2004, 2006 and 2007, the Grand Slam in 2009 and back-to-back Six Nations Championships in 2014 and 2015. By mid-2015, they were the number*

Opposite: Gregor Townsend prepares to kick to touch against Ireland in the 1996 Six Nations.

two ranked side in the world behind World Cup holders, New Zealand.

There is no equivalent publication about Scottish rugby in the professional age. From the SRU's professionalisation of the four traditional districts, to their compression into two 'Super Districts', to the expansion to three professional teams with the reintroduction of the Borders, and then the reversion back to two with its closure, Scottish professional players have rarely had a moment to settle in anything close to a stable environment. For most of the first two decades of professionalism, resources were stretched to the limit and the purse strings held tightly by Murrayfield; as a result, Edinburgh and Glasgow flourished only in blips and achieved very little of any substance. Edinburgh qualified for the Heineken Cup quarter-finals in 2004, the semi-finals in 2012, finished second in the Magners League in 2009 and over the years have beaten just about every top side in Europe – but have often only when their own hopes for qualification to the latter rounds of various competitions have been snuffed out. Glasgow, too, have taken some eminent scalps over the years, most notably Toulouse's at the Stade Ernest Wallon in 2009, and qualified for the Magners League's inaugural semi-finals in 2010. But for much of their existence as professional entities, they have remained a minnow in European rugby. All that started to change, however, when Gregor Townsend was moved sideways from his position as Scotland backs coach to take over the reins at Glasgow Warriors in 2012. Townsend succeeded Sean Lineen, who had taken Glasgow from a side that often struggled against the bigger teams from Ireland and Wales into a team that regularly finished the season in the top-half of the league; there was some vocal opposition that Townsend had failed to prove himself with Scotland and that the Glasgow job was simply an unmerited golden handshake given to him by his old cronies at Murrayfield. Townsend said nothing, but got to work. And very soon he showed just what an astute operator he was. They made it to the semi-finals of the league in 2013, before losing the Leinster; in 2014 they went one further and qualified for the final – but again lost to Leinster. 2014-15 was the breakout season, however, as they finished the league in top position, defeated Ulster in the semi-final and then coasted to a comfortable victory over Munster in the final to deliver the first piece of major silverware for Scottish club rugby in the professional era. Their home ground of Scotstoun is now a fortress. And Townsend is hell-bent on continuing the trajectory of the Glasgow Warrior project.

Edinburgh have fared less well in recent years, but they made it to final of the European Challenge Cup in 2015 and are working hard to emulate the success of their rivals along the M8.

It has been a tumultuous two decades for Scottish rugby since Rupert Murdoch's News International Company signed the SANZAR (South Africa, New Zealand and Australia Rugby) nations on board for his Tri-Nations and Super 12 tournaments in 1995 – after which the other world unions jumped desperately, and on the whole blindly, aboard the professional ship as it set sail for a new dawn. Any potential tome on Scottish professional rugby would no doubt ponder the merits and deficiencies of the myriad decisions that were made under intense time pressure by the SRU in 1995. Should the domestic leagues have gone professional, or was the professionalisation of the districts the correct way forward? Were the amalgamation of Edinburgh and the Borders into the Edinburgh Reivers, and

Glasgow and Caledonia into the Glasgow Caledonians the wisest utilisation of limited resources? Was the third team, the Borders, ever really given a proper chance to establish itself when it was resurrected in 2002, or should there have been a team set up in Stirling, Perth, Dundee or Aberdeen instead? And then there was the rebuilding of Murrayfield into the mighty stadium that it is to today – the cost of which plunged the union into debt to a tune of over £20 million which crippled development of the domestic game for more than two decades. Should the SRU have taken on this redevelopment itself, or should it, as the IRFU have done with Lansdowne Road, have held out until the government stepped in to finance the project?

Throughout all these machinations, the SRU, its employees, its structure and its very role in the Scottish game have come under constant scrutiny, both within its own ranks and without. Serious questions about professionalism, player welfare, team and league structures and so on were asked in 1995, and have continued to be asked every year since then. They will continue to be asked until consistent success is established across the board, replicating the achievements made across the Irish Sea and in the other major unions around the world. For in the professional era, victories, titles, trophies, qualifications, rankings, performance-based business viability and the provision of entertainment for the paying fan is what the game is now about; indeed, they are the only barometers of success. It is no longer just about a player pulling on a jersey and giving his all for his teammates, his supporters and the badge on his chest. The essence of the game has changed and what it means to pull on a professional club or international jersey has a different edge to it than in days gone by. Whether that has been to the benefit of the greater good of the game is, and perhaps always shall be, open to debate.

Interesting times, indeed.

Gordon Bulloch (Scotland 1997-2005, 75 Caps plus 2 Caps for the Lions): In 1996, we were sent letters which said we were being offered an SRU contract and that you were either a grade one, two or three player, which meant you had a salary of £20,000, £30,000 or £50,000. It was done en masse; we all went in to negotiate together, so as soon as the senior players at that time were happy we all signed. That meant that there was no real succession planning for when the guys who had signed for £20,000 or £30,000 became senior players, and it ended up with some individuals who had won 30-odd caps still being on £20,000.

We would turn up on Monday morning for training and everyone had to wear a shirt and tie, because we didn't know what you did as a professional rugby player. We'd get changed and do two minute runs, because that's what athletes did – no one knew how to train professional rugby players to get fitter.

Nowadays the coaches are told how long they can have a player by the medics and by the strength and conditioning team. Back then you were run into the ground by the coach and then passed over to the medics and fitness guys after the coach was done with you. It has gradually evolved since then. Marty Hulme came in and started introducing specific training depending on your body shape, position and so on.

We were on a learning curve in terms of nutrition as well. At one stage during the 1999 World Cup, if we'd been served boiled chicken and red pasta sauce one more time, there would have been a riot. You'd walk down the corridor in the hotel at half-past-nine at night, and there would be empty pizza boxes discarded outside all the rooms. It took a while to recognise that you have to entertain guys and give them some sort of quality of life. You can't expect guys to live and breathe rugby, rugby, rugby, just because you say they are rugby players.

Keith Robertson: The SRU made the decision to invest in the professional game, but they didn't know how it was going to develop and they didn't have the people who could take it forward. That's why they have lost so much money along the way. They just threw good money after bad. That has had a massive bearing on where we stand now as a country, a union and in terms of the quality of rugby we have produced throughout much of the professional age.

John Rutherford: The professional game took off in other countries so much faster, but it just hasn't happened here – at least not until 2015 when Glasgow won the Pro12. I still don't think that two professional teams are enough. I'm envious of what has happened in Ireland because they seem to be flying at the moment. And to think, we used to be so far ahead of them.

Rowen Shepherd (Scotland 1995-98, 20 Caps): Some of the training sessions were very long in those days. Because we were full-time we were expected to be on the training paddock more-or-less full-time – but if you look at the way the professional boys are handled these days, that's not the way it works. Training sessions are shorter and they are far more specific.

It could have been handled better in terms of introducing the players to the professional environment. We got bombarded with all the fitness and dietary advice, and there wasn't much support for what was really a huge change in lifestyle. I mean, one day we were amateurs then the next we signed a bit of paper and we were professionals with all that that entailed. Nobody seemed to have worked out what it was going to be like, and more importantly, what it needed to be like. And it wasn't just the players who were having to learn on the hop. The coaching team – Jim Telfer, Dave McLean, Richie Dixon, David Johnston and so on – were searching for the right formula as well.

Doddie Weir: I thought it was a ridiculous decision for the SRU to close the Borders for a second time and amalgamate them with Glasgow. It just didn't make sense and I couldn't understand the reasons given for it. The SRU had put a lot of money into redeveloping the pitch at Gala and had signed a long-term deal to maintain it; the ground had superb parking, the facilities at the Border College that the team used for training were great, and there is a niche market in the Borders because rugby is the major sport there. The pitch, changing rooms and facilities in Glasgow were dreadful, parking was a nightmare and the interest level is mainly in football. Even though things have improved with Glasgow in the last couple of years, I still think it was crazy for us not to have a third team – especially when the facilities were already there and up and running.

Donnie Macfadyen (Scotland 2002-2006, 11 Caps): I was part of the first generation of Scottish players whose career was one hundred per cent in the professional era. Having said that, when I first came into the Glasgow ranks, professional rugby was still a very new concept so what was considered as being professional in 1999, when I started, was night and day to what it is now. Now it is a properly professional sport, while back then it was essentially amateurs training slightly more than they normally would and getting paid for it; it took a long time for that transition into full professionalism to take place.

The amount of analysis that goes in now as well as the strength and conditioning of players are the two things that I really noticed develop during my time at Glasgow and with Scotland. As far as the analysis went, when I first started it was all videos, so the picture wasn't necessarily all that brilliant and you had to stop the tape and rewind it and all that kind of thing – but now every player gets DVDs of their games and their training and the computer programmes calculates how far they run and so on. The programme breaks the game down and you get clips of every bit of play that you're involved in – and it's the same with the opposition players that you're coming up against that week, so you can study how they run and step and pass, or you can study lineout and back-row moves. It's a different world.

The players now all train with GPS trackers on so that the coaches and fitness guys can track the work that they're putting in at training, and they wear heartmonitors to make sure that they're always working as hard as they can – if the heart rate is too low then the fitness guys know that player needs to increase his intensity; there are no hiding places any more. They also use drones so that the coaches can watch the movement and patterns and so on of the players from an aerial viewpoint, which is so much better than just standing on the side of the pitch. And the advances just keep on coming.

Rowen Shepherd: When I came into the side in November 1995, replacing Gavin Hastings after the World Cup, we played Samoa at Murrayfield in our first Test match as professionals and drew 15–15. There wasn't a lot of rugby getting played at that time. I remember Toony was getting moved around so we didn't really have an idea about what kind of team we were trying to be. I think that because of the type of player he was and that he was now a professional, they figured he could play anywhere they wanted him and he would always play to his optimum, which was a ridiculous attitude to have. But then they seemed to see sense and he got a run of games at stand-off during the 1996 Six Nations – and things that season took off from there.

Gregor Townsend: While 1995 was a great year because we won in Paris, 1996 was even better. We had this young team and we just had this great belief in ourselves. I was playing in my favourite position at stand-off, with Bryan Redpath, a good friend of mine, at scrum-half; and with guys like Rowen Shepherd, Craig Joiner and Kevin McKenzie coming into the side, there was just this great feeling. Everybody wrote us off, but we played a great brand of open rugby – which I think is the type of rugby Scotland need to play – and we were really successful.

Rowen Shepherd: We went to Ireland first-up, and that was at a time when Ireland couldn't buy a win off Scotland. Naivety was a good thing for us. Mike Dods, Craig Joiner and myself were the back three, and we had decided we were just going to have a go. It was pouring with rain and we should never have been counter-attacking but it worked. I remember with five minutes to go there was a really positive feel, the crowd on the terraces had gone quiet, and I said to Scott Hastings, 'We've got this one.' He snapped back, 'No we haven't, not until the final whistle goes.' He had been there and done it, and he gave us young bucks a bit of a reality check. But we held on to win 16-10, which was a great start to the campaign.

We played France next, and I think David Johnston and Richie Dixon must have been shitting themselves because we were playing against Émile Ntamack, Phillipe Saint-André and Jean-Luc Sadourny, so they brought in a psychologist called Richard Cox to speak to Craig Joiner, Mike Dodds and myself. He just said, 'Right, you're on the same wavelength, you're going to have a go, you're going to play France at their own game.'

And we just nodded our heads and said, 'Let's do it then.'

Knowing no better, we just let rip and had a go. Toony was on fire and everything we tried worked, and we won 19–14 in the end. I spoke to Saint-André about it a few years later and he said that was still reeling from that match. It was his second match as captain and he was sure he was going to lead France to the Grand Slam that year, and Scotland was not a match they expected to have a problem with.

Rob Wainwright: In 1996 we felt that we could beat anyone. It was the best season I had. Richie Dixon was under a huge amount of pressure from above and I don't really know where it started to go wrong for him. The difference, psychologically, between the England game in 1995 and the France game at Murrayfield in 1996 was stark – we knew right from the start of that 1996 match that we would win. We scored two tries in twenty minutes through Michael Dods; people talk about the Murrayfield roar and the noise that went up for those two tries and throughout the game was the best I'd ever heard it.

Gregor Townsend: A lot of that was down to how we started the game. We called a 'miss-one-blind' from the kick-off. It's quite a gutsy call with a miss-one, and then the blindside winger coming outside the centres and being missed as well. We ended up making a huge break off it and that set the tone. The whole game was pulsating. I remember Rob Wainwright catching a high ball in our twenty-two and running it out, and Shep was running at them all day.

In the lead up to Mike Dods' try, I remember Basil [Bryan Redpath] chipping forward and running past Laurent Cabannes, one of the great exponents of this open type of rugby, as if he was at half pace. The French couldn't live with the speed we were going at. We dropped the ball over the line three times that day, and with other missed opportunities we could have scored a few more than the five tries we got against France in 1999. I remember Jim Telfer saying after the game, 'Yeah you were good boys, but you should have won by thirty points.' And he was right.

Rowen Shepherd: Next we went down to Wales and I had heard people talking about breathing out of their backside before but I didn't really understand what they meant until I played in that match. It was totally harum-scarum. They had clocked the style we wanted to play, with Townsend playing flat and Ian Jardine hitting up the middle to provide quick ball, so they slowed us down pretty effectively and it was harder to get round them. It was exciting from the point of view that it was erratic, not because it was great rugby – there were a lot of mistakes.

Stewart Campbell (Scotland 1995-1998, 17 Caps): It was the last time Scotland played at the old Cardiff Arms Park. I remember we had a line-out near to their line and we couldn't hear the codes, we were screaming in each others' ears but still couldn't hear a thing because the Welsh were making so much noise and it was just bouncing down off the roof of the old stand.

Arwel Thomas missed with the last kick of the game, which would have got them the draw, we were all standing together under the posts but nobody celebrated. It was just a huge sense of relief because we should have won comfortably but ended up almost throwing it away.

Rowen Shepherd: We were all a bit shell-shocked. We were three from three and were suddenly favourites to win the Grand Slam. England had lost their first game to France in Paris and hadn't played particularly well against Wales in their last match, but they had recalled Dean Richards at number eight and he was the difference that day. He was like a honey pot at kick offs. He got under everything and slowed it down.

Because we were such a young team we maybe weren't aware of what we were involved in. I think the occasion slightly got the better of us. It was my fifth cap and a lot of the guys in the side were in the same sort of position – apart from Scott Hastings, the rest of us were all still trying to find our feet. If you look at the Scottish sides that won the Grand Slam in 1984 and 1990, there was a lot of experience there which helped them cope with the occasion as well as the rugby match.

It wasn't a great game. I think if we had got something out of Gregor's breakout from our twenty-two early in the second-half then that might have opened things up, but in the end it was a total anti-climax. England came up, strangled the game brilliantly and went away with the win, 9–18.

The English had Will Carling and Jeremy Guscott in the centre, and to this day I'm still amazed at how little they were used – but I suppose they just didn't fancy running at Jardine and Hastings because those two boys could tackle.

It was a disappointing end to the tournament and we not only missed out on the Grand Slam but also the title because of point difference. It was then that the mistakes we made dropping the ball over the line against France really came back to haunt us.

Rob Wainwright: Richie Dixon and David Johnston developed the most amazing feeling in the squad while they were in charge. They rarely receive the plaudits that they deserve for their time in charge, but I want to go on record to say what a great job they did. Often their training sessions were led by the players. Great teams are not led by coaches but by the players and a strong core of leaders within that. That was a team in the truest sense of the word because it was so much more than the sum of its parts. We all worked really well together and had a great bond; unfortunately the team started to be tinkered with in terms of personnel – partly due to injury – and that great feeling and bond seemed to die a little. It started when we went to New Zealand and our top-scorer from the Five Nations, Michael Dods, wasn't included because Jim Telfer, who was the tour manager, didn't think he was big enough for the professional era, which given Scotland's limited resources seemed a pretty luxurious attitude. As the tour rolled on, a distracting rift developed between the tour management and the players and coaches.

Stewart Campbell: It was the tour from hell. The food was the main thing – our management phoned ahead to every hotel and all we got to eat was either boiled chicken or boiled salmon with rice – and tour morale just went through the floor. Then in one hotel we got an apple pie and we were all cheering, but they hadn't put any sugar in it so it tasted horrible. You felt like a machine – they completely overlooked the importance of the players being in a good place psychologically.

I was sharing with Barry Stewart and it was his twenty-first birthday. There was no party or anything like that – but we sneaked out to get a KFC for a treat. We climbed out the window of our room and when we came back we were like two little kids hiding behind cars with our party bags full of greasy chicken bits because we were sure Telfer would be keeping his eye out.

Don't get me wrong, I know you have to take in the right stuff, but when you are training that hard you can get away with eating a bit of the wrong stuff once in a while because you burn it off the next day. When you spend weeks on end being told you can't do this, and you can't do that, you end up rebelling against it.

We went from an amateur environment to going completely overboard, and I think they missed the boat from a mental wellbeing perspective – which is huge in rugby. There wasn't a fall-out, but there were a lot of disgruntled players.

It is strange because at the World Cup in South Africa in 1995 it was the same management set-up, but it was just a wee bit more flexible. Maybe they saw that trip as a way of imposing the new way of doing things, whereas the World Cup was not the place for mixing things up.

Rowen Shepherd: It was the first professional tour so Jim Telfer was keen for it to be done properly and he had us on strict diets which included absolutely no alcohol. We were drinking hot chocolate in the pub and Jim was coming round checking our mugs. The media heard about it and it became a bit of an issue, but we understood the situation. I would say that the one lesson from the tour was that we should maybe have been treated a bit more like adults as opposed to naughty kids who couldn't be trusted.

There is a great respect for New Zealand rugby and we didn't want to look like we were shoddy, and I don't think we did. But Scottish players, generally, are always very honest and relatively well behaved, and maybe being treated with a little bit more respect might have allowed everyone to work through the process of turning professional together. It was a little bit them and us.

There was one meeting in Southland which was kind of heated. I think Scott Hastings and David Johnston were just saying, 'Look, there is happy medium here, if the boys want to have a glass of wine with their meal, or want to stay up a little bit later and relax and chat, then it should be allowed.'

Doddie Weir: Telling grown-ups that they're not allowed to drink is not the way to do things. It brings out the rebellious side in you. At the end of the tour we were told that we could eat whatever we wanted because the tour was over and you found that you didn't actually want to eat a load of rubbish; you would never have a massive drinking session the night before a game, because you could never play as well if you had had a skin-full and it might mean that it would be the last time you would play – and also, we were all desperate to beat the All Blacks, so no one was going to do anything outrageous before the Test matches. But that responsibility was taken away from us and it got a lot of players very annoyed. Looking after yourself is just common sense, but the fact that we were told we weren't allowed to do this or that like a bunch of little kids got a lot of backs up. It was the wrong way to do it. Drinking sessions can pull you together as a group. In the old days, between 1990 and 1996, we would meet up on a Wednesday before a Five Nations game, train and then go out on the town. It would pull you together as a group.

Peter Wright: Scotland had always been very relaxed when on tour. We didn't have curfews and things like that – we were just trusted not to get too carried away. Then suddenly we were being told to be in bed by 10pm, we couldn't drink and things like that. So it was a huge culture shock. I remember travelling by bus from Wanganui to

Auckland and we watched the movie *Road House* on the video. At the team meeting that night Jim Telfer lost the plot about that, he just couldn't understand why we wouldn't want to watch rugby videos – because that is the way he did things. But we weren't used to living and breathing rugby every woken hour – we needed some release.

One Tuesday night, a few of us – Derek Stark, Gregor Townsend and myself – got speaking to the manager of the hotel in Hamilton we were staying in and ended up asking him to take us into town for a couple of beers. He told us to meet him in the reception at 8pm, but we said we'd meet him at his car in the car park so we could sneak out the back door. We met him and got in the car and as he was reversing back out of his parking space he looked in the mirror and realised he couldn't see any of us because we were all ducked down. He said, 'What's wrong?' – thinking there was a drive-by shooting or something happening. But it was because Jim was at the front of the hotel and we were hiding from him. We went out and had a couple of beers and came home, it was nothing major. Because we were being told what not to do, it made us more determined to do it.

Tony Stanger: I would never criticise Jim or the other coaches about that tour. It was the first tour of the professional era so how could they possibly know what was required? But it was a pressure cooker environment so we needed some sort of release and having a few drinks and letting your hair down is a good thing to do. It was a mistake calling it a dry tour because that wasn't what touring was about at that time. Towards the end of the tour we did manage to negotiate a bit of a night out, not getting smashed but a few drinks and a bit of a laugh together – and it made such a difference to the trip. It was all a learning curve.

Rob Wainwright: It wasn't really an alcohol issue as such, it was a player–management issue. On the 1997 Lions tour the management was just fantastic. For me, Fran Cotton was the most important man on that Lions tour because of the way he ran things. In the week-long camp before we left for South Africa he sat us all down and told us that this was our tour and so we, as players, should be making all the rules. We thrashed out a set of rules that we were all happy with and we abided by them.

Jim's management was very different to Fran's. He told us about the alcohol ban, he didn't ask us about it – if he had asked, most of us would have bought into it. He told the press that the tour was going to be dry and then he told us. If he had come to us first to talk about it I would certainly have argued a case for a slightly more relaxed approach than the one he took, but still have supported the idea.

Jim was an amazing forwards coach, just unbelievably good at making forward units the best they can be – people go on about how good the '97 Lions' backline was, but as much as Fran and Geech, Jim was the most important man on that tour because he guaranteed the provision of the ball to those backs because of the work he did with the forwards and his contribution to the whole thing was amazing. But he fell down as a manager; it just wasn't his thing.

Jim was one of the most incredible speakers I've ever heard when his gander's up, he is incredibly impassioned and moving in what he says. As a manager those speeches would sometimes be slightly farcical but some were amazing. I remember being in Dublin a few hours before playing Ireland at Lansdowne Road and Jim sat us down at about 11am after our morning run-through and gave the most impassioned speech that had the players climbing the walls, it was just brilliant. And as captain, I just remember thinking, 'Jim, why have you told us this four hours before kick-off when we're usually trying to keep the guys calm? This should have been saved for just before we go out to play.' But that was just the way things were organised at the time. On the Lions tour he gave some amazing speeches, many of which have been recorded for prosperity on the tour video, but he actually gave his speeches the night before the Test matches and they would have been so good to hear just before we went out of the changing room. Looking back, I wish I had had the courage to go and speak to him about it and asked him to make his speech in the changing room – it would have been even more sensational for us as players.

Jim Telfer: The idea of the tour being alcohol free was decided by the management as a group – we wanted to do everything we could to give the players a credible chance of beating New Zealand – which was the whole point of touring there in the first place. Before we left we sat down and discussed the idea of trying something different when we went on tour there because all our previous efforts had ended in failure in the Tests. David McLean, our fitness coach, was doing everything he could to educate the players on diet and nutrition, trying to pull them into the professional era, and he had studies that proved how detrimental alcohol was to player performance. They were still allowed to have fun on tour – play golf and do trips and have a drink at the weekend – but the idea was that they would be more physically prepared to take on the All Blacks if they kept their bodies free from alcohol during the week before a match. It was hardly rocket science, but the players really made a fuss about it in the aftermath of that tour. They were clinging on to amateur ideals which didn't belong in the professional era. Professionalism was new to us all and as a management group we thought it was the best way forward. The All Blacks didn't drink in the build up to the Tests, I can tell you that, and time has proved that this is just basic preparation for Test match rugby in the professional era. I got a lot of stick about it at the time, but my methods were proved to be correct in the end – every country in the world has that outlook these days.

Gregor Townsend: I actually really enjoyed that trip. It was the first time I had been to New Zealand and I was playing really well. It was a dry tour and it was a mistake telling the press that because they jumped on it and from then on they were keeping their eyes peeled for anyone breaking the curfew.

I don't think Jim appreciated at the time what New Zealand players do after games. When we were there four years later in 2000, we went out after the first Test and were playing drinking games with Justin Marshall, Andrew Mehrtens and Taine Randell.

That is the way rugby is; you have to bond as a team and drinking together can really help that. To his credit, Jim was assistant coach on the 1997 Lions tour to South Africa, and when the players making the rules said that going out for a few beers was an important part of the team bonding process he was all for it – so he clearly realised he had maybe got that a wee bit wrong in 1996.

We set a proud record on that tour of scoring the most points ever to be scored against the All Blacks up to that point, during the first Test in Dunedin. Unfortunately that coincided with the dubious distinction of having surrendered more points than any other Scotland side had ever conceded. We lost the game 62–31.

Rob Wainwright: Scoring thirty-one points away from home against the All Blacks, especially in a stronghold like Carisbrook, but still ending up on the losing side and with a record margin posted against us, was pretty difficult to accept at the time. We had worked hard and pretty effectively for much of the game, especially around the ruck and maul area, but their back three of Christian Cullen, Jonah Lomu and Jeff Wilson were just incredible and they tore us to pieces whenever they got the ball in space.

Gregor Townsend: In the second Test, in Auckland, we played really well into a horrible gale in the first-half and we came in at half-time trailing only 17–7, and we all thought we were going to beat the All Blacks, but they just screwed us into the ground in the second-half.

Rowen Shepherd: I scored our first try in that Auckland game. Zinzan Brooke sclaffed a clearance kick and it was a dreadful day with a sodden pitch but I ran it back to their twenty-two anyway, then sent a kick up in the air. Peter Wright has told me that the subs were all on the bench, burying their heads in their hands and muttering about what I was doing. It took one bounce between Craig Dowd and Ian Jones, squirted up into my hands and I scored under the sticks. So it went from, 'For fuck's sake, Shep . . .' to 'Ya beauty, Shep!' in a matter of nanoseconds. That's the way rugby works out, sometimes.

The following season was hellish. Our opponents knew what to expect and things didn't quite click, so we struggled a bit from the dreaded 'second-season-syndrome'. The previous season, we were unbeaten in the autumn and then got off to a good start against Ireland away from home so we were on a roll. Whereas in 1997, with more or less the same team, the momentum went the other way – we lost to Australia 29–19 in November and then struggled against Italy just before Christmas before winning 29–22. I don't remember anything specific being wrong with that season as opposed to the year before, except perhaps that the opposition had sussed us out. We had a great game against Ireland which we won 38–10 at Murrayfield, which salvaged that season and probably the next for the players, but we had gone from genuine Grand Slam contenders to find ourselves in a major slump.

And because we had signed contracts there wasn't the same understanding from the public – they felt they were entitled to expect better. A switch had been flicked and all of a sudden we were expected to be professionals. You shouldn't drop the ball and you shouldn't make mistakes because you were a professional, but we weren't very professional in our approach. The Scottish game was doing its best, but compared to the likes of New Zealand, Australia and South Africa, and even England and France to a degree, the set-up was not geared up for the transition. You look at players now and most of them take a long time to establish themselves in the pro game – you are told that guys are on a year-long conditioning programme, they're certainly not expected to be the finished article straight away – yet with one signature we were pros and that was it . . . and a lot of us were amateurs in the truest sense of the word trying to be pros.

Jamie Mayer (Scotland 1998-2000, 8 Caps): When I learned that I'd been selected for the Scotland tour to South Africa in the summer of '97 it was just the most brilliant news I could have imagined. It was essentially a development tour and there were no Test matches because it was on at the same time as the Lions tour, but wherever we went the whole place was just rugby mad and the atmosphere around the country was incredible. There was a great moment when Tony Stanger was called up from our squad to join the Lions for the last ten days of their tour and played against the

Doddie Weir towers over his teammates at a lineout at Lansdowne Road, 1997.

Northern Free State. If ever there was a tour to capture your imagination about the magic of international rugby, it was that '97 Lions tour.

I remember sharing a room with Stuart Reid and, having never been on a tour like that before, I wasn't sure what the etiquette was regarding getting undressed in the room – did I get naked and go to the bathroom or did I get undressed in the bathroom and go back to bed with a towel round me? Anyway, Stuart sensed my dilemma and in true touring tradition decided to wind the naive new boy up. So when I came out of the bathroom he threw back the covers of his bed and patted the mattress. 'Come on Jamie,' he purred, 'there's room in here for two.'

Duncan Hodge (Scotland 1997-2002, 26 Caps): My first start was against Australia in the autumn of 1997. I had been part of an extended 25–man squad, but I was one of three guys that got cut from that. Then Rowen Shepherd was injured in a club game the week before, so I got called in on the Tuesday and was picked to start at fullback. I had only ever played two minutes at fullback but the management played down my inexperience by saying I had played at fullback quite a bit. Australia were some team, but luckily they didn't test me out too much. They put one high ball up and I took it cleanly, but they weren't bothered about whether I was playing out of position and fairly inexperienced – they weren't going to alter how they played for that. They kept the ball in hand most of the time and if they kicked it tended to be short dinks over our defence. It worked like a dream for them and they blew us away. That was Scott Murray's first Test and I think he scored from a driven line-out and we went into the lead at that stage, although it didn't last long.

Scott Murray (Scotland 1997-2007, 87 Caps): I started playing rugby for Preston Lodge when I was about sixteen and was selected for the Scottish Schools squad to play Ireland, but didn't get on the pitch. I then quit rugby for a while to focus on basketball, which I absolutely loved and which helped hone my handling skills as well as my athleticism – all things that really helped me in the line-out when I returned to rugby. I was first capped against Australia in 1997 – alongside George Graham, Stuart Grimes, Adam Roxburgh, Grant McKelvey and James Craig. We were thumped pretty convincingly – I remember that monster Willie Ofahengaue running all over the place causing chaos and then George Gregan, Stephen Larkham and Joe Roff all scoring tries as well – but it was a pretty special moment for me because I started that match and scored a try.

Rowen Shepherd: Things went from bad to worse when we played South Africa in the following game. You are always going to take a hiding now and again from a southern hemisphere team which is on top form – I just wish it hadn't been by that much. 68–10 it finished. It was so frustrating. I'd liken it to standing in the middle of the racetrack at Silverstone, one moment Percy Montgomery is flying past you, and you have only just recovered your bearings and then James Small flies past your other shoulder. It was pretty hard going.

We got quite a tough reception that night, we stayed in the hotel and a few fans gave us a bit of stick. They had a point – from their point of view we were dire – but you have to appreciate what we were up against as well. The southern hemisphere big three transformed the game by having pace and power outside. Guys like James Small and Pieter Rossouw from South Africa, as well as Christian Cullen and, of course, Jonah Lomu of New Zealand burst onto the scene. These guys were different animals to anything we had encountered before.

Gordon Bulloch: That was my first Scotland match and obviously it was a baptism of fire. But people forget it was only 14–3 at half-time – then all of a sudden it was 68–10. In your first game in international rugby you are just trying to stay afloat so maybe it wasn't as tough for me to take as it was for some of the more experienced guys, who had a better appreciation of what it was all about.

Craig Chalmers: You don't often hear this but it was a game where I was almost pleased to get injured. It turned into Scotland's record defeat. They were a good side, a better team than the one that had won the World Cup a couple of years before.

Rob Wainwright: Percy Montgomery put in one of the finest display I've ever seen by a fullback in that game. He was just a devastating attacking force. The Springboks were so powerful that autumn; they wanted to put a marker down after losing to the Lions in the summer and those performances really made people sit up and take notice – they scored a record fifty-two points at the Parc des Princes, a record twenty-nine points at Twickenham, and then sixty-eight against us at Murrayfield. It was some revenge on the northern hemisphere.

Stewart Campbell: I've managed to block most of that game out of my memory, except for one of their tries, when we kicked off and Andre Venter caught the ball and ran right back through our whole forward pack to score. I had a hugely strong urge just to walk off the pitch, I was so annoyed with myself and with everyone else. It was the only time I ever felt like that on a rugby pitch. It was horrible.

NINETEEN

A FOND FAREWELL TO FIVE
1999

1999 was the last ever Five Nations Championship. And what a way it was to see off the grand old tournament before it became the Six Nations in the spring of the new millennium. After the hammerings from Australia and South Africa in the autumn of 1997, 1998 started no better, with Scotland falling to a 22–21 defeat to Italy in Treviso in a precursor to the Five Nations Championship. This result cost Richie Dixon and David Johnston their jobs as coaches and Jim Telfer, reinvigorated by his success as part of the Lions brains trust, returned to the fold in their stead.

Rob Wainwright: In 1997 the team was tinkered with again and then after a run of poor results, which culminated in us losing to Italy in January 1998, the coaches were cut and I was dropped as captain. The SRU's dealings with Richie and David were not handled well, but I don't suppose there is an easy way to strip out your team management. What made it worse, from a personal point of view, was that I wasn't only stripped of the captaincy, but I was also stripped of my decision making roles, such as calling the line-out and the back-row moves from scrums. They gave the task of calling the line-out to Simon Holmes, who was a fantastic player, but an open-side – not the most appropriate person to be calling a lineout – and I thought that that was just daft. Morale was low.

In terms of the captaincy moving to Gary Armstrong, I wasn't too disappointed because I thought that Gary was a fantastic leader and he had been a very important player for me during my time as captain. When he was made captain I remember that Gary used to give me a wry old smile in the changing room after matches when he had just had to do the post-match interviews and I remember him once saying, 'There are some jobs that I wish you still did.' It's a difficult job doing those post-match interviews. It's pretty hellish to have to talk about a game that you've just lost, and you want to be respectful to the opposition when you win – I remember getting seriously annoyed reading or watching post-match interviews with winning captains who just dismissed our performances as a side-show to how well his own team had done. But I also remember John Beattie giving me a row once because I apologised for our performance after we lost to Italy in 1998. He said that I should never apologise – perhaps he thought it undermined my authority as captain – but it was something I wanted to do; we had just put in the most appalling performance and I wanted to apologise to all the fans. It was just how I felt.

Telfer's impact was far from revolutionary, however, and Scotland's 17–16 victory over Ireland at Lansdowne Road was the last to be posted for a year. The team was humiliated

Opposite: Alan Tait celebrates with Stuart Grimes after the lock forward scores against Ireland in 1999.

51–6 by France at Murrayfield, lost 19–13 to Wales at Wembley (the hosts' temporary home while the Millennium Stadium was under construction) and 34–20 in the Calcutta Cup. Then came another summer from hell. The team travelled to the southern hemisphere to play Fiji in Suva and two Tests against Australia in Sydney and Brisbane. All three were pitifully one-sided, Fiji running out 51–26 winners and Australia hardly breaking sweat as they recorded 45–3 and 33–11 victories. The poor results were, however, somewhat silver lined as Scotland were able to blood a number of youngsters and implemented a more expansive style of play which, although coming unstuck in the Test matches, started to show promise in the midweek games, particularly against Matt Williams' New South Wales side in Sydney, which Scotland won 34–10.

Duncan Hodge: We had a great time on that summer tour and although we struggled in the Tests, we did pretty well against the midweek teams. I remember playing against Queensland in Brisbane and Jim Telfer gave us an absolute rollicking before we went out, picking on players and saying how bad they had been playing in previous games and that if they ever wanted to play for Scotland again then they would have to pull their socks up and go out and perform, which luckily we did and I remember Glenn Metcalfe having a fantastic game. Jim's bollockings were pretty scary – even though a lot of the older boys said that he was mellowing by that time, but you still didn't want to get on the wrong side of one of his bollockings.

The trip to Fiji was ridiculous. We left the dirt-trackers in Melbourne for three or four days to have a great time while the match squad flew over to Fiji. We arrived at around midnight the night before the game and didn't manage to have a run-through or anything beforehand. It was meant to be one of these SAS in-and-out jobs but it completely backfired. We were in bed late and then the next day we had this four-hour long trip in a roasting bus, got to this massive bowl of a ground which was as hard as concrete and then took on a Fijian team that were totally in their element.

Rowen Shepherd: I came on as a sub and it was a classic Scottish disaster. We had all flown to Australia for a week acclimatising on the Gold Coast, which we thought was the dog's bollocks, then twenty-two of us flew to Fiji to play in that game, and we were caught cold. We'd had to sit in a rickety old bus with no air-conditioning – windows open to try and generate a draft – right across Fiji; turned up at the ground without a clue as to what to expect and discovered a hard, bumpy pitch; the crowd were going crazy as every bounce of the ball went their way; they were throwing it about all over the place and we were chasing shadows. Back then teams didn't run it from their own twenty-two and off-load the ball like they were doing, and against rugby like that you have to be up to speed from minute one because you can't play catch-up. It finished 51–26.

Stewart Campbell: The ground in Suva was basically a big natural bowl, no seats just huge grassy slopes, with about 20,000 folk there. And if anybody made a mistake, all the crowd did was laugh at the top of their voices. It was the weirdest sensation, because you were expecting the sort of groan we were used to at Murrayfield, but they would just hoot with laughter. It didn't matter if it was us or the Fijians who had messed up, they just found it hilarious. They were good supporters – there was no noise when the kickers were lining up their shots at goal – and when they laughed it wasn't malicious, they were just enjoying themselves.

Rowen Shepherd: It was a bit of a wake-up call because we ended up having quite a good tour of Australia. We beat New South Wales in Sydney, a very young midweek team lost to Queensland by a single score, and quite a few guys earned their spurs on that tour – which was valuable for the next season.

Jamie Mayer: The tour itself was mainly dry, but we still had one or two great nights out, particularly in Melbourne while the Test squad were in Fiji and again at the end of the tour, and those nights were fantastic for bringing a young squad together and integrating them with the old hands.

Glenn Metcalfe (Scotland 1998-2003, 38 Caps): I came to Scotland to play club rugby with Glasgow Academicals as the coach at the time was the former Waikato rugby coach Kevin Greene. My gran was from Glasgow which allowed me the work permit to stay and also qualified me to play for Scotland. My initial intention was only to stay for a year or so and travel Europe at the end of the season. But I landed a district contract with Glasgow, got selected for an extended Scotland training squad and then went on the summer tour to Australia – so suddenly I went from bumming around Europe for a year and playing a bit of club rugby to getting a chance to play international rugby. It wasn't something that had even crossed my mind as a possibility six months earlier, so it was a real whirlwind experience.

I remember after not being selected for the Fiji match the remainder of the squad flew to Melbourne while the Test squad flew out to Fiji. We had a great night out in Melbourne and I think it may have ended with some tackling practise in the hotel hallway . . . which resulted in a rather large hole made in the wall. When the Test squad returned from Fiji the hotel management had a word to our management; Jim Telfer wasn't in the best of moods after the Fiji trip and this just made matters even worse. So all the dirt trackers were summoned for a meeting with Jim. Well, I thought my tour was over before it had started as he completely tore strips off of us. He was furious. I can't remember what he said now – I think I've blocked it from my memory – but I'm sure you couldn't print it anyway. After that I never used the hotel lift at all just in case I got trapped in it with Jim.

I was selected for the Victoria and New South Wales matches and after having won both games well I gained selection for the first Test against Australia. I couldn't believe that in such a short space of time I was about to run out in an international match. I admit I went from brimming with confidence to being a nervous wreck at kick-off. It wasn't really a memorable result as we were trounced by the Wallabies but playing Test rugby was the most thrilling feeling ever.

Rowen Shepherd: The Tests against Australia were fairly credible despite the scorelines and a big learning curve. I remember David Johnston trying to get the backs to play a bit more of an expansive game. It was one of the last old fashioned type tours – we went to play New South Wales Country away out in the sticks and Victoria down in Melbourne. And I don't think it is any coincidence that we had quite a good season after that trip.

Rowan Shepherd makes a point to his teammates during the 1998 Test match against Australia at Ballymore.

When the team returned home, their captain Rob Wainwright announced that the time had come to hang up his boots. He was a major personality in the squad and a hugely important player, but the team was fortunate enough to have a number of ready-made leaders in place to alleviate the impact of his loss. Bryan Redpath assumed the captaincy in November, for South Africa's return to Edinburgh, but despite improvements in performance, an annus horribilis was sealed as they were steamrollered by the powerful Springboks 35–10.

Duncan Hodge: We got back and Rob Wainwright decided to retire. There was a bit said in the press about it – such an influential guy deciding to retire when we were only a year out from the World Cup – but in the squad we just got on with it. When a guy decides to retire, it's very much a personal decision. For whatever reason – be it a physical thing that the body just can't take it any more, or a personal reason that the fire for the game has gone, or for family reasons or whatever – once that decision is made you can't feel aggrieved about it. Rob was a great player and a great leader, but there are always guys coming through that will step into any retiring player's shoes. It's the nature of the game. No, we were all sad to see Rob retire, but no-one questioned his decision; it was his to make and he was able to retire on his own terms, which is a rare thing in this game.

Rob Wainwright: If the game had still been amateur I would have announced my retirement after the last Test against the Wallabies. I had been reinstated as captain on that tour because Gary was injured and it had been nice to lead the team again. But as it was, I felt that I needed to speak to Jim Telfer about my decision to see what he thought. He said that I was still an important player and he wanted me to carry on for another season. It was a nice boost to my ego so I decided to stay on, but by the time the autumn came around I knew that my time was up – my body just couldn't take any more punishment – and I realised that it would be better for the team if I dropped out. Martin Leslie obviously then came in in my stead and although I didn't approve of the manner in which he was brought in, he was a fantastic player and great servant to Scottish rugby and his brother helped create the most exciting midfield Scotland have ever had. Seeing the success they had the following season wasn't frustrating as such – I felt no desire to be out there, so I knew my decision to retire had been right, and I was so pleased for them to achieve what they did because I was still very close friends with many of them – but at the same time, when Wales beat England I just thought, 'Why couldn't they have done that in 1995 or 1996?' because a result like that would have allowed me to experience a Championship win with Scotland, which I think those teams in '95 and '96 deserved.

Thanks to the advent of professionalism, the movement of players looking to ply their trade abroad increased significantly. Either through residential qualification or through ancestry, a growing number of players from the southern hemisphere began to seek out new careers abroad with the hope that they might achieve recognition on the international stage.

Representing a country other than the land of one's birth was not a new phenomenon of the professional era. From English-born James Marsh who played for Scotland in 1889 while at Edinburgh University before switching his allegiance to play for England against Ireland in 1892, to the prolific Melbourne-born and New Zealand-bred Ian Smith, who scored twenty-four tries for Scotland from 1924–33, to the Kilted Kiwi Sean Lineen, and with over 130 internationalists being capped out of London Scottish, Scotland have fielded a substantial number of players born beyond its borders. During the 1925 Grand Slam season, for example, the Scotland selectors picked the Oxford University three-quarter line en masse, which contained a New Zealander, two Australians and only one Scot. So importing players from outside Scotland had always occurred – and now a new generation of faces from around the world were lighting up Scottish rugby and adding depth to the club and international squads. Among the influx were South African prop Matthew Proudfoot, and Kiwi back-row Gordon Simpson and his compatriot winger Shaun Longstaff, each of whom made significant contributions to the Scottish cause both domestically and internationally. Arguably, however, the three most influential imports in the new professional age came in the shape of fullback Glenn Metcalfe and centre and back-row brothers John and Martin Leslie, sons of former All Black captain Andy Leslie, who qualified through their Linlithgow-born grandfather.

Metcalfe's intelligent angles of running, his accurate passing and kicking, and his ability to jink and step at speed made him a dangerous attacking weapon from fullback, where his defence was also of the highest standard. John Leslie captained Otago to the NPC title in October 1998 and he and his brother travelled north to Scotland shortly afterwards. John was selected for Glasgow Caledonians against the touring Springboks and impressed immediately with an outstanding individual performance. He was then selected to play against the same opposition in the Murrayfield Test match on 21 November while his brother took a place on the bench. Martin Leslie was the perfect replacement for the retired Rob Wainwright – a powerful ball-carrier, a canny operator at the breakdown and a player who always led from the front.

Jim Telfer: We are not the only team to scour the earth looking to strengthen our quality and depth by finding players born outside our borders. And it is not a new phenomenon either – it has been going on for years all over the world and the teams like New Zealand and Australia are probably the best at doing it by recruiting all the Pacific Islanders, but they get little or no real flak for it. Guys like Glenn Metcalfe and Shaun Longstaff were playing club rugby in Scotland and you could see that they would make a difference to our team on the international stage. They were qualified, so they were selected. Simple as that. We did look to bring in some other players, though, but I was comfortable with that as long as we didn't go overboard with the concept. We were lacking real depth in some positions and so were recommended players who qualified for us – like tight-head Matt Proudfoot and back-row Gordon Simpson. They all bought into Scottish rugby and were fully committed to the cause. I was as happy to select them as I was to select Damian Cronin or Budge Pountney. They committed themselves to Scotland and were legitimately qualified, so that was all I needed to know.

Martin and John Leslie had great pedigree and were keen to come to Scotland and they made an immediate impact. In his first game for Glasgow Caledonians against the touring Springboks, John looked like the only home player who actually wanted to take the game to the South Africans. He was intelligent and forthright and made of exactly the right kind of stuff that I wanted in a centre. I knew that he would help raise the standards of those around him, and the same was true of Martin – he was hard working and abrasive and a very intelligent player.

Jamie Mayer: I will never forget that game against South Africa in the autumn of 1998. I was twenty-one years old and was winning my first cap in my home stadium against the world champions. It was the most incredible experience. And the speed of the game was something else. I remember being tackled by Bobby Skinstad early in the first-half and then getting up and sprinting across the field to the next breakdown . . . only to see Bobby running past me and beating me to the breakdown with some ease. I knew then that Test rugby was a completely different ball game to anything I had been involved in before. That game was a hard lesson in international rugby for the whole team, but it gave me a salutary lesson that I would have to raise my game at least two or three notches just to be competitive.

So where were the team to turn as the last year of the twentieth century hove into sight? And a World Cup year no less; the tournament would be hosted by Wales and Scotland would play their pool and quarter-final games at Murrayfield (should they qualify for the latter rounds). Performances had to improve beyond recognition in order for Scotland to pose any threat in the Five Nations and build confidence before the World Cup. The media believed Scotland had no chance of being successful in the 1999 Five Nations tournament and the bookmakers had them at 100–1 to lift the trophy. Yet it is often in times of extreme adversity that a team finds its true sense of collective purpose.

In the build-up to the Five Nations, Telfer had adopted many of the lessons he had learned with the 1997 Lions and had made a point of empowering his players as much as possible, encouraging them to take leading roles in training, during the match day preparations and, crucially, on the field of play itself. One of the initiatives that the senior players concocted as the tournament loomed was to mix up their approach to kick-offs; they wanted to play as unpredictably as they could, to keep the opposition guessing at every turn and to be bold in their attacking play. The first fixture of the campaign was against Wales at Murrayfield.

Gordon Bulloch: For a lot of guys, 1998 had been their first Five Nations, so in 1999 they were a bit more experienced. On top of that the Leslie brothers had arrived from New Zealand, which gave us a lot more nous around the field. Toony was at his peak, Taity could always sniff a try out, and John Leslie was the missing link we had been crying out for to get that backline really firing. He and Toony were on the same wavelength and I think they saw things – opportunities – that nobody else in the team would see. We scored sixteen tries in four matches that year which is an unbelievable statistic when you think about it.

John Leslie (Scotland 1998-2002, 23 Caps): I have great memories and I feel very privileged to have been given the chance to play for, never mind captain, Scotland. I knew quite a bit about Scotland from my dad, and the personalities of the two nations are definitely very similar. New Zealand have an advantage in that rugby is the number one sport there and that is not the case in Scotland, other than in the Borders. When the sport is number one, there are more players in that sport, and so more competition at every level, but it also means the most naturally athletic people choose to play rugby in New Zealand before anything else. Many of the most skilful or athletic youngsters in Scotland aim for football, or maybe athletics, or something else before rugby.

I remind people in New Zealand that the player base in Scotland is not very big – there are more people playing rugby just in Canterbury than in Scotland. New Zealanders don't realise that, yet they all believe Scotland is a big part of world rugby, because of the history, the enthusiasm Scots have for it, even if it's not the number one sport, the pride and passion in-built in Scottish teams, and because it produces seriously tough guys. Rugby is a natural fit in Scotland.

But New Zealand also has the fortune of a great mix of cultures with Polynesians, White Europeans, Maori and others, which is superb for sport and rugby in particular. The All Blacks get criticised for having different roots in the team, but that is the beauty of this country – people have settled here from all over the world. Scotland doesn't have those resources which means it will always be an underdog.

When I came to Scotland, I didn't know what to expect and I probably worried more than my brother Martin did. But Scotland had a good squad, both on the park and off it too, and they welcomed us both in.

When you think about it now it was some back line to become a part of – Gregor Townsend, Alan Tait, Kenny Logan and Cammie Murray, complemented by Glenn Metcalfe at fullback, and, of course, the junkyard dog himself, Gary Armstrong, who was such a great leader; someone we loved playing for.

The forwards had the experience of Paul Burnell, Eric Peters and Stu Reid, Budge Pountney of course, and great young guys coming through, Tom Smith, Gordon Bulloch, Steve Brotherstone, then Stuart Grimes and Scott Murray.

It was a good environment, a bit like New Zealand – Jim Telfer encouraged everyone to have an opinion and contribute. We clicked very well as a team in 1999 mainly because we had guys who all wanted to play for each other.

And that's the thing about any successful team, particularly in Scotland. There was flair in that squad, but the flair guys were also prepared to roll up their sleeves and get stuck in, and that's what made the difference I think. When you get that blend, Scotland can be very dangerous. I had an absolute great time and feel very privileged to have been a part of that time.

Gordon Bulloch: The forwards were all good, good players and we worked well as a unit. Scott Murray and Stuart Grimes were a tremendous partnership in the second-row, Paul Burnell had been there and done it all before and in Tom Smith we had the best loose-head prop in the world.

Tom Smith (Scotland 1997-2005, 61 Caps plus 6 Caps for the Lions): When I joined Dundee High after I left school at Rannoch, there was an old prop, a bit of a local legend, called Danny Herrington. Danny took the view that a young prop should have his share of bad experiences before trying to inflict them on other people and he basically shoved my head up my arse in training twice a week every week for what seemed like years. In my position, you need brute strength and a highly-developed survival instinct. That's what Danny taught me. It was a hell of a learning curve and the lessons that he taught me were carried through the rest of my career.

I've suffered from epileptic seizures – grand mals, they call them – since I was 18. Until around 2006, the attacks always happened in my sleep, but then I had a waking attack, which meant I had to forfeit my driving licence for twelve months. I had to be careful not to return to rugby too quickly after an attack, because the short-term memory loss can be very acute. I played a Calcutta Cup match after having a seizure on the day of the game, which was not the best idea I've ever had and it definitely affected my performance. But I am incredibly fortunate to have had such a long career in professional sport in spite of my epilepsy. I am involved with a number of charities these days and I think that it's very important to talk of it openly because I want other sufferers to know that epilepsy doesn't have to be a barrier to achievement. You just have to manage your life in a different way, but that is something that all sorts of sportsmen and people in other walks of life have to deal with as well, and it should never inhibit your aspirations to achieve your goals.

Gordon Bulloch: Momentum is everything, and we got the 1999 Six Nations off to the best start we could possibly hope for against Wales with John Leslie scoring that try within ten seconds of kick-off. We had decided beforehand that we wanted to use the kick-off as an offensive weapon – whereas now they tend to use the restart to establish field position. We also knew the right winger, Matthew Robinson, was coming in for his first cap, and with a huge atmosphere the last thing he would want was to get stuck under a high ball.

So it was a planned move for Hodgey to kick it that way and fortunately it came off – Shane Howarth came forward to cover for Robinson but it was just too far for him to take it comfortably before John snatched the ball away from him and galloped home unchallenged to break the record for the fastest try in the history of international rugby. It gave us such a huge boost. When something you have worked on earlier in the week comes off it is great for confidence.

We went in at half-time and we were losing [13-8] but then Hodgey was unlucky and got injured and we had to swap our backline around and, almost by accident, found an amazing combination of players.

Duncan Hodge: We got a penalty about ten minutes into the second-half and I kicked to touch . . . and missed. Shane Howarth caught it and started running towards me and all that I can remember going through my mind was the video

John Leslie stretches his legs as he prepares to make history with the fastest try to be scored in international rugby.

analysis we had done on him – that he always stepped off his right foot. He stepped off his right foot, I adjusted my weight to hit him with my right shoulder but my studs caught in the ground. All my weight went to the right but my foot stayed where it was and snap . . . there went my fibula.

Alan Tait (Scotland 1987-1999, 27 Caps plus 2 Caps for the Lions): So Hodgey went down, Gregor went into stand-off and I came on at outside centre. I knew that the 1999 Five Nations would be my last Championship, so I wanted to try and go out in a big way, and when I came off the bench, that was my motivation. And it worked out really well. John Leslie was a world class centre and I knew from watching him that we would work well together – he always made the right decision, either to give you the ball at the right time or to hit back into the forwards if it was bad ball. And when Gregor moved to ten he proved once again, like he did for the Lions in South Africa, that stand-off is his best position. And all three of us just gelled. Gregor scored after picking up a loose Welsh pass, then he put me in for a try, and then we sealed it when Scotty Murray scored off a lineout.

Scott Murray: 1999 was my first Five Nations. I had been in and around the squad for a while, but that was my first taste of the Championship – and to experience it for the first time at home against Wales was a great way to start – and then to score just capped it all, it was brilliant. It was my first win for Scotland at Test level; I had also played against Wales eight times at various age-grade levels, but it was the first time I had beaten them, so all-in-all it really was a fantastic day.

Gregor Townsend: The way we built up that season demonstrates what Five and Six Nations rugby is all about. We hadn't performed particularly well during the autumn, losing pretty heavily to South Africa, and our first game of the Championship was Wales at home. They had pushed South Africa all the way in November and had beaten Argentina fairly comfortably, and were one of the favourites to win the Championship that year. But we completely outplayed them.

Combinations are very important in selection, which doesn't necessarily mean picking your best fifteen players but getting guys who play well off each other, and we were lucky because that injury meant we stumbled upon a formula that worked during the rest of the Championship. We were actually 13–8 down when that change was made and we went on to win 32–20. Winning that first game gave us so much momentum because the pressure was off and we felt we could try things a bit more.

Jim Telfer: It was a huge relief to beat Wales – that was the overriding feeling. A lot had been said in the press in the build up to that game that Graham Henry had got Wales back to their best, so it was widely felt that if we beat them it would be a sign that we were starting to turn the corner and that after a few tough years, Scottish rugby would begin to regain some credibility.

Gregor Townsend at 10. John Leslie at 12. Alan Tait at 13. It was a combination that clicked so seamlessly that it was as if they had been playing together for years. Townsend was the conjuror, Leslie the steady and intelligent co-conductor, Tait the bustling powerhouse outside them. All three were capable of magic with ball in hand and incisive running angles in attack, and together they proved to be an obdurate brick wall in defence.

Throughout the tournament, the front-row of Tom Smith, Gordon Bulloch and Paul Burnell were powerful and dynamic. The second row of Scott Murray and Stuart Grimes were maestros on their own lineout ball, rapacious snafflers on the opposition's throw, and athletic around the park. The back-row combinations of Peter Walton, Martin Leslie, Eric Peters, Budge Pountney and Stuart Reid were powerful, cunning and skillful. Gary Armstrong, the bull-necked controller at scrumhalf, was the perfect link between his mobile forward pack and his mesmeric backline, and out wide the running skills of Kenny Logan and young Cammie Murray combined wonderfully with the mazy running of Metcalfe.

The following week, Scotland travelled down to Twickenham for the Calcutta Cup. In the opening quarter of the match, it seemed that Scotland would be blown away as Nick Beal and Dan Luger ran in two quick tries and the Scottish pack were pounded by their physically superior opposition. But the self-belief garnered from the win over Wales had penetrated deeply, and the will to attack with flair, speed and aggression had been imbedded throughout the Scotland squad. Minutes later, Eric Peters secured a loose ball at a lineout and it was swiftly fed by Armstrong to Townsend who was flat on the gainline. He offloaded out of the tackle to Martin Leslie who in turn slipped the ball out of contact to Scott Murray and the lock was able to deftly move the ball just as Tait was hitting the line outside him to cross for the score. It was full of energy and skill and was thrilling in every way.

The teams retired to the changing rooms at half-time with England ahead 17–7 thanks to Jonny Wilkinson's penalty adding to his two conversions of the early tries. Despite the ten-point deficit, Scottish confidence remained high. They were beginning to gain parity in the forward exchanges and their angles of running were causing the English defence all manner of problems.

Shortly after the match was resumed, Townsend ran a wrap-around move with Armstrong and used John Leslie as a decoy runner to release Tait into space. The former rugby league giant hit the gap like a bullet train and then arced away from the covering defence. As he surged to the try line, he was met by Luger and as if in defiance to the winger's earlier try celebrations he stepped towards him, dipped his shoulder and thumped him back as he crossed to score.

England extended their lead through a converted try by Tim Rodber, but Townsend soon ensured that the match would finish with a thrilling dénouement as he intercepted a pass between substitute scrum-half Kyran Bracken and Mike Catt to dart home under the posts.

In the end, England held out to retain the Calcutta Cup and to extend their unbeaten run of victories at Twickenham over Scotland to sixteen with the 24–21 scoreline. It could have been different had Logan, who was carrying a leg strain, not missed three eminently kickable penalties, while Wilkinson – as he would do so often during his career – produced an immaculate kicking display.

Gregor Townsend: We went down to Twickenham next, and were dismantled by England's huge pack in the first quarter; but the self-belief from the Wales game helped us fight back, and although we never led we came really close to stealing our first win down there since 1983. It was really frustrating, but we had done enough to feel that our growing self-belief wasn't misplaced.

Alan Tait: Going down to London for the England game was my first and last game at Twickenham and, again, I wanted a big performance. So it was great to score two tries. The first was really just getting on the end of a broken play move and the second was from a set-piece move that we had improvised on the Friday before the game during our run through, and it worked like a dream.

Jim Telfer: That game at Twickenham was disappointing to lose in so many ways – we had bounced back to get into the game and scored three tremendous tries with Alan Tait going in at each end and Gregor Townsend picking off a lovely intercept and racing in from halfway. We converted all three but unfortunately Kenny Logan missed with a couple of penalty attempts. It was during that game that I first really registered the impact of the Leslie brothers. At half-time I said a few bits and pieces and then John took the backs into one corner and Martin took the forwards into another and they laid out exactly what had gone right and wrong in the first-half and told the rest of the players what they needed to do to beat England. All the other players listened and understood what they were being told and then they went out

Dan Luger, Richard Hill, David Rees and Matt Dawson can do nothing to stop Alan Tait from powering over for his second try in the Calcutta Cup clash at Twickenham.

and did it – and very nearly managed a famous victory. Both John and Martin were very technical and analytical in their approach and they knew exactly how to go out and win games against different opponents.

Gary Armstrong: Looking back, it was a real missed opportunity at Twickenham. Not many Scottish sides have gone down there and won and when the dust settled after the last game, we realised the implication of not winning that game because it could have been another Grand Slam – we ended up four points away in a game that we should have won.

Glenn Metcalfe: I guess in all the highlights of my international career, that 1999 season ranks right at the top. We were actually pretty close to a Grand Slam and looking back on that result at Twickenham is a bit of a sickener as we were only a few points away from toppling England.

The balance that we had throughout the team that year was perfect for our game and playing at fullback I could see the experienced decision making and skill of John Leslie amplify the talents of Gregor and Taity around him – I was in the best position in the world to see the holes the three of them would open up against seriously talented opposition. I was happy for my mate Gregor to have such a great season as a lot of people were critical of his play prior to that year, even though he had guided the Lions to a Test series victory in 1997. People were often on his back about the risks he would take and the mistakes that would sometime come from those risks, but that year he really came into his own and his performances against Ireland, England and France were almost impossible to fault.

Ian McGeechan: In a sense, the problems that Gregor experienced as a playmaker were not his problems at all. He was branded as a 'mercurial' player, but the fact of the matter was that his thought processes always tended to be half a yard in front of everyone else's and if the other players were not on their toes, his best ideas could backfire. I wasn't involved with Scotland for that Five Nations, but watching it from the outside I could instantly see the difference that John Leslie had made to Gregor's play – they had an intuitive understanding with one another about how they wanted to play the game and it worked well with Alan Tait outside them, too. They were a super combination and Gregor was really able to show the breadth of his talent.

Scotland had a month's break between the England game and Ireland coming to Edinburgh in March. The SRU arranged a fixture at Murrayfield against Italy on 6 March, which Scotland won 30–12 thanks to tries from Logan, Cammie Murray and, again, Townsend. It was a stuffy game, as Scotland-Italy fixtures tend to be, but it provided a good work-out for the team in preparation for the Ireland match.

Ireland were also a team full of confidence, with a monstrous and talented front-five, and wit and skill out wide. Ulster had won the Heineken Cup in 1998 and their domestic game was in rude health. They were captained by Paddy Johns and boasted several Lions in the talismanic Keith Woods, Paul Wallace, Jeremy Davidson and Eric Millar, and in fly-half David Humphries they had one of the finest controllers of the game in Europe. The game was only minutes old when Humphries scored a try to put the visitors in the lead. In the first three rounds of the competition they had lost to France and England at Lansdowne Road but had beaten Wales at Wembley and were playing some decent rugby. For the crowd, things looked ominous. And then Scotland came alive. Over the next seventy-five minutes they played with control, ambition and wondrous skill, battering their visitors with relentless waves of cleverly angled runs, superb territorial kicking, quick rucking and offloading, eating up the yards towards the opposition try line with a seemingly unstoppable rhythm and tempo. The majesty of their play that day was epitomised by a length-of-the-field try which began in the shadow of their own posts and swept irresistibly up field before Stuart Grimes dived over in the corner. Townsend continued his impressive scoring run, dotting down after collecting an offload from John Leslie and stretching through a despairing tackle from Keith Wood. Two tries for Cammie Murray plus two conversions and two penalties from the boot of Logan saw Scotland home 33–13 and into second spot on the table behind England.

Gregor Townsend: We beat Ireland 30–13 at Murrayfield in what was the most accomplished allround performance by a Scotland team I was ever involved in. John Leslie, Alan Tait and myself in the midfield were getting a lot of praise, but Glenn Metcalf and Cammie Murray were also excelling in the backline, and we were all benefiting from the quick-ball the forwards were consistently producing. We had great leaders all over the park, which made a huge difference. The Leslie brothers were fantastic to have around and then we had guys like me, Taity, Tom Smith and Gary Armstrong who had all been around and achieved great things with Scotland and with the Lions. That kind of leadership and experience is very hard to come by, but it tends to be one of the key ingredients to any successful side.

The team was full of strong personalities who wanted to play rugby so we were as player-led as we had ever been. Nowadays, teams are even further down the line in terms of the players making decisions, but back then coaches would still have a big say right up to the moment you ran out onto the pitch. But we had the experience there to say, 'We are going to play it this way because we know it's going to work.'

The try Grimesy scored against the Irish was epic – we started it under our posts and went the length of the field, inter-passing all the way. It was electric stuff.

Stuart Grimes: I got up from the bottom of the ruck that we had turned the ball over in and saw Gregor making a break out of the twenty-two and I just legged it after him – I was lucky that the ball just came my way in the end and it was nice to get the final touch because Kenny Logan was right beside me and he had never scored in a Five Nations match, so it was good to help keep that record in tact – although I had to put up with all manner of abuse from him later that night.

And so the final weekend of the tournament approached. Ireland had completed their fixtures at Murrayfield, leaving Scotland to play France in Paris and Wales to host England at Wembley. Scotland's preparations for arguably the toughest venue in the whole competition were marred by Tom Smith's leg break in the Ireland match, followed by the withdrawal of Eric Peters after he shattered his kneecap playing for Bath. David Hilton was brought in for Smith and Budge Pountney and Stuart Reid came in to win their second caps at blind-side flanker and number eight.

Although France were having a disappointing season by their standards, they had won back-to-back Grand Slams in 1997 and 1998 and were always incredibly strong when they played at home. The partisan French crowd were in the mood for blood and the game was barely two minutes old when Thomas Castaignède, the elfin genius of the French backline, sniped through the Scottish defensive line and deep into their twenty-two before setting up a ruck from which a series of delightfully delivered passes released Émile Ntamack to score in the corner.

Away from home Scotland had leaked two soft tries to England and then fought back to the brink of victory. Against Ireland they had opened their arms to allow Humphreys to score early before surging back into the ascendancy. Going down by five points to France was not ideal, especially in somewhere as imposing at the Stade de France, but there were still seventy-eight minutes on the clock. They would strike back, they were sure. No one, however, not even the players, imagined that they would strike back in quite the manner that they did.

In the act of setting up the ruck from which his team scored, Castaignède had twisted his knee and was carried from the field. His departure cast a shadow over the French while serving as a catalyst to galvanise the Scottish effort. And what followed was perhaps the most extraordinary seventeen minutes in Scottish rugby history as the team scored five mesmerising tries and four conversions. Attacking from deep with the flair and élan normally so associated with their hosts and with an accuracy that had typified so much of Scotland's play during the season, they scored three tries in the space of just six minutes from Martin Leslie, Tait and Townsend – who, in doing so, completed a remarkable run of scoring in every Championship match that year, making him only the fifth player ever to achieve the feat, and the first British player since Scotsman AC Wallace in 1925. Martin Leslie's try came only two minutes after Ntamack's opener and Tait's almost immediately after the resultant kick-off thanks to a coruscating break by Metcalfe after he was released by a deft offload from Tait, who returned the ball to the British & Irish Lion seventy metres later to score.

French number eight Christophe Juillet then added to the score-fest off the back of a powerful scrum on the Scottish line, but in the spirit of this truly bizarre match, Tait crossed for his second try only minutes later after another dazzling break from Metcalf and just minutes later Scotland were on the attack again, Townsend scything through the French ranks on a fifty metre run only to be brought down just shy of the tryline. He popped the ball up to the supporting Martin Leslie who slid through to score his second.

As the final moments of the first-half drew to a close, Christophe Dominici lanced off his wing and through flailing Scottish tackles to score the eighth try of the half and to raise *some hope for the home team. When Clayton Thomas blew for halftime the score stood at 22–33.*

If the first-half had been an exhibition of attacking flair and dynamism, the second-half was an outstanding display of attritional and full-blooded defence. 55 points had been scored in the first-half; in the second there were only three – one penalty from the boot of Kenny Logan – and at no point did the Scottish defence look like breaking. They left Paris triumphant, joint top of the table with England and with their highest-ever points win over their Gallic cousins.

John Leslie: It was a great, maybe lucky start to the Five Nations, but we played good footy against Wales and England – we were unlucky to lose by three points at Twickenham – then beat Italy at home pretty well with three backs' tries and played well against Ireland, so we went to France full of confidence.

Gregor Townsend: It was Scotland's first appearance at the Stade de France, which is an incredible venue. I wonder if we were slightly overawed by the whole experience of playing there because we were very loose in the first five minutes, and lost an early try. Then, suddenly, players started reading off-loads and anticipating breaks – the understanding was just there and everything began to click again.

We called the same 'miss-one-blind' move as we had called at the very beginning of the 1996 game against France. This time Alan Tait got smashed just as he passed to Glenn Metcalfe but he got the ball and away and Glenn ran seventy-five yards up field and we scored off it. Rugby is all about fine margins. If you get caught in your own twenty-two while trying to execute a move then the next time you are in that position you are less likely to try and move it, but if you go through with it – if your skills are up to the job – then all of a sudden the whole team are looking to have a go. And fortunately, on both those occasions our willingness to have a go paid off.

When we came in at half-time the buzz was amazing and the coaches didn't know what to say – they couldn't possibly have planned for that scenario. We wanted to keep playing with the same pace and flair but it was inevitable that France would come back at us. In the end we won the second-half 3–0, which is almost as impressive as what we achieved in the first-half because we defended so well.

Jim Telfer: I had never seen anything like it. It was as if every time we had the ball we scored a try. For a time it was like the other team wasn't even on the park. That first thirty, forty minutes was just unbelievable. It was all down to the positivity of the players – the more positive you are in attack, the more chance you will have to get the result.

Gary Armstrong: We wanted to play a wide game, the sort of game that they used to such good effect against us the previous year. It worked, and we cut through them like a knife through butter.

Glenn Metcalfe slices through the French defence on a glorious day in Paris.

On Sunday 11 April, Wales hosted England in the last ever match of the Five Nations, eighty-nine years after the tournament had expanded from the four Home Unions to include France among their number. The following year, Italy's inclusion would see the tournament rebranded as the Six Nations. As the Scotland players, management and fans awoke bleary-eyed from celebrating their Parisian triumphs, thoughts turned to their place in the Five Nations table. They were currently top after their win over France, ahead of England on points difference. If Wales were to do the unimaginable and topple the English, Scotland would win the tournament. It was a wild speculation. A dream.

England, however, were in no mood for the speculative optimism of those from the north. They were heading into the match full of confidence, looking to seal their twelfth Grand Slam. Despite enduring their own summer of hell in 1998, they had recovered their poise and class to defeat South Africa 13–7 in the autumn, to hold out in their tournament opener against Scotland, and then to overwhelm Ireland 27–15 at Lansdowne Road and France 21–10 at Twickenham.

Wales, after promising so much at the outset of the season, had had something of a mixed tournament. They had lost to Scotland and Ireland, but had then defeated France 34–33 in a thriller and then thumped Italy 60–21 in a friendly in Treviso.

England started the match at Wembley as strongly as they had done against Scotland at Twickenham, scoring two scorching early tries through Dan Luger and Steve Hanley. They were all power and speed, dominating proceedings with muscle and intelligent running angles and passing. But despite their supremacy, they couldn't shake Wales from their coat-tails. The prolific boot of fly-half Neil Jenkins kept his team in the game three-points at a time. As half-time approached, Jenkins had pulled back the deficit to bring the score level at 15–15. A Wilkinson penalty and a converted Richard Hill try looked to re-establish some breathing space for the English going into the break, only for Jenkins to strike again with another penalty to take the teams in at 18–25.

Wales burst back into life after the break after and at last crossed the English line through Shane Howarth. Jenkins' conversion took the score to 25–25. But England were soon back in the ascendency again with two quick-fire Wilkinson penalties and were beginning to look stronger and stronger as the closing stages drew in.

The clock ticked to seventy-five minutes. And the final quirk of fate in Scotland's campaign showed itself. England were awarded a penalty halfway between the Welsh twenty-two and the ten-metre line. A penalty kick at goal would stretch their lead to 34–25, more than a converted try clear of their opponents. Captain Lawrence Dallaglio glanced up at the posts and tossed the ball to Wilkinson. 'Go for the corner,' he said. 'We'll take the try.'

Ninety seconds later, after a powerful rolling maul, Mike Catt hoisted a Garryowen under the Welsh posts, which was only just gathered by Welsh centre Mark Taylor. Tackled in the process of taking the catch, Wales were awarded a scrum; Rob Howley swept the ball to Jenkins who put in a booming kick, and the Welsh lines were cleared.

Wales had survived. But time was running out. They were six points adrift and needed a converted score to steal the victory. Save for a few rampages from the giant brothers Scott and Craig Quinnell and Howarth's try, the English defensive line had held strong all afternoon. The talismanic figure of Scott Gibbs, a hero of the Lions tour two years previously, had been well-marshalled by the English midfield and back-row and his efforts to scythe through their ranks in the way that Tait had done at Twickenham just a few weeks earlier had been met by staunch English tackles time after time. There seemed no way through.

But then Tim Rodber offered a chink of light with a high tackle on Colin Charvis forty metres from the Welsh line, which gave Jenkins the opportunity to stab a penalty kick down to the English 22. Two minutes to go.

Chris Wyatt won a shortened line-out, Howley fed Scott Quinnell, Quinnell juggled the ball for control and managed to slip it to Gibbs who hit an identical line to the one Tait had taken off Armstrong at Twickenham. He burst through Rodber, fended off Neil Back, arced his run around Matt Dawson, slid past Wilkinson and skipped past Matthew Perry, raised his arm in triumph and dived into history. 30–31.

Jenkins lined up the ball for the conversion. Stepping back, he picked a bit of mud from his studs, wiped his palms on his shorts and waved a guiding hand towards the posts. Three steps. Contact. The ball sailed straight and true.

There was less than a minute left on the clock as England kicked-off. They were lucky. Wales spilled the ball and England were awarded the scrum. There was still time for them to snatch the win. Dallaglio controlled the ball at the base and Dawson fed to Catt, who struck a drop at goal. It went wide. Howarth gathered, called the mark and then rifled the ball into the sea of red beyond the touchline. The Championship was Scotland's.

Jim Telfer: I think we had a vague notion at the back of our minds that we could still win the Championship, but it was no more than that. Everyone expected England to stroll to victory over Wales and although I knew many of the Welsh players very well from the Lions tour and knew how good they were, I also knew many of the English players and couldn't see them fluffing their shot at a Grand Slam.

We travelled back from Paris that morning and each of us managed to get home or to a pub or a clubhouse or wherever to watch that final game of the tournament. I was back at home in time for the kick-off and settled in for what I thought was the inevitable England win. But even at the hour mark of that game Wales were still very much in it, although I still thought that England would pull away at the end. Neil Jenkins was keeping them in it as only he could and then when Scott Gibbs crashed through to score I nearly hit the roof.

Alan Tait: I looked up at the TV screen in the pub to see Gibbsy flash through the line and I just started jumping all over the place. People started saying that it was too early to celebrate because there was still the conversion to go, but I knew Jenks well from the Lions and I knew there was no way he was going to miss it – he was the best kicker I'd ever seen.

Jim Telfer: It was a tricky conversion to take the lead, but I knew Neil would get it. He slotted it and they held out to deny England at the final whistle. It was quite something to suddenly realise that we were champions, and the phone didn't stop ringing for hours.

Crowds flock to Murrayfield for the trophy presentation.

TWENTY

TELFER'S LAST STAND
1999

Scotland were Five Nations champions and looked to be in a strong position going into the 1999 Rugby World Cup – they had battled through the adversity of injury and defeat to England to win the Championship and were playing a thrilling brand of rugby.

Instead of scheduling a run of major Test matches in the build-up to the World Cup, Scotland elected instead to tour the provinces of South Africa with a development squad in an effort to build some strength in depth. Most notable of the young players to travel were future captains Jason White and Chris Paterson. The tour was a mixed success results-wise, with Scotland defeating Border and Northern Free State Griffons but losing to Mpumalanga and the Golden Lions, yet it proved invaluable for introducing several young players into the international set-up.

In the weeks before their first Pool 1 match, Scotland played Argentina at Murrayfield, losing 22–31 before facing Romania at Hampden Park in an encounter which they won 60–19 but at which barely 5000 supporters turned up to watch – an ominous signal of what was to occur during the World Cup itself. Jim Telfer had indicated the previous year that he was only taking the head-coach role until the conclusion of the World Cup, after which he would return to his job as director of rugby for the SRU. After a long and eventful career with Scotland and the Lions, the World Cup was to act as the final chapter in Telfer's esteemed coaching career. Fate and luck had conspired so wonderfully for Scotland in the spring, allowing them to overcome the trials of injury to emerge, ironically, even stronger. But luck is a fickle thing and fate's wheel was beginning to turn.

The injury that Tom Smith suffered against Ireland and which ruled him out of the sensational victory in Paris also ruled him out of the World Cup, and while Doddie Weir had recovered from a broken ankle he had sustained against Wales in the Five Nations opener, he was still some distance away from full fitness. Finally, Scotland were struck down by another serious leg injury that reduced their chances still further. John Leslie, the pivotal rock of the midfield, twisted his ankle against South Africa in the opening pool game and was ruled out of the rest of the tournament.

Gordon Bulloch: Jim Telfer was a world class coach, one of the very finest that Scotland and the Lions ever had, but he would sometimes try to push things on to us that had worked for him – and he is a very different character to most human beings; not many people can be as single-minded as he was.

Jamie Mayer: What was Jim Telfer like as a coach? He was a very good man – although I was probably too young to really understand him and his style at the time. He expected the highest standards of skill, effort and commitment and I believe that any great and

Opposite: Jim Telfer bids farewell to his role as Scotland's head coach.

well-respected coach gets that delivered consistently from his team. Jim's teams over the years, whether as a player or a coach, always displayed these qualities and that, above all else, is a testament to the kind of man he is.

Gordon Bulloch: We spent the Welsh World Cup of 1999 in the Dalmahoy Hotel just outside Edinburgh. We didn't go to the opening ceremony, we didn't do anything, and we played all our games at Murrayfield. The last game against New Zealand was fabulous but in the quarter-final play-off we played Samoa on a Wednesday afternoon in front of 15,000 people – it was a bizarre experience. You couldn't really buy into the excitement of being at a World Cup because Edinburgh, as a city, wasn't really that fussed about having a few World Cup games there. Come game day it was good – for the South Africa and New Zealand games, at least – but apart from that you didn't really feel you were at a World Cup.

Gregor Townsend: The crowd for three of our games was less than 20,000, which was shocking. We were European champions and playing at our home ground in what was meant to be the biggest event on the rugby calendar, but Edinburgh as a city hadn't really been enthused with the World Cup spirit and a few of the games were on weekday afternoons so people were naturally at work. More people had turned up to see us collect the Five Nations trophy a few months earlier than for two of our World Cup games. In South Africa's pool match against Spain only 6000 turned up at Murrayfield and crowds throughout the tournament in Scotland were hugely disappointing. Things got so desperate that the SRU started to filter recorded crowd noises through the speakers at the stadium. It was embarrassing.

Duncan Hodge: It was a real shame. The ticket pricing and match scheduling were all wrong. It was just a nondescript tournament. It was very disappointing. The World Cup is supposed to be one of the highlights of your career and we were playing in front of crowds of five or six thousand. We didn't even go down to Wales once, all our games were at home and we were staying out at Dalmahoy. It was all just really weird and a huge disappointment.

Jamie Mayer: The squad's preparation for the World Cup was very good and we worked hard to get ourselves into the best shape we could, even though it was a bit weird being in Edinburgh while the rest of the tournament's focus was in Wales. But we just had to get on with things and focus on our own preparations. We knew that despite winning the Five Nations that the World Cup would be another step up altogether, particularly as we had to play South Africa in our opening game. I got injured in a training session down in Troon and I genuinely thought my World Cup was over before it began. Fortunately over the next few weeks the physios, particularly Stuart Barton and Stephen Mutch, worked absolute wonders and helped me back to full recovery in time for the tournament's opening.

Jim Telfer: We opened against South Africa, which was fairly huge to have first up – they were the defending champions and had put more than a hundred points on us in our previous two encounters. But we were the reigning Five Nations champions and despite losing to Argentina in one of our warm-up matches, we looked in good shape. We played pretty well to begin with and went in at half-time with a 16–13 lead, but we lost John Leslie to an ankle injury, which was a huge loss, and South Africa stepped it up a level after the break.

John Leslie: I can still remember running on to a beautiful chip-kick by Gregor over the South African defence, seeing the ball bouncing for me and the line just metres away, when someone landed on my back. I went down and something in my ankle popped.I was lying there in agony trying to keep the ball, trying to get to the line, but it wouldn't happen. I think we might have beaten them if we'd scored then, but I was stretchered off, we lost by a bit, and that was the start of a long injury haul for me.

The Springboks moved into a different gear and swept the hosts aside, finishing the game with six tries to their name and a 46–29 win over their main rivals for the pool.

Jim Telfer: The lead exchanged hands a couple of times after tries from Martin Leslie and Deon Kayser and then we were ahead for the final time after Kenny Logan scored with a penalty. They then scored two tries within three minutes which was a fairly killer blow and except for a nicely taken try by Alan Tait after a neat offload from Gregor, they went on to sweep us aside after that. Bobby Skinstad, Joost van der Westhuizen and Brendan Venter were all very influential that day and they looked strong contenders for the World Cup at that stage.

In the aftermath of that game we played Spain and Uruguay and won comfortably in both to set up a play-off game with Samoa.

Scotland's matches against the pool minnow were little more than training exercises as the home team ran out 43–12 agianst Uruguay and 48–0 against Spain. Finishing second in their group behind South Africa, Scotland played Samoa in a quarter-final play-off at Murrayfield. In the opening ten minutes Scotland won a scrum on the Samoan line. After the scrum was collapsed by the Pacific Islanders, Scotland were awarded a free-kick and elected to re-scrum. Over the next few minutes the scrum either collapsed, awarding the home team another free-kick, or was reset for a technicality. Scotland, trusting their superior fitness and technical ability, elected to scrum and scrum and scrum. It was tactic that was limited as a spectacle but was a tactical master-stroke which resonated through rest of the match, as it not only depowered the fiery Samoan forwards, it also sapped their energy, negating the impact that they had in broken play over the next sixty-five minutes. Scotland dominated proceedings and went on to win 35–20 to book a quarter-final place with the All Blacks at Murrayfield.

Jamie Mayer powers through the tackle of Terry Fanolua
during Scotland's victory over Samoa.

Glenn Metcalfe: Playing in a World Cup is just an awesome experience. In '99 we had a good season and took a lot of confidence into the tournament. We really needed to hit the ground running against the Boks; we came up short in the end but played some great rugby in that match; a key moment was when John Leslie was injured out of the tournament. He was a huge loss to the campaign.

Duncan Hodge: After one training session we went into this team meeting out at Dalmahoy and everyone sat down. Then Jim grunts at Grimesy and says, 'Come with me.' They went to the room next door, and Jim asks him to roll up his sleeves, the Jim gets out a red marker pen and starts scrawling up and down Grimesy's arm. Then he rolls his sleeves back down and sends him back to the team room.

Then during the meeting Jim says that some people just can't believe they are at a World Cup, they've been pinching themselves so hard they are bleeding. And he makes Grimesy roll up his sleeve to show us this arm with red pen all over it. It was just bizarre. You knew what Jim was trying to say but he wasn't trying to be funny, so you didn't know how to react to it.

Jim had some odd ways about him sometimes. It was quite hard keeping a straight face because he would have a bit of a problem remembering guys names or not pronouncing them properly – he used to talk about Darren Garforth and call him Darren Garfield, or would be telling us about Lawrence Dallaglio and pronounce his name Lawrence Dall-aj-leo.

He had an all-encompassing presence in the squad when he was head coach. Unlike today when training is mainly position-tailored, so the front-row do different training drills to the back-row and the backs mainly run through game situations, it used to be full squad sessions under Jim so that the backs would be hitting as many rucking pads as the forwards – we would do hours of rucking training, while in a game I would be lucky to hit one ruck in eighty minutes.

Jamie Mayer: Some of my best memories were getting together with the boys during downtime in the hotels and just talking through the opposition and the strengths and weaknesses of the guys we were coming up against. I then loved playing out these pre-game discussions on the pitch, and that was particularly true of the Samoa game – I do not think there is a more satisfying feeling that when a plan you've been working on comes together. We knew that we had to depower them up front and then target guys like Tuigamala, Brian Lima, Stephen Bachop and Pat Lam to make sure they never got into their stride. They were fantastic players, real stars, and although we weren't able to hinder them completely, for the vast proportion of that match they had nowhere to go and we felt comfortable all the way through.

Gregor Townsend: We played our best rugby of the tournament against Samoa, but again the crowd numbers were bitterly disappointing – only 15,000 supporters turned up to watch us. Fortunately they have subsequently done away with the quarter-final play-off game because none of the three teams who won those fixtures progressed beyond the quarter-final stage. I'm not saying that the results in those games would have necessarily been different, but it certainly hampered our chances, as well as England's and Argentina's, as we had to play an extra fixture just four days before the quarter-final while our opposition in those fixtures were able to rest and focus their training without distraction.

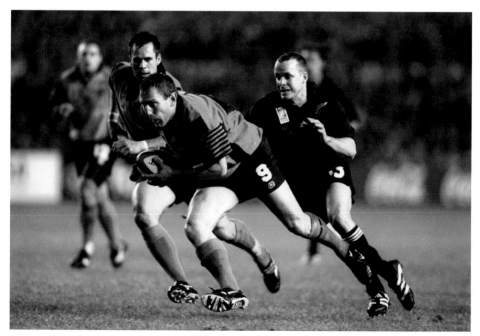

Gary Armstrong snipes past Christian Cullen in the World Cup quarter-final.

On a wild and windy night in late October, the All Blacks showed their outstanding class and superior skills in dreadful conditions to extinguish the Scottish challenge by half-time, where they retreated to the changing rooms with a 25–3 lead under their belts. Scotland showed enormous courage to rally in the second-half, scoring fifteen points to New Zealand's five, but they had too much ground to make up and the 30–18 defeat was a disappointing way for Telfer to bid farewell to his role as Scotland head coach and for the curtain to fall on the international playing careers of three mighty servants to the Scottish cause. Gary Armstrong, Alan Tait and Paul Burnell all bid an emotional farewell to the Murrayfield crowd as they and Telfer performed a final lap of the pitch and the lights dimmed on their theatre of dreams for the last time.

Jim Telfer: The atmosphere at Murrayfield for the quarter-final against the All Blacks was incredible. It was one of the best feelings from a crowd there that I had felt in years and the atmosphere in the dressing room was just as powerful. It was my last game in charge and the last game for several of our leading players – and it was some challenge for us to face the favourites for the tournament.

The weather was dreadful and I think our players froze a bit in the first-half, giving them too much respect before trying to implement our own game – and New Zealand were away and gone by then. When we turned it on we played some great stuff, but the All Blacks were just flawless and deserved the win. They scored three outstanding tries – one where Christian Cullen flipped the ball out the back of his hand to Tana Umaga, which would have been impressive on a bright summer afternoon, let alone a freezing October night in Edinburgh in the lashing rain.

Duncan Hodge: That last game has long stuck in my mind. Before we went out Gary Armstrong made this speech about his career coming to an end and what it meant for him to play for Scotland. He was hugely emotional about the whole thing and it really made me realise what it was that I was a part of, playing rugby for Scotland. Right from that letter I got when I was a teenager telling me that I had been selected for Scottish Schools, I was in the system and it just carries you along, you barely have time to really think about it. But that speech that Gary made really made me take stock of what I was doing and where I was and I carried that with me for the rest of my career. When someone like Gary spoke, you listened. In his own way, that quiet way that he has, he remains the most passionate Scotsman I have ever met, the most passionate rugby player I've ever played with. He laid it on the line what it meant to him to play for Scotland and he was in tears talking about it and after that I never took anything for granted. He really put everything he had into the jersey when he played and the emotion on his face when he came back into the changing room after the game . . . it's something that I'll never forget.

Gregor Townsend: We went in at half-time 25–3 down and I remember saying to Jim Telfer that I didn't think that we could play any better than we were; we were playing right at the top of our game but they were just on a different level and we both knew it. But Jim said that we couldn't let up in the second-half. It was a World Cup quarter-final and you can never just lie down in a fixture like that.

Jamie Mayer: It was a horrible wet day at Murrayfield but the All Blacks seemed to be able to handle the ball like it was dry summer's day and they constantly played out in the wide channels, while we struggled a bit in the conditions; we were having to use our bodies to receive the ball and because of that we were limited to a tight game. But you have to remember that this was one of the best All Black back divisions of all time. Marshall and Mehrtens had been at their heart all through the late nineties and to see them in action was incredible. They played Ieremia and Cullen in the centre and while many felt that Cullen was wasted there, they ended up having an amazingly quick partnership that worked really well together. Lomu, Umaga and Wilson in the back three . . . need I say more? Those three scored all their tries which, given the weather, was some feat. Jonah scored eight tries in the tournament and really was a superstar, but he was backed up by some fabulously evasive running from the 'lightning bolt' Jeff Wilson and the guile, strength and clever feet of Tana Umaga. They were some team and I still can't believe that they didn't go on to win the tournament.

Glenn Metcalfe: I remember lining up against the Haka and feeling a bit odd facing it as an opposition player. That was one game that I would love to play again. My whole family had flown over for the World Cup and to have them there in the stand at Murrayfield dressed in Scotland rugby tops and scarves, cheering us on, was great, but I had a poor performance out there and felt I offered very little to the team that night. As a whole we played fantastically in the second half to outscore the All Blacks, even though we went on to lose – but maybe we took too much out of the ABs as they lost to France in the next match!

Gordon Bulloch: I was very proud of the way we played in the second-half, we kept them to one try and scored fifteen points ourselves. Martin Leslie went over, which was a special thing for him, and it was a great moment when Cammie Murray made that break late in the game and dummied Jonah Lomu to go over. The noise in Murrayfield was like a thunder storm.

It was an emotional moment for the guys who were retiring and it was a super testament to them that despite the weather and the result that so many of the crowd wanted to stay on and cheer them farewell. Gary tried to make a speech to us in the changing room afterwards, but he couldn't manage it. All those years of putting everything into the jersey and he was about to take it off for the last time. Everything that it meant to him was written across his face. Sometimes, you don't need speeches.

TWENTY-ONE

THE LION MASTER'S SCOTTISH SWANSONG
2000-2003

As one old master retired from the post as Scotland's head coach, so another stepped back into the breach. In the build-up to the World Cup, Ian McGeechan had come aboard the coaching panel with Telfer, John Rutherford and Hugh Campbell and he took over from his old partner in crime at the conclusion of the tournament to become commander in chief of Scotland's fortunes. Scotland's first game of the 2000 Championship was momentous as it welcomed Italy into the tournament for the first time – an event that was celebrated in style in Rome as the home side were kicked to victory by their Argentina-born maestro Diego Dominguez. It was a devastating blow to the defending champions.

Tom Smith: There were factors we couldn't control in 2000. We had a few injuries. John Leslie was out after only playing a few minutes of the opening Six Nations game; Gary Armstrong, Alan Tait and Paul Burnell had retired; and there was a change of coaches as well. Our environment changed and unfortunately our performances did too. Ideally you want to have a legacy where you have enough people knocking at the door that success becomes continuous and you can survive the loss of star players, and maybe we were a little bit fragile on that front. Maybe we spent too long patting ourselves on the back after we won the Championship the previous year instead of saying that this time we want the Grand Slam. It took us a while to build confidence in the 1999 season and I think maybe we forgot how tough it was grinding out those performances before it clicked. Having won the last Championship expectations were quite high, but we went down to Italy for game one of the new Six Nations and got brought back down to earth with an almighty bump – and things deteriorated from there. The whole 'Grannygate' thing was blowing up at the time – Shane Howarth and Brett Sinkinson, the Welsh players, had no link to Wales through their grandparents' as they had claimed, and the IRB's rigorous checks that followed revealed that David Hilton's grandfather's birth was registered in Bristol, rather than Glasgow, which was where all his family had believed him to have been born. David was forced to withdraw from the Scotland squad, but he took the decision with incredible bravery and fought for his place by qualifying through residency a couple of years later. It was tough on David and tough on the squad, but it wasn't a mitigating factor in our performances.

Jim Telfer: The situation with David Hilton was incredibly unfortunate and devastating for him because he and his family were convinced of his qualifications. David still maintains that his grandfather was born in Scotland several weeks before his birth was registered in Bristol.

Opposite: After ten long years of trying, Scotland, at last, regain the Calcutta Cup.

David Hilton (Scotland 1995-2002, 42 Caps): There was never any doubt in my mind at the time that I was Scottish qualified, none at all. I was so confident that right after the Welsh game I offered to produce my grandfather's birth certificate. Dougie Morgan had told me to be careful what I said to the press but I told them, 'There's absolutely no problem'. I phoned up my dad and he said he didn't have a copy of the birth certificate but the Edinburgh registrar could easily get it. So I got in touch with them and they said they needed my great grandfather's name, which was a bit odd. They found his name but not my great grandmother because she was married three times and it was a bit of a struggle to discover which name she was under. Then eventually they told me there was no record of a Walter Hilton being born in Edinburgh. I asked, 'What about rest of Scotland?' and she said, 'That does cover the whole of Scotland'.

Even then I was hoping and hoping. Then my dad eventually got hold of the death certificate and there it was, Walter Hilton had been born in Bristol. We'd always thought he was born in Edinburgh but he was registered in Bristol and his birth date and date of registration were 16 weeks apart and a lot could have happened in that time. The reason I got banned was because we couldn't prove that he was born in Scotland but in the same breath no one could prove that he wasn't.

It wasn't just the shock of the news that made it so hard but also the pressure from the press – I've never known anything like it. A lot of journalists came down to Bristol to research my family and I'd never have dreamt people would want to do all that, there was even something on TV where they traced my great grandfather back to Glasgow.

I had always felt a sense of pride, I always thought I was qualified. It was devastating to find otherwise and I couldn't get my head round it for a time. It screwed me up completely for a few months. No one has ever said a bad word to me, but it's hard to get this feeling that you are a fraud out of your body.

Duncan Hodge: That first game was obviously huge for Italy and they played very well to win, but we really didn't help ourselves. There was the saga of John Leslie playing when he had hardly trained after coming back from injury and was named as captain, and then after only a short time he broke down injured and had to go off. It was a shambles, the whole thing, but none of us were at the races.

Budge Pountney (Scotland 1998-2002, 31 Caps): To be honest, if there was one game in my whole rugby career that I could erase, the first match against Italy at the start of the Six Nations in 2000 would be the one. Definitely. Horrendous.

There was so much fanfare around the first-ever Six Nations match and Italy were loving it, being part of the whole thing, which should have been great. But you could just feel us as a team starting to get nervous. Nobody would say anything about it, but you could feel it. I have no idea why. We had finished the last championship as champions for god's sake, and then we'd had a difficult World Cup, but reached the quarter-finals and lost to New Zealand.

But in Rome that day things got tight, and as we got further into the game I remember thinking, 'Shit, this isn't right; we could lose the first game of the Six Nations to the Italians'.

I don't think we under-estimated them, and that's not meant to sound arrogant, but they were not up to Six Nations speed at that stage. They were very physical, got away with a few things, but that's the game, and they worked hard buoyed by a passionate, excited crowd. And that was it. Diego Dominguez – kick, kick, kick, kick . . . And I broke my nose, so it was painful game mentally and physically. And every time I went back to Northampton from Scotland games that season, the boys were playing the theme tune from *The Italian Job*; every bloody week.

Tom Smith: After losing to Italy we went to Ireland and started well, with Kenny Logan scoring a cracking try – his first ever Championship try, would you believe – but then it all fell to pieces. Brian O'Driscoll started to show what a special player he was going to be over the next decade and they just ran wild.

Gregor Townsend: Those first games were tough, really tough. After the high of the previous year we really sank to the depths – like many of the Scottish teams of the past, the season following a Grand Slam or Championship win has tended to be something of a disaster. We seemed to forget that all the glamour play of the year before had been built on hard work and graft. It didn't help that Kenny missed a lot of kicks in Rome or that John Leslie wasn't fit when he took the field as captain – he had only had one week's worth of training in him before we travelled to Rome because he was still coming back from the ankle injury he picked up at the World Cup. He didn't last the first quarter of the game before he went off. But the blame didn't rest at their doors – the whole team's performance was dreadful and we were all accountable for the result.

Against Ireland we tried to pick ourselves up and had a good start, but we were completely outplayed after that. Nothing we tried worked and confidence dropped through the floor.

France came to Murrayfield and we improved on our performance in Dublin – although that wouldn't have been hard – but they ended up winning 28–16.

John Leslie: I got rushed back from injury for the next Six Nations and was made captain. I suffered a badly bruised hip and had to come off in the first game, in Italy, we lost and I had to face the media.

It was an incredible honour to be named Scotland captain, but it was very controversial for a lot of people, and when I couldn't contribute as I wanted to I found it hard. You get ups and downs in rugby, but what really hurt was the criticism – I got 'wasn't giving my all', or 'wasn't showing pride in the jersey', they said.

I tried to play, but we lost to France and Wales and the team didn't perform – the only win we got was in the last game against England. I've always been quite serious and introverted about my rugby. I say what I have to when I'm with players, when necessary, but as captain you have all the public stuff to deal with too.

I was asked lots of questions, but I felt it wasn't for me to tell Scottish rugby what to do – I was captain of a team, not in charge of the whole of Scottish rugby. But some people took that as me not caring about the team, and wrote that I wasn't passionate about Scotland or rugby, and that hurt. It doesn't matter anymore. I had some great times in Scotland, and I still feel passionate when I see the guys out there at a full Murrayfield.

Gregor Townsend: We went to Wales hoping to take advantage of the furore surrounding Sinkinson and Howarth, but it seemed to galvanise them; we were starting to play much better but we still ended up losing 26–18.

The media had completely written off Scotland's hopes going into the final game of the 2000 season. England were determined to put right the errors of the previous season when they had lost out on a Grand Slam and the Championship by losing to Wales at Wembley and to atone for their exit from the World Cup when South Africa's Jannie de Beer had spectacularly kicked them out of the competition at the Stade de France with a world record five drop-goals. England were unbeaten that season as they travelled to Edinburgh and had seared through every previous match in the tournament. In The Sunday Times, *esteemed rugby journalist Stephen Jones wrote: 'Will England be denied as they were in 1990? The odds are against such a notion. No miracle, just a massacre. In the Six Nations showdown at Murrayfield, England to win by 44 points to take the Grand Slam today.'*

After a relatively mild start to the year, the heavens were open and a chill wind had swept across the east coast of Scotland as the plane carrying the English team touched down at Edinburgh airport. For twenty-four hours the rain fell, covering the city in a thick, swirling miasma. In the hours before kick-off the rain at last relented and watery sunlight filled the cavernous bowl of Murrayfield. But at two o'clock, just as the anthems were drawing to a close, the clouds began to gather once more, pressing in over the Firth of Forth and rolling out over the city, bringing with them a light but persistent drizzle which set in over Murrayfield towards the end of the first-half. By the time the second-half kick-off was hoisted high into the darkening sky that drizzle had developed into a downpour. Very soon it became a deluge. Despite conceding a soft first-half try off the back of a scrum to Lawrence Dallaglio, Scotland were succeeding in their tactics to stifle the English quick-ball and slow their backs' lightening attack at its source. And as if to make up for the tragedy that had struck him the previous season – which had inadvertently acted as the catalyst for Scotland's Championship success – the rugby gods cast their eyes over that Calcutta Cup match and through the mists and swirls of rain, resolved that the day should belong to Duncan Hodge.

Duncan Hodge: I got into the team for the Wales game and we actually played some really good stuff and I remember Glenn Metcalfe just carving them up from all over the field. I hit the posts a couple of times and we ended up losing by eight points, so it was a tough one to take. We were obviously staring down the barrel of the gun at the wooden spoon then and were completely written off by the time England came to town.

Tom Smith: By the time we met England, they were chasing the Grand Slam and we were facing a white-wash. They were extremely confident and let the whole world know how confident they were – despite having had a bit of a shake-up the year before when they lost to Wales at Wembley to gift us the Championship.

We all went to the cinema the night before the match to see the Al Pacino film *Any Given Sunday*, which is all fire and brimstone about inspirational sport. I don't know what effect that had on us. I know that when we woke up on the morning of the match and looked outside to see it bucketing down that gave us all a huge boost. In fairness to England, they still wanted to play rugby. Clive Woodward had had a few moans about our pre-match entertainment and things like that. He'd had done quite a good job of irritating everybody as only he knew how.

Everyone was pretty low and it took a little while for the belief to start to develop. England kept trying to run it out of positions where they probably should have just hoofed it up the park, and we kept pinning them back, and slowly everyone stated to think maybe . . . just maybe.

Duncan Hodge: It was the end of a nightmare season, and that was the first time ever we were given a day off during the week leading up to the game. I think it was because it was a Sunday game. We went clay pigeon shooting.

We'd actually played fairly well the week before down in Wales. We had a bit of a go and hadn't been beaten by a lot. In the lead up to the game I can remember certain bits of analysis. Dawson was massive on his quick taps, so McGeechan said

Duncan Hodge looks up to see whether referee Clem Thomas
has awarded his clinching score against England.

that whoever was back ten – which was more likely to be a winger or the fullback – was to come in and smash Dawson. And that was pretty important – Glenn Metcalfe took it upon himself to cover Dawson during those tap-penalties and he completely neutralised that threat.

During the game, it was all England. The first half went almost all their way, then just before half-time we got a penalty five yards from our own line, we ran it then kicked it to around about halfway and we got another penalty which we kicked for three points. So it could have been 17–6 but we went in at 10–9. Then in the second half we started well, and the silence amongst the English boys was deafening. Whereas in the first half they had all been chirping away, and swaggering around, there was then no chat whatsoever. Everything so far for them that season had been on Easy Street and all of a sudden, for the first time – partly because of the weather, partly because of us, partly because they weren't playing the conditions as well as they could have – they were in a situation that they hadn't been in before, and for all the experience that they had throughout the team, they didn't know how to change track to Plan B. Plan A had worked every time and they kept thinking that eventually it would click and come right and they would start running in half a dozen tries or more. Their tactical play was as poor as ours was good in the conditions. For the first time they were thinking to themselves: 'Hang on a minute, we're in a serious game here.'

Tom Smith: On a day like that, it is all about blood and guts and territory. Skill doesn't really come into it. And I think England misread it by trying to play great rugby inside their own half. Scotty Murray and Richard Metcalfe were doing a tremendous job on their lineout which meant that they were struggling to secure any set-piece authority, which they had been enjoying all season – and it rattled them. We kept up in their faces the whole time, keeping possession for long spells and when we kicked we kept it low and awkward. Andy Nicol did one great little grubber through which had their defence at sixes and sevens.

Duncan Hodge: The rain really set in and it started to hinder their attack – they had been throwing the ball around at will in the previous games, but our defence and the rain were slowing them down. As the game wore on and the weather got worse, they struggled to impose themselves and their lineout really started to struggle.

Tom Smith: All through the second-half the rain was just bucketing down – it was like standing in an ice cold shower – and we just kept on pressing them. Duncan Hodge kicked brilliantly and kept us in it. Then towards the end we really started to camp out in their half. We pushed hard to their line with some bursts through the forwards; the ball squirted out just as we were inches away, but Gordon McIlwham reacted the quickest and secured the ball back. Hodgey had come forward to gather the same ball and he grabbed it from Gordon and dived over.

Duncan Hodge: It was just luck that I was there – I was following the play in as we approached the line hoping to help, but suddenly the ball was there, I grabbed it and I dived over. The ground was so wet that the ball slid out of my hands as I touched it down and for a moment I wasn't sure if the ref was going to give it. I have a picture at home of me looking up at the ref to see what his decision was going to be and it was a great moment when he signalled the try. It was something really special.

Gregor Townsend: It was great to beat England in 2000 because it was the only time I managed that in ten years in the international game – but, speaking personally, it doesn't really stand out in the same way as some of the other notable successes of that era. That season we only won that single game out of five – so you have to remember to keep it in that context Having said that, it was a fantastic performance, with Duncan Hodge immense at stand-off – he controlled the game really well. They were Grand Slam favourites, but we matched them physically during the first-half when it was still relatively dry, then in the second-half when the weather deteriorated we managed the conditions really well.

It was the coldest I have ever been on a rugby pitch. I was at outside centre and the ball just didn't come out that far. Afterwards, I was one of three or four outside backs who just ran straight into the changing rooms and jumped into the showers with all their kit on. So we weren't there to witness Andy Nicol being presented with the Calcutta Cup outside.

Duncan Hodge: It was a Sunday and there was just a buffet after the game, so everyone just had a quick bite to eat and then went off to do their own thing. All my family had been at the game so we went to Montpeliers in Bruntsfield. I was sitting at this table with my family and three or four different strangers came up during the time we were there and put a bottle of champagne down at the table. I was saying, 'What are you doing?' And their answers were all pretty much the same: 'You don't need to ask that. You and the team have made our day. Just drink it and enjoy it.' Then they'd just turn around and walk away.

That was a big moment of realisation for me. Because you are so immersed in international rugby, you don't realise, or you forget, what it means to other people.

In the summer, Scotland travelled to New Zealand for a five match tour which included two Tests against the All Blacks in Dunedin and Auckland. It was a chance to blood new players: Ross Beattie, Iain Fullarton, Graeme Beveridge, Steve Scott, Jon Petrie and Nathan Hines and to give some more game time to the recently capped Chris Paterson, Jason White, Richard Metcalfe and James McLaren in the toughest rugby environment on the planet.

Jon Petrie (Scotland 2000-2006, 45 Caps): Despite a fairly dismal Six Nations, Scottish rugby was nevertheless on a bit of a high after reclaiming the Calcutta Cup for the first time in ten years. My first cap came at a time when I wasn't really expecting anything at all. It was only my second year as a pro and I somehow squeezed onto the New Zealand tour during the summer of 2000. I was twenty-two years old and there were a lot of older guys who had been there for a pretty long time, so I suppose a few people would have viewed me as being there to make up the numbers. But once I got out there, it was like nothing I had ever experienced before, it was kind of hard not to get overawed by the whole experience.

It was one of the last tours to have games outside the Test matches and it gave us a chance to establish some patterns of play and get used to playing with each other – either as new players or as players coming together for the first time since the Six Nations. We travelled all over New Zealand, playing matches against East Coast/ Poverty Bay, the Maoris, the New Zealand Barbarians and then Tests against the All Blacks in Dunedin and Auckland. All of those games were incredibly tough and we only managed to post one win all tour, against East Coast/Poverty Bay.

Duncan Hodge: It was the last long tour that Scotland have done. There were midweek games in North America and in Australia in 2004 but since then it has just been Test matches. We were away for six weeks in New Zealand and travelled all over the place playing games. It was a great experience, but very, very hard to do after a long season. Your body is just in pieces and your knackered all the time – and there are simply no easy games in New Zealand, every team was very, very strong.

Jon Petrie: In the Tests, the All Blacks were just unstoppable – I remember sitting in the stands during the first Test and watching Anton Oliver, the hooker, rampaging in like a train from the halfway line, just swatting our defenders aside.

Scotland line up to face the Haka at the House of Pain in Dunedin.
Carisbrook's nick-name once again rang true for the tourists.

Usually they'll give you a hint that you might be coming into the team or being dropped out of the team before the final selection meeting, but nobody had spoken to me at all. Geech read out the team for the second Test, and when they read these things out you are listening intently for your own name, and I was picked at number eight which tends to be the last name read out, so I didn't have any knowledge for about a day and a half afterwards of who else was in the team. It was a fairly long meeting, with a discussion about tactics and the mindset we needed to adopt, but I had to go to Geech afterwards and ask him to give me a summary because I hadn't heard anything. It does get a whole lot of emotions going. Obviously you are really excited and you know your family are going to be really excited as well. I phoned my Dad at 4am UK time, and I think he thought someone had died.

That second Test was played during a horrible night up in Auckland with gale force winds and the rain just lashing down. It was one of the proudest moments of my life. I had read French at university in St Andrews but cut short my studies after my third year when I was offered a contract with the Caledonia Reds. It had been a hard decision to make as I was only a year away from graduating with an honours degree, but I realised that the opportunity might not arise again and my burning ambition was to play for Scotland. You can never tell if you're going to be good enough to make it, if you'll get the luck of the bounce in front of the selectors and all the rest of it. So to finally pull on the jersey was a magnificent feeling and one that I knew I would cherish forever.

I remember the first kick-off and Andy Nicol was at scrum-half so we were standing close to each other. Andrew Mehrtens launched the ball way up into the floodlights, it seemed to hang there for an age, and as it started to come down I remember Andy shouting, 'Your ball, Jonny.' So that was my introduction to international rugby, collecting this slippery ball which was plummeting to earth like a meteor, with the entire All Black pack running at me. I suppose it is good to get into these things straight away.

To be capped against the All Blacks at Eden Park, in a starting jersey, is about as good as it gets. We were playing at night in this iconic stadium, facing a Haka from the likes of Christian Cullen, Tana Umaga, Andrew Mehrtens, Justin Marshall, Jonah Lomu, Anton Oliver, Todd Blackadder, Norm Maxwell, Reuben Thorne and Josh Kronfeld – all of them absolute legends of the game, many of them the best-ever to have played in their positions. They completely outmuscled and outran us, of course, but we did well to score a couple of tries through Cammie Murray and Chris Paterson.

Duncan Hodge: We were destroyed in both the Test matches, but I look back now at that team that we played against and it was just phenomenal. In the backs alone you had Justin Marshall and Andrew Mehrtens at half-back, you had Pita Alatini and Alama Ieremia in the centre who were perhaps not legendary names but were still decent players, and then you had a back-three of Jonah Lomu, Tana Umaga and Christian Cullen, which would be a lot of people's all-time dream team back-three. We weren't close in any of those games at all.

I remember after we got hammered in the first Test Jim Telfer flew into New Zealand on the Monday. We had a training session on the Sunday morning and then got flogged by Jim as soon as he arrived. The dirt-trackers played on the Tuesday, but Cammie Murray got injured, so I had to go on and play about an hour of that game; then on the Wednesday Jim got the Test team together and he flogged us again and we didn't have any days off so we were training on the Thursday and Friday too. There was no categorisation of training at that point – so we all did big sessions together no matter what and they were killers. And for three or four of us who had to back up games with the midweek team because of injuries, it was even harder. So I remember running out onto Eden Park on the Saturday night for the second Test and just thinking how completely shattered I was and wondering how on earth I was going to make it through an entire match against the best team in the world. I have never played as tired as I was in that match.

Jon Petrie: After the game I asked to swap jerseys with my opposite man, Ron Cribb. Cribb said that because the All Blacks only ever play in white when they play Scotland or France, he might not get another, so he wouldn't swap. I went back to the changing room a bit disappointed – I thought that it was a kind of standard etiquette. I was sitting in my space in the changing room, starting to take my boots off when there was a knock at the door. In walked Josh Kronfeld, who had just won his fiftieth cap for the All Blacks. He walked over and congratulated me on a great game and on winning my first cap . . . and handed me his jersey. 'You hold on to yours,' he said. 'I'm sure it'll be the first of many, but the first one is always special.'

We went out in Auckland that night with all their players and had a superb time. The life of a professional player can be fairly robotic, and in many ways it needs to be because to achieve anything in the game you have to be very disciplined in your approach to training, diet, lifestyle and playing. But at the same time, it is a game played by young men and if you restrict yourself too much you miss out on a lot of the things that you need to properly enjoy in your teens, twenties and your early-thirties like anyone else.

At the start of the new season, Scotland defeated the USA and Samoa but were unable to overturn the Wallabies despite virtuoso performances from Scott Murray, Stuart Grimes, Simon Taylor, Jon Petrie and Gregor Townsend.

Results in the 2001 Six Nations improved on the previous year and after losing narrowly 16–6 to France in Paris, the Scots drew 28–28 with a strong Welsh team at Murrayfield thanks to Tom Smith's late equalising score. They were hammered 43–3 by one of the all-time great English performances at Twickenham, but recovered their composure to defeat Italy at Murrayfield. Because of the outbreak of the Foot and Mouth epidemic in the late spring of 2001, the tournament went into hibernation until September. On the 22nd of that month Ireland at last arrived in Edinburgh, chasing a Grand Slam. In a remarkable performance, Scotland completely outplayed the visitors to win 32–10 and scored four scintillating tries through John Leslie, Budge Pountney, Tom Smith and debutant Andy Henderson.

Duncan Hodge: The 2001 Six Nations was a really mixed affair. Gregor got injured after about five minutes against France and there then followed a whole goal-kicking debacle that lasted for a few matches. In that France game I came on for Gregor and Kenny Logan was doing the kicking and took a couple while I was on and then a message came on that I was to kick the goals. Then in the next game Kenny was kicking the goals against Wales and he kicked something like three from eight and I remember at around seventy-five minutes when Tom Smith scored, Andy Nicol turned to me and said, 'You take the next kick,' and I looked at the scoreboard and realised that it was 28–26 to them and I had to kick the goal to draw level. So it was the only kick I had taken all day and there was obviously huge pressure on it, but I managed to get it, which was a huge relief – although in the very last act of the game I had a drop-goal to win it, which was charged down. It wasn't to be, but the organisation of it all from the sidelines wasn't good.

Tom Smith really showed his full range of skills in that game. He was bossing the Welsh scrum and the lineout was functioning really well – and he was charging all over the place in the loose. At one stage he got the ball down the blindside wing and he and Mossy [Chris Paterson] were on their own and outnumbered by about four or five Welsh defenders . . . and Tom put in this beautiful grubber kick behind them that Mossy dived on to score. And then, right at the death he took a ball out in the centre again and broke away from their defence on the twenty-two and rounded Neil Jenkins to score. It was some performance.

Jon Petrie: That was my first Six Nations game at Murrayfield. We were 18–6 down at half-time and we just sat in the changing room and I don't remember anything anyone in particular said, but I remember the feeling that it was going to have to be all or nothing. We knew we had to put everything out there. There was just this collective sense that we didn't want to lie down. That's the thing about international rugby, you get so drained physically and mentally out there that sometimes you are left thinking that you don't know how you are going to manage to get back to your feet. It's not that you don't want to, it's just that you don't know where the energy is going to come from – but there is something that makes you do it.

Duncan Hodge: We went down to Twickenham for the next game and were absolutely stuffed. They well and truly got their revenge on us for the previous season and the way they played was one of the best performances I've ever seen. I remember that we were about thirty points down and they had been running us ragged and they brought on Jason Robinson for his first cap with about fifteen minutes to go, which was the last thing we needed to see. He came on and within about thirty seconds had made a sixty-yard break out his twenty-two and had set up a try. And then he did it again virtually from the kick-off. There can't be many first cap impacts like that one.

We played Italy next and it wasn't a great game, but we did what we had to do and won – I kicked six kicks from seven and Tom Smith picked up another try and we managed to put them away – although it was far from a classic.

And then the Ireland game was called off because of Foot and Mouth. When we played them it didn't really feel like a Six Nations game, more of a one-off Test, but it was a great performance.

After a towering performance bustling with skill, Tom Smith slides in for the score to draw the match with Wales at Murrayfield.

Ian McGeechan: Our victory over a strong Ireland was no fluke – it was good rugby, played well. We put in another strong performance against Tonga and then fell away against Argentina and the All Blacks, but it should be remembered that we lost our middle five to injury around that time. If you can't put your best back-row and half-back combinations on the field, you will invariably struggle, especially against teams like Argentina and New Zealand, who excel in that area. We were entering something of a transitional phase at the time, with new players coming into the set-up and a change of focus developing on the way we wanted to play the game. The results were mixed at the time, but we came third in the 2001 Six Nations, which was probably higher than most people expected us to, and it remains one of the highest finishes we've had since the tournament expanded in 2000.

Jon Petrie: That was a year and a half since we had been Five Nations champions, we had beaten England in April of the previous year, so at that stage there was still a fairly high level of expectation. And despite suffering a massive loss to England, who were just on a different level that day, we recovered to beat Italy at home and then, once the authorities were satisfied that the Foot and Mouth epidemic was under control, we played Ireland at Murrayfield and absolutely stuffed them. It was tremendous performance and one that I still remember very fondly, even though I didn't start the match. Things were looking up for the squad, but then things turned a bit sour in the autumn with the whole Brendan Laney affair.

Scotland opened their autumn international programme by beating Tonga 43–20 in a game where debutant fly-half Gordon Ross controlled the game expertly and kicked flawlessly at goal. But this opening win would be the only one in the series as the team went on to lose 25–16 to Argentina before being obliterated by the All Blacks 37–6. That latter game was particularly memorable as it saw the introduction of New Zealander Brendan Laney into the Scotland team, just a short time after his arrival from his native shores. McGeechan had originally picked him for the Argentina match but after concern from the senior players that this act would not be received favourably by the wider squad, the media or the fans, McGeechan changed his mind and selected Laney instead for the A team encounter with New Zealand. However, after Scotland fell to the Pumas, the head coach felt that the team needed Laney's Super 12 experience and selected him to play against his countrymen for the second time in a week. The decision was, as predicted by his senior players, widely derided and cast a long shadow over both the remainder of McGeechan's term as coach and, unfortunately (for he was not himself at fault for the decision), over Laney's career in Scotland.

Gregor Townsend: Several of us let Geech know about our concerns surrounding Brendan's selection, but he seemed absolutely determined to play him. I think he looked at the almost instant success that John and Martin Leslie had been and thought that Brendan would do the same. And unfortunately there had been a precedent set there – John and Martin had only played one game for the Caley Reds before they were picked to play for Scotland against South Africa – and we all thought that it was a dangerous road to take. Geech placated us for a week by putting Brendan in the A team, but it was pretty obvious what his thinking was when Brendan was subbed halfway through the game – he was clearly being rested for the Test team. So no matter how Derrick Lee played against Argentina, it seemed a foregone conclusion that Brendan would take his place the following week.

Duncan Hodge: I was kind of caught up in the middle of the whole thing because I was captaining the A team at the time and Graham Hogg was basically told that he had to play Brendan against New Zealand as soon as he arrived. It was tough on Dezzie [Derrick] Lee because he got awarded man of the match against Argentina and was then dropped for Brendan – and it had nothing to do with Brendan either because he wasn't the one picking the team. It was just so short-sighted. There was no way that one guy was going to make the difference between us beating the All Blacks or not. Even if he had been a new Christian Cullen, it still wouldn't have been enough – no one player can make that kind of difference on his own. It was totally pointless throwing him in like that and it had a huge impact on how he was regarded in Scotland – when he could easily have missed that game and had three months earning his stripes at Edinburgh before the Six Nations and been integrated into the Scotland squad then.

It was a tough time for everyone involved. I like Brendan a lot and always enjoyed playing with him, he was a good player and he was a great talker and communicator and was great at taking the ball up hard and flat – a typical New Zealand-reared rugby player – but he was put in a nightmare situation as soon as he got off the plane.

Gregor Townsend: It wasn't Brendan's fault. There aren't many people who would turn down a chance to play international rugby and he wouldn't have wanted to anger the coaches by refusing to play – he might never have been selected again. It was tough on everyone – Derrick and Stuart Moffat were shoved down the pecking order and there were strong feelings of animosity from the crowd and the media that lasted for the rest of his time in Scotland; it was felt that he hadn't earned the right to wear the jersey and he became a caricature of the rugby mercenary.

Brendan Laney (Scotland 2001-2004, 20 Caps): To be honest, I should maybe have been firmer and refused to play that first Test match – and I really did think long and hard about that – but I had just arrived in the country, wanted to make a good impression and push for international honours as soon as I could. Hindsight is a wonderful thing. I know that I should have played a few games for Edinburgh and for Scotland A before even being thought about for Scotland, but if you're handed the opportunity to play against the All Blacks, how do you turn that down?

Glenn Metcalfe: I thought it was odd to rush Brendan into the Scotland set-up so quickly. He was undoubtedly a very good player and we all knew he could bring something positive to Scottish rugby, but the manner in which he was introduced wasn't ideal. I think it put him in a really hard position. But from someone who has trodden that path before him, I think that it would have been a lot better for him to have served out an apprenticeship of some sort in the Scottish club game. Without doing that I don't think there is any way that you can go into Test rugby with any affinity to the jersey you're wearing or to the players you're playing with – especially when wearing that jersey means so much to them. There should be no easy routes to Test match rugby. And also the game is very different in Scotland to the rugby played in New Zealand. Every country has a different culture and approach to the game and you need time to settle into that environment and attune yourself with the type of rugby that your teammates and coaches are playing.

Ian McGeechan: New Zealand still pose the ultimate threat to any team on the planet's psychological and physical well-being: they can destroy you, at any time, in a dozen different ways. Every team in the world has experienced it when playing them. Over the years, Scotland have played some of their best rugby against the All Blacks – basically because the players know that if they don't raise every aspect of their game, they know that they'll be blown away. More often than not, the game can be fairly even for much of the eighty minutes, but the All Blacks excel at sucker-punching teams out of the game with relentless efficiency near the try line. So often they score two or three tries in the space of just a few minutes, which wipes out the hopes of the opposition, even if the rest of the game is fairly evenly matched. It is a clinical efficiency that every All Blacks team seems capable of. That is the challenge that you have to meet, prevent, and then implement yourself if you are to stand a chance of victory. When the All Blacks are in full flow they make it look so easy. Passes are timed to perfection, running lines carve open space and it all looks so simple. When they are in full flow they play rugby the way it is supposed to be played.

Jon Petrie: Jim Telfer was back coaching for those November games. When I first came in he had moved upstairs to be director of rugby, and you could see him up in his office with a pair of binoculars looking out, then after a few weeks he started coming out and standing in his suit at the side of the pitch, then it got to the stage he was standing at the side of the pitch with his boots on, and eventually he was back in the thick of it.

On the morning of a Test match the forwards used to go out and do some line-outs on the hotel grounds, then Jim used to take us into the team room to give us his big motivational speech. I remember before the All Blacks game in 2001, we were staying at the Roxburgh and he decided to sit all the forwards in a circle facing out the way, and he was marauding around the middle of the circle going through his speech and he kept on slapping boys on the back of the head. It scared the daylights out of you. He went through every player, telling them how tough they were and what he expected them to do to the opposition. Then he got to Badger – Gordon Simpson – who had been brought in when Simon Taylor was injured, and he'd run out of things to say, so he ended up slapping him on the head saying, 'Badger, we didnae want you in the team, but you're the best we've got.'

England were the first opponents scheduled to play Scotland in the 2002 Six Nations and they won comfortably 29–3 at Murrayfield, and although Scotland also lost in Dublin and against France in Edinburgh, they defeated Italy and Wales on the road.

Brendan Laney: I really enjoyed my first Six Nations, which was in 2002. I felt more comfortable to be in the team having got some game-time for Edinburgh under my belt. I got my first Scotland man of the match award when we beat Italy in Rome and managed to score twenty-four points, which was a record haul at the time for a Scottish player. I then played pretty well when we beat Wales in Cardiff, which was a great experience. We really took the game to the Welsh and snuffed out their hopes through our forwards – Gordie Bulloch got two tries from driving mauls – it may not have been pretty, but that's how you win on the road.

Donnie Macfadyen: I was first involved with the senior Scotland side when we toured

North America in 2002. It was a good young squad that went out there and we had a great time as well as getting our first experience of the Test match environment. The coaches on that tour were Pat Lam and Ian McGeechan and I thought they were brilliant – although at the same time I had grown up watching Ian McGeechan in charge of Scotland and the Lions, so to begin with I was a bit awe-struck by the whole experience.

Mike Blair (Scotland 2002-2012, 85 Caps): My first game for Scotland was against the Barbarians at Murrayfield in the summer of 2002 and although we lost, I started and scored a long range try which was a great boost for my confidence – especially as it was my first involvement with the senior side. But all these things are about luck and right-time-right-place opportunities because Bryan Redpath had decided not to tour North America that summer and Graeme Beveridge was injured, so I got selected for that tour and was suddenly number one scrum-half for the Test matches – while in other circumstances I might easily have not made the squad at all.

remember before my first cap against Canada I had all these visions of scoring a similar try to the one I'd scored against the Barbarians. We had a driving maul from about five metres out and were just about to plop over the line when I joined the maul, knicked the ball and fell over – so it was great to score on my debut, but it was not in quite the manner I had envisioned. When you dream about what your first cap might be like, I definitely didn't imagine it to be the experience that I ended up having. We played in a field which was in the middle of nowhere in Canada with about 2000 people watching. It was baking hot and we lost. It wasn't the best of starts.

The following week we played against the USA, went 7–0 down after five minutes and then Wagga [Nathan Hines] got sent off for punching. All the new guys were just thinking, 'Thanks for that, Wagga!' But we were able to pull it back and ended up thumping them, so it was a good way to haul the trip back on track.

Brendan Laney: Coming back from the summer tour and preparing for the autumn internationals I really started to feel that I was beginning to change people's perceptions about me. The autumn series was just fantastic that year, something really special to be a part of. I equalled Gavin Hastings' record of reaching a hundred Test points in nine matches, which was a proud moment for me, and then to go unbeaten through all three games of the series was a real achievement and to beat a side like South Africa was epic. It was a really gutsy team effort and we deserved to win on the back of the courage that the guys showed out there.

David Hilton: It took to 2002 until I was cleared to play for Scotland again and I won my forty-second cap against South Africa at Murrayfield. After trying for two and a half years to get this goal it was given to me through an unfortunate injury to Mattie Stewart. I was not at my best but it was great that Scotland didn't turn their back on me and I was very determined to prove I should be there. I played fifteen minutes off the bench and the crowd reaction was brilliant.

It was one of my favourite games for Scotland and the pride I had at helping us beat South Africa for the first time in thirty-three years was unbelievable. I didn't win any more caps after that but it was all worth it.

Gordon Bulloch: The game plan was pretty straight-forward, we were just told to go at them up front right from the start and to put as much pressure on them in the midfield as we could. It's probably the same game plan that's totted out every time anyone plays the Springboks, but we went for it and got results.

Simon Taylor (Scotland 2000-2009, 66 Caps): We pressurised them into mistakes in the backs, which gave us field position and then the donkeys up front did an incredible amount of work to get in amongst the Springbok pack and cause them all sorts of problems – from the set-piece to the contact area. We got lucky with the tries, but we earned that luck with the way we played.

We controlled most of the territory in the first half and Brendan kicked a couple of penalties for us. He could have put us 9-6 up at half-time but missed and there was a small doubt in the back of my mind that that might come back to haunt us. Fortunately it didn't.

The Boks came out with a bit more purpose in the second half and Butch James made a big break but Bryan Redpath cut him down with a great tackle. I think that was a real turning point in the game; they could sense that nothing much was going for them, we were pretty fired up, and decisions started to rack up in our favour.

Bryan Redpath: Yeah, we definitely had the momentum in the second half. I think we

The squad celebrate their victory over the Springboks at Murrayfield in November 2002.

took a lot of confidence from the amount of territory we had in the first half and that, even though we were level with them at the break, we had the making of them.

After a series of attacks on the South African line, Budge Pountney was driven over. The TMO couldn't ascertain whether Pountney had grounded the ball, so referee Nigel Williams went with his initial, and probably correct, instincts and awarded the try. If the legitimacy of that score was contentious, however, it was nothing compared to Scotland's second try. As the South African backs over-complicated their exit strategy from behind their goal-line the ball spilled loose and Nikki Walker pounced to score – although TV replays later appeared to show that the winger had missed the ball completely.

Nikki Walker (Scotland 2002-2011, 24 Caps): I had been briefly unconscious a few minutes before so I really don't remember much about my try but I definitely got a fingertip to the ball.

Simon Taylor: If Nikki says he got a touch on the ball . . . I'll take that. Please just don't make me watch the replay again.

In the build-up to the 2003 Six Nations, captain Budge Pountney announced his retirement from the Scotland team. It was an acrimonious affair as Pountney renounced the shambolic set-up of the SRU, citing unprofessional conduct that was detrimental to the progress of the team. Among his grievances were simple incompetence such as a lack of water at training and a continued reissue of an invoice from the SRU for a tie that he had given away to a young fan after an international, to more serious ones about player welfare. This concluding point had come to a head when Telfer had flogged the forwards to a standstill in the wake of their victory over the Springboks and had then berated them for a poor performance against Fiji, which Pountney had vocally claimed was down to fatigue brought on by Telfer's brutal training sessions.

Budge Pountney: It was amazing to play for Scotland and to captain the team was such a special experience that it's impossible to put it into words. It is one of the greatest honours, perhaps the greatest, you can be asked to do. I see it on the captains' faces now, the pride they feel, and being given that honour even once is just amazing. So I do wish my Scotland career had ended differently, but I still stand by my decision. I made it for the right reasons, at least in my head. If you'd asked me a couple of weeks after the decision, I'd still have said I loved playing for Scotland, but I just didn't like the crap behind the scenes that I felt stopped the team achieving what it was capable of and maybe if I hadn't been captain, and didn't feel the responsibility I did for standing up for the guys, it might have been different.

I think, looking back, that it was perhaps the contrast between professional rugby on the field, which was moving at a very fast pace, and the game being stuck in the amateur era still behind the scenes and the SRU not being able, or willing, to keep up. I really felt for the lads. They were a great bunch of boys and we had a great team ethic, a great laugh and got on really well, which is sometimes difficult when lots of different cultures come together. You always have a few dust-ups here and there, but that team really worked hard for each other, for that Five Nations Championship in '99 and put everything into playing and trying to win for Scotland.

But I just couldn't take it anymore. Players work very, very hard to be the best they can be, but in those days it felt like we were treated like second-class citizens by the SRU. Every week before an international was like a fight – a fight to get simple things like water after training, food, kit, studs, whatever. I know it was a difficult financial climate, but when opposition sides were only worrying about the game, many Scotland players were involved in stupid squabbles until kick-off.

I took some flak, but I kept in touch with many of the players afterwards and things got a lot better afterwards. I'm not saying that's down to me – maybe it would have happened anyway. I thought it was pretty crass of people [at the SRU] to question my state of mind – they had known me for five or six years, but obviously didn't know me very well at all – but I knew exactly what I was doing. Of course, I felt terrible for my team-mates and Scotland supporters when I took that decision, and I missed hugely not playing for Scotland, but the roller-coaster had started and I had other things to keep my mind active. Sport is a wonderful thing and I was always someone who viewed rugby as a fantastic sport, but there is life outside it. I love it to bits, but you always need perspective; it makes you a more balanced and healthy sportsperson.

Brendan Laney: We thought we would do better in the 2003 Six Nations than we did, but we picked up good wins at home against Italy and Wales and controlled things well. We lost to Ireland in the opening match at Murrayfield and to France and England away, but all three of those teams were hitting a purple patch, especially England and France – and looking at their impact later in the year, you could see how well they were building towards the World Cup at that stage.

Mike Blair: Bryan Redpath got stitches in his eye after about twenty minutes of the France game and I came on for my Six Nations debut – and I was absolutely shitting myself. The noise in the Stade de France is one of the most unbelievable things I've ever heard, it's like the Millennium Stadium when the roof is closed – thunderous, thunderous noise and this incredible energy. The atmosphere at Murrayfield is a different kind of environment; in France and Wales there's a real carnival mood during the build-up to the game, but at places like Murrayfield and Twickenham there's a much more eerie, almost pre-battle kind of atmosphere.

So I came on, shaking to pieces and almost immediately a gap opened up at the side of a ruck and I sneaked through it and hared off up field on this forty metre run before eventually getting hunted down. There's a point on the video that you see me running and the only other people you can see around me are these ten French guys that are about to jump on me. I remember speaking to Simon Taylor after the game and he said that he had had the weirdest thought when I made my break because he hadn't really been aware that I had come on; he had got up from the ruck and looked around and the first thought that he had was: 'Why is the ball boy running away with the ball?' I was barely pushing eleven stone, had a ridiculous haircut with a Tintin quiff and looked about twelve years old. I probably haven't changed all that much physically over the years, but at least the quiff has gone.

Gregor Townsend: We toured South Africa in the summer and although we lost both Tests we played some of the best rugby that I had experienced with Scotland – it was right up there with the '99 season. Our forwards picked up where they had left off when they last played the Springboks and really took the game to them physically. The back-row of Jason White, Simon Taylor and Andrew Mower were just brilliant and our back-play was pretty electric too. In the first Test we outscored them three tries to two, with Andy Craig, Chris Paterson and Jason all scoring. We were leading 25–12 at one stage, but Louis Koen was keeping them in the game with his kicking – and a freak moment from one of his kicks got them right back in it. He took a penalty from around thirty or forty yards out and hit the post – Trevor Halstead had been following up the kick and he reacted quicker than we did and got to the ball to score. They then pushed on and got into the lead after Stefan Terblanche scored another try. Going into injury time we were just four points down and were pressing on their line for several minutes. Eventually Nathan Hines picked up the ball and reached out through the ruck to score . . . but he just dropped it before grounding it. It was a real gut-wrencher that we were that close and we definitely deserved more from our performance than that.

We headed to Ellis Park in Johannesburg the next week and the Springboks played much better than in the first Test. I think the biggest difference came down to our fitness levels. They were ahead of us at that stage and they were able to close out the game in the final quarter.

Mike Blair: We had a couple of weeks at home after we got back from South Africa and then we began our pre-tournament training for the World Cup – which was all pretty novel. We flew out to the Olympic training camp in Spala in Poland for ten days of cryotherapy-based training – which basically involved heavy training sessions followed by three-and-a-half minutes in a cryogenic freezer, with temperatures at around -140 degrees centigrade while we just wore shorts, earmuffs and facemasks and a pair of clogs. The idea is that such extreme temperatures allowed for better muscle recovery after an intense work-out, allowing you to fit more training into a day. Those are the longest minutes and seconds of your life when you're in there. I found the whole Spala thing a bit weird, to be honest. You go out there for ten days and because of the whole cryotherapy thing they tell you that instead of doing five sessions in a week, you can do ten sessions. But they fail to tell you at that point that you then need a week to recover. So I always thought that we should just have stayed at home and done ten sessions over two weeks as normal.

Once we were back in Edinburgh and began training again we started doing a load of cardio work on bikes and rowing machines in the Botanic Gardens so that we got used to the heat and humidity levels that we would be facing out in Australia. We played one game in Townsville where the humidity was meant to be at its worst – but it wasn't humid at all. We then played the rest of our games in Brisbane and Sydney and again there was no humidity, so all those sessions in the Botanics had been a bit pointless.

Looking back, the South Africa tour earlier in the year had kind of felt like our break-out tour. We weren't miles away from the Springboks then we did all the training in Poland and the warmup games in Edinburgh and things just felt like they were building and building . . . and then it never really happened in Australia. I'm not sure if it was a case of pressure, or what, but we never got into our stride and only showed in very occasional glimpses what we were capable of.

Jon Petrie: A lot of people made a lot out of the atmosphere in the camp and claimed that we were not very professional while we were out there, but I would completely disagree with that. We were out there for seven weeks so there were a few occasions when a few guys went out for a few beers, but these would be the guys that weren't playing that week. Everyone knew they were at a World Cup and understood what an honour that was.

Gregor Townsend: I really enjoyed the 2003 Rugby World Cup. The way the Australians organised it was brilliant. The USA game was a highlight, which you would never have expected, with 50,000 people in Suncorp Stadium on a Monday night.

Gordon Bulloch: While we had a great time at the tournament, one of the harder things to take was when Martin Leslie was suspended for twelve weeks after the USA game because he'd banged his knee into an opposition player's head as he cleared out a ruck. We all felt it was a pretty harsh punishment because there hadn't been any intent and the guy he hit wasn't injured, so for some reason we decided to pay tribute to him by mimicking his facial twitch as the camera came down the line past us during the national anthems for the France game. And we were absolutely slated for doing that by the press. I suppose, if we had won the game it would have been forgotten about – but we got fifty points put on us and suddenly you were left thinking, 'Jeez, that wasn't too good an idea.'

Gregor Townsend: It's a tough one because I know certain players back home thought it was a bit disrespectful. But if you want to judge how Scotland performed after doing that then look at the score after thirty minutes, we were only 6–3 down – it was only in the secondhalf that game really got away from us. We wanted to make a statement that we were a strong group and we thought the punishment was harsh.

Jon Petrie: We'd had quite a long build-up out there but it just didn't click in the first game against Japan in Townsville. We came round to it a bit more in Brisbane against America, and then there was the France match. We didn't cover ourselves in glory at that World Cup, we made it to the quarter-finals but only by the skin of our teeth after we had been hammered by France at Stadium Australia. We just didn't play very well.

Chris Paterson (Scotland 1999-2011, 109 Caps): I loved my time out in Australia – it was the best six weeks of my international career up to that point and we all had a great time. The French game was obviously a huge disappointment and on the back of that there emerged all these reports that there were problems in the camp. But the truth of it was that France were outstanding and deserved to win that well. After that game I genuinely thought that they would go on to win the tournament.

Mike Blair: In the wake of the France game it was decided that Mossy [Chris Paterson] would get a run at stand-off for our last pool game against Fiji. Geech said in a press conference that it had always been our intention to play him at ten at some point during the tournament, but it seemed to come a bit of the blue for all of us, including Mossy, because he hadn't trained in that position even once during the any of team training runs. But fair play to Mossy, he took it all totally in his stride and really showed his class as he looked completely comfortable and confident out there controlling things.

Gordon Bulloch: Fiji was a must-win match after the France debacle. They were a strong side and the conditions in Australia were suiting them perfectly – they were throwing the ball around and having a go from everywhere. Their forwards were massive but could sprint as fast as most international backs and their skills were unbelievable. And in Rupeni Caucaunibuca they had one of the stars of the tournament. He was short and barrel-like, almost chubby, but he could shift, really shift. He had scored the most unbelievable try against France from around seventy-five yards out, so we were well aware of what he could do and were determined not to give him any space . . . so of course he went on to score two tries against us.

Stuart Grimes: We were staring down the barrel of a gun then. They were running it from everywhere and Caucau was just on fire. Going into the final five minutes we were 20–15 down and looked like we might be exiting before the quarter-finals for the first time in our history. Basil took us aside and said that we had to keep it tight and look to score through the forwards, which was where Fiji were at their weakest. It wasn't a pretty way to win the game but it was immensely satisfying. We worked incredibly hard to get ourselves into position and then kept our heads to force Tom Smith over; Mossy had to kick the conversion to win and he kept his cool – and we were through.

Jon Petrie: Caucau, was at his peak and could have scored a barrel-load of tries, but Glenn Metcalfe tackled like a demon that day. He absolutely wrecked his body, throwing himself at guys who were about to score in the corner. We were actually quite lucky to sneak through.

Stuart Grimes: So we had the hosts, who were also the defending champions, in the quarter-final. It was about forty minutes before the match and the kickers were already out on the field getting a bit of practise in. Then the rest of us started heading out of the changing room for the warm-up and as we walked up the tunnel we saw Chris Paterson getting carried past us in the opposite direction. He was one of our main men, playing stand-off that day and our main goal-kicker, so we were wondering what the hell was going on. It turned out Mossy had been practicing his kicking, with Ben Hinshelwood returning the ball to him. And Ben had launched this huge torpedo kick which had struck Mossy right on the side of the head just as he was lining up another kick. He collapsed on the spot – out cold.

They got Mossy into the changing room and were splashing his face with cold water, saying, 'Oh my god, what are we going to do?' Andy Craig was called down from the stand: he was in his number ones and was struggling a bit after being out on the tiles the night before. His boots were back at the hotel, which was half a mile away, so someone was sent to get them.

But in the meantime Mossy began to recover his senses, and with only five minutes to go before kick-off they decided to go with him. He played a blinder and struck one of the finest drop-goals ever by a Scottish player, but we ended up losing 33–16.

Gregor Townsend: It was 9–9 at half-time, but we were lucky to be level. We were playing our hearts out, but Australia were a much better team and we were still in the game largely by dint of their mistakes. We were unlucky in a couple of facets of the game – Kenny Logan had broken free to score but Steve Walsh, the referee, brought us back for a penalty which he awarded to us because he hadn't see that Kenny had made the break. Australia scored a fairly dubious try that then lifted their confidence and they then ran amok for fifteen minutes. We fought back and scored a try through Robbie Russell, but it was too little too late.

It was an emotional end to the game. We did a lap of honour to thank the fans, and Bryan Redpath and Kenny said their goodbyes as the tournament was their swansong before hanging up their boots. It was also the end of the coaching road for Geech and Telfer; Telfer was finally standing down from the SRU and Geech was moving up to become the director of rugby. Matt Williams had already been named as his replacement and we had been implementing some of his structural play and tactics during the World Cup. Many of his instructions had been confusing and somewhat over-elaborate, often over-complicating areas of the game unnecessarily, which was a terrible decision to try and introduce mid-tournament. We weren't particularly impressed by very much of it, but had little choice but to get on with things. In retrospect, it should have served as a warning of what was to come.

TWENTY-TWO

THE AUSTRALIAN REVOLUTION
2004-2005

As he moved up to take the helm as director of rugby from Jim Telfer, Ian McGeechan's final act as head coach was to appoint the Australian Matt Williams as his successor. McGeechan would not last long in his role behind a desk at Murrayfield – the siren call of the tracksuit and the training paddock would prove too strong and he was soon heading south to take up a new position with English and European champions, London Wasps, an appointment which, in turn, would eventually lead to his return to the Lions den, first as midweek coach on the 2005 tour to New Zealand under Sir Clive Woodward and then as head coach for the 2009 tour to South Africa.

As part of a continued shake-up at the SRU, chief executive Bill Watson was sacked and team manager Dougie Morgan stepped aside. Matt Williams had been brought in as a technical advisor during the 2003 World Cup so that some of his systems and initiatives could begin to filter into the team. He appointed former All Blacks skipper, and the incumbent Edinburgh captain-coach, Todd Blackadder, as his assistant. Alan Tait had been working with the squad as defence coach, but Williams wanted to take on that role himself, and so the Kelso man was soon on his way out of Murrayfield as well.

The Australian had a mixed track-record as he came into the post as Scotland's head man. He had been head coach of New South Wales from 1997 to 1999 and in his first season in charge he took the Waratahs to their worst-ever Super 12 position of ninth. In his final season the team finished their campaign with a dismal six losses in their last seven matches, extinguishing any hopes that they had held earlier in the season of a semi-final place, and he left the post with a year still to run on his contract.

From Sydney he moved to Dublin to become assistant coach to Mike Ruddock at Leinster and succeeded the Welshman the following year. After an inauspicious first season in charge, when his team finished third out of four in their Heineken Cup pool, he led the Irishmen to the inaugural Celtic League title as well as the Irish Inter-Provincial championship, and followed this up by guiding them into quarter and semi-final appearances in the next two Heineken Cup campaigns. On the back of these performances he was approached by McGeechan to ascertain his interest in moving into international rugby and was finally named as his successor on the eve of the World Cup.

Williams was initially affable and charismatic in his dealings with the media and could certainly talk a good game; his eloquent southern hemisphere cadences added weight to his statements about how he thought Scottish teams should play the game, and helped expound his vision for Fortress Scotland – an initiative to strengthen the domestic teams by only selecting players for the national side who plied their trade within Scotland – as well as his targets for 'up-skilling' the players who were now under his charge. No one could hide from the raw truth of many of his statements – Scotland had been underperforming

Opposite: George Gregan gets the ball away during the summer 2004 tour despite the attentions of (*from left to right*) Ben Hinshelwood, Scott Murray and Donnie Macfadyen.

for a number of years, and save for an upsurge in the 1999 Five Nations, had been on a downward spiral since the mid-nineties. However, there were some doubts cast about his approach when he claimed that the Scottish rugby public should not expect to see any notable improvement in the team for some eighteen months as the players adapted to the new systems and worked on improving their skills; he predicted that throughout this transitional period there would be very few, if any, positive results registered. The revolution would be painful, he said, but in the end the team would emerge into a bright new dawn to bathe in success for years to come.

As with every revolution there are casualties. Dougie Morgan and Alan Tait had already been cleared from the management and coaching side. Now Williams turned his attention to the playing staff. Following his announcement that huge improvements would have to be made in every position in order for the team to stand a chance of success in the future, Williams phoned Glenn Metcalfe, James McLaren and Gregor Townsend, three of the most experienced players in his squad, and recommended that they should each take the opportunity to announce their retirements from international rugby on their own terms – as he had no intention of picking them for any of his future squads. With little option before them, all three players duly announced their retirements, immediately removing 144 caps worth of experience from the squad.

For all that the coach may have been misguided in jettisoning many of the more experienced campaigners that were still willingly at his disposal, he certainly didn't hold back in his promise to give youth its head by selecting a team brimming with young talent for the 2004 Six Nations opener against Wales at the Millennium Stadium.

In the months preceding the World Cup, and during the tournament itself, Mike Blair was seen as the heir apparent to succeed the retiring captain, Bryan Redpath. Williams wasn't so convinced, and as he studied the players in the Scotland squad and compared them with their rivals in the opposition ranks, he came to the conclusion that the Scottish pack was going to struggle to impose themselves in any of the forthcoming Tests. Williams believed that Blair was getting something of an armchair ride at Edinburgh; Chris Cusiter at the Borders, however, was getting anything but that. In selecting Cusiter ahead of Blair for the opening match of the 2004 Six Nations, Williams said that he needed a scrum-half who was used to playing under the pressure of a retreating scrum. There was no doubt that Cusiter deserved his shot at glory and he went on to prove his class for both Scotland and the Lions, but it was a mixed message that Williams was sending out – it boosted Cusiter's confidence certainly, but it also revealed that he did not rate his forwards as an international unit.

Other youngsters brought into the team included centre Tom Philip and back-rower Ally Hogg, and in a bold move he selected Chris Paterson as his stand-off and captain. As well as the added responsibility that the role of captain brought, there was a lot of pressure on the Gala man to repeat the form that he had shown at fly-half during the World Cup while simultaneously leading a team shorn of much of its experience. To compound matters, Williams had devised what he believed to be an ingenious defensive system whereby Paterson would retreat to fullback in defensive situations, centre Andy Henderson, who was playing out of position on the wing, would shuffle into the number twelve channel while Philip moved to stand-off, and fullback Ben Hinshelwood would come into the vacated wing birth. In reality the system was disjointed, confusing and added doubt in the minds of the players as they lined up to stifle the Welsh attack. In the end, the hosts were able to unpick the system with relative ease. This type of over-complication became emblematic of Williams' tenure in charge of the national side. Despite positive showings from Cusiter, Philip, Hogg and a late introduction by the Australian-born stand-off, Dan Parks, Wales strolled to a 23–10 victory.

It was a story that would become a trend throughout the remainder of the tournament as Scotland finished the Championship without registering a single win.

Gregor Townsend: Coming back from the World Cup, I was excited and invigorated about the season ahead. I was very pleased with the way that Mossy had finished the tournament at stand-off and although I still wanted to contest for the jersey with him, I could also envisage us building a new partnership with him at fly-half and me outside him at inside centre – in a kind of mentoring position. But then I received a call from Matt Williams. He told me that we had a dearth of international experience in midfield and that he wanted to blood new players in that position so that they could start building that experience. He was about to announce his Six Nations training squad of 44 players . . . and I wasn't in it. I told him that I wanted to fight for my place but he was worried about the PR side of things – that the press would focus in on my exclusion rather than his positive selections. He said that because of my reluctance to just disappear into the background, he would publicly pick me for the squad but that, in reality, I was banned from attending any training sessions and that I would not be considered for any match day squads. Where was I to go from there? For all that I was prepared to fight it out for my place, it was clear that no matter how well I played over the next few weeks and months, I wasn't going to be picked. I went to Murrayfield for a meeting with him and said that I had decided to retire. What else was I to do?

Mike Blair: Gregor was put out to pasture when he was only 30. He was also, at the time, the most capped player Scotland had ever had. All that experience and class just went out the window. It also didn't help that guys his same age were still getting picked in the squad – guys like Brendan Laney and Derrick Lee – and yet he had been told that he was now too old for the international game.

Simon Webster: I think it was a big mistake axing all the experience the way they did. The guys who were told their careers were over were a big loss because we were a largely young and inexperienced team, and those guys could easily have played on; it took a long time for us to recover from that.

Andy Henderson (Scotland 2001-2008, 53 Caps): When Matt Williams took over, as a changing room, we were keen to be positive about it. We were excited about the prospect of a new challenge. But things didn't really work out. One of the big things for me was that training was simplified an awful lot, and broken down to basic skills. When you come together before an international match you really need to be working on what you are going to do as a team and not spending your whole time practising your spin passing, which really should be the sort of day-to-day stuff you do at your club. I always thought that was a bit bizarre. As things went along a growing issue was the drop-off in confidence within the squad – which in international sport is probably the most important factor in teams realising their potential. It is a vicious cycle because unless you win a few matches it is really hard to instill confidence, but without belief you are going to struggle to win.

Chris Cusiter (Scotland 2004-2014, 71 Caps plus 1 Cap for the Lions): It was a surprise to get the elevation into the Scotland squad so soon after signing for the Borders and I definitely didn't expect to be the first choice for the opening game of the Six Nations. Standing there in the Millennium Stadium gave me a feeling that I had never felt before and I had a tear in my eye during the anthems. After you taste international rugby all you want to do is experience it again and again. After I picked up my first couple of caps I reassessed my goals and it became incredibly important to me that I held on to the shirt from all-comers. I wanted that number nine shirt and I would work as hard as I possibly could to keep it.

Mike Blair: Every generation seems to have had its major battle for the Scottish scrumhalf berth, and ours was no different. There was me, Cus [Chris Cusiter] and Rory Lawson all fighting it out for that one shirt. It was a challenge, but if you were picked to start you knew you'd definitely earned it to get ahead of those other guys.

I hadn't played well during the World Cup and there was a bit of a hangover from that. I was obviously massively disappointed not to be starting under the new regime, but Cus definitely deserved his chance – he was playing very well for the Borders and although I didn't agree with the coach's reasons for picking him ahead of me, on playing merit he certainly deserved his shot. But the thing that really annoyed me about it all was that Matt Williams told me about six weeks before the Wales game that Cus was going to be starting. There wasn't much I could say to change his mind. He'd said that line about Cus getting the nod because he was playing behind a weak pack, which I found pretty baffling, because while Edinburgh were having a good season that year, our forwards were hardly beasting teams.

Dan Parks (Scotland 2004-2012, 67 Caps): I think I was fortunate that I turned up at a time when the team was losing a lot of experienced players – top backs like Gregor [Townsend], Bryan Redpath, Kenny Logan, James McLaren and Glenn Metcalfe were all retiring after the 2003 World Cup, or had just retired, and there were holes to fill. In that December, there was a national camp with a lot of new faces, and myself, Chris Cusiter, Tom Philip and Ally Hogg were all put straight into the first Test match of

Chris Cusiter in action against Ireland at Landsdowne Road.

2004, down in Wales, and guys like Hugo [Southwell] and Sean Lamont and the next year Rory followed.

Tom Philip (Scotland 2004, 5 Caps): For the young guys, most of us just thought we were there to make up the numbers at training, so it was hard to believe it when I was selected to start against Wales for the 2004 Six Nation opener.

You just can't imagine the noise that hits you in Cardiff, , it's unbelievable. In modern sport, and especially in rugby, much of the game is based on communication, but in a place like the Millennium Stadium, you can't hear anything that anyone else is saying to you – it was one of those games where guys would be running the length of pitch long after the whistle had been blown because they couldn't hear anything. It was an amazing feeling to be right at the centre of it all.

Simon Webster: The Wales game in 2004 was unbelievable. We went in there with a new coach and pretty much a new team and the excitement levels were massive, but we really didn't help ourselves with some of the tactics we used. There was this huge defensive system that basically revolved around Matt being nervous about Mossy – and then Parksy – defending in the ten channel. So on set-piece defence the ten would leave the line and go and stand at fullback and everyone else would shuffle along. In theory that's fine, but somehow you've then got to get your ten back into the line and your fullback dropping back into position after the first phase or two and very quickly the whole system just fell down.

Tom Philip: I was moved to the stand-off channel defensively because I always liked making big hits and I was looking forward to them sending guys down my channel, but it never happened – they moved the ball wider and exploited us out there. It didn't work out the way we thought it would – which was pretty much the story of that whole Championship. It was a hard, hard season.

Simon Webster: I think Simon Cross must get the award for the closest anyone will ever come to winning a cap and not actually doing it. Five minutes to go in that Wales game, most of the subs were on and Crossy gets the call that he's going on – he strips, is standing on the sideline, the touch-judge knows what is happening and tells him that at the next set-piece he'll be on. But the final five minutes of that game were an uninterrupted series of phases. When the ball eventually went dead the game had gone into eighty minutes and the referee blew for fulltime. And Crossy was just standing there on the sideline. The next week Jason White was fit, Crossy lost his place on the bench and he was never there again. He's a mate so I find it funny and I take the piss out of him for it – but the truth is that it's heartbreaking; I wish they could even give him something like a half cap.

Tom Philip: I remember Will Greenwood was playing at inside centre against me in the Calcutta Cup the following week and he looked over at me from the half-way line just before the kick-off and gave me a wee smile to say have a good game – it was a nice thing to do, but at the time I think I just scowled at him . . . I wish I had been more comfortable in the whole environment to smile back, but I was still pretty new to it all.

There was a lot of anger going around the camp towards the end of the Championship because we were playing some quite good rugby at times but just weren't getting the results, and the coaches and the players were getting the blame to varying degrees from the press and the public – and we were all just annoyed that it wasn't happening for us. I remember going out for the final game against Ireland in Dublin and I was just really, really angry, desperate to win, and I hit Brian O'Driscoll with a pretty dodgy tackle early on . . . I was lucky not to get carded for it and he was nice to me afterwards about it, which was decent of him. We should have won that game and again there was this incredible sense of frustration that things just weren't happening.

During the summer, the team recorded their first victory under Williams against Samoa in, uniquely, Wellington, but then crashed to two defeats to the Wallabies, going down 35–15 and 34–13 in Melbourne and Sydney.

Chris Paterson was injured during the Samoan match and was replaced as captain by Scott Murray for the remaining two Tests. When Paterson returned to the team later that year he regained neither the fly-half shirt nor the captaincy; he was selected on the wing and on-field leadership responsibilities were passed to hooker Gordon Bulloch.

Donnie Macfadyen: The opening Test was played in Wellington because it has the highest Samoan population outside Samoa and it wasn't too far for us to travel from our main base in Australia, so by hosting it there it guaranteed a good crowd. The atmosphere throughout that whole match was brilliant and we played some really good running rugby that night and scored some great tries.

Simon Webster: The summer tour in 2004 to New Zealand and Australia was great, it was almost a bit like an old-fashioned tour because we had mid-week games, which I thought were brilliant. Todd Blackadder had also come on board as part of the coaching group and I was a massive fan of his. He was a great leader at Edinburgh when he was playing; he was in the twilight of his career by then but you'd look at his stats on a Monday morning and they were unbelievable. He transferred that aura he had to his coaching and was absolutely top-drawer.

Donnie Macfadyen: In the Test matches against Australia I was up against my old under-21 rivals in Phil Waugh and George Smith, who both established themselves as two of the greatest open-sides the game has ever seen. In both Tests I remember battling away against George Smith for around an hour and then just as we were both beginning to tire, they would bring on Phil Waugh; I remember standing there and just thinking, 'Oh come on, give me a break!'

Those games also showed me just what a canny operator George Gregan was. He always seemed to pick the right option and was in total control of every facet of the game that he was involved in. But he was also a master of gamesmanship. I was running around for the whole game trying to win as much ball on the deck as I could and I remember in one ruck, going in on a fairly isolated Aussie player and was just about to turn the ball over when all I heard was, 'Hands off blue seven!' Obviously not wanting to get pinged by the ref I let go and backed off and when I looked up I saw that the ref was about twenty yards away and Gregan was just grinning to himself as he box-kicked the ball clear.

Chris Cusiter: I remember when I first got to Watsonians I got picked to play in a second XV game alongside Scott Hastings, who was still going at that stage. And I was so excited, I thought it was going to be amazing to play alongside him – something I could tell my Dad about – but the game got called off and I remember being a bit gutted about it. So if I thought playing with Scott was going to be exciting – and no disrespect to Scotty! – but coming up against a hero of mine in George Gregan on that tour was just amazing. He was a legend of the game, the best scrum-half in the world, and the whole thing was a bit surreal to come up against him. But I loved it. It was always a real privilege to play against all these kinds of guys and to measure yourself against them. Working alongside Bob Easson from the Scottish Institute of Sport, I had studied videos of him passing, from all angles and at different speeds, maybe one year before. I remember making sure I swapped shirts with him afterwards; but then I remember when they came over to the UK in the autumn – we played them four times that year – and I asked him to swap shirts again and he said no. Probably fair enough, in retrospect.

Alastair Kellock (Scotland 2004-2013, 56 Caps): My first cap was against Australia in the autumn 2004. I went to bed at seven o'clock on the night before the match because I was so nervous. When I got to my room I found Gordie Bulloch, the team captain, had put a letter under my door. He was basically wishing me luck and saying that I should do what I had been doing at club level because that's why I had been picked. I don't know if he did that for every player on their first cap, but I thought it was a really nice touch. It helped settle my nerves.

George Gregan gets the ball away at Murrayfield despite the attentions of Chris Cusiter and Gordon Bulloch.

Donnie Macfadyen: One of the few victories we had under Matt Williams came against Japan at McDiarmid Park. We racked up what remains the highest Scotland score in Test rugby. I think there was always a feeling in the camp that we were always going to struggle to overturn the big teams, and in retrospect that was probably partly to do with the fact that the management were continually telling the press that we weren't ready yet as a team to beat those kind of sides.

Andy Henderson: We played Australia four times in 2004 – twice on tour in the summer and twice in the autumn. I remember coming out for the team run the day before the fourth match of the year, and the old touchlines at Murrayfield had been painted over and new ones had been put in, meaning the pitch was a good few metres narrower than it normally was. It was pretty obvious for everyone to see because the lines which had been painted over were a completely different colour to the rest of the pitch. The coaches obviously wanted to stop Australia going wide and although I didn't think about it too much at the time, it sent out another dispiriting message to us all. Apparently we weren't good enough to defend against them on a full-width pitch; it was humiliating that they felt they had to go to such extremes to cover our deficiencies.

Donnie Macfadyen: And in the end it made no difference because they still trounced us. It was so embarrassing, the whole thing, and it did really make you question how much faith the coaches had in the team.

Chris Cusiter: I remember when they came over that November, we narrowed the pitch and I think grew the grass a bit longer, but we were never close to beating teams like Australia back in those days. Matt had retired a lot of the more experienced guys in the squad, so we had a really young team and just weren't in a place to challenge the top teams at the time. We could be competitive for large parts of the game but were never really in any danger of beating them.

Williams' attempts to contain the expansive Australian game plan by reducing the width of the Murrayfield pitch to its legal minimum failed to make much impact as his countrymen ran out 31–14 winners. The team then had something of a morale boost with the victory over Japan in Perth, but normal service was soon resumed when they lost yet again to Australia, 31–17, before facing South Africa in the fourth and final Test of that autumn series. The visitors atoned for their 2002 defeat in Edinburgh by scoring five tries in a 45–10 victory to conclude a wretched year for the Scots.

Tom Smith: I missed the November 2004 internationals with injury but came back in again before the 2005 Six Nations. We went to Stobo Castle in the Borders for a team get-together and that's when I really noticed that something had changed. They did a review of the South Africa game and it was a really unhappy atmosphere. They had lost the game, Matt was picking the team to bits on the video, but there was a variety of contradictions in what he was saying.

You can go to a player and say, 'That was the wrong decision, you got away with it that time but nine times out of ten you wouldn't have.' Similarly, you can say, 'That was the right decision, nine time out of ten it would have worked, but on this occasion it didn't. You were unlucky.' But Matt would judge an action by its consequences and not by whether it was the right decision. He would fire into a player for doing the wrong thing because it didn't work and then five minutes later another player would do exactly the same thing and if it worked he would say nothing to them. A bit of an argument sparked up with a few players pointing out the inconsistency of this, and it actually got quite unfriendly.

The 2005 Six Nations campaign opened with a moment of promise as Scotland ran France close in Paris and had Ally Hogg not been called back for a much debated foot-in-touch, the Scots might have recorded a famous victory.

Chris Cusiter: My first couple of years of Test rugby were pretty disappointing in terms of results. Going into the 2005 Six Nations I had picked up thirteen caps but had only won against Samoa and Japan. It was a frustrating time, there were games when we didn't perform as well as we could have, but there were others, like the France game in 2005, when we played well but still ended up losing. We defended very well and they got a lucky try late on when Hugo Southwell's clearance kick was charged down and Damien Traille flopped over to score – while at the other end, Ally

Hogg had been called back earlier in the game for a foot in touch, which was a pretty dubious call – on the replay it definitely looks like he kept himself in play. It felt like everything was conspiring against us. It was a tough time.

Gordon Bulloch: As captain I felt caught between a rock and a hard place. You are trying to support the coach and support the players at the same time but at one stage they were pulling in completely opposite directions.

Any hint of progress was dismissed the following week, however, when Ireland came to town and hammered their hosts 40–13. Two weeks later, Williams finally broke his Six Nations duck by defeating Italy 18–10; for all that it was positive for Scotland to claim the win in what had already been dubbed the wooden spoon play-off, it had once again been an uninspiring performance from the home side who had clawed their way to victory thanks to the steady boot of Chris Paterson. The lack of any real progress was once again highlighted the following week when Wales came to Edinburgh and, as Ireland had done, inflicted a humiliating defeat over the hosts, running out 46–22 winners as they marched towards the Grand Slam.

Jon Petrie: I always felt that Matt was a good guy, and you could see he was trying to bring a Clive Woodward type business approach to it – but it didn't work. And in that particular game against Wales, everyone had got so hacked off with it, that the attitude was: let's just go out there and play.

Williams was holding true to many of the promises that he had made when he was appointed coach. He was encouraging players back to Scotland, preferring to pick home-based players over those who played from clubs abroad; he was implementing his own style of play and tactics and was sticking firmly to his guns that his was the right way for Scotland to play; and his team had managed to achieve just two wins, against fairly limited opposition, during the entire course of his tenure. Now, in the wake of the Welsh defeat, Williams claimed that it might well be another year before the team would make its breakthrough.

Mike Blair: We had been hammered in the first-half and Wales were leading 38–3. It was humiliating. So we decided in that half-time talk to just go out and have a go and forget all the structures that were in place. We scored three tries in that second-half and the fact that we had done so was definitely in the back of our minds as we went into half-time at Twickenham in the next game.

England were on the wane after their triumphs in Sydney two years previously, but they were still a mighty and intimidating prospect for a Scotland team at such a low-ebb. 26–10 down at half-time, a decision was made after the coaching team had left the changing room to discard the over-regimented game-plan; the result was probably already beyond them; they had nothing to lose.

Mike Blair: The tactics just weren't working – they were wrong for us, so we decided to change our style, just as we had done against Wales. Again, it worked and it showed us even more clearly that the style, the structure, the whole system that the coaches were trying to enforce on us wasn't right.

Tom Smith: I think, essentially, Matt didn't have enough faith in the players around him. He didn't trust them to do the right thing. It became very much a 'them and us' environment. Ultimately, it was inevitable that the wheels would fall off.

Simon Webster: That period is badly thought of but the coaches did have some decent ideas. Matt was primarily a backs coach and some of the things he taught me about standing positions in attack and defence were really good and I carried them through with me for the rest of my career. If he was just taking a backs session, he was decent – it was the overall job he struggled with. I don't blame the SRU for employing him, he had very good credentials and I think he was a decent choice, but you just don't know what someone will be like until they get into the job.

Ian McGeechan: I have to hold my hand up and admit that I made a mistake in taking on Matt Williams as my successor. He talked a good game and I was impressed by that, but when he took over he never respected Scotland or the players and spent most of his time telling them what they couldn't do. That's the wrong approach to take to coaching and it totally misses one of the keys to unlocking Scottish sporting potential – we'll always be the underdog, but we relish that and we'll always put up the biggest fight. It was something that Matt totally missed and the team suffered badly as a result.

Andy Henderson: In fairness to Matt Williams, he brought in guys like Chris Cusiter, Allister Hogg and Ross Ford, who went on to have big careers for Scotland, but if you are told enough times that you are not very good at something then eventually you start to believe it. So that was a big change when Frank came in, he talked the team up and that had a huge effect as we saw in his first season.

Chris Cusiter: I find it hard to speak badly about Matt because he gave me a chance that a lot of coaches wouldn't have and he stuck with me. He launched my Scotland career, gave me my first seventeen caps or so, and then just over a year later I was a Lion, which was just an unbelievable time. Matt was only ever good to me. I recognise that the regime and the set-up didn't work out; it wasn't a successful team and things ended up falling apart, but he helped me realise my dream of playing for Scotland and in doing so helped me become a Lion; I'd been on the 2001 tour as part of a Watsonians tour and the idea that I would be a player on the next one was just inconceivable at the time – but Matt had helped make that happen for me. Despite the losses, I have really good memories from that time. Everything was new, I was playing against the best players in the world in these incredible stadiums, and the whole occasion is just mind-blowing. How can you not enjoy that?

SCOTLAND v ENGLAND
25-02-06
Jason White
943

TWENTY-THREE

OLD SCHOOL VALUES
2005-2008

Back to basics. That was the mantra of the former master of Merchiston Castle School who was appointed interim head coach alongside Hugh Campbell, forwards coach George Graham, backs coaches Steve Bates and Sean Lineen and defence coach Alan Tait. Frank Hadden's remit was to rebuild the battered confidences of the Scotland team. From his seat as head coach of Edinburgh, he had watched the disintegration of his players' performances as they moved from club to international colours. They were all good players, he knew that first hand. Yet when they took to the field for Scotland something was missing – their spark had been dampened, their nerves were looking frayed. They had the skills – he knew it as their coach and he also knew it as a Scotland fan for he had seen the demonstration of their skills as clearly as anyone else when they played on their wits in the secondhalves of the Wales and England games. Having spoken to his senior players and conferred with his new assistant coaches, there was a realisation that the Matt Williams and Willie Anderson regime had stifled the players' creativity and had shot their confidences to pieces. They had witnessed what the team could achieve with just a modicum of belief that they could play. So Hadden reverted to his schoolmaster's pastoral past and began the rebuilding of the Scottish team's battered psyche.

That summer, Hadden and his coaching staff led Scotland to their first-ever victory over the Barbarians on a beautiful afternoon in Aberdeen. The players looked invigorated under the new coaching system and ran in five tries for an emphatic 38–7 win. Two weeks later they flew to Bucharest for a one-off Test match against Romania. It saw first caps for Kelly Brown, Scott Lawson, Phil Godman, Euan Murray and Andy Wilson, and a first captaincy stint for the experienced war horse Jon Petrie. The squad's preparations were hardly affected by the Lions tour to New Zealand as only Chris Cusiter, Simon Taylor and Gordon Bulloch had been selected in the original squad of 44 players, while Jason White would fly out as a late replacement in the last week of the trip. The only particularly significant change was at scrum-half where Mike Blair took advantage of Cusiter's absence to regain his place in the team. Blair then held on to the shirt, more or less, for the next four years, until, ironically, he himself was selected for the Lions in 2009 and Cusiter took advantage to grab the starting place. In a commanding performance over the Romanians, Scotland emerged 39–19 victors.

Jon Petrie: When Frank came in it really was like a breath of fresh air. His whole attitude and approach made my job really easy because it was such a refreshing change. If you tell people they are crap enough times they are going to start believing it and they don't play well, and that is what happened with Matt. All Frank did was come in and say, 'Actually, you know what guys, I am going to put faith in you to play the

Opposite: Jason White celebrates with the Calcutta Cup during Scotland's 2006 Six Nations campaign.

game as you see fit. I'll give you the shape but you express yourselves. Go out there and play rugby, you are good players.' And that was all it took to turn things around at that stage. It made my job a hell of a lot easier because we had guys playing rugby with a smile on their face for the first time in a long while.

Mike Blair: With Matt Williams it was all about structures and angles and detail, with loads of meetings all the time. Frank came with a very simple game plan – let's just enjoy ourselves and throw the ball around. I think the massive contrast between them was that around Frank everyone was just able to relax and play their own game. As opposed to being told how crap we were all the time and focussing or what we couldn't do, Frank developed a game plan around what we could do instead of trying to foist a completely alien style of play on us.

I remember before we played New Zealand in 2005 we didn't do any video analysis on them. Frank sat us down and said that he could show us reams of film showing how good they were or he could show us film of them dropping passes and missing kicks etcetera, but in the end neither really mattered – what was important was how we played and the type of game plan we wanted to implement.

You can over-analyse things. Often when you analyse a team you don't watch the bad stuff that they do. You can over-do the analysis to a point where you begin to wonder how you could ever possibly beat the team you're watching – because all the flaws in their game are removed. You forget that they're fallible, so Frank was trying to dispel that whole aura around the All Blacks and it was very refreshing. In the end we lost the match, but New Zealand were a great, great side that year. They destroyed the Lions in the summer and that autumn they completed their first Grand Slam tour since 1978. But Frank's approach really liberated us and we felt invigorated going into that match – and that attitude definitely helped set things up for the success we enjoyed the following season.

Simon Webster: Losing to anyone was crap, and it didn't make it any easier that it was the All Blacks. You always think you can go out and win and make some history. I'd hate for any fan to every think that we don't feel that way every time, no matter if it's the All Blacks or whoever. We always go out expecting to win and losing hurts, no matter who is it against.

When you play against New Zealand you see how clever they are on the field, and that's what really sets them apart from everyone else. We would play to a formula, especially during the Matt Williams era, but to a degree we would play to certain formulas no matter who was coach – so if there was a scrum in a certain part of the field, before the scrum had even packed down we would have called a set move, and because we had set plays for certain situations everyone in the backline knew what the move would be before the ten even called it. But you play against the All Blacks and the ball would be in the scrum and their whole backline would still be discussing what they were going to do. 'Move in, move in . . . I'm going wider . . . I'm going to slide . . .' They would watch what we were doing in defence and how we were set up, and then when the ball came out they had worked out the perfect move for finding space and attacking where we were exposed. I played against all of the top sides; the All Blacks, every time, were a whole level above every one of them.

As the 2006 Six Nations loomed, the pack was reshuffled and Jon Petrie dropped to the bench, with the captaincy handed to Jason White. It would prove to be an inspired appointment. Scotland's first fixture was against France at Murrayfield. It has been a long established rule of thumb that France started slowly in the tournament before getting on a roll: if ever there is a good time to play Les Bleus, it is first up and at home.

In a pulsating encounter, Scotland scored two superb tries in each half through Sean Lamont. Scotland's defence was aggressive and the back-row of White, Ally Hogg and Simon Taylor were immense, while out wide Mike Blair and Chris Paterson combined magnificently on more than one occasion to scythe through the French ranks and the wide passing of centre Marcus di Rollo had their defence stretched. Having led 13–3 at half-time the home team held onto the lead to secure a famous 20–16 win.

Andy Henderson: France at Murrayfield was the first game of the 2006 Six Nations and expectations weren't too high because we hadn't done particularly well under the previous regime. But there was a feeling of confidence in the squad at the way we were being asked to play and the clarity and freedom of the game-plan; so it was a very different mood, but we still realised that we were huge underdogs.

Mike Blair: We played some really great rugby against Franc eend our expansive style took them totally by surprise. I think the French expected to just turn up and thump us, and they just weren't prepared for that open style we played. There were a lot of gaps around the rucks and mauls and I remember making several breaks down the fringes which got us in behind their defence. They really started to look shaky in defence and there were times when we were just lacerating them all over the park.

The biggest moment was the driving maul that Sean Lamont scored his second try from. We drove from about twenty-five yards out against one of the most respected forward units in the world – and by the end we had them running backwards. I was trying to get my hands on the ball so that, like any good scrum-half, I could capitalise from all the forward's hard work and claim the glory, but Sean had the same idea and he flew in at the last moment, pinched the ball and flopped over.

Alastair Kellock: We were delighted that we had scored, but not overly happy that Sean had come off his wing to steal our forwards' try. He got pelters.

Mike Blair: Mossy was running great lines from fullback and kicking like a dream and our ball-carriers were all over the place giving us options off nine, ten and twelve, and in the wide channels as well. It was just brilliant rugby and the crowd noise was

Sean Lamont dives over to score the first of his two tries against France in 2006.

incredible. When you break a team like that, when every part of the game is going your way, it's a great, great feeling. And to do it against the third or fourth best team in the world at the time made it all the sweeter.

A week later the team were in Cardiff and were looking good until Scott Murray was knocked to the ground without the ball by Ian Gough. Murray flashed a leg out in frustration and connected with Gough's head; he pleaded that it was accidental, but he was shown a red card and left the field with more than an hour left to play. Scotland's fourteen men were eventually over-powered by the fifteen of Wales, despite a late rally which brought tries for Hugo Southwell and Chris Paterson.

Alastair Kellock: We competed pretty well considering Scotty Murray got sent off and we played with fourteen men for most of the game; we began to think that we might even sneak it at the end, but it wasn't to be and they managed to close the game out 28–18. But we were playing some really positive stuff and I have no doubts that we would have won if we had had our full complement of players on the field for the full eighty minutes.

Scott Murray: It was a stupid thing to do, but it was reactionary. I didn't mean to kick him in the head. I got a three week suspension because the disciplinary committee didn't think that it was accidental which was a pity because it was. Ian was very decent about it and he and several of the Welsh players came out in support to say that they didn't think that I meant to do it, but it didn't cut any ice.

Jason White and Simon Taylor flatten Ben Cohen during the 2006 Calcutta Cup.

Alastair Kellock: Then came the Calcutta Cup match, which was . . . just . . . unbelievable. Scott MacLeod and I started in the second-row, I think it was the first time we had played together. We were both pretty young and skinny playing against a typically massive English pack – so we were under the cosh all afternoon. But we stuck in and all I really remember is the massive feeling of elation afterwards.

Andy Henderson: I remember pitching up for training before the England game and seeing big queues outside the ticket office at Murrayfield – which was probably the first time that had happened in a while. It was a tough old game, but we deserved the victory. England were famed for their forward power and their backline at the time was also pretty huge, so to neutralise their physical threat was a great.

Mike Blair: You could argue – as many in the press did afterwards – that England played into our hands in that Calcutta Cup match. They said that they should have kept their tactics simple and pinned us back with a solid kicking game. Maybe they should have; but sometimes you just know a game is going to go your way and as we jogged down the tunnel, I just had this confidence, which you could sense through the whole team, that we were going to win.

The defence in that game was one of the most outstanding I've ever been involved in with any team, and the back-row were on a different level. The impact that Simon Taylor, Ally Hogg and Jason White had on the game cannot be overstated – they were just unbelievable. Ally stole and slowed down so much ball, all three carried really well and some of the hits that Jason and Simon put in were just incredible – it was like watching the England boys running into a swinging sack of bricks; they were smashed back every time they tried to break through. And the most impressive thing is that it didn't let up for a moment – even right at the end, Joe Worsley ran into Jason who lifted him up and hammered him backwards. When the guys on your team are making hits like that you gain such a level of confidence – and with it the crowd noise rises and that lifts your spirits even more. The noise that day from the stands was amazing and it really felt like we had a sixteenth, seventeenth, even an eighteenth man on the pitch with us.

I think the tackle stats were something like one hundred and twelve tackles completed by us to their thirty-six, which is astonishing. And Mossy's kicking was flawless – he kicked five out of five attempts and Parksy got a drop-goal. It was a game of attrition, but the satisfaction that comes from grinding out a win like that was huge. It was a real case of punch and counter-punch from both teams. It was savage. But the key was that we never backed down and against teams like England, that is exactly how you have to take them on. The atmosphere was incredible – it was suffocating for them and completely energising for us.

Alastair Kellock: We went out in Edinburgh afterwards and I remember walking home and people were shouting out the window to us, calling us legends and that sort of thing. We were getting clapped into pubs, which, looking back, was a bit cringe-worthy, but it was great at the time. Normally when you go out in Edinburgh or Glasgow no one recognises you, but that night we were the toast of the town.

Scott Murray was back from suspension and Nathan Hines had come out of retirement by the time we played Ireland, so I got dropped to the bench and Scotty MacLeod was dropped out of the squad altogether. I remember getting the phone call from Frank on the Monday morning telling me to come and see him, and it was devastating.

The Monday morning call is the worst. They don't phone you to say, 'Congratulations, you're playing really well and you're in the team.' It is just torture. Other players claim it doesn't bother them, but I wake up and I just can't help but stare at the phone, waiting for it to ring. There was also a time when Frank used to stand at the bottom of the lift in the hotel and wait for you coming down to breakfast. You'd come out the lift and try not to look at him, it's almost as if you are thinking, 'If I don't make eye contact he can't see me and he can't drop me.'

In the final round of the tournament, Scotland faced off with Italy in Rome. As has so often been the case with this fixture, the encounter was something of a slugfest and very low on entertainment value, but the visitors crawled their way to a 13–10 victory with a try, a penalty and a conversion from fullback Paterson and a drop-goal from Gordon Ross, which took Scotland to third-place in the Championship table and, in terms of points, their best-ever finish in the Six Nations.

In May, Scotland scored nine tries at Murrayfield in a record 66–19 win over the Barbarians which set them up for their summer tour to South Africa. While both Tests were lost, 36–16 in Durban and 29–15 in Port Elizabeth, Scotland once again demonstrated their attacking capabilities and ran the home team much closer in the second Test than the score-line suggested.

Simon Webster: The 2006 summer tour was amazing. It was probably when I was at my peak as a player and we had a really great team. We should have beaten the Springboks in Port Elizabeth. There was a kick into the back field and the ball was bouncing really awkwardly; I put my hand on it and as I did, the ball kind of stopped where it was. Play went on and Mossy went the length of the field and scored – and then we all saw that the touch judge had his flag out because he reckoned I had knocked the ball on. I've watched that video back a hundred times, it wasn't a knock-on. They then scored off the resulting scrum, so it was a fourteen point swing that should never have happened. It was really tough to take, that one. But I think we all went away after the tour and thought, 'You know what, there's something here in this team. We could really start to do some special things if we keep working hard.'

That autumn Scotland faced Romania, the Pacific Islands and Australia. They won the first two games comfortably, 48–6 and 34–22, and although they then lost heavily to the Wallabies, 44–15, the coaches had used the series to hand a number of new players their first caps, including Johnnie Beattie, Rob Dewey, Dave Callam, Jim Hamilton, Rory Lawson and Alasdair Strokosch, all of whom would become important players in the squad over the following years.

Mike Blair: We were still playing with adventure on the summer tour and were causing the Springboks real problems when we threw the ball wide from side to side and stretched them. We carried that style of play into the Romania and Pacific Islands games in the autumn of 2006, but we found that, as a style, it was beginning to creek when we lost heavily to Australia. They played a wide game as well but they were also very physical and their backs outmuscled ours at the gain-line contacts.

The success that we had with that wide style been brilliant and we all enjoyed playing that way, but continuing to play that way definitely affected us the following year because other teams had cottoned on to what we were doing and analysed our wide game, so they would work on pressurising us around the breakdowns to prevent us getting quick ball and many teams adopted a press defence coming from out to in so that the wide channels were cut off unless we threw a long looping ball to the outside centre or the wings, or kicked it in behind the defence for those wide players to run on to it – both of which are unpredictable tactics and can cost you possession or put you under a lot of pressure.

It was when that started to happen that the coaching staff started to look at a more physical and confrontational style of play. That was aided by some injuries and we had guys like Jim Hamilton coming into the team, we had Rob Dewey at inside centre, the Lamont brothers out wide, it was a huge team. And bigger our team got the more we focussed on keeping things tight and dominating through our size and the less we began to throw the ball around as we had been doing. Some people felt that it was wrong to change our tactics, but we had been worked out so we had to mix it up. What we needed to do, looking at the whole situation retrospectively, was to work on a balance between physicality and the wide game – which is what teams like the All Blacks have always done so brilliantly.

In 2007 the team endured a poor Six Nations, only managing to secure a victory at home to Wales. They began the Championship with a 42–20 drubbing in the Calcutta Cup at Twickenham before making something of a recovery to defeat the Welsh 21–9 at Murrayfield.

Andy Henderson: The Calcutta Cup match at Twickenham was our first game of the 2007 Six Nations and Jonny Wilkinson's first game back since he had kicked the drop-goal to win England the World Cup – it had been something like thirty-nine months that he had spent out of the England starting line-up. It was something of a fairytale comeback for him and a complete nightmare for us. They absolutely destroyed us. It was disappointing to lose so heavily after our efforts to wrestle the Calcutta Cup from them twelve months earlier – especially as the try that Jonny scored should never have been given. In the replay and in a whole ream of photographs that came out after the match, you could clearly see that his foot was well in touch before he placed the ball over the line. But these things happen and you have to look back on them after a while and be philosophical about it. Jonny had been through a torrid time with injury and if anybody deserved a bit of luck to swing back his way, it was him. But Christ it hurt.

On 24 February the Italians arrived in Edinburgh and took part in one of the most memorable opening quarters ever witnessed at Murrayfield. For the home team, it was for all the wrong reasons. In seven extraordinary minutes Italy were gifted three tries – one from a charge down of a Phil Godman chip which was snaffled by Mauro Bergamasco, and two interception passes thrown by Chris Cusiter, who had reclaimed the scrum-half jersey from the injured Mike Blair. Although Scotland fought their way back into the match with tries from Rob Dewey and Chris Paterson, the visitors sealed a 37–17 win – their first on the road since joining the Championship – with a late try from scrum-half Alessandro Troncon.

Phil Godman (Scotland 2005-2010, 23 Caps) : During the week leading up to the Italy game we worked on this game plan of going wide quickly to lap their rush defence, and to kick over them as well, and it had gone like a dream in training. Then I got the ball in the first minute and I remember thinking at the time that I might be a bit deep – I was right on our own line – but at the same time a well executed chip kick would have really caused Italy problems because there was absolutely nobody there, and we could have been scoring at the other end. It was a risky option, but it was only a matter of inches away from being the right one.

I had played against Mauro Bergamasco before and all he did was hit me all afternoon, whether I had the ball or not. He was an animal. So I knew he was going to come at me and as soon as I hit the chip I knew I hadn't put enough on it. And even when he got the charge-down I was thinking, most of the time charge-downs don't result in tries. But it bounced perfectly – and all you could hear was this big groan reverberating round the ground. But I wasn't panicking at that stage.

Chris Cusiter: Then I threw two interception passes – and they scored off both. The first one wasn't a planned move. I was at first receiver and I just tried to draw the man and pass, but Andrea Scanavacca read it and was left with a clear run to the line. The other one was off a move from a line-out. One of the options we had discussed was throwing a pass over the top, and I chucked it because there was nothing else on. I don't know if somebody had run the wrong line or not, but it didn't come off. In retrospect it was the wrong decision.

Phil Godman: Suddenly we were 21–0 down and you're standing there wondering how this could have happened. The chat under the posts was not to panic, but in that situation it is hard not to. Anyone who played in that game will agree that it was the strangest rugby experience of their lives. We had the ball but were gifting them the scores. We got back into it – but there was an element of shellshock there, which was hard to cope with at the time.

Chris Cusiter: It was horrible, but at the same time you are conscious that there is another seventy-five minutes to play so you have plenty of time to make up for your mistakes if you keep your focus. You know that the only good thing that can come out of the game is coming back and winning it, so you have no choice but to knuckle down and get on with that. There is no place to hide out there in front of 50,000 people. All I could do was try to block what had happened out of my mind and concentrate on helping Scotland get back into it. You don't have time to think about the implications of what is happening when you are out there. It is only afterwards that everything catches up with you. At one point we got back to within one score of them, but they upped their game and we had worked so hard to get close that there was nothing left in the tank. It was really tough.

Kelly Brown (Scotland 2005-2014, 64 Caps): It was the most surreal experience. I remember jogging up to the halfway line after the third try, looking up at the scoreboard and thinking to myself, What the hell is going on here? It was like an out-of-body experience. You were genuinely wondering if it was all a dream . . . or should I say nightmare. We had only made three mistakes but they had all led to tries. It took quite a while to get past that.

The very foundations of Hadden's new feel-good administration were beginning to tremble. And the situation did not improve in the final rounds of the tournament as Ireland squeaked a 19–18 win at Murrayfield and France overpowered Scotland 46–19 in Paris. The downturn in results opened up the pressure valves in the coaching set-up – and as the 2007 World Cup loomed, Hadden began to compromise.

A relentless training camp made sure that the squad would come second to none in terms of strength; but at what cost? The emphasis on player freedom had disappeared and the limited style of play Hadden was looking to enforce was reflected in his comments before the team's last game of the 2007 Six Nations, when he spoke gleefully about the three-quarter line being the biggest ever assembled by a Scotland team. Few would ever question the strength and courage of Sean Lamont, Rob Dewey, Andy Henderson and Nikki Walker but as an attacking unit there was precious little guile there. Scotland could now physically compete with any side in the world, but the confidence in their strength and power meant that they focussed on bludgeoning sides rather than combining their new attributes with the running game they had employed so successfully in previous seasons. It wasn't pretty rugby, but it was effective. Scotland swept past Portugal and Romania and then fielded a weakened team against the All Blacks. This caused outrage in both Scotland and New Zealand as well as other corners of the rugby world, many feeling that the decision to rest players against the All Blacks to keep them fresh for the crunch game against Italy was demeaning to the Scottish shirt, negligent to the paying fan and undermining to the spirit of the World Cup. But Hadden simply stated that he was ultimately judged by how the team finished in the tournament. It was doubtful that even his first team would be able to run the All Blacks close and to risk them to injury before the Italian game would serve no one. A brave fight against the Kiwis and a loss to Italy might placate the ire of the purists, but it would cause even greater anger to the majority of Scottish supporters than that incited by the fielding of a weakened team against New Zealand.

Chris Cusiter: I remember not really understanding why we changed tactics going into the World Cup. The wide, off-loading game we had played in the previous two Six Nations had worked well for us and I think it suited our players. It was a similar pattern that Edinburgh had played under Frank, which was quite structured, but it got results – and I didn't think at the time that the game had moved on so much by the 2007 World Cup that we needed to change that. That said, it was probably the most enjoyable pre-season that I've done. Mark Bitcon was brilliant – he was great at motivating the players, everyone got really big and that was the fittest I've ever felt. Also, I suppose you can't keep doing the same thing the whole time, your game has to evolve – people will have analysed Scotland and seen that we had been playing a wide-wide game under Frank, so he obviously wanted to change that going into the World Cup so that we could keep teams guessing, but I felt that we maybe went a little bit too direct and tried to outmuscle teams. At some points it worked; we played Ireland in the warm-ups and it seemed to confirm that it was working. But I don't think that will ever be the way forward for Scotland, especially when competing with countries like South Africa, New Zealand or the Pacific Islands because you're very rarely going to be able to be more physical than those teams.

Jason White (Scotland 2000-2009, 77 Caps): Mark Bitcon used to call himself the Guru and he put together an absolutely tremendous programme for us in the build up to the World Cup. He was well supported by guys from the Scottish Institute of Sport and the whole thing was just superbly structured and managed. It allowed us to compete physically with any team in the world, whereas before we maybe suffered in one or two games because we were outmuscled. The only drawback was that we began to rely too much on that power game to the detriment of our wider attacking plays.

Simon Webster: There was a bit of a change of personnel with Scotland and in the mindset as to how we were going to go out and play. We only managed one win the Six Nations, against Wales, but going into the World Cup we felt we were getting back some form because we smashed Ireland in the warm-ups and then pushed South Africa pretty close – and they went on to win the whole thing.

I was a big Frank Hadden fan. He wanted us to play an expansive game, but that was based on the fact that he thought it suited the playing personnel he had at his disposal. He looked at the players when he first came in and figured that the best way for us to win was to play a wide game, with offloading, trying to stretch teams. Things changed as we went into the World Cup because his players changed. We got bigger and because of that he figured we were then better suited to a tighter, more attritional game.

My game, like a lot of the backs in the team, was based around speed and agility, but our programmes changed and it was all about bulking up. Ultimately, I think it affected the way I played quite a bit. I got heavier, I didn't feel as sharp, and I certainly felt that I was slower. I think a lot of players were affected like that.

Chris Paterson: That game against Ireland before the World Cup was brilliant in many ways, because size and being dominant physically was something we had lacked before and we really showed what a difference it could make in that game because Ireland were completely blown off the park. That lack of physicality had cost us games in the past. But because it worked so well that day against Ireland, I think it held us back over the next couple of years. It took away other parts of the game that had been really quite effective for us.

Mike Blair: The way the rules were working at the time of the 2007 World Cup, particularly surrounding the tackle laws, teams that were kicking well were tending to be the ones that were winning games. Teams like Argentina, France, England and South Africa progressed through the tournament because they kicked superbly and then used a fast, aggressive defence to push up and force turnovers or penalties.
As a result, Dan Parks was fantastic for us during the World Cup. He was one of the best in the world when it came to putting boot to ball; he could do the most unbelievable things when he kicked – the kind of things he did in training, little tricks and so on,

were incredible, and he could literally put the ball on a sixpence. In the aftermath of the tournament we all voted for our Scottish player of the World Cup and it deservedly went to Dan. He had a tumultuous time in a Scotland shirt, he went to darker places than many of us could imagine and some sections of the public and the media were appalling to him for a time, but his positivity despite all of that was inspiring.

Kelly Brown: We improved throughout the World Cup, certainly. We came into it having recorded a good win against Ireland and come pretty close to South Africa. We weren't particularly great against Portugal or Romania, but each game showed positive signs of improvement. For all the fuss that was made about our team selection for the All Blacks game, I still thought that we might have a chance to do something special against them because we had been written-off. In the end they took us apart, but they had a nearly full-strength team and we had a few injuries – Mossy went off early with a head bang. That loss was disappointing, but it wasn't a disaster. We blooded some new players and guys on the fringes got to have a run-out. The big game was always going to be against Italy and that's exactly how it worked out.

Jason White: We had a short turn-around between the New Zealand and Italy matches so the decision had to be made as to whether we would field a full-strength team or not against the All Blacks; in the end we decided to rest a number of our first-choice team to allow them plenty of time to recover from the first two games and prepare properly for the Italy game.

It was a pretty tough environment for John Barclay and Alastair Dickinson to win their first caps, but they both really stood up for themselves and looked comfortable out there among some of the very best players in the world. There was a bit of talk about us throwing lambs to the slaughter and I can understand people's arguments, but I think it was the correct tactical call; and after all, it paid off in the end.

Chris Cusiter: If I was the coach, would I have done the same thing? I think I probably would have. Except Mike would've been in the 2nd XV.

The All Blacks ran amok in Edinburgh as a under-strength Scottish fifteen fell to one of the favourites for the tournament 40–0. And so the focus turned to the Itlay match in Saint-Etienne. On a cold wet night Scotland fell behind to a controversial Alessandro Troncon try as Andrea Masi took out Rory Lamont in the air as he went to gather a high ball, allowing Italy to establish a platform on Scotland's line from which their talismanic captain slithered over.

Thanks to the steady boot of Chris Paterson, however, who impressively finished the tournament with one hundred per cent kicking accuracy, Scotland pushed on to secure a narrow 18–16 win. It wasn't beautiful, by any means, but it was effective, and Hadden had secured Scotland another quarter-final place that just two years earlier had looked a distant dream.

Mike Blair: The Italy match was a huge game for many reasons – we had to win to go through to the quarter-final, we had backed our whole pool strategy around that one fixture, we were the only Celtic nation still in with a chance of making it out of the pools, and Italy had something of a voodoo sign over us – especially after the debacle during the Six Nations. It was do or die for both teams. Italian centre, Gonazalo Canale, referred to it as 'the match of death' during the build up.

We were 6–0 up after only four minutes or so. We might have scored a try shortly afterwards after Troncon had a poor clearance kick but Mauro Bergamasco put an end to things with a professional foul and was yellow carded. Not that that did us much good – a few minutes later Ramiro Pez fired up a Garryowen and as Rory Lamont went to take it in the air he was smashed by Andrea Masi; Italy won the ball and it was chaos for a few seconds before Troncon forced his way over. They converted and then added a penalty and out of nowhere, it seemed, they were 10–6 ahead.

Mossy pulled us back in it before half-time with a couple of long-range penalties and we went in 12–10 ahead, but it was a nervous old time.

Jason White: The game ended up being dominated by kicking and trying to dominate territory, which was the absolutely correct thing to do in the conditions. You have to play what's in front of you, no matter what the game or the opposition.

Mike Blair: Mossy and David Bortolussi exchanged penalties in the second-half and going into the final few minutes we were 18–15 ahead. Then, with only a couple of minutes left, Italy were awarded a kickable penalty.

It was real stomach-in-your-boots time. It was a tricky kick – out to the right of the posts near the ten-yard line and it was cold and wet, which would make the flight of the ball heavier and there was a bit of a breeze, but you can never tell. Those moments are agonising because there is nothing you can do to influence the kicker – you just have to stand there and just hope and hope and hope.

Jason White: It was a bit nerve-wracking at the end, but Bortolussi put the kick wide and we came through and that was the important bit. Our target was the quarter-finals and we made it – which is something that neither Ireland or Wales managed, so it shouldn't be underestimated as an achievement.

It was tight, tighter than we would have liked, but the win was the thing that mattered. We knew that we would have to improve against Argentina the following week to have a chance of progressing to the semi-finals, but at that stage we were more than happy to accept substance over style.

The Pumas had been the surprise package of the World Cup and had become a fan favourite at the tournament. Their pack were monstrously effective and in the backs they fizzled with skill and pace, with the luminous Juan Martin Hernandez, Felipe Contepomi, Ignacio Corleto, Lucas Borges and Agustin Pichot dazzling on the fields of France. They had already shocked the tournament hosts by beating them 17–12 in Paris and had turned over Ireland 30–15 on their way to the top of Pool D.

Again, Scotland looked to out-muscle their opponents but they were soon trailing the South Americans 13–6 thanks to a charge-down try from number eight Gonzalo Longo and the boot of Contepomi. In the final quarter of the match Scotland finally seemed to realise that the most effective way to play the game was to imitate the style of their opponents – to combine their new-found physicality with a wider running game. As the ball began to fly across the width of the pitch, the Pumas soon began to look stretched and Chris Cusiter, on as a late replacement for Mike Blair, fastened onto a ball from Kelly Brown after a wonderful break from prop Craig Smith to slide in at the corner. Paterson's boot was clawing Scotland back into the game and as the final seconds ticked in Dan Parks delivered a cross-kick into the Argentinean dead-ball area for a match-clinching try . . . but Sean Lamont was unable to gather the punt before it went dead. Thirty seconds later, Pichot kicked the ball high into the Paris stands and the Latin locomotive steamed into the semi-final. In that last twenty minutes, Scotland played with a style and panache that was reminiscent of the way they had played when Hadden had first come on the scene in 2005 and many felt that if they had just held onto that style while combining it with their new power, things might have been turned out quite differently. There was a lingering sense of frustration that the team's tactics against Argentina in the quarter-final seemed to have been geared around avoiding defeat rather than securing victory – at least until it was too late.

Allister Hogg: In the build-up to the quarter-final we really felt that we had the beating of Argentina. We had some real chances in that match to seal the result but we let them slide and didn't play as we might have, so it was hugely disappointing not to go any further in the tournament. They were a good side, well drilled and knew each other very well – as a team they had been together for a number of years. We tried to play a bit of a territorial game, but it didn't come off. We should maybe have tried to throw the ball around a bit more earlier on.

Simon Webster: I enjoyed playing in the centre at the World Cup, but you look back now and see issues that cropped up from the fact that it wasn't my regular position with Scotland and that we weren't always that slick as a backline unit. I remember against Argentina, Rob Dewey was in a ruck so I moved into the inside centre position and me and Parksy ran a simple cut; we hadn't ever really run one them together before – not that you should have to, it's really straight-forward – but you can get timing issues if you're not used to each other's running lines, and we got it wrong and I dropped the ball. We were on their twenty-two and there was a seam to run through and if I had got through there it was just one-on-one with their fullback with thirty metres on either side, and I'd have always backed myself in a situation like that. In a tight game like that . . . Man, these things stay with you.

Dan Parks: We probably started to play too late in the game – and we had a chance at the end but didn't take it. It was a heart-breaking way to go out, but they took their chances and we didn't. At the end of the day that's what rugby so often comes down to. They lit up that tournament and deserved to go through.

Mike Blair: Unfortunately we looked to counter the way Argentina played rather than looking to impose our own game on them. Our game plan was to kick into their half and once we had any set-pieces in their half we would attack, go wide and get a decent balance in our play of ball carriers and wide runners. The only problem was that we didn't get a set-piece in their half for about sixty minutes. They didn't create very much – they got a few penalties and a try from a charge-down clearance. But we were as guilty of a lack of creativity. You look back now and consider the styles of play that we had in 2006 and 2007 – the wide game and the physical game, with almost exactly the same personnel, give or take a few players. If we had married those two styles we could have been in the semi-final of the World Cup and would have been a dangerous proposition for any team. In terms of a path to a World Cup semi-final, you couldn't have asked for much of a better one than the one we had that year. So yeah, it's pretty hard to look back on now and know what we missed out on.

Chris Cusiter: When you're that far behind in a game you really have nothing to lose so you start to throw the ball around a bit more. It's easy to look back now and say we should have been playing like that before then, but games are completely different in the last twenty minutes, especially when one team has a lead because they tend to stop playing as much and become a bit more defensive so the other team gets more ball, and that's what happens.

I managed to get a score in the corner and that gave us a chance in the final few minutes to steal the win. Parksy went for a cross-field kick to Sean Lamont in this big all-or-nothing play and unfortunately he overcooked it and we lost the game. I remember being so disappointed afterwards because although Argentina were good and they had a great team spirit, they were fairly limited and I think that if we had played a better game on the day, we could have beaten them and made it into a semi-final. You don't get opportunities like that very often. It's something that I think we'll all always look back on and think, 'Jeez, what if?' We were in a position to score and win that game and we just couldn't quite do it.

Jason White: In many ways it came down to experience on the big stage and Argentina had more players who were used to performing at the highest level, particularly for their clubs – but also in that competition because they had faced the hosts in the opening game, a huge, huge occasion, and had won and then they had beaten Ireland as well, who many people had as dark horses for the competition. And they backed up how good they were by giving South Africa a bit of a scare and then beating France again to finish third.

Andy Henderson: We lost our opening game of the 2008 Six Nations to France at Murrayfield and didn't play at all well. We then went down to Cardiff and lost again and then had to travel over to Ireland to play at Croke Park on the back of Ireland's massive – and historic – win over England the week before.

Frank picked Mossy at ten for that game and we had a brilliant opening ten minutes when we were all over them and Mossy was looking really good. But then, as that Ireland team always seemed to do at the time, they rode the storm and managed to stop some of our more promising attacks by giving away penalties, and then they broke against the run of play and scored up at the other end. I think that both of Tommy Bowe's tries and Rob Kearney's try were all scored after we had been on the attack and they turned the ball over. It's always a fairly shattering moment when you get yourself into a good position and you think that you're going to score, only for someone to drop a ball or get turned over at a ruck or for a kick not to go to touch and the other team are suddenly sixty yards up the other end of the pitch scoring. It felt that that happened to us a lot in 2008.

Mike Blair: Jason White was injured against Wales, so I was made captain against Ireland and England. I remember standing in the tunnel before the England game waiting to go out and the lights were mostly off in the stadium and this lone piper was playing up on the top of the East Stand and all I could see was the rain pouring down almost horizontally because the wind was so strong.

That was another sensational defensive performance. It was a kind of re-run of the 2000 game in terms of us having gone through the Championship without picking up a win and then playing to the conditions. It was funny, just like the 2000 and 2006 victories, I was astonished by the fact that England didn't change their tactics to suit the weather or to counter the way we were playing. They had these experienced core in Jonny Wilkinson, Iain Balshaw, Andrew Sheridan, Phil Vickery, Simon Shaw and Steve Borthwick, who had all been there and done it before at the highest level – and who had also lost to us in the same manner in 2006, and some of them again in 2000 – and yet they didn't say, 'Look, this isn't working, what we have to do is change this and do this . . .' They just carried on playing in the same way and that suited us perfectly. To lift the Calcutta Cup as captain is something I'll treasure for the rest of my life.

Simon Webster: I think my favourite memory from my career was when I came off the field after we had beaten England in 2008. It was my birthday and we had just won the Calcutta Cup; it hadn't been a great game, the weather conditions had been poor and it was a typical Scotland-England game at a wet Murrayfield, so not exactly a great spectacle. But I remember looking up at the stands full of fans celebrating, and I could see my English mum bouncing up and down, waving a Scotland flag and punching the air and blowing kisses and going crazy at the result. And I won't ever be able to really describe how that moment made me feel.

We had the meal at Murrayfield afterwards and then got the team bus to George

Mike Blair hoists the Calcutta Cup aloft after another mighty defensive performance from the home team seals the bragging rights over England for the second time in three years.

Street and piled into a bar. The whole downstairs was packe and the place just stopped, the music stopped, everything. And everyone in there started applauding us, shaking our hands, asking for photos, giving out high-fives. Do you know what, just thinking of that day again, it gives me goosebumps. That's what makes it so special playing for Scotland because you see the pleasure that you can bring other people and you can see how it makes them feel.

I suppose as an international player you eventually start to compartmentalise things, certainly once you retire – you put all the bad memories of losses and all the rest into one box and all the good things into another. And opening up that box of good memories is as special as it gets. As I said before, international players are just fans who have lived a dream that we've all had since we were little kids. And that's an incredible thing.

In what would prove to be a sign of the changing of the guard, there was something of a shake-up in the coaching panel that summer. Andy Robinson came on board from Edinburgh along with Glasgow's Sean Lineen to assist Frank Hadden as the team travelled to Argentina for a two Test series. They lost the first match 21–15, but roared back in Buenos Aires to win 26–14 with outstanding performances from centres Graeme Morrison and Ben Cairns, the front-row of Allan Jacobsen, Ross Ford and Euan Murray, the back-row of John Barclay, Ally Hogg and Alasdair Strokosch, and halfback pairing Mike Blair and Phil Godman.

Alastair Kellock: They mixed things up by bringing in some new coaches to assist on the tour. It was refreshing to work with Andy Robinson as well as my club coach at the time, Sean Lineen. They brought in new ideas and focus, and Andy's attention to detail – especially for the forwards – was very impressive. Little things like adjustments in technique and little tricks really helped to improve our technique and efficiency in the set-piece and around the contact area.

I came off the bench in both those Tests and to win the second match was a brilliant, brilliant feeling. It was also one of the toughest, most physical games I've ever played and the crowd were mental. There's real passion in Argentinean rugby, right from the clubs and the crowd through to the players. They all stick together like brothers in the trenches and that sense of a team ethic was very inspiring. The challenge when you play them is to match that passion and the ferocity that they bring to a game. Their sense of loyalty to each other keeps them fighting for the full eighty minutes and they never give up thinking that they will win.

Mike Blair: It is always so satisfying to see the hard work done during an intervening week between matches come out and we were more intense and more precise and we played a quicker ball in the dangerous areas. Playing good rugby to achieve only the second-ever Test victory Scotland had had in the southern hemisphere was a tremendous experience.

Graeme Morrison (Scotland 2004–2012, 35 Caps): To come across to somewhere like Argentina where rugby's a very passionate game, the crowd were pretty hostile; both arenas we played in in each Test were pretty intimidating. So to bounce back from the defeat in the first Test to win in the second was a very memorable occasion and to score made it all even better. Dan Parks had just come off the bench and he intercepted a pass inside our half and ran about forty yards into their territory, then just as he was about to get tackled he looped a lovely ball inside to me and I had a clear run to the line.

John Barclay (Scotland 2007-2015, 45 Caps): Everything just went right for us in that second Test and it was one of the most enjoyable games that I played for Scotland. We played some great rugby and I never felt at any time that we looked like losing, which is a fantastic feeling to have in somewhere like Argentina with the crowd going crazy all around you and their players throwing everything at you.

Simon Webster: Argentina was an amazing place to tour. Really passionate supporters; I suppose the best way to describe it is that it's more of a football environment than a traditional rugby one.

I remember we went to watch [Club Atlético] Lanús play Boca Juniors in a mid-week game in Buenos Aires; I'd been to plenty of football games but never experienced anything like that before. It was an unbelievable atmosphere. It was at Lanús' home ground and Boca Juniors won 3-1 and afterwards we piled on our bus and started making our way out of this tiny stadium and into the backstreets of Buenos Aires. But as we were slowly making our way out, all the home fans came out too and thought we were the Boca Juniors players trying to make a quick exit. A few things started getting launched at the bus and then pretty soon they'd surrounded us and were hammering on the side, throwing more stuff, and we were all starting to think, 'Uh-oh, we could be trouble here.' There were probably a couple of hundred people surrounding us by that stage.

Then the driver and the guys who were looking after us started plastering the windows with Scotland flags to show we had nothing to do with Boca Juniors. Fortunately it was before the President [Cristina Fernandez de Kirchner] was really making a big thing of the Falklands again and before the Top Gear guys had gone over and really flared things up, so we got away with showing we were a British sports team, which might not always have been a sensible alternative to Boca Juniors! They mob backed off and let us go, but for a split second or two, we were shitting ourselves.

In November, New Zealand, South Africa and Canada came to Scotland and although the only victory that was posted was against Canada in Aberdeen, the team had only just fallen short of South Africa and the front-row had announced their credentials to the world with magnificent performances against the All Blacks and the Springboks. On the back of these showings, much of the Scottish pack and a number of the backs were heralded as certainties for the Lions tour to South Africa in the summer of 2009, and Mike Blair became the first Scottish player to be shortlisted for the prestigious IRB Player of the Year award.

Mike Blair: At the start of the following international season we had a good run-out against Canada up in Pittodrie. I like it when games go to other venues around Scotland – although sometimes the weather up in Aberdeen can make it a fairly arduous experience. In the days leading up to the match there had been blizzards all across the country and when we arrived to play the game they were shoveling snow drifts off the pitch – so it was bloody cold and really soft under foot. To make matters worse, the ground staff at Pittodrie had decided to paint the pitch-markings red to help distinguish them from the snow – but the only problem for me was that I'm colour blind so I couldn't see any of the markings at all. I had to go through the whole game trying to guess where the lines were from the flags – and I wasn't all that successful, to be honest.

Euan Murray (Scotland 2005-2015, 66 Caps): The autumn of 2008 was fantastic, although it was bitterly disappointing not to beat either the All Blacks or the Springboks considering the dominance we had over them in the set-piece. Those games were the biggest challenge I had faced in my career at that point and as a team it was the biggest challenge of most of our careers. I wish we'd had New Zealand last in the three-Test series though, because I really feel that we could have beaten them if we had had a few run-outs before facing them.

Mike Blair: We started that game very strongly and took the game to the All Blacks right from the off, which is something that I don't think they expected. I took a quick tap in the first minute or two and put Mossy through after he took a great angle off my shoulder and he was dragged down just short of their line. A wee while later we had a scrum right on their line and Ally Hogg picked up, drew their back-row and passed to me – I was on the move, ready to accelerate to the line with Thom Evans outside me and I think we would have almost definitely scored . . . except I knocked the ball on. It was a killer moment in the game. It was just before halftime and would have taken us in at 13–18 and with our tails up, but as it was we went in 6–18 and all our possession and dominance had barely registered on the scoreboard. The All Blacks scored some clever opportunist tries, as they always do, and the game got away from us in the end. But the forwards had stood up and sent a message to the world about the kind of power we possessed and in the backs we made some nice breaks and got into good field position.

It was agonisingly close against South Africa the following week. We had played superbly during the first-half and were winning 10–0 at half-time after Wagga [Nathan Hines] went over by the posts. But inevitably the Springboks powered their way back into the game and kicked well and we ended up losing 14-10.

Going into the 2009 Six Nations, hopes were once again flying that Scotland could make a push for the title. They had a huge pack, the best goal-kicker in the world, and a number of exciting and powerful strike-runners. The signs all looked positive.

Phil Godman: We went into the 2009 Six Nations pretty confident. We had shown in the autumn that we had a pack to compete with anyone in the world and we were starting to get a fluid running game coming together with some really dangerous strike players out wide. We had a huge choice of players in the back three, all who were proven match-winners and who all brought different qualities to their position – Thom and Max Evans, Sean and Rory Lamont, Simon Danielli and Simon Webster, Nikki Walker, Hugo Southwell, Chris Paterson. So the way we played against Wales at Murrayfield was a bit of a shock.

Mike Blair: The Wales game was a confidence killer. It was the first game of the Championship and after the autumn series and the way that both Edinburgh and Glasgow were playing in the Magners League and the Heineken Cup, we genuinely thought that we were dark horses for the Championship. We were missing Euan Murray and Nathan Hines, but we still had a strong squad and Geoff Cross, who came in on the tight-head for his first cap, had been playing really well for Edinburgh. It was a fairly demoralising debut for him in the end. About twenty minutes in, he chased an up-and-under clearance kick and knocked himself out on Lee Byrne's knee as Byrne leapt to take the ball. We all watched the replay as a team afterwards and you can see that Geoff was just charging up field, thinking that the ball was probably going to land about thirty metres further away than it did. It was a fairly sickening impact to have to watch in slow-motion. He was stretchered off and given a yellow card at the same time for dangerous play.

Geoff Cross (Scotland 2009-2015, 40 Caps): Starting that game for Scotland was one of the proudest moments of my career and I remember everything about that game – for the first twenty minutes, anyway. I remember the huge emotions during the anthems and the tears rolling down my face; I remember preparing for the kick-off and focusing all my thoughts on doing well in the scrums and at the lineouts, winning the contacts and collisions and sticking with our planned shapes of play. I remember everything until I ran into Lee Byrne's knee. It was hugely disappointing that I made a poor decision but it's a game and these things happen. It was my first cap so I was very pumped up and it affected my decision-making.

Mike Blair: Shortly after Geoff had gone off Byrne scored – and they scored again a few minutes later. Our scrum was struggling because we were still a man down and Wales won a strike against the head and after a few phases Alun-Wyn Jones went over. We were 3–16 down at half-time and the second-half was no better than the first. Jamie Roberts was huge all day for them, cutting great lines and busting through tackles. Leigh Halfpenny went in at the corner and ten minutes later Shane Williams was scoring for them again. It was a shocker.

Simon Taylor: That was the last time I played against Wales; every one of their breakdowns seemed to produce lightning quick ball, making it impossible to set our defence, and we were chasing shadows from the first kick-off. Meanwhile, Mike Phillips, charming fellow, found the time to tell me that I was embarrassingly crap. Hurtful, but essentially true.

Alasdair Strokosch (Scotland 2006-2015, 47 Caps): We made a big improvement in our attitude from the Wales game when we went to Paris. We upped our intensity and did much, much better in the collision area and dominated much of the physicality of the game. In the end we lost again, but we had definitely improved. We had two tries disallowed, which would have changed the whole face of the game. But at the same time we gave away a lot of penalties and made a lot of errors which cost us the result. Over the years you could probably use that whole description to describe dozens of Scotland matches – which, as a player, is immensely frustrating.

Phil Godman: We rattled France in the first-half and felt we were in the ascendency – but we did an almost typically Scotland thing of letting in a soft try at the start of the second half that should never have been given. The whole thing was a bit of a mess – the ball was pin-balling around on the ground and it bounced up into Lionel Nallet's hands and he fed it to Maxime Médard who cut a lovely angle to our line –

but the space for his run was created because their flanker, Fulgence Ouedraogo, was running a block on our defence and then as Médard was tackled he gave a blatantly forward-pass to Ouedraogo to score.

Ross Ford (Scotland 2004-2015, 95 Caps plus 1 Cap for the Lions): The level of effort and the way we approached the France game was more of where we wanted to be, although we still ended up on the losing side. We knew that we would have to up it again for the Italy match. Fortunately we did and we ended up winning 26–6; we were making progress in the competition but it was nowhere near the levels that we had produced in the autumn and that was incredibly frustrating.

Mike Blair: We had Ireland up next at Murrayfield and they were two games away from sealing only their second-ever Grand Slam. That tells you how the game went. It was a pretty tight match and it was effectively decided when Jamie Heaslip went over to score the game's only try. It was off the back of a great little bit of opportunist play by Peter Stringer. In the build up to the game there was a bit of controversy about the fact that he had been picked because he had fallen down the pecking order somewhat in Ireland. But he was a player of huge experience and he wouldn't have appreciated the way the press were talking about him. Well, I think they probably said much the same about him before Munster played Biarritz in the 2006 Heineken Cup final – and he scored the decisive try when he picked and went from the back of a scrum to score. He took a ball off the back of a lineout against us and John Barclay moved out to attack O'Gara, opening up a gap between him and Stroker . . . Stringer saw it and he slipped through and then released Jamie Heaslip to score. Mossy had kept us in the game with his kicking but it was Ronan O'Gara's boot that settled the result.

We had to go to Twickenham for the final game and although things hadn't been going well for us that season, we still felt that we might be able to cause an upset down there. We'd done well against England over the previous ten years and we really thought we could win. We started brightly and Thom Evans almost got in to score – it was a cracking tackle by Ugo Monye and great work to come over from his wing to haul Thom down. I think the try Ugo scored and then that tackle, all within the space of around five minutes, sealed his place on the Lions tour that summer and in fairness to him it was a super bit of attacking and defensive skill. They then scored another try through Riki Flutey which was well-worked, but we were still very much in the game and it was only a late, late try for Matthew Tait that sealed it for them and put a bit of gloss on the result that made it look like we were well beaten, which didn't tell the whole story. It was often a case of fine margins, but those margins went against us during that Six Nations.

The result at Twickenham, although spirited, was the final nail in Hadden's coffin. Now roundly criticised in the media, it was felt that the head coach had brought the team as far as he was able. He had resurrected their fortunes in 2006 and guiding them to some memorable victories; although hounded at the time for his decisions during the World Cup, he had nevertheless taken the team to the quarter-final and had Sean Lamont collected Dan Parks' crossfield kick, Scotland might well have snuck through to the semi-final. The last two seasons of his reign had been less successful, but he had secured Scotland's second-ever win in the southern hemisphere by guiding his charges to victory over the Pumas in Buenos Aires and had come incredibly close to toppling the world champions in 2008. But it was felt that the time had come for a change and although the SRU touted the names of Australian Eddie Jones and South African Jake White around as they conducted their interviews for Hadden's replacement, there was already a man waiting in the Murrayfield wings ready to step back into the limelight of international rugby.

Jon Petrie: I suppose the honeymoon period can only last for so long, because eventually things start going against you and at that stage you have to have a plan B, and that's when things started to fall down a bit under Frank Hadden.

Mike Blair: I felt very bad for a lot of the flak that Frank copped towards the end of his time as head coach. He had really turned things around after Matt Williams had been in charge and had helped us enjoy our rugby with Scotland again – which resulted in some famous victories and our best-ever finish in the Six Nations table. He got us through to the quarter-finals of the World Cup and within touching distance of a semi-final spot. And then luck turned against him. We had a lot of injuries in the squad in 2009 – and losing Nathan Hines and Euan Murray for much of the Six Nations was a real blow – and some of us weren't playing as well as we might, myself included. I stressed it at the time – and it wasn't just a case of the captain supporting his coach – I said that it wasn't Frank or any of the other coaches out on the pitch making the simple errors that cost us games; it wasn't any of them dropping passes or missing kicks to touch or falling off tackles. It was us. People have said that the time had come for a new man to come in with a change of attitude and ideas – Andy Robinson's impact with Edinburgh spoke for itself, he totally transformed the club's performaces while he was in charge, so maybe there was some truth in that statement. But the level of abuse that went Frank's way was totally unmerited. He did all he could to help us win, but it wasn't him out there making the mistakes that meant that we ended up losing in those final games of his tenure. He saved Scottish rugby when it was at one of its lowest ebbs and he did great, great things to bring our game back out from that depression. Some of my fondest memories as a rugby player happened because of Frank and the fans who watched those games will never forget the results we had while he was in charge, particularly our win against France and our two Calcutta Cup triumphs.

But it's always the man at the top that gets the chop and every coach and manager in any sport goes into the role in the knowledge that his head is first on the line when things go wrong. Andy Robinson was a very different character to Frank and brought different credentials with him. Once it was decided that Frank's time was up, there was really only ever going to be one man for the job.

TWENTY-FOUR

POACHER TURNED GAMEKEEPER
2009-2012

Andy Robinson was made Scotland head coach in June 2009. While he was at pains to stress that his tenure would be a case of evolution rather than revolution from the Frank Hadden era, one thing that would definitely change was that Matt Williams' Fortress Scotland policy would be entirely disbanded. While the policy had been watered down somewhat by Hadden, there continued to be a preference to select home-based players over those playing elsewhere if all other factors were equal; under Robinson, players would be picked entirely on merit, no matter where they were based.

With a coaching style epitomised by a furious intensity and attention to detail, Robinson declared that his primary remit was to empower his players while seeking to 'inspire the nation' through their performances. His tenure got off to a very promising start. In the autumn of 2009 Scotland defeated a Fijian team ranked above them on the IRB table, and then beat Australia for the first time since 1982 thanks to an incredible defensive display, before falling just short against Argentina in a close-fought battle.

Alastair Kellock: One of Andy Robinson's first acts in charge was to lead a Scotland A party to Romania for the Nations Cup in 2009. There was no main Scotland tour that year because of the Lions tour to South Africa, so we took a pretty strong team to the Nations Cup. He asked me to be vice-captain and it was a great trip, really enjoyable – helped no doubt by the fact that we won the tournament and played some decent rugby.

Chris Cusiter: I was captain and we did well out there, playing some good rugby to win the competition and I think that stood me in good stead while Mike Blair was away with the Lions. It was a competitive environment among the scrum-halves but we always got on well with each other. It was a funny thing that we both got starting places when the other one went on a Lions tour – me in 2005 and Mike in 2009 – and I think that it balanced itself out. I think that if Mike had been the starting scrum-half for Scotland in 2005, then he would have definitely gone on the Lions tour that year, and I think I could have done the same in 2009. Because we're seen as the weakest of the four Home Nations, you're not going to get on a Lions tour unless you're starting. You might if you're playing for England because they have so much more depth, but not if you're Scottish; so unless you're starting you're definitely going to miss out, and that's what happened with us, even though I think we were both good enough to go on both those tours. It's just the way it was. The consolation prize in 2009 was that tour to Romania. Not quite a Lions tour but it was actually a lot of fun and I really got to know Andy Robinson well which stood me in good stead for the following year.

Opposite: Dan Parks celebrates his winning penalty against Ireland at Croke Park in 2010 as the ball is still mid-flight towards the posts.

As a trio of scrum-half options for Scotland, Mike, Rory Lawson and I were all different. I don't think we ever tried to adapt what the others could do, we just worried about playing our own styles. Mike was probably more skillful and more tactical than I ever was, but I felt my strengths were in being a bit more physical and getting involved in the nitty gritty a bit more, I think he liked to come off the pitch a bit cleaner than me! He was a great tactical reader of the game and we just had different styles and Rory was a bit of an all-rounder, no real weaknesses, and when he played he did really well and was involved in a lot of really big Scottish wins; so it really depended on what the coach wanted from each game. We all got on well, but we all get on better now, for sure. We're not competing with each other and we socialise now, which we didn't back then, which is nice because we've experienced a lot together.

Anyway, we played Fiji first up in the autumn and they are always tricky to play against – all their players are big and fast and athletic, with great ball-handling skills. We scored an early try through Johnnie Beattie that was well worked and set the tone. Graeme Morrison scored a try in the second-half that was perhaps a little fortuitous, but we generally controlled the game and deserved to win.

The plan going into the Australia match was to spread the ball wide a little bit more, to be ambitious, and to speed things up with quick taps. We knew that we needed to be ambitious to beat a side of that quality.

Alastair Kellock: Before the Australia game we spoke about passion, about the need to lift the crowd by giving absolutely everything. Andy had made a big thing about inspiring the nation in the build-up and we all knew what a difference it could make to your performance if you could get the crowd lifted and cheering you on. We really worked hard in defence all afternoon. They had gone ahead with an early penalty but we got two back through Phil Godman, one of which was an absolute belter from the right-hand side; a great kick. Chris Cusiter had also pulled off a wonder-tackle to hold Stephen Moore up over the line, although he got injured in the process. Then Mossy sent over a drop-goal and we just began to wonder if it might be our day.

They were battering away at our line in the final minutes and then they scored a try in injury-time. I thought it was all over, but when you defend like that you deserve to win games and maybe all our efforts had helped to knock Matt Giteau out of his comfort zone because he missed the conversion and we snuck the win by a point. It was an incredible feeling.

Phil Godman: We showed ambition in attack but it was the way we stuck in in defence that really won it – it was comfortably the best defensive performance I was ever involved in. By the end, when they went over after two or three minutes of defence, the whole experience was a bit surreal. We were all so shattered after working so hard that we just stood there as Matt Giteau lined up the conversion. I was in a bit of a daze, and was shocked to see it not go over, but the feeling of realising that we had won the game was just incredible.

Rory Lawson (Scotland 2006-2012, 31 Caps): I only found out that I would be on the bench the day before when Mike failed a fitness test on his ankle, which was a great shame for him but a great opportunity for me. And again, it was tough for Chris that he had to go off with a head-bang, but it gave me a chance to show what I could do and to be involved with a game like that was just unbelievable.

It was a strange feeling after the game. It was a real high, but we also knew how close we were to recording another valiant defeat – which would have taken away from the defensive effort, from the guts and the passion, and everyone would be continuing to talk of the decline of Scottish rugby.

Alex Grove (Scotland 2009, 3 Caps): When Ryan Cross went over to score for the Wallabies late on, there was a few of us saying, 'It's still 9-8, we're still winning,' but everyone's heads were down – even

Alex Grove and Nick de Luca celebrate as Matt Giteau realises the consequences of his last-minute missed kick.

with the kick still to come we were pretty sure it was all over and we were going to be robbed of a famous win.

But my best memory, and one that will probably live with me forever, was Al Jacobsen in a three-point stance, ready to chase down the kick. Matt Giteau was standing over the ball, ready to take the kick, and we all charged up as soon as he moved to strike – but I think Chunk outpaced everyone!

Chris Paterson: You have to take that win with a pinch of salt – we won because of a mistake at the end. Yes, we played our hearts out for eighty minutes and defended well, but we had very few opportunities to score tries and it very nearly went the other way. It was a great win, there's no doubt about that, but we were a long way from going into games against the likes of Australia expecting to win. We said under the posts that we would rush out and try to charge down the conversion, but I still expected Giteau to kick it. I turned at the last second and saw it go wide, but I didn't jump for joy – it wouldn't have been courteous, especially to a player of his standing.

Great defence and great tenacity, that's what I remember most about that game. As I say, the fact that it ultimately came down to them missing a final kick to win the game slightly took the gloss off things, but it was still a great result. I spoke with Jason White after the match and we realised that the only top-ranked team that the Scotland team of the 2000s hadn't beaten was the All Blacks – so for all the doom and gloom that had gone around Scottish rugby over the years, that was something pretty significant to bear in mind.

Alastair Kellock: The third game that autumn wasn't much of a spectacle, but credit to Argentina, they did exactly what they needed to do to win. They disrupted our ball at every turn in the rucks and mauls and they played to the referee's interpretation, which shut us out the game and broke down any momentum we tried to generate. It was frustrating not to complete the hat-trick of wins that autumn as it would have been a great – and well deserved – achievement, and it was all the more frustrating because we knew exactly what to expect from Argentina and still didn't manage to combat it.

In the 2010 Six Nations Scotland finished a disappointing fifth in the table, but the devil was in the detail. They came as close as any other team to beating eventual Grand Slam champions France at Murrayfield and but for two defensive lapses might well have caused an upset. In Wales, they suffered a severe injury to Chris Paterson, who sustained deep bruising and two tears and lacerations to his kidney only fifteen minutes into his hundredth cap, an ankle injury to Rory Lamont that ended his season, and a near-fatal spinal injury to wing Thom Evans which forced him to announce his retirement from the game a few months later. It was horrific. In what will be remembered as one of the most extraordinary conclusions to a game, Wales recovered from 12–9 down to sneak the win 31–24 in the last seconds of injury time against a thirteen-man Scotland.

Unsurprisingly shell-shocked by their Cardiff encounter, Scotland tumbled to a limited Italian side in Rome before picking up the pieces to draw 15–15 with England at Murrayfield. In the final round of the competition they travelled to Dublin for Ireland's farewell match at Croke Park before their return to a redeveloped Landsdowne Road. A wonderful try from Johnny Beattie and the metronomic boot of Dan Parks ruined the Irish party but sent the Scots into raptures as they claimed a famous 23–20 win, their first in Ireland since 1998.

Chris Cusiter: After the autumn, we had built ourselves up for a big opening game in the Six Nations against France, but it didn't come to anything. Our scrum struggled a wee bit and France kicked a few penalties, and Mathieu Bastareaud went over for two pretty soft tries. People made a big deal out of the fact that Euan Murray had elected not to play on Sundays because of his religious beliefs and so missed the game, but I thought Moray Low did very well against a French pack that proved they were the best in the competition that year.

Mike Blair: The players and coaches all accepted Euan's decision not to play on Sundays. Everyone knew how serious he was about his religion and we backed him up, there was never any sniping about it.

Euan Murray: I took a nasty head knock playing for Glasgow against Munster in 2005 and had convulsions on the pitch. I don't remember anything about it, but I've seen the video. In the aftermath of it all I was just thankful to be still alive. It was pretty scary – the other guys on the pitch told me afterwards that they thought I was going to die. The seizure made me realise that life is short, so I started to question things like, 'What are we here for?' and, 'Where am I going when I die?' And then I started reading the Bible and my life was transformed. On the day of the France match I went to church, I cooked, and I didn't watch the game until the next day. I don't know how many of my team-mates agreed with my approach, but I was happy with my decision and they seemed to accept it. They had all been with me through good times and bad and seen both sides of my life and they knew how important it was to me.

Chris Paterson: That game against Wales was my 100th cap. You stand on that pitch in Cardiff with 70,000 Welshmen singing and shouting and making this great din . . . and there are only fifteen of you staring up at them all . . . but that's what it's all about, that's why you play the game – you want to take them on and if you can silence that crowd, you know you're doing well. To win my hundredth cap there really was special. It's a shame that the game itself didn't exactly go according to plan – although it will be remembered around the world for a very, very long time.

Mike Blair: We started that game really well and John Barclay had a storming run that took him right through James Hook and Gareth Cooper to score. Dan Parks controlled things brilliantly at ten – he gave an absolute masterclass in tactical play. We scored two tries, two drop-goals, two penalties and a conversion in that first-half. It was fantastic.

John Barclay splits the Welsh defence to score in Cardiff

But the injuries were just horrific. Mossy took a knock that looked at the time like he may have cracked a rib or something – but he had actually lacerated his kidney. Things were still looking pretty bright for us despite Mossy going off. But then Thom Evans got injured.

Thom Evans (Scotland 2008-2010, 10 Caps): I've watched the incident a few times and it didn't look too bad from the TV angle. I kicked the ball ahead and chased and as I got to it again Lee Byrne came up to cover and we collided. My head hit his torso and I went down. It looked fairly innocuous on TV but the pain was terrible. I hit the ground hard and I just couldn't move; it was the most awful feeling I've ever experienced. I tried to get to my knees but nothing would move, not even my arms. Then after a few seconds I began to get some movement back but at the same time there was this searing pain between my shoulder blades. It felt like I'd been shot. The next thing I remember is James Robson, the Scotland doctor, at my side talking to me. I could respond to him, but my breathing was so fast that it felt like my insides were being crushed. James told me not to move and he stayed with me, trying to keep me calm. In the end he saved my life. If the injury had occurred even a millimetre further away I would have been paralysed and I'm extraordinarily lucky that I'm able to walk. I was taken to Cardiff's University Hospital and had an operation on my neck just a few hours later. A few days later they gave me the option of a second operation to help stabilise the injury, so I went for that and they inserted a steel rod into my back – which put an end to my rugby career.

Mike Blair: Max Evans was our main utility back and he was already on for Mossy. There was just me and Phil Godman left on the bench, so I was put on as a winger. We held the line pretty well for the remainder of the half considering that there had been such major reworking of the backline and we went in 18–9 up and then got a penalty in the first minute of the second-half to move 21–9 ahead.

Chris Cusiter: There were a couple of things that we couldn't quite nail in the second half and that let them back into the game. There was a cross-field kick to Kelly Brown and Rory Lamont and Shane Williams managed to out-jump them both for it and took it brilliantly above his head; then there was two v one and Sean Lamont's pass to Kelly was called forward. If we'd scored either of them we would have been out of sight.

Dan Parks: I'll never forget a kick Stephen Jones put over Sean Lamont, who was tracking back, and then the ball did something I'd never seen one do before. It basically bounced straight back over Sean's head into Leigh Halfpenny's hands for him to run in and that was the start of the collapse. It was our day for 74 minutes; it was just a shame about the last six. But it was one of the best matches I played in. A classic.

Mike Blair: Dan had to go off because he had cramp, so Phil [Godman] was on at stand-off. Wales went on the attack from deep and Lee Byrne kicked ahead – Phil jumped up to try and charge the kick and just caught Lee with his foot. I was covering the kick from the wing and caught the ball and when I looked up all I saw was Lee on his face on the ground about ten metres away from Phil and the referee was signalling a penalty – and then he yellow carded Phil.

Phil Godman: It was never a trip. I'll swear that to my dying day. I jumped up for the ball and my toe had the slightest of contacts with his leg – and five or six metres later he was sprawled on the ground behind me. It didn't merit a penalty, let alone a sin-binning. That one decision really put the nail in our coffin.

Mike Blair: They kicked the penalty and we were all square at 24–all. We were down to twelve men, so Alan MacDonald, our substitute flanker, came on in the centre.

Chris Cusiter: By the time they scored the try and kicked the conversion that made the game level, our tanks were just empty, we were done. The clock had ticked to eighty minutes at this point but for some reason George Clancy felt we still had to restart the game. I don't understand why, but he did. We couldn't kick it deliberately out on the full otherwise they would get a penalty. I told Mike, who was playing stand-off now, to kick it in-field. The idea was that we would pin them back in their half and maybe sneak a penalty.

Mike Blair: They worked their way back to our twenty-two and I thought we might be able to just hold out but a couple of quick rucks later Shane Williams was in under the posts. To lose in that manner … it was just devastating.

Chris Cusiter: It was so gut wrenching. If we'd got a win down in Cardiff it would have been one of those real career highlights. And then you get off the field and you hear about the severity of all the injuries and the whole thing just takes this terrible turn for the worse. Those injuries put the result into perspective almost instantly, it was horrific what had happened. None of us cared about the game anymore, there were much bigger things going on.

Max Evans (Scotland 2008-2014, 44 Caps): At half-time I knew that Thommy had been hurt and there might be something to do with his neck, but it was very vague. I only found out after the game the severity of it. I got my stuff together as quickly as possible and went straight to the hospital. I saw him as he went into the operating theatre. As I got there they were reading out the clearance form, the waiver, whatever, so I knew it was pretty serious then. James Robson told me that if Thommy had been moved by even a millimetre it could have been fatal or he could have been paralysed. He said it was the worst injury he has ever been involved in.

Mike Blair: There's not a lot to say about the Italy game that followed. We were all so deflated after Cardiff and were a bit shell-shocked with all the injuries. We still thought we would win and although the game was a typically turgid Scotland-Italy encounter, I thought we deserved to edge it. Chunk [Alan Jacobsen] swore blind that he scored from a maul, but the video ref didn't give it. It was another disappointing afternoon in Rome.

Max Evans: I drove back through to Glasgow the night before the Calcutta Cup match to pick up Thom. We met the rest of the team and Thom said a few words before presenting Dan Parks with his fiftieth Test jersey and James Robson with his own match jersey from the Wales game, as a thank you for everything he did for him in Cardiff. Thom did really well to get through all he wanted to say because it was very emotional and all the boys appreciated it – it gave us all a massive lift.

Chris Cusiter: Playing against England at home is as big as it gets for a Scotland player and I think the crowd feels that way too. That was maybe the best I've ever heard Murrayfield. We were in control for large parts of the game; in the first-half we had a lot of possession and we were attacking really, really well and causing them a lot of problems. We went into half-time with a 9–6 lead and felt that we were in a good position to push on from there. The set-piece functioned really well and was a great source of possession for us and we made a number of line breaks and came close to scoring on several occasions, but England's defence was solid. It was a draw and strange sort of result to digest – on the one hand we were desperately disappointed not to have gone on and won it which we felt we could have, but at the same time they missed a late penalty and had a drop-goal charged down for them to win it, so we were also glad to hold on.

Johnnie Beattie (Scotland 2006-2015, 38 Caps): It was an odd feeling afterwards. It's not something that occurs very much, a draw in international rugby, and especially in a Scotland-England match. It was good to get some points on the table but disappointing not to push on and get the win which we all felt we deserved.

Mike Blair: Our back-row were sensational all through the season and against England they were brilliant again. They turned-over their ball on at least five occasions at the ruck and we didn't get turned-over there all game, which shows how much we dominated that area. Dan had two kicks rebound off the uprights and Toby Flood missed a couple of kicks as well and we basically battered ourselves to a draw, so it was probably a fair result. After losing the first three games that year in the manner in which we did, seeing Rory Lawson charging down Toby Flood's drop-goal as he went for the winner was a great moment. A draw allowed us to stabilise and look to build towards Dublin.

Chris Cusiter: I remember in the build up to the Ireland game all that anyone seemed to be talking about in the press was that it was going to be this big celebratory send off for them from Croke Park and we were basically going there just to make up the numbers. There was one Irish journalist who basically gave our team talk for us – he wrote an article saying that we were OK players but that Ireland were better than us in every facet of the game, individually and collectively, and that we didn't stand a chance. It was exactly the kind of motivational thing you want to read before a game, it fired us all up so much. I was seething when I read it.

To win there was just incredible, especially considering the occasion. What a try Johnnie Beattie scored and then Parksy had that kick to win it, in a big windy stadium and he just struck it perfectly. It was awesome.

Rory Lawson: We had a shakey start and Brian O'Driscoll scored a try after a forward pass from Jonny Sexton, but then we started playing with some composure and Johnny Beattie's try was brilliant and Dan Parks' kicking and all-round control was superb. It may have come down to that final kick of the game, but we thoroughly deserved the win. It was nothing more than we deserved after the Championship we had had and it gave us a great boost as we started to prepare for our tour to Argentina in the summer.

Dan Parks: When we first got to the ground I walked around the stadium before the game and the breeze was going across the pitch – but at each end it was going different ways. I'd had a penalty early in the second-half just short of fifty metres and it moved to the right when I thought it would have drifted left. When I lined up the final kick I thought I'd aim it to the left to account for the breeze and it went through. It was a great moment.

Jonny Sexton was very gracious after the game. I went over to swap shirts with him; he didn't have a Scotland jersey at that stage but he wanted me to take his shirt and wouldn't swap. He said, 'It's your day'. That was pretty special of him.

In the summer of 2010, the team travelled to South America for a two-Test series against Argentina. The country had been a happy hunting ground for Robinson on his previous trip there as assistant coach with Scotland in 2008, but that second Test win, although very welcome, had been achieved against a home side lacking many of its best players, who had been playing club rugby in France. For the 2010 series, the Pumas were at full-strength. On a balmy afternoon in the rugby hotbed of Tucumán, where Argentina had never lost a Test match, Dan Parks kicked Scotland to a magnificent 24–16 victory and, in doing so, also picked up his fourth man of the match award in five consecutive Test matches – a remarkable feat considering he had only been on the winning side twice in that time.

The tour was completed with the second Test in Mar del Plata, and a win that gave Scotland their first run of three consecutive wins on the road since 1982, as well as their first-ever series triumph in the southern hemisphere. In a match that was played out for much of the eighty minutes in driving rain, Parks's kicking game came to the fore once again while his pack dominated a highly experienced Argentinean unit. An early Jim Hamilton try and eight points from Parks' boot gave the Scots a 13–9 victory.

Dan Parks: The noise of the crowd in both Tests in Argentina was crazy. Some people say that it can be intimidating, but I didn't ever try to shut it out, even when I was kicking for goal. I actually enjoyed it. It was the same feeling that I had in Cardiff and Dublin that year as well – it's what Test match rugby is all about – the ferocity of the noise and the way that the crowd really takes part in the game. And then once you kick the points it suddenly goes silent and I loved that most of all.

Scott MacLeod (Scotland 2004-2011, 24 Caps): I hadn't played for Scotland since 2008 so when I was recalled in 2010 for the tour of Argentina, it was honestly the biggest moment of my career. I hadn't got on in the first Test in Tucumán but they put me on with about ten minutes left of the second Test. Right at the end Argentina kicked a penalty to the corner, five metres out, trying to win the match. We were going to drive, but I said to the boys, 'Put me up.' I got a one-handed steal. We put it out and won. It's something to tell the grandkids about. It meant so much to me to come back and play for Scotland and have such a big impact.

Dan Parks: It's a small shift psychologically, but the confidence was there after the win in Dublin and that result made a huge difference to the mindset of the squad. The biggest difference was in the first Test in Tucumán – we went behind but knew what we had to do to get back in front and we knew that we could do it and in the end it felt pretty comfortable, even if the scoreboard was pretty close. In the second Test, especially in the conditions, we showed great character, and the confidence in the squad was the best I'd ever known it. They were two very different games. The first match was played in dry conditions so both sides were able to throw the ball around a lot more while the second was played in heavy rain and was a real dog-fight, so it was good to know that we could win well in both sorts of conditions. It was a great way to finish the season and gave us good momentum going into the autumn – when both those different types of conditions came into play in big matches.

In November 2010 the All Blacks, the Springboks and Samoa filled the autumn Test schedule and after a disappointing – although perhaps predictable – mauling from the Kiwis, the Scots pulled off a famous victory over the World Cup holders South Africa, and backed it up with a win over Samoa in Aberdeen.

Richie Gray (Scotland 2010-2015, 52 Caps plus 1 Cap for the Lions): Having won my first three caps off the bench, it was a great moment to get selected in the starting team against New Zealand, but I was absolutely devastated at the end. I think the biggest shock was just that we felt very confident going into those games, and while losing by that margin [49-3] in any game is devastating it hurt more because of how that confidence was just . . . I don't know; it just didn't happen.

Rory Lawson: The loss to the All Blacks was a real knock to everyone's pride. No coach or player likes to be on the end of a result like that. But the beauty of the autumn Tests is that you get to focus your attention very quickly onto the next task in hand – which was pretty much as hard as you can get after the All Blacks, because we had South Africa up next, who were the reigning world champions.

Dan Parks: Although there was some embarrassment at the way we lost to New Zealand there was also a genuine belief we could beat South Africa the following week. We had to get back to basics and try to get more territory. That meant playing only when it was on to do so and getting the defence right.

Rory Lawson: The key for me was that extra yard, the willingness to work for that extra yard, whether it was beyond the tackle, off the line in defence or to fight for it with the ball. That was the most important thing to me. We went behind early and that's the last thing you want to do in a game like that, but Parksy got things all square again with a couple of penalties and then he pushed us ahead with two more.

The conditions had a massive part to play. As the game went on the conditions got worse and worse, and it became a game of trying to get territory and keeping our noses in front. It's fair to say that the forwards got a rocket through the week after the All Blacks game and they all knew that they were about to come up against one of the best packs in the world, so there was huge motivation. And, fair play to them, they worked incredibly hard. Obviously, Dan knocked over the goals, but so much work was done by the pack, they were awesome.

Richie Gray: The rain and Victor Matfield are the two big memories I have of that game, and coming off to cheers around Murrayfield – that was special. To get a win against the world champions and to be part of one of the very few Scotland teams who have beaten South Africa was very, very special. It was a brutal, bruising game, but I loved it. I'll never forget the feeling of that win.

Nathan Hines (Scotland 2000-2011, 77 Caps): Forward dominance is the Springboks' plan A, so you have to take that away from them and make them think outside the box, make them come out of their comfort zone. We did that by really getting in their faces. It wasn't as quick as the previous week against New Zealand, but it was more physical, and we helped ourselves by being more dominant in defence. I knew at half-time that we had to put the foot back on the gas to try and stop them getting into our half, and we did that pretty well. They scored at the end but that was through a bit of luck and it gave the scoreboard a tighter finish than we perhaps deserved because we played well and controlled things for most of the game.

Ross Ford: We knew it wasn't a day for fantastic rugby; rather it was about managing the conditions. We tried to play an open game the previous week but weren't at the races. Against South Africa we were a bit more clinical at the breakdowns and followed through with plans to meet their players toe-to-toe. We talked beforehand about not letting them go at us. All around the pitch we refused to let them get a foothold and when they attacked we defended very well and turned over a bit of possession. It was about getting into the right areas of the field and when the penalties came our way we knew we could rely on our goal-kicker.

Dan Parks: Sometimes if there is nothing on you just have to keep chipping away with drop goals, which I did. They weren't always the most pleasant strikes and some of the kicks looked pretty nasty, but it was all about keeping the scoreboard ticking and then kicking well for territory and off the tee when we won penalties. It all went well and to get a win against the Springboks was a real career highlight for everyone involved.

Richie Gray: The third Test that autumn was against Samoa in Aberdeen, which was a really cold, tough game and they really pushed us hard. Jacko [Ruaridh Jackson] came on late in the game and had a kick at the death to win it. He nailed it, in his home city, which was special too, and we all went crazy. It was a great couple of weeks.

In the spring of 2011, Scotland faced Wales, Italy and Ireland at home and England and France on the road before the preparations for the 2011 World Cup in New Zealand began in earnest. The 2011 Six Nations was disappointing, with Robinson's men only managing to record a single win over perennial wooden spoon rivals Italy, winning 21–8 at Murrayfield.

After that it was all eyes on New Zealand and the World Cup. With a summer of pre-tournament training under their belts, Scotland faced an intriguing pool containing England and Argentina as their main rivals for a quarter-final berth. They also had a proud record of having reached at least the quarter-final stage of every World Cup to date

Dan Parks successfully kicks one his goals en route to a famous win
for Scotland over South Africa.

to defend. On paper it all looked set-up for Scotland to challenge for the pool. They had a strong, experienced squad with a nucleus that had performed well in the 2007 World Cup. They were also presented with virtual warm-up matches for the key games with their first round fixtures against Romania and Georgia in Invercargill before playing Argentina in Wellington and England in Auckland. It was therefore expected that they would sweep aside both Romania and Georgia, but it did not prove so simple. After a high tempo start against Romania which saw Mike Blair score under the posts after just a few minutes, the team then laboured to a 34–24 victory before performing with a similar malaise, albeit in dreadful conditions, against Georgia, eventually winning 15–6.

Chris Cusiter: From a personal point of view, the pre-season for the World Cup wasn't enjoyable for me at all, to be honest. I was struggling with a calf injury which wouldn't go away and I wasn't able to participate in many of the group sessions. It was stressful having battled back from a bad knee injury which had kept me out almost the whole season only to pick up a calf strain picked up on the very first day back. I don't think I was the only one who found the whole pre-season slightly unenjoyable – it felt like we were getting flogged half the time; pre-season is tough no matter what, but if it's not enjoyable it just becomes a killer. Andy Robinson, who is one of the best rugby coaches I have worked with, for some reason took over some of the fitness drills. I think we were doing some drills he used to do at Bath when he was playing! Old school, to say the least.

Greig Laidlaw was on the scene by then and playing well and I was coming back from injury so I was pretty lucky to scrape into the squad. Andy put a bit of faith in me and put me in the squad which I was extremely grateful for, but I didn't actually play all that much.

Alastair Kellock: A World Cup in New Zealand is so special, and the amount of interest there is inside the country is hard to believe unless you witnessed it first-hand. Yes, there were ups and downs in terms of selection, but there are ups and downs with selection wherever you are. I took a lot from it – some of it was from the tough times, but most of it was from the good times.

We were in Invercargill to start with and the whole town took us on as their adopted country. The support was massive. I think we probably got a tough deal with some of the weather conditions. We played two of the biggest forward packs in the tournament – Romania and Georgia – in pretty wet conditions. Everybody looked at those games like we should win them and we did that. It might not have been as pretty as people would have liked but I think we played pretty good rugby in the circumstances. So it would have been nice to be a wee bit further up north.

Chris Cusiter: I remember being on the bench against Romania and coming on and it was a really tight game. We were losing until quite late on and then Simon Danielli got a couple of tries to salvage the win for us, which would have been a disaster if it had gone the other way. We were playing down in Invercargill and it was freezing cold, the weather was awful, and I remember thinking how unfair the way the pool was organised because England were playing their games in Dunedin under a roof, while we were playing in conditions that really leveled the playing field for the minnows. It was ridiculous that in a tournament where bonus points counted, England got to play in perfect indoor conditions and we had to slog it out on a heavy pitch in the wind and the rain.

We played Georgia in the pissing rain and they are stuffy team at the best of times, but the weather was a real leveler and we only just scraped past them as well. People gave us some abuse for our lack of attacking rugby, but you can't play attacking rugby in those kinds of conditions. But they were horrible, nervy games and we were pretty pleased to come through them, even though we weren't playing well. But we obviously didn't get anywhere near to scoring a try bonus point – although I really do think that was largely because of the conditions.

And so it was to Wellington for the first of the key games. Argentina were familiar opposition by now. The summer tours in 2008 and 2010 had followed the 2007 World Cup quarter-final clash and although the 2011 vintage weren't quite the dazzling Puma team that had finished third at the 2007 tournament, they remained a formidable opposition. For two teams that knew each other so well and also knew the importance of the result to their chances of making the knock-out stages (Argentina had, by this time, already lost to England in an earlier pool game), the match was predictably tight. At no-side the South Americans had sneaked the win 13-12 and Scotland faced a do-or-die match against England at Eden Park.

Chris Cusiter: We had the first of the must-win games, against Argentina in Wellington, in the rain again. Rory started that game at nine and Mike was on the bench, so I was watching from the stand, but we looked pretty comfortable out there for a lot of the game, but then they ran in an amazing try where half our backline seemed to just fall away from tackles. And we had a chance to nick it but Parksy was rushed into a drop-goal and he missed; it looked like Felipe Contepomi was miles off side when he charged at Parksy, but we didn't get a penalty from it, which would have won us the game. If we'd won it then we would have qualified for the quarter-finals and would have gone into the England game in a complete different state of mind.

Dan Parks: Contepomi was totally offside, but I wasn't actually calling for the ball. It just came to me quite suddenly, and I couldn't go off my right foot because there was too much pressure, and I don't know if I'd ever attempted a left-foot drop-goal in my life. Argentina got away with it that day; it's hard to look back on, but it's just one of those things.

For large swathes of this final pool match the contest was evenly contested and thanks to the boots of both Chris Paterson and Dan Parks, Scotland had pushed out to a 12–3 lead on

55 minutes. But Jonny Wilkinson pulled England back into contention with two penalties before, with just two minutes remaining on the clock, Chris Ashton darted down the wing to score in the corner and break Scottish hearts. Toby Flood's conversion made the final score 16–12. So it was that the class of 2011 became the first Scotland side to fail to emerge from the pool stages of the World Cup – albeit by the narrowest of margins.

Alastair Kellock: In the game itself we went out there and threw everything we possibly could at England, and we got very, very close. We made decisions in that game that we wouldn't have made if we were just going for the win, but we had to try and stop them getting a bonus point and chase one ourselves, so Parksy putting up an up-and-under towards the end of the game when we were already winning was not something you would generally do – it was a real Hail Mary play. Then we made mistakes defensively that allowed them to score, but we were working so hard to get the points we needed in attack sometimes something has to give.

Dan Parks: We had a chance against England where again we played very well for long periods, but there was quite a bit of pressure because we had to beat them by at least eight points. Scotland-England games around that time were always really close affairs and we hadn't beaten them by a margin like that for years. But the mathematics didn't matter at all in the end because Chris Ashton went over for a late score to win the game at the death. We got close but it wasn't to be.

Chris Cusiter: It was tough to take. It made us the first Scotland side not the qualify for the quarter-finals. Not a great first to be a part of.

Mike Blair: Obvioulsy it was hugely disappointing not to make the quarter-finals but I thought the fall-out from it was a bit over-the-top. We were in a pool with two teams ranked higher than us and although we pushed them both close, we performed exactly as the world rankings predicted we would. That's just where we were at the time.

Andy Robinson's time in charge of both England and Scotland was marred by an accusation that he was a great technical coach but a poor selector of teams; it was a charge that was also laid at his door following the World Cup exit after he had selected four different XVs in the pool matches. But for all that he drew the ire of pundits and fans alike for the make-up of his teams, he retained the loyalty and respect of his players throughout his tenure. This spectre of poor selections, however, reared its head once again in the spring of 2012 when he persuaded Dan Parks to postpone his planned retirement after the World Cup. Robinson felt that he needed Parks' experience going into the new campaign – only for the fly-half to suffer significant criticism in the opening match of the year, the 13-6 Calcutta Cup defeat at Murrayfield. Following the game and a storm of negative reactions, Parks did indeed retire, no doubt wishing he had never listened to Robinson's enticements to prolong his career.
A more spirited performance against France, albeit in a narrow loss, provided flashes of

hope for the Scottish public between defeats in Wales and Ireland, before the tournament came to a calamitous end in Rome with one of the most insipid performances delivered by the national team in many years.

Dan Parks: I had already made a big decision to leave Cardiff for Connacht at the end of that season and, to be honest, part of the deal was that I wouldn't be playing international rugby any more. Andy spoke to me and asked if I would make myself available for the first couple of games of the 2012 Six Nations. Any chance you get to play for Scotland, especially if you're needed, you obviously want to play, but I knew I was retiring from international rugby that year. I don't know if it affected my performance, but my head wasn't perhaps where it needed to be because I knew I was only back for a very short-term period. We were so much the better team against England, but I got charged down by Charlie Hodgson and they scored a try. I would have liked to finish on a more positive note, but it wasn't to be. That's life. I don't regret it, because it gave me another opportunity to play against England, and I honestly believed that we were going to win that match. I still to this day don't understand how we didn't. The highs and the lows are just part of the privilege of playing international rugby and I am just proud I had the chance to experience it.

Nick de Luca (Scotland 2008–2014, 43 Caps): We played well in patches in the 2012 Six Nations, but morale just began to seep away after the England game. I got sin-binned in Rome, and when I was watching from the side it just didn't look like the team and the boys I knew. It was weird because we'd gone into the Six Nations with such high hopes and it all just fell completely flat.

Remarkably, despite the disappointments of the Six Nations where they finished bottom of the log, the team then enjoyed another hugely successful summer tour, recording an historic southern hemisphere clean sweep: defeating Australia away for the first time since 1982 before overcoming the challenges of Fiji in Lautoka and Samoa in Apia.

Chris Cusiter: I remember the torrential rain coming down as we ran out of the tunnel into the stadium in Newcastle where we were playing Australia and Nick de Luca shouting, 'It's a sign boys, it's a sign!'

It was pretty cold that day. Nothing compared to a wet January day in Scotland, but cold. When I came on, Will Genia was visibly shivering as he was waiting to put the ball into a scrum. It felt OK to me.

Alastair Kellock: I remember standing for the national anthems and thinking this was the wettest I had ever been on a rugby field – and that was before the game kicked off. Because they don't generally see that much rain there the pitch held up to the moisture, so it wasn't like we would get in Scotland where you would be playing in six inches of mud – but it didn't make life much easier when you were trying to handle the ball.

Ross Ford didn't have his best days in the line-out – in fact, he'd probably tell you himself, that he had one of his worst! We were trying every trick in the book to win the ball – throwing it at waist height to the prop at the front, all that sort of stuff.

Greig Laidlaw (Scotland 2010-2015, 46 Caps): It was a nightmare night, pouring with rain, an icy wind blowing around the place. But there was actually some pretty decent running rugby from both sides – but that was partly because you couldn't kick very far if you were playing into the wind. It was nip and tuck all game, both teams slogging it out in horrendous conditions, and we just hung in there.

Chris Cusiter: We were going into the wind in the second half so to get any kind of field position was almost impossible. It was so wet and windy and so to try and run it out of your half you had to put loads of meaningful phases of play together to make any ground and it was so windy that to kick the ball was almost impossible. The only reason we got that field position we did at the end was because Rob Horne had tried to put up an up-and-under and it had gone seventy metres and rolled off the end of the pitch – so suddenly we had a scrum deep in their twenty-two, which was about the only bit of decent field position we'd had that entire half. Our scrum was going really well so suddenly we went from thinking, 'Can we hold on for a draw,' to, 'Wait a minute, we might actually be able to win this thing.'

I remember trying to put pressure on the referee to say that they'd dropped the scrum and he gave it. But that kick . . . Even though Greig is one of the best kickers around and it wasn't that far out, it was a huge kick to make with that wind and the pressure of the moment and what it meant. He had to strike it perfectly.

Greig Laidlaw: So we won the penalty and I suddenly realised, 'Jeez, I'm going to have to kick this to win the match.' It was probably the most-pressurised kick I've had to do in my career. I've got a bit of a draw when I hit my best kicks, so I always try to aim just

Grieg Laidlaw slots the winning kick against Australia in Newcastle in 2012.

inside the right post, no matter where I am. Stay nice and tall and make sure I follow-through. The wind was pretty much straight down the pitch towards us, so it was one of those kicks that you need to commit to one hundred per cent and kick through the wall. It wasn't very far out but with the weather conditions it was a tough one.

Joe Ansbro: When Greig hit that kick over we all just went crazy and rushed him in this great pile of bodies. Me and Stroker [Alasdair Strokosch] charged in from opposite sides and jumped up at the same time and clashed heads. I think that got as much replay time as Grieg's kick. Probably more – it became a bit of an internet sensation.

Chris Cusiter: The euphoria was just unbelievable. We'd been reading in the papers that week all about the fact that the last – and only – Scotland win in Australia had been in 1982, which was the year I was born, so we suddenly realised that we had just made history. Those are such special times. We'd done something incredible and were part of a great group of boys who all got on with each other, and we were away on the other side of the world; we went back to the hotel and everyone was there having drinks and celebrating and it was great, really, really great. That's what makes all the sacrifices and the work worthwhile.

Joe Ansbro: It was probably the first time I'd ever celebrated, like properly celebrated, a win. It meant so much. Without a shadow of a doubt, they underestimated what we were going to bring to the game. The weather certainly helped, kept the game nice and tight for us, and allowed us to strike in the last play.

Chris Cusiter: In Fiji it rained for the whole week when we were there. For the two days before the game it was torrential and everywhere was flooded. We were wondering if the game was going to go ahead and then some of the boys started getting ill. Max Evans and one or two other guys got some horrendous food poisoning and were really struggling. Then on the day of the game the rain cleared up and it ended up being ridiculously hot and humid. But we got the win, which was fantastic.

Alastair Kellock: Fiji and Samoa were two of the hardest games I ever played in. The conditions were just unbelievable. It was as hot as I had ever trained or played in (apart from maybe Romania), and humid as you had every trained or played in, and they'd just had their rains so the underfoot conditions were like Allan Glen's on a Tuesday night in January back in the bad old days.

Rob Harley (Scotland 2012-2015, 17 Caps): Samoa was the third game and one I'll always remember because I won my first cap – but what made it all the more special was that I scored the winning try.

Alastair Kellock: We probably should have done better in that game but we won it thanks to a Rob Harley try at the end, so it was an unbeaten tour, which is a great achievement – although we didn't play brilliant rugby. Sometimes things just line-up for you and momentum is on your side and you get results because you believe you are going to get a result. Maybe we don't feel like that enough in Scotland.

In the autumn, New Zealand and South Africa came to Murrayfield and Tonga travelled to Aberdeen. After being blown apart by the All Blacks and Springboks the Scots looked to salvage some pride against the Pacific Islanders in a city, and at a time of year, which has historically suited the home team more than the visitors. But Scotland were as appalling as Tonga were inspired and Kelly Brown's men fell to a 21-15 defeat. It was the death knell for Robinson's time as Scotland head coach; he resigned his position a few days later.

John Barclay: We beat Australia in the autumn of 2009, we beat Ireland away from home in 2010 and won our first Test series in the southern hemisphere against Argentina. We should have won a few more games than we did in the 2010 Six Nations and it was fantastic to beat South Africa and Samoa that autumn. The 2011 World Cup was disappointing, but we then had that fantastic summer tour in 2012 and went unbeaten, then it all went wrong again in the autumn, especially with that loss to Tonga in Aberdeen. The highs of lows of playing for Scotland really can be massive.

Greig Laidlaw: All credit to Tonga, but that was a disaster for us. They battered us. The lowest feeling ever. The worst. The changing room was mayhem, boys crying and people saying, 'Where do we go from here?' We knew we'd let down the jersey, let down the country. Andy [Robinson] said afterwards that a game like that is a coach killer. We'd come off the back of a good tour and maybe went into it thinking we'd already beaten Fiji and Samoa away so it won't be that hard a game and they caught us on the hop. It was unacceptable. Totally unacceptable. It's a horrible memory.

Alastair Kellock: It was a really sad end to the Andy Robinson era, not least because it wasn't his fault. There was maybe an accumulation of things which contributed to him deciding to step down, but you can't blame the coach for a performance like that.

I think he decided overnight and I knew pretty early in the morning. We had a team meeting and talked it through – and I don't think any of us were in any doubt that, ultimately, what we did on that park cost him his job. If you look at the bigger picture, there were maybe other things going on – but if you isolate it into the players' perspective, it was on our heads and that is a horrible feeling. I phoned him the next day to say sorry.

I believe he was very good for Scotland. He came from a no-excuse culture which he translated into the Scottish set-up. That is a very important legacy from his time up here. He was always clear that you had to work hard and operate at the standard expected of you, but the SRU also have to make sure that everything is in place whereby you can go out and perform to the best of your ability. I'm not sure that we had really properly embraced that idea in Scotland before Robbo came along.

TWENTY-FIVE

RETURNING TO THE TOP TABLE
2013-2015

2013 and 2014 saw another period of transition. Scott Johnson had been employed by Robinson as a skills and attack coach at the start of the 2012 season and took on the head coach role after the Englishman's abdication. Johnson in turn employed the services of former England international turned Sky TV analyst Dean Ryan on a short-term contract as his forwards coach for the 2013 Six Nations and the hurriedly assembled coaching team pulled a rabbit out of the hat in leading Scotland to third in the table – the highest finish they have enjoyed since occupying the same position in 2006 (although the 2013 team recorded just two wins to the 2006 team's three – and one of these was a daylight robbery one-point win over an otherwise dominant Ireland at Murrayfield).

Johnson came to Scotland with a mixed reputation as a popular skills coach but with mixed results as a head coach. After negotiations with the SRU following the 2013 Six Nations, it was revealed that he would remain as temporary caretaker coach and would, in time, move 'upstairs' to the SRU's Director of Rugby position, last occupied by Ian McGeechan in 2005. With the announcement of Vern Cotter as his long-term successor as head coach, a whole new controversy ignited when Cotter's employers, Clermont Auvergne (who had been unaware of the SRU's advances), blew a gasket and insisted that Cotter see out his contract to the summer of 2014. So Johnson remained in charge for the 2013 summer tournament in South Africa with the host nation, Samoa and Italy, the autumn Tests against Japan, South Africa and Australia and the 2014 Six Nations before handing over the reins to Cotter for the summer tour to north and south America and South Africa – and the road to the 2015 World Cup in England. Clearly, for a team that had struggled to string a series of victories together in the professional era, the foundations on which the team was trying to build consistency were manifestly unstable. But the players simply had to accept the coaching merry-go-round and get on with things.

Despite this instability and sense of uncertainty in the coaching structure, some of the attacking play during the 2013 Six Nations was exceptional. Against England in the opening game, Sean Maitland marked his debut with a try down the blind-side wing after some wonderfully ambitious attacking play, before a turnover on the Scotland line by Kelly Brown unleashed a counter-attack normally only seen by the classic French teams of the '80s and '90s. The ball went from Brown to Stuart Hogg to Ruaridh Jackson to Matt Scott, whose quick hands unleashed David Denton – and all this done behind the five metre line. Denton carried the ball just beyond the twenty-two and very nearly ended the move when he ignored supporting runners. But as he was felled by Mike Brown he popped the ball from the floor to Jackson, who showed the same dexterity as Scott had done just moments before to slip the pass wide to Maitland. Maitland found himself in space but was aware of the covering defence tracking across to close him down; he was also aware that he had Hogg

Opposite: Mark Bennett slides over to score against Australia in the 2015 World Cup quarter-final to take his side into the lead with just four minutes remaining on the clock.

on his inside, so carried the ball up field to the ten metre line and stabbed a grubber into space for his fullback to chase. Hogg put on the afterburners, showed fabulous footballing skills to hack the ball on and then beat the despairing cover of Toby Flood to score in the corner. It was to be voted try of the tournament.

The attacking intent was wonderful, but the defence was often stretched and the set-piece creaked under pressure from a dominant England eight. In the end, those were the margins that decided the fate of the match and England won 38-18, a scoreline that was more than a disservice to the Scottish efforts.

Mike Blair: I decided to retire shortly before the 2013 Six Nations. It was a hard decision to make, but it's one that I felt lucky that I was able to do. Every time I pulled on the Scotland jersey it was an incredible honour and a privilege.

There's a plaque in each players' cubicle in the Murrayfeild changing-room which bears the name of greats from the past who have previously worn the shirt. Seeing those great names, I was always reminded of something that Jim Telfer once said: that the jersey is never really yours; it belongs to the nation and to the history of the team . . . you are only ever borrowing it for a time.

I used to recreate David Sole's slow march of 1990 in my garden, used to hear Bill McLaren's voice commentating as I ran around with the ball. I think that when any player pulls on their international jersey, they wear it for their friends and family, for all the fans that support them around the world, for the great players that have worn it before them, for their school teachers and for their club coaches and so on; but they also wear it for that boy inside of them who has played a thousand games in his head, and for those who even now run around their gardens with a dream that they might one day wear that same jersey. For me, that was what playing for Scotland was all about. Forget all the lows. It was an amazing ten years; I lived a dream.

Jim Hamilton (Scotland 2006-2015, 63 Caps): After the England loss Dean Ryan dished out a pretty brutal analysis. There was no crisis meeting but he spoke to every forward and asked us to tell him what we felt our primary role was as an international player. None of us did our job properly against England so we had to strip it back and sort it out. Rugby is a simple game and if you don't do the basics right you won't win the game; there's no point looking pretty, running around and offloading if you don't get the win.

Against England, we were a bit off our game and they were very, very good – they played a completely different game to what we had trained for and what we expected. You have to give them credit, though: they won the contact area so well that we had to go away and have a good long look at ourselves.

The backs had impressed at Twickenham and they continued where they left off when Italy came to Murrayfield, tearing the Italian defence to shreds as they scored tries through Tim Visser, Matt Scott, Stuart Hogg and Sean Lamont in a 34-10 shellacking.

Stuart Hogg (Scotland 2012-2015, 38 Caps): I really enjoyed my try against Italy because it was another length of the field effort and had been a bit of a gamble. Italy had broken through and they had a two-on-one against me – and I decided to go for the intercept. It was a pretty big call and I could have made a complete mess of it if Luciano Orquera had thrown a dummy. It was a fourteen-pointer, as they say, because if it didn't come off then they would have scored under the sticks. Orquera had broken into space and I was set up pretty square against him, so it made sense for him to try and keep me fixed and then give the scoring pass to Tommaso Benvenuti. I had the option to either try and tackle Orquera man-and-ball to try and stop his pass, to slide onto Benvenuti but risk Orquera dummying and scoring himself, or to go for the intercept. Luckily it came off and eighty metres later I'd scored at the other end. It's a great moment when you back your instincts and your skills and things like that work out for you.

Greig Laidlaw: We played Ireland next and with the way we were playing we felt really good about our prospects. We wanted to win and we wanted to win the respect of the Irish boys as well. We'd probably not given them much reason to respect us in the recent past, so we wanted to change that. Unless you beat them you can't expect respect from them. It was a bit of a scrappy game; they went ahead after we let in a pretty soft try from Craig Gilroy, but we kept in amongst them and kept chipping away at the scoreboard. We showed some decent dog that day and hung in there and we managed to get our noses in front near the end and stayed there.

Jim Hamilton: It was a strange game, I think they had seventy-five per cent possession and I think we stole ten out of fourteen of their lineouts, which was obviously a huge base for them. Ireland are always very structured in what they do and rely on their set-piece a lot. But if you can counter that you set yourself on the road to beating them and that's exactly what happened in 2013.

Although the team continued to play in an expansive fashion in the next two fixtures, against Wales at Murrayfield and France in Paris, the defence was porous and small errors on the part of the Scots were ruthlessly taken advantage of by their opponents as Grieg Laidlaw's team lost both Test matches 28-18 and 23-16 respectively.

In the summer, the team travelled to South Africa for a quadrangular tournament featuring the Springboks, Samoa and Italy. The opening match was against Samoa in Durban, where preparations were hampered slightly – albeit in a positive way – when prop Ryan Grant received a call up to the Lions tour in Australia. The late change in the front-row could not be blamed for the result that followed, however, as the big-hitting South Sea Islanders overpowered the Scots to win 27-17.

The bruised squad then had to try to pick themselves up to face the might of the tournament hosts at Nelspruit, but they had picked up a number of key injuries in the squad and Kelly Brown, Pat McArthur and Geoff Cross were all forced to return home. The South African media had written off the challenge of Scott Johnson's side, but the match wasn't nearly as one-sided as it had been predicted, with Scotland sparkling in attack to score some sensational tries through Matt Scott and Alex Dunbar. The injury woes continued, however, as Scotland lost not one but two stand-offs during the course of the match, with Ruaridh Jackson and Peter Horne both sustaining serious knee injuries, and in the end the greater power and experience of the Springboks told as they secured a 30-17 victory to meet Samoa in the tournament title decider.

A bloodied Kelly Brown raises the Centenary Quaich after defeating Ireland in the Six Nations.

Matt Scott (Scotland 2012-2016, 33 Caps): The South Africa game in the summer of 2013 was a big turning point for me. Scott Johnson had given me a hard time all week after we lost to Samoa, and one day he took me to one side and said, 'Look, you've got thirteen caps now, you're not new any more. If you don't start growing up and acting like a player with thirteen caps, one who can boss the game and start believing that you are good enough to be here, then we're going to pick someone else.'

It was a huge kick up the arse, but he was right; subconsciously I was still immature, still not being loud or assertive enough. Against Samoa I'd been too chilled, but before the South Africa game I wrote loads of notes and distilled them into five or six key points which I kept reading over and over. In the warm up I was very focused and animated, much louder and more vocal than usual.

I was so motivated and pumped – although getting up for that game was easy as the South African media spent the week speculating on whether we could keep the margin of victory to less than 50 points – and I had a very good game against Jean de Villiers, one of the best centres in the world. The way I played gave me a big confidence boost; I felt a genuine change inside of me, and I often reference that game in my own mind.

Tom Heathcote was installed in the pivot-role as the team, virtually held together by medical tape, took to the field in Pretoria to face Italy. The match couldn't have got off to a worse start as Leonardo Sarto crossed for a converted try after just two minutes – but Matt Scott soon made amends by scoring a delightful try a few minutes later, converted by Greig

Laidlaw. It was a pattern that was to repeat itself throughout the match, with both sides edging ahead at various times without ever breaking free of the other. As the game closed out and crept into stoppage time, Italy were six points to the good.

Scotland attacked inside the opposition twenty-two and the Azzurri defensive line looked solid, yet a simple one-out pass to Alasdair Strokosch saw the blindside flank trundle past the despairing tackle of prop Lorenzo Cittadini with barely a finger laid on him to score beside the posts. Laidlaw's conversion saw the Scots steal the game 30-29.

Scott Johnson (Scotland head coach 2012-13): Going into the autumn the squad was suddenly a lot more competitive. We blooded a lot of players during the summer, ten new caps, and then a new crop of younger players were coming through from their clubs – Alex Dunbar was playing great footie with Glasgow, Mark Bennett's form was superb, and Jonny Gray was coming through. Seeing that happen was an important step for the growth of the team. The older guys were getting pushed, but the younger guys also knew that if they played well we would show faith in them and give them a shot.

Alex Dunbar didn't play well in the first Test against Samoa – by his own admission, and mine! But he came of age against South Africa, against formidable opposition, and he went on to prove over the following year just what a class player he is.

Alex Dunbar (Scotland 2013-2015, 14 Caps): I asked my grandpa to build some rugby posts for me when I was little. I grew up on a farm and I wasn't the type for staying inside and watching TV. I was playing outside at every opportunity and used to love spending hours outside with a ball pretending I was playing for Scotland. It was an extraordinary moment when you actually fulfil those childhood dreams and do it for real.

I was a bit disappointed with how I played against Samoa on that tour, but played much better against the Springboks and it was great to get on the scoresheet, dotting down in the corner. Again, it was disappointing to lose, but we were beginning to show the kind of attacking ability that we had and would go on the show over the next few seasons.

Scott Johnson: We went into the autumn Tests that year with a lot of new guys pushing for inclusion and that was great. It was an interesting set of fixtures – we played Japan, who were really starting to take their rugby seriously. They have a professional league that has a lot of money invested in it and they have a large number of very high-quality foreign players plying their trade in it, plus they had great coaches in charge of them – as they showed at the 2015 World Cup – and they have the World Cup there in 2019. We knew we had them in our group in the 2015 World Cup, so it was important to put down a marker against them, while also seeing what kind of things they had in their armoury. They were fast, played some adventurous rugby and scored some decent tries against us, a couple of wonderful tries – even if the final score was a pretty healthy 42-17.

Since the scare we gave South Africa over in Nelspruit, their form had been superb

– a combination of brute force and a bit more flare than we're sometimes used to seeing from them. And then Australia were coming in on the back of a disappointing Lions tour and a change of coach, but we knew how much potency they had in attack.

Ruaridh Jackson (Scotland 2010-2015, 27 Caps): South Africa did what they do best – they smashed us pretty hard in the contact and when we gave them a couple of chances they took them, while we had a few chances and didn't manage to do anything with them.

David Denton: It was immensely physical against South Africa, as it always is – and that's really where I think we lost the game, in the first-half set-piece and around the contact area. It's no surprise that was how they were going to play, but it's one thing knowing it and another to successfully do something about it. We managed it before when we beat them in 2010, and we've run them close a few times over the years, but they are one of the world's top sides and very few teams can live with them when they get into their patterns of play and are as destructive as they are capable of being.

Greig Laidlaw: The following week against Australia was also pretty disappointing, having beaten them on the previous two occasions. We put a lot of energy into the game, but came up short. Quade Cooper put Israel Folau through for a pretty soft score and that was really the different between us. We struggled a bit on our lineout ball and I think if we had done better there then we would have caused them all sorts of difficulties and the result could have been different.

Jim Hamilton: We played significantly better than we did against South Africa and got ourselves into a position with a lineout to win the game with five minutes to go – and we lost the lineout. It's agony when it comes down to stuff like that, when it's a case of just not being clinical enough and not controlling the controllables, like winning your own lineout ball.

Another Six Nations loomed. Almost inevitably, another disappointing campaign awaited. It wouldn't be Scotland's worst, but once again they were just bit-part players and were out of the running for the title early on. As the saying goes, you can't win the tournament in the first week, but you can sure as hell lose it.

The opening fixture against eventual champions, Ireland, in Dublin saw the visitors show great intent but very little attacking verve, and their inability to trouble the scoreboard allowed Ireland to get into their stride. Once the hosts had a hold on the game, they didn't let go, and finished the match comfortable 28-6 winners.

If the attack had seemed a little tepid in Dublin, it was to sink to new depths of toothlessness for the Calcutta Cup. With the Murrayfield pitch infested with nematode worms that destroyed the turf's basic structure, a hugely underwhelming performance was played out on a quagmire that was unfit for Test match rugby. Both sides were awful on the day; England were just slightly less so, and thanks to a couple of small sparks of creativity, they were able to get tries on the board through Luther Burrell and Mike Brown before trudging to a dismal 20-0 victory.

The trip to Rome was now a certain wooden spoon decider. In the warm spring sunshine, Scotland at last unleashed some attacking brilliance through the hugely impressive Alex Dunbar, who scored two sensational tries. Matt Scott, Stuart Hogg and Sean Maitland also contributed to a fine backline display and it seemed extraordinary that Italy had found a way to edge ahead on the scoreboard as the final seconds of the match closed in. Duncan Weir rescued the game however, with a sweetly taken drop-goal at the death, to edge the game 21-20.

David Denton: It was a complete rollercoaster. After the first game against Ireland we didn't feel that bad. Maybe it looked different from the outside but we thought we'd played some pretty decent rugby. We were unlucky with a few calls and the bounce of the ball didn't favour us. We came out of that one with a bit of positivity.

But the England game was devastating. I can't tell you what it feels like to play in a Scotland-England match, how excited you get before it, the incredible atmosphere. Everything's amplified against England; so many more people watch that one. And to know you've disappointed all of them – it's really tough to handle. We were never in that one, never looked like scoring, never threatened their line. But credit to England: they got right in our faces.

I was devastated when I was dropped for the Italy game. I sulked but I knew that if I was going to win my place back I couldn't be anything less than my best coming off the bench. Alan Solomons [the Edinburgh head coach] gave me good advice: 'Don't try to be a world-beater. Don't try and fit eighty minutes into your twenty. You'll only give away penalties.' I think I did my bit in the lead-up to the penalties we got and Duncy's [Duncan Weir's] drop-goal.

With a spring in their step, the team travelled back to Edinburgh to welcome France. There was genuine hope that the side could claim their first victory over Les Bleus since 2006 and the signs looked promising as Stuart Hogg created a try from nothing for himself after launching a towering up-and-under into the French in-goal area before reclaiming it to dot down. Tommy Seymour got in on the act shortly afterwards, but the French struck back through wing Yoann Huget and in the end the superior goal kicking of scrum-half Maxime Machenaud decided matters as the French nudged their way to 19-17 victory.

David Denton: The France game was so tough. We were in complete control. Even when France got that intercept and led by a couple of points, I wasn't worried because we had a stranglehold. Maybe we showed naivety not closing up the game but we were still unlucky. We definitely deserved to win that game.

And so to Wales for the final match. A record win for one side, a record defeat for the other and a red card that overshadowed the whole proceeding. Stuart Hogg was the villain of the piece when he was dismissed on the twenty-third minute after jumping clumsily into the path of Dan Biggar, the Wales fly-half, and clattering him in the face with his shoulder. Jérôme Garcès showed him a yellow card and then, upon review of the television replays, changed it to red. Scott Johnson, strangely, did not decide to substitute one of his forwards for an outside back, despite having a ready-made fullback replacement in Jack Cuthbert on the bench, and thus he left his backline exposed for the remainder of the game. With captain, Kelly Brown, already off with a concussion injury when Hogg was sent off, Johnson didn't feel that he could risk removing another forward to make up the numbers in the back division. And the Welsh took full advantage, running rampant as they scored seven tries in a chastening 51-3 victory.

Greig Laidlaw: The final match was a humiliation. Hoggy got sent off early on for a late shoulder charge on Dan Biggar and they hammered us.

Alasdair Strokosch: We got humiliated and we had them swan diving over the line and singing to each other at the after-match meal. It was a big insult, a big slap in the face. Anything that could have gone wrong did go wrong. You look back and a lot of people blamed Hoggy for that defeat, but one player going off is not an excuse to lose fifty points. It's a bit harder playing with fourteen, but it's not fifty points harder. It's the worst defeat we've ever had against Wales. The manner in which we folded over . . . The team didn't do itself or the jersey justice. It was an embarrassing display to be a part of. It's tough to describe. You're angry, upset, gutted, disappointed at the same time. But you just have to try and pick yourself up and move on; consign it to the history book. As painful as it remains in your memory.

Stuart Hogg: I'm a really passionate player and all I want to do is win. I found myself really frustrated with the kick I tried to execute which Biggar caught and I just had a moment of madness. I've never been a dirty player by any means and so it was really disappointing to find myself in that situation.

It's hard to put into words the feelings that whole incident caused. It was the lowest point of my career – I let a lot of people down.

In the twelve months before Vern Cotter officially took up the reigns with Scotland he could be seen from time to time stalking around Murrayfield, observing training and talking to players and coaches – but he did not take up a hands-on role until the squad gathered in advance of the 2014 summer tour. That tour would prove to be something of a baptism of fire as the squad was faced with an extraordinary schedule that would see them play Test matches in four countries – against the USA, Canada, Argentina and South Africa. And with the final game falling outside the IRB window for summer Test matches, any players based outside Scotland were forced to return home to their clubs.

Cotter and his coaching staff decided to name two separate touring squads (with one or two players crossing over between them) in order to reduce the impact of thousands of miles of travel and the risk of injury and fatigue.In light of the circumstances, Scotland did remarkably well to record three wins out of the four fixtures, with the only defeat coming, rather inevitably, at the hands of the Springboks in the final game. A number of replacements were flown out to join the squad, but the headline-maker among these was twenty-year-old Adam Ashe, who was flown in from New Zealand where he was playing club rugby as part of the Macphail Scholarship. He was parachuted into the starting Test team – without ever having started a match for his pro side at home, Glasgow.

Action from the match at Port Elizabeth. From left to right: Stuart Hogg, JP Pietersen, Handre Pollard, Nick de Luca, Peter Horne and Fourie du Preez.

Adam Ashe (Scotland 2014-2015, 6 Caps to date): I was in New Zealand on the Macphail Scholarship, being mentored by Reuben Thorne and playing club rugby, when I got a text from Duncan Weir. It just said, 'There's a rumour you're coming across to South Africa.' Then the next day I got an email from Gregor Townsend and I was off the next day. It was surreal – one minute I was lodging with a family in Christchurch and had only had two competitive games for Glasgow, both off the bench, and the next I'm playing against South Africa against two of my idols in Duane Vermeulen and Schalk Burger. We got smashed 55-6, but it was an incredible experience.

It proved to be an important summer for Scottish rugby. As well as recording morale-boosting wins over the USA, Canada and Argentina, the tour gave valuable game time to a number of emerging players, in particular to rising star Finn Russell at stand-off, who had been playing club rugby for Ayr just a season earlier, as well as Adam Ashe, Jonny Gray and Mark Bennett. Back in Scotland, Glasgow were hosting the Commonwealth Games and the SRU released some of the fifteen-aside stars to play for the abbreviated team at Ibrox. Among these were Bennett and Stuart Hogg, who had drifted into the wilderness at Glasgow after a fall-off in form following his return from the 2013 Lions tour to Australia and the ban that followed his red card in Wales; the Games would prove inspirational to the players and a catalyst for Hogg to rediscover his world class form – and played a vital role in spreading the rugby gospel to new audiences around the country.

Stuart Hogg: I got a three match ban and then I struggled to get back into the Glasgow team. I think I played something like a hundred minutes for the rest of season. And so I was really fortunate to be selected for the summer tour – but I think the summer tour and the chance to play in the sevens at the Commonwealth Games really helped me to find a love of the game again.

Matt Scott: Vern's an interesting guy and I was really looking forward to working with him when his signing was announced. He's not really a prescriptive coach. He doesn't play rugby by numbers. He gives you a structure and expects you to do your homework – to analyse how we should be playing and things like that. We've definitely got a bit more leeway, I think. Also he just says, 'Don't be afraid to make mistakes and try things,' which I think is an important philosophy. Even from coaching kids, that should be the philosophy – don't be scared to try things. Sometimes in professional rugby you can get caught up in playing with a lot of structure and playing safe, a lot of kicking, things like that. Obviously, there's a time and a place for that, but the way Scotland play best is utilising our skills in a fast-paced offloading game. Vern has been good at highlighting that. There's obviously a balance. You don't want to be flinging miracle passes on your own line. If there's a logical reason for what you've done, a grubber kick or a crossfield kick and you can say, 'I saw a winger come up or the fullback was not going to get across and I saw space in behind,' and you kick it out on the full – if reasoning is something logical like that, you should reward players.

Gordon Reid (Scotland 2014-2015, 15 Caps): Vern is the quiet assassin. When he comes into a room and has something to say, everybody else shuts up. He doesn't blabber on. Some guys just say stuff for the sake of being heard and some other guys will always have something to say. He isn't like that. He lets you get on with it in training, but if you have missed a tackle, oh boy will he let you know about it. He is definitely a one-off.

Rob Harley: Vern's attention to detail is forensic and the emphasis is very much on making sure that every rep is as close to perfect as possible, from measuring our power and depth in the gym to every lift we do at lineout practice. There was also a lot of emphasis on improving your skill-set and decision making in open play. Vern is very strong on playing what is in front of you and placing the onus on all the players to read the defence and pass or carry depending on the situation.

Finn Russell (Scotland 2014-2015, 15 Caps): Before I signed for Glasgow, I was awarded the Macpahil Scholarship alongside Sam Hidalgo-Clyne and we spent a few months out in New Zealand. It was a great thing for me; it challenges you in all sorts of ways. You're away from home, on the other side of the world, and it's a completely different environment than you're used to. I was playing for Lincoln University and it was brilliant to get to train with all these great players and every week you've got boys coming back from the Crusaders' Super Rugby set-up or the Canterbury province team to play with you and against you, so the standard is really high and you have to adapt to that quickly.

I came back from New Zealand and didn't really play for Glasgow, I was mainly playing for Ayr at the time, but managed to get into the Glasgow team during the Six Nations. I then went back to Ayr for one game and was then with Glasgow for the rest of the season. I got a phone call two weeks before the summer tour to say I was selected to go and because it came so quickly and everything was still such a whirlwind playing for Glasgow, I didn't really know what to think or how to react. I didn't get time for it to sink in because although there were a couple of weeks before we left, we had the semi-final and then final of the Pro12 to play with Glasgow, so that took up all my focus.

We played the Pro12 final and then flew out at four or five the next morning to America for the summer tour, had about five days prep for the game and then played against the USA on the Saturday and did the same the following week for Canada. And to be honest, I really didn't have any time to think about it at all, that I'd achieved my childhood dream of playing for Scotland. I think, even now, I've never really had a chance to think about it and let it sink in – winning my first cap, playing at Murrayfield, playing the Six Nations, playing in a World Cup, any of it. I think when people ask what it was like winning my first cap, I'm like, 'Oh, it was good,' but I kind of missed the emotional build up to it because it happened so fast.

In the autumn, Scotland welcomed Argentina and New Zealand to the newly named BT Murrayfield, and Tonga to Rugby Park in Kilmarnock for the first-ever Test match to be played on a purely synthetic surface.

All three matches contained impressive performances from Scotland, with Argentina dispatched 41-31 with the hosts scoring five tries, the All Blacks pushed all the way before they scored a late try through Jeremy Trush to win 24-16, and Tonga were defeated 37-12 to avenge the loss in 2012.

Finn Russell: Making my debut at Murrayfield really sticks in my memory because that's what you imagine doing when you're growing up, playing at Murrayfield rather than out in the America on a summer tour. I came back from a shoulder injury just before the Argentina game, played a couple of Pro12 games for Glasgow and a couple of European games – which I'd not done before, either – and then we were into the autumn Tests. I'd played at Murrayfield once before in an under-18s match, but this was a bit different – it's quite a surreal experience: 60,000 people, under the floodlights, the pipe band, the whole thing. We played really well and beat a top quality side. It was good fun. I had a wee dance at the end when I came off.

Greig Laidlaw: It was an honour to be handed the captaincy for the autumn Tests. Vern wanted Gilco [Grant Gilchrist, who had captained Scotland in the summer but was injured for the 2014-15 season playing for Edinburgh]. Injuries happen, but I got the opportunity and because of that, the Gray brothers had their chance to play together and they were fantastic.

Jonny Gray (Scotland 2013-2015, 19 Caps): Richie is five years older than me but when we were growing up we were always competing with each other. It was great for me to see him progress through the ranks and do really well. He was always telling me stories about how much he was enjoying it, so from an early age I always wanted to be like Rich: he really inspired me, got me hooked.

Rich is quite chilled but when it comes to rugby he's really switched on, so I got to see first-hand his work-rate, how hard he had to work. All of the extras he did – extra fitness, extra weights and a tailored diet – showed me how hard you had to work to get there. I saw the rewards too. Just seeing Richie playing age group for Scotland was massive. I remember watching him on TV at the U20 World Championship, and I was really proud. I remember the whole family sitting down and everyone getting pretty emotional. If that doesn't inspire you, what will?

Richie Gray: I'd never played serious rugby with Jonny before we made it into the Scotland set-up together. I always looked at him as my little brother, but then I started training with him and I saw him put in a hit or use some sleight of hand and I thought, 'This kid can play. I'd better buck up my ideas here!' So it was great having him around in the Scotland set-up and seeing him do so well.

Jonny Gray: It's hard to put into words what it was like to find out I would be playing alongside my brother against Argentina. It was so special – to be named in the team next to Rich was something I never thought would happen. People never believe me when I say this to them, but I never expected to rise to this level. When my brother started making it, people kept saying to me, 'Oh, you'll be up there with him one day,' and I just laughed it off. I just thought that people were being nice.

At the match it was pretty emotional, there was so much going through my head. To be playing for your country is incredible, but to stand there next to my brother made it that bit more special. Singing the anthem next to him for the first time is something I'll never forget. And to both get on the scoresheet in that match was a pretty special follow-up – and then to win as well as we did and to have a such a great team performance, was terrific.

Greig Laidlaw: The first game against Argentina was great. They'd just come off the back of the Rugby Championship and had won their last game against Australia, so they were going well. We were playing our first game since the hammering from South Africa on the summer tour, so we were in pretty different places – but we ran them ragged, played some great rugby, scored five tries. We got a bit lax at the end and they scored some soft late tries, which was a bit annoying, but on the whole the performance was very pleasing.

Jonny Gray: Each of those autumn games was very different, and I learnt a lot from them, tactically. To play against the All Blacks, the best team in the world, was very humbling – a great experience. To face the hakas from Tonga and New Zealand was amazing because you've thought about it loads before, so I just tried to absorb it all and

Brothers in arms: Jonny Gray and Richie Gray in action at a lineout during the New Zealand Test match (with Rob Harley, far left).

remember every sensation and feeling. When we were young Rich and I would watch the All Blacks do it on TV, turn it up full blast and scream along. So to be facing it was an experience that's etched in my mind.

Finn Russell: We had a guy come in to talk to us who had done a walk to the North Pole and he spoke about taking time to remember things about these occasions – like the first step he took and various things along the way – because when you're in that environment, like playing a Test match, it can go in a blur and you can sometimes remember very little about it. So I try to be aware of the occasion and to consciously remember bits and pieces from it; but at the same time, you don't want to be doing that all the time. Test matches are huge occasions, but you can't focus on that too much. You have to also try and treat it like any other game.

I think the only time I really found it a bit weird, but probably without realising it, was when we played New Zealand. I'd obviously been out there just a year earlier, so I was going from playing club rugby down there to facing the All Blacks. Dominic Bird was playing for them that day and we'd played together, so that was pretty cool. But I remember warming up and seeing them come out and it was a weird feeling seeing all these guys who I'd been watching for years on TV. My mate Bob Wyllie was in the

crowd and although I thought I was warming up normally Bob said that when Dan
Carter was warming up I kept looking over at him, same with Sonny Bill Williams,
Julian Savea, Richie McCaw . . . it's funny, I totally didn't realise I was doing it.

Greig Laidlaw: As a country we've been playing New Zealand for over a century and
never beaten them in a full Test. A couple of draws is as close as we've got. So every time
you play them you know you have a chance to make history. We started off really well
and went up early when Tommy Seymour grabbed an intercept and scored.

Tommy Seymour (Scotland 2013-2015, 22 Caps): Yeah, I was pleased with that. I
got an intercept the week before against Argentina and I could see it coming again.
The All Blacks love to tip the ball on and I could see that Richie McCaw would try and
ship it wide quickly – which he did and I was there to grab it. There's no doubt that
it was a great feeling to score and to get us back in the game, but the disappointment
is huge that we didn't complete the job.

Greig Laidlaw: The All Blacks are just a class act, you know. They just know how to
hit you back, keep in the game, and find a way to win. It was pretty agonising, to be
honest. They pushed ahead and then went over for a late score and the history books
remain untroubled. 24-16. It was a tough one, that. Very disappointing.

Finn Russell: We all knew that we'd never beaten the All Blacks before and an hour
into the game and we're still in it . . . you don't think about the history and because it's
the All Blacks you don't get ahead of yourself, but I think we'd all be lying if we didn't
think we were maybe going to do something special. I got subbed off with around
twenty minutes to go and sitting on the sidelines is the worst because there's nothing
you can do to alter what's going on. And then it was a kind of typical All Blacks thing,
they took their chances when they came and were just so accurate and composed
when it mattered. We had a penalty and missed it; they had a penalty and got it and
then not long afterwards scored the try that sealed the game.

Stuart Hogg: We got a good run-out afterwards at Rugby Park in Kilmarnock against
Tonga. Played well on a fast track; it was good fun. We scored some decent tries and
finished the series strongly. It was disappointing that we didn't make a bit of history
by beating New Zealand, but it was a good autumn and we were showing what we
could do as an attacking team. We had scoring threats all over the park.

Greig Laidlaw: After the positive performances in the autumn, it was the reverse in
the Six Nations. We played well, but very much felt that luck was against us. Each of
those losses to France, Wales and Italy were incredibly tight. In any other competition,
that would have been three bonus point losses. And we were in a position to win each
of those games – just as we had been against the All Blacks in November. So it was

painfully disappointing. Even the England game – it started off pretty badly but we recovered and were right in it. It was a case of so close yet so far. With the exception of the Ireland game, it was one of the best whitewashes ever, you could say.

After an industrious showing in Paris that had been filled with vim and attacking sparkle but which had ended in a narrow 15-8 defeat, Scotland came out all guns blazing against Wales at Murrayfield in round two. Stuart Hogg put the hosts 7-3 ahead after an excellent turnover from Finn Russell released him down the blind-side wing; Wales chipped away at the lead through Leigh Halfpenny, but the real momentum swing in the game occurred when Wales fly-half Dan Biggar sent a Garryowen high into the bright spring sky. Russell ran forward to collect the kick but was beaten to it by Biggar, who jumped as he went to regather; the Scotland ten tried to pull out of the challenge when he realised that Biggar was going to make it to the ball first, but couldn't avoid a collision that sent the Welsh fly-half spinning to the ground. Referee Glen Jackson had little choice but to issue a yellow card and it took Wales just a few minutes to make the numerical advantage count, as scrum-half Rhys Webb crossed for a try. Momentum – and tries – swung back and forth throughout the match and Scotland were agonisingly unlucky to have Mark Bennett's late effort disallowed for an apparent knock-on. In the final minutes Jim Hamilton muscled his way over, and Russell's conversion took the score to 26-23 in Wales' favour. There was still time on the clock for the restart, but Jackson inexplicably blew his whistle to conclude events, much to the surprise of all thirty players on the field.

Sean Lamont (Scotland 2004-2015, 101 Caps): The high ball is a highly effective weapon. Biggar is good at it and got his rewards that day; he shows how good he is at it all the time with the Ospreys and he did it again at the World Cup. When he did it against us, not only did he win the ball but we ended up with a man in the bin for ten minutes. So when you are good at it, it's definitely a great tactic. There is nothing worse when you are standing under a ball that's dropping on you and you know you can't get any more than a standing jump. If you are facing someone running at pace, you know they are going to out-climb you. It's physics. If you're throwing yourself up at a ball, and you're going above and putting your centre of gravity above someone, then yes, you can topple over with somebody just standing under. It's got to work both ways. I think the law was brought in to protect the receiving player, somebody jumping into someone, but it's become such a good weapon, the attacking kick, that people can throw themselves up and make it a 50-50 ball.

Finn Russell: It was a bit disappointing but these things happen and it's all about how you put it behind you and move on. There wasn't much I could do about it, any of it, the incident itself and then what happened afterwards. The citing pannel decided to upgrade my yellow to a red card, which meant that I missed the Italy game. We gave it a crack in the hearing but they didn't see it the way we saw it. They've changed the rules now so it wouldn't be a red; but in many ways that makes it even more annoying.

Chris Cusiter: It was a tough one for Finn because there was obviously no malice. It seems anyone who goes to contest in the air and the other guy ends up hurt, it is a yellow or red card. It's a complicated issue. It could have been worse for Finn, he could have been given a red but it was costly because Wales scored when he was off. But for me, it's a really tough decision to say he did the wrong thing there.

Jim Hamilton: When the citing panel upgraded his card to a red, it meant that we had to change things around pretty late in the day before the Italy game and Pete Horne came in at stand-off.

Peter Horne (Scotland 2013-2015, 15 Caps): It was the proudest moment of my life belting out the national anthem before the Italy game and a huge moment for me to be the playmaker for that match. It was a tough game, the lead kept changing hands and finally we were ahead going into the last few minutes. We had a series of scrums on our line and then the forwards won a penalty and that looked as if that was game won.

My legs were feeling pretty sore by that stage and I just didn't kick the ball very well. Regardless of the fact that I had cramp in my calves – which is something I have been guilty of for years and I have tried everything to fix it – I just didn't get it right. It looks like I was going for length but that wasn't the case at all, I just didn't want the line-out on our own five yard line. In reflection I should have just dinked it twenty metres and got the line-out. Anyway, I miss-hit it and two minutes later, the Italian forward pack mauled the ball over the line and scored and we lost the game.

It was devastating and every time I think about it I still cringe. I had my whole family there that day, I was so proud of my first game at Murrayfield, played stand-off and felt I did pretty well – and then that happened. All I can do is put my hand up and accept that I got it wrong. I was dropped after that game. Vern spoke to me afterwards and just told me to go away and knuckle down with Glasgow and learn from the experience. At the time I worried that I would never play for Scotland again, but then you have to recognise that one bad kick didn't make me a bad player.

The game should have been out of sight by that point and even after I missed touch we could have got out of jail. As Rob Harley pointed out afterwards, we made the tackle on the halfway line so they had a long way to come to get that penalty try. I'm not trying to pass the buck, but there should be some perspective.

Finn Russell: It's funny to look back on how the mood in the squad changed over the course of the Six Nations. We had gone to France really confident that we could get the win, played well but just lost. At that stage we were all kind of like, 'That was disappointing, but there are still four games to go.' Then we played Wales and I got yellow carded and we just lost the game. So we went into the Italy game and thought, 'Well, if we win this we can get back on track.' We lost that and the pressure started to build without us really noticing. When we went into the Ireland game the pressure was on us not to get the Wooden Spoon and I think that's what led to us getting beaten so badly – we froze under the pressure, we went into our shells because we were so worried that whatever we might try might go wrong and we would lose. It was the wrong attitude to have, but it was one that just kind of crept up on us over the tournament because we were playing well but losing narrowly, we just couldn't quite grind out the win. If we'd gone out against Ireland with a view that we had nothing to lose, then I think we would have played differently.

Jim Hamilton: On paper, it didn't look like we did too well in the Six Nations as we didn't win a game, but I think it is fair to say that we were definitely showing that we were on the up. We had some fantastic players coming through. Jonny Gray was just twenty-one midway through the tournament. Adam Ashe, Hoggy, Finn, Fraser Brown, the centres [Alex Dunbar, Matt Scott and Mark Bennett]. We all knew were building an unbelievably good squad of players and playing some great stuff, even if we weren't getting the results.

Look at the England game that followed that tough loss to Italy – we were swamped by them early on, conceding a converted try in the first four minutes and then a penalty, so to turn things around to be winning 13-10 at half-time just showed the maturity that was developing in the squad. We were scoring some really exciting tries, some of them were fantastic.

We knew it was just about tying everything together. Against Italy, we struggled in the maul. Against England, we dominated the lineout and dominated all the scrums bar the first. Tying everything together was the next thing to do. It's not that we were not scoring tries. It's not that we were getting bullied up front, which we have been in the past. We had all the tools and had some unbelievable players coming through. That's something that I hadn't seen in the past as much as I was seeing then.

Vern was the best coach I ever worked with. We all felt that once we got everyone back fit and with the guys coming through, we were definitely going to be in a good place. The Ireland game at the end of the Six Nations was hugely disappoitning, but then we showed enormous improvements between that game and the World Cup warm-up in Dublin a few months later. Then we went out to Turin and didn't play fantastically, but got the win over a decent Italian side.

Ross Ford: The Six Nations hurt my pride. I was pissed off that we hadn't performed as we should and I knew that we all needed to knuckle down in the build up to the World Cup to do something about it.

We'd been saying the same thing for years. We'd play really good stuff and have sides in all sorts of trouble, but then we wouldn't build on it. We'd shoot ourselves in the foot. People see the final scoreline and after a while some of them forget about the little moments that were critical, the tiny mistakes we made at the wrong time that cost us.

We live with those moments. People see the end product and get frustrated because we're not winning enough and they're absolutely right to feel that way, but they don't see the hard work that goes into it behind the scenes and how frustrating it is for us as players. I've been around for over ten years. I've never had a good run in the Six Nations when we've threatened to win something – a Triple Crown or a Championship. I've not had a sniff of silverwear of any kind. Haven't had it.

What was incredibly frustrating was that we had beaten a lot of the top teams. South Africa, Australia a couple of times, England, Wales, Ireland, smashed Argentina. But we never backed it up. We know we can do it against the biggest teams because we've done it, but we just haven't done it nearly enough. We'd have a decent performance and then we let ourselves down. It's maddening.

The fans deserve something they can get their teeth into. When you think about it, 1999 was when we won our last Championship and none of our players were around back then. The supporters have always been great regardless of how we've struggled. They turn up in big numbers to watch Scotland and it's not like they're coming and expecting a win as is the case for other teams. Do you know what, I wish they could know what it's like for us to hear them as we run out into the pitch. It's immense. Knowing that a whole stadium and a whole country are behind you is a very powerful thing, but it makes the sense of frustration all the greater when we don't deliver the victories that we all want.

Geoff Cross: When you look back, you could ask, 'What is there to say about getting whitewashed in the Six Nations?' On paper, nothing much – zero from five games. But there's always more to it than that. Apart from the Ireland game, they were all close-fought things. The challenge for us as players after a tournament like that is execution as much as anything else. There's no secret to why we lost those games – it was dropped balls, penalties, inaccuracies in the contact area, all of that. But we also knew that we had one of the most exciting attacks that Scotland had had for years. The job then was to focus on was stringing all the good parts together and not undo all the good work we were doing with errors.

Adam Ashe: I don't know why the Six Nations went so badly wrong. I think the loss of Finn, followed by the defeat to Italy, was so hard to take and really affected confidence. We did well at club level, but struggled to replicate that for Scotland and I think it's a Scottish thing where we give people too much respect and drop down a level rather than maintaining our best in every game.

I felt really positive in the autumn, but the end of the Six Nations was something I'd not really been used to before – losing. There were harsh words afterwards, deservedly so.

Finn Russell: We had a three hour meeting after the Ireland match. It was pretty brutal. But ultimately, at the end of it, we said, 'That's out the way, it's onto the World Cup now.'

Adam Ashe: I think the younger guys all felt much the same thing – and this is not to be disparaging to the older guys – but we felt that we needed to be the ones to step up and start taking the lead because the older guys had been there for a lot of years and got stuck in a mindset where they expected to come off the pitch having lost, whereas the younger guys like me, Finn, Jonny Gray and the others, we weren't used to that.

Finn Russell: We were used to winning with Glasgow so our focus was to transfer that mindset to Scotland. I don't get nervous before games, I just want to go out and play and I expect us to win, no matter who we play. It's just the way I am. It's not arrogance, it's just confidence – I don't feel any fear when I go out to play. I just feel relaxed.

Stuart Hogg: We had an amazing season at Glasgow that year. We finished the regular season top of the table, then had an great game at Scotstoun to beat Ulster in the semi-final, then went to Belfast and played outstandingly well to beat Munster pretty comfortably in the end to win the Pro12. I don't think the importance of winning that title for Glasgow and Scottish rugby can be underestimated. From a Scotland squad point of view, it allowed us to bounce back from the Wooden Spoon and have something really positive to focus on going into the World Cup training. The atmosphere during the camp was great and we played really well with a largely second-string team against Ireland in Dublin, where we almost got the win, and against Italy in Turin, where we snuck it.

Richie Gray: We all felt that despite the end results in the Six Nations, we were building well. We'd managed to show how good we could be in patches, but had still to deliver a performance where we could say, 'That was pretty decent.' The November 2014 game against Argentina sticks out, where we had a good first half and scored some good tries but it trailed off in the second half. The All Blacks game was much the same, and we had flashes in each of the Six Nations matches, but we were still to give it a full one.

It's interesting to compare the preparations for the 2011 and 2015 World Cups. It was really tough in 2011 and was the first of its kind for me. 2015 was quite different, we camped out high in the Pyrenees and the aim of the camp was to focus on being comfortable in uncomfortable situations, and looking to develop the tools to get yourself out of those situations. By training hard in a very intense environment, if it gets to the seventy-ninth minute in a match and you need to pull something out of the bag, you have the reserves in the tank to do it.

Finn Russell: We had an overnight exercise up in the mountains and that was brutal. We had one fleece blanket each to last us in five degrees or something like that. It was a long, long night.

In 1987, Scotland's World Cup campaign was severely debilitated when John Rutherford went on a pre-tournament jolly to play in an exhibition match in Bermuda and wrecked his knee. Twenty-eight years later, the ghosts of that incident looked as if they might be coming back to haunt Scottish rugby.

Finn Russell: We were in France for two weeks and after about ten days we moved from the mountains down to the beach at Canet-en-Roussillon near Perpignan. When we got there we had the afternoon off and then the next morning off, so we all went out for dinner that night, had a few drinks, and naturally ended up the pub afterwards, had a few more drinks, and before we knew it we were at a beach club and Ashie [Adam Ashe] was DJing and it was a great fun night out. So we got back to the hotel later and, just mucking around, I picked Ashie up and then fell over and hurt my knee. I knew it wasn't good at the time. In the morning it really wasn't feeling good at all. I didn't feel like I'd properly ruined it, but I'd defiantly tweaked something pretty badly. The doctors and physios were really good, they looked after me really well. But it was a worry for a while.

I was only fit for contact a week before the warm-up games, came back and hurt it again in a contact session. So then I was thinking, 'Oh no, if it goes now, I'm really going to be struggling to make the World Cup.' But we managed to get it right for the final warm-up matches against Italy and France and luckily it held up.

Peter Horne: People find it hard to believe but in the Six Nations you are only coming into the camp a week or so before the first game, so this was the first real period we had spent together under Vern. The summer before he had just joined the set-up so was just scouting it out, and then during the Six Nations it is about patching players up and trying to throw together a game plan for the next game. Whereas during the summer before the World Cup, we spent hours upon hours upon hours out on the training field running through all of our shapes and getting to know everything inside out, getting to know people's body language, learning to understand instinctively what the guy next to you is thinking and what he is going to do. It was a brilliant summer and by the end of it we were in great physical shape.

We should have beaten Ireland in that first warm-up match with a really young side and a lot of new caps. We scored three tries, having struggled to get over the line in the Six Nations, and I certainly felt like Vern's philosophy on the game was starting to come to the fore.

We then picked up an encouraging win over in Italy in tough circumstances before absolutely pummelling them at home, which really showed what we were capable of if we could match teams like Italy physically. From a personal point of view it was great that four months after that horrific miss-kick to touch I was back at Murrayfield as part of a team putting fifty points on the same opposition.

Richie Gray: We worked hard in pre-season putting our skills to the test under fatigue – we'd go through brutal fitness sessions and then go through skill-based sessions, having

Finn Russell returned from injury to lead the Scottish backline with aplomb against Italy at Murrayfield.

to keep the standards up when you're in pain and your lungs are struggling and all you want to do is take a break. It was fascinating to see the differences it made in the boys, how they improved over the course of the summer. And it was interesting seeing the influence of new guys in the set-up, particularly guys like Josh Strauss and WP.

Willem Petrus 'WP' Nel (Scotland 2015, 8 Caps): Yeah, so I was the first 'project player' to get capped. There have obviously been a lot of guys capped in the past who have done so after qualifying by residency, but I was one of the first guys signed with a view to qualifying. The move to Scotland was a clean break for me and it gave me a chance to do something completely new. I think it came at the right time for me in my career. It was difficult to get a chance to play for South Africa and the opportunity was there to play for Scotland, so I looked at it very carefully, decided it was going to be the right thing for me and my family, and we went for it.

It took me almost a year to adapt to northern hemisphere rugby, particularly the scrummaging. It was different to come from Super Rugby and then be met with the weather conditions as well. Scrummaging is more technical here, while in South Africa it is more a case of players getting the ball in and out as quickly as possible. So I was doing regular work with Massimo Cuttitta while he was here as Scotland scrum coach and he helped me a lot. And Stevie Scott had us all working hard at Edinburgh and it made a big difference. Winning my first cap in an all-Edinburgh front-row out in Turin definitely helped me settle in.

Ross Ford: We had the advantage of playing seventy minutes week-in and week-out with each other as a front-row unit at Edinburgh, against everybody. So we almost instinctively knew what to do against different opposition. We could feel what was happening in the scrum and reacted to it accordingly. The way WP plays, he's really good to scrum with, he's so aggressive, he wants to go forward all the time which always makes my job a lot easier. Around the pitch he throws himself about. He brought his family across here and both his kids were born here; he made a statement by doing that and it showed that he was committed, so it was really good to see him get that first cap and grow into the squad. By the end of the World Cup we were regarded as one of the best front-rows in the tournament.

Finn Russell: We were all pretty pleased with how the pre-World Cup games went. We played pretty well against Ireland in Dublin and just lost, then had a good win against Itlay in Turin, smashed them the following week at Murrayfield, then played well again against France in Paris. We had a chance to go for a draw at the end of that game and if it had been a Six Nations game, we would have taken it, but it was a friendly so we thought we should at least try to get the win with the last play of the game. We were cutting them open but just didn't manage to finish it off and so ended up losing the game; we were disappointed with the result, but were pleased with how a lot of the game had gone – and, importantly, we had managed to come through all four games without picking up any injuries. So it had been a good summer and we were all just looking forward to getting into the World Cup after that.

Ever since the World Cup draw had been made two years previously, it had seemed a certainty that Scotland would enjoy two easy pool matches against Japan and the USA before taking on the likely pool winners South Africa in round three before facing a probable winner-takes-all fixture against Samoa in the fourth match.

But sport is wondrous because of it unpredictability. Japan pulled off the greatest upset in World Cup history when they defeated South Africa in the opening pool game, 34-32, in Brighton, and while Samoa dispatched the USA on the same weekend, they had been forced to dig deep to do so. With the so-called 'minnows' performing so well, the potential for another World Cup disaster loomed large for Scotland.

Sam Hidalgo-Clyne (Scotland 2015, 8 Caps): After such a disappointing Six Nations we were under no illusions that we would be the team that every other side in our World Cup pool would be targeting. The USA and Japan would have looked at our game as the one where they could cause an upset and Samoa would have been the same as us and realised that whoever won that game would probably come second in the group after South Africa. So we knew that every game would be incredibly tough, but that's the way it should be in a World Cup.

There is no doubt that Scotland benefited hugely from World Rugby's scheduling of matches, that pitched Scotland into action against Eddie Jones's Japan just four days after the Brave Blossoms' heroics against the Springboks.

Arriving on a wave of momentum at the Kingsholm Stadium in Gloucester, Japan continued where they had left off against South Africa by playing some wonderful attacking rugby that resulted in the only try of the half for Amanaki Mafi after a well-executed rolling maul. But despite this set-back, Scotland still looked tactically very assured. They were not going to be caught out like South Africa were.

The Scottish players worked hard for each other, played one another into space, backed up breaks and half-breaks and took their chances very coolly. The line-out wobbled a bit, and an old issue with restarts reared its ugly head again, but the scrum went well and, in spite of Mafi's try, the rolling maul was subsequently well contained.

Tactically Scotland got much of their play spot on and moved through the gears well in the second half, pushing out to 45-10 lead. Had the game lasted another five minutes or so, they would probably have gone past the half century mark. They ran at shoulders, their support runners held their depth knowing that the Japanese chop tackle technique would affect their usual running lines by a half second or so, they used inside and the outside runners and they cut against the grain at the right moments. Finn Russell mixed up his game superbly, using short pops, long passes, dinks and chips and well angled punts, and he stood up well to the big ball carriers sent down his channel. He looked dangerous every time he touched the ball and you could tell that a try was coming for him – which it duly did as the Japanese defence began to buckle at the knee late on – and it was thoroughly well-deserved.

Outside Russell, Matt Scott and Mark Bennett marshalled the midfield defence well and made ground just about every time they had the ball and Bennett took his two tries brilliantly, while the back three were potent, with Tommy Seymour crowning an industrious afternoon with a try.

In the forwards David Denton carried strongly, Ryan Wilson was an energetic nuisance and the front five worked hard all day to secure quick ball for man of the match Greig Laidlaw, who kept the scoreboard ticking and the tempo of play at a steady rhythm.

And in amongst all of this was the tumbling ball of energy and cool aggression that was John Hardie. The Kiwi had been parachuted into the squad during the pre-season camp, straight off the back of a Super Rugby winning campaign with the Otago Highlanders. His inclusion in the squad at the expense of John Barclay, Rob Harley and (initially) Blair Cowan angered many fans, recalling the spectre of Brendan Laney, but Hardie was soon to show just what a class act he was. He was everywhere against Japan and it was his clever Hail Mary to keep the ball in play as he was being tackled into touch that led to the ruck on Japan's try line from which Hardie himself then scored Scotland's first try. In two moments within that single passage of play, Hardie had wrestled the momentum back into Scotland's favour. The world's best players always seem to get the bounce of the ball, but that is because they make their own luck – and that was exactly what Hardie, Bennett, Russell and Seymour all did.

The magic had been with Japan on the Saturday against the Springboks; on the Wednesday it was all with Scotland. As it would turn out, the points margin of this game would make all the difference as Japan became the first side in World Cup history to be knocked out at the pool stages despite picking up three victories out of four matches.

Tommy Seymour: Before we had even arrived at the World Cup, we were very aware that it was going to be a very difficult game for us – not only because we were going to have a bit of a wait before our first game. We had been studying them during the summer and seen that they were making a lot of waves with the way they were performing and the results they were getting. They were clearly a very well-drilled and structured side, who also played with a lot of controlled passion.

Then, watching the South Africa game, we knew that we were going to be in for a real battle. That was, without doubt, the biggest upset the game of rugby has ever seen – so, although we were well aware that Japan should not be taken lightly, that was a real eye-opener.

You couldn't help but lose yourself in that game. In terms of Scotland's World Cup campaign, we should have wanted South Africa to beat Japan, but at the end we were all on our feet cheering them on.

Finn Russell: I remember with the Japan-South Africa game, I was on FaceTime with my girlfriend and I was trying to keep an eye on both of them as the game went into the final quarter. Eventually I just had to say that I had to watch the match!

I remember going into the game just thinking, 'They can't beat us.' Nothing against Japan, but I just thought, 'We are going to win this.' And even when it was close at half-time, we knew that we still had a lot to come in the second half. We just knew it. So there was no panic. We came out in the second half and we ran over them, scoring five tries. And that was great for us because there had been so much hype coming into the game after they had beaten South Africa and their coach, Eddie Jones, was making a lot of noise about us not being any good and that they would win. Obviously the four-day turnaround was tough for them, but we had much the same between that match and our next match against the USA. You know, it's not ideal, but pretty much every team had to deal with something like that at some stage. You just have to make do with the schedule that you're given and get on with it.

John Hardie (Scotland 2015, 5 Caps): I came over to Scotland and people said it was a big risk, but I didn't think it was a risk, I thought it was an opportunity. I knew it was going to be tough and I knew I had to work really hard to prove myself. I was out of my comfort zone. I'd been with the Highlanders for seven years and I was in my comfort zone. Coming over to Scotland really brought the best out of me as a person and I think it's helped my rugby as well.

When I first came over I did a lot of research on my family tree. My grandmother went over to New Zealand in 1925 on a ship and I've seen her name and her signature on the shipping list. We looked up all that sort of stuff and it was really cool to see where she came from. I printed it out and presented it to my mum and dad when they arrived over for the World Cup. Having them there to see me play against Japan was amazing.

Finn Russell: Like most Kiwi players, John just knows rugby really well and it's been brilliant to play alongside him. Straussy [Josh Strauss] is the same; he's a real leader on the field, especially at Glasgow, and he's growing into it with Scotland. Neither of them are the kind of guys to always talk loads in meetings but when they have a point to make it tends to be a good one. There was a lot said about them coming into the side, along with WP, but they are class players and have made a real difference to the team.

Tommy Seymour: During the first half of that game the nerves were evident. We had waited so long to get going, and then with Japan doing what they did against South Africa, there was a lot of pressure. Then they scored off the maul to go ahead, and we couldn't get over the try line in the first half. I nearly got over towards the end but was smashed in the corner by their full-back

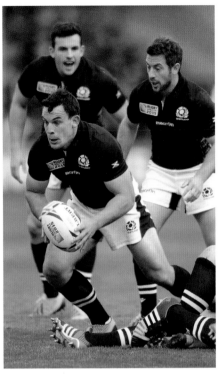

Watched by Matt Scott and Grieg Laidlaw, John Hardie picks the ball from the base of a ruck against Japan and snipes down the fringe.

– and that really reinforced how much they wanted another big result and to get out the group.

We settled into our game well in the second half, and once the second try came we eased up and started to play some good rugby. We held them out at the end as well. So it was a nice start against tough opposition.

Just four days later, Scotland endured yet another difficult first forty minutes against the USA. Stuart Hogg looked to have dragged them back into the game when he made a searing break from within his own half to create a two-on-one for Tim Visser just before half-time, but his pass to the flying winger was a shocker and Visser was unable to collect the ball. Scotland went into interval trailing the Eagles 13-6.

The USA's rush defence had caused Scotland no end of issues in the first half and had flustered the backline, while the forwards had struggled in the set-piece. Vern Cotter made changes in the front-row that shored up the scrum and lineout and allowed his pack to regain a foothold in the game. From there the backline were able to recompose themselves to address the issue of the American rush defence.

Peter Horne: It was a really tough game. They were a big, physical team and they really came out the blocks at us – having clearly identified us as an opportunity for them to claim a scalp. There was a lot of talk afterwards about us not playing very well in the first half, and there were a few passes that didn't go to hand, plus the set-piece struggled a bit – but in international rugby it can take a wee bit of time for things to settle down. They were really fired up and they got the rub of the green on a few occasions, so we had to weather that storm. Once we broke them down in the second half, we put them to the sword and got the bonus point.

There was certainly no panic at half-time. Vern spoke to us about keeping our composure and assured us that so long as we didn't retreat back into our shells then the tries would eventually come. So, we were frustrated but we knew it was going to click eventually.

Finn Russell: In the first half we never really got going, never got into our stride. At half-time they showed a feed from our changing room on the TV coverage and it looked like Vern was having a real go at us. He wasn't really, he was just being direct in telling us what he wanted. He basically just told us that we needed to be more direct and not throw the ball about as much as we'd be doing – which was my fault! I'd thrown a couple of wide passes and boys had got smashed. So we needed to go through them a bit more and try and dominate them physically before going wide. Which for the first try is what we did – we had two forward hits and then went wide and scored. It was pretty simple rugby but it was effective. He was saying, 'Why are you trying this, when all you need to do is this and it's gonna work.' As you've probably heard, he's quite a straight talker; he wasn't shouting at boys but he was saying, hit it up, take on that responsibility, then we can go wide and we're going to score. Which was good for us to hear; he'd analysed it and just cut straight to the point. He's always positive but was just telling us what we need to do to make the break-through.

The team emerged at half-time clearly fired up and with a focus not to butcher chances as they had in the first half. The forwards and backs combined well to carry the ball deep into the USA's territory and then exploit the blind-side as they had done against Japan four days earlier: Henry Pyrgos released Hogg at pace, who drew the last defender and then freed Visser, successfully this time, to score in the corner. The fact that the initiative had been so decisively dragged back into Scotland's favour created a huge momentum shift in the match. Scotland suddenly looked focused and authoritative.

Finn Russell took a more controlled approach, using his forwards running inside and outside of him to check the defence before steering balls behind runners to his supporting backs who, in turn, were standing a few steps deeper than they had during the opening forty minutes, which allowed them to pass their way around the on-rushing defensive line and release the ball into the hands of the back-three players.

Scotland had been forced to defend for long periods in the first half and struggled at the breakdown, turning over a lot of ball and giving away penalties. Hooker Fraser Brown did admirably well in the second half to come into the back-row to play more of a fetcher's role in the absence of John Hardie, who was missing from the side having failed a pre-match concussion test. Brown helped secure Scotland's ball at the ruck and sped up the supply to Greig Laidlaw who also emerged off the bench to good effect.

Laidlaw controlled his forwards well, using runners off his shoulder, commanding his pack to pick-and-go around the corner, and marshalling the rolling maul to suck in the fringe defenders. The variety of play Scotland's play through their halfbacks opened up an array of different attacking opportunities for Scotland in the second half and they were extremely efficient at capitalising on them, scoring three tries in just sixteen minutes to banish the threat of another 2015 World Cup upset and putting them firmly in control of Pool B – which was augmented further by the bonus point try scored brilliantly by Matt Scott before the icing was added to the cake with Duncan Weir's late five-pointer, giving Scotland maximum points from their first two outings.

Coming into the third round match against the Springboks, Cotter had some decisions to make. Did he put out his first-choice team (or as close to it as possible as Finn Russell was ruled out with an ankle injury and John Hardie with concussion), or did he follow Frank Hadden's 2007 plan and put out a team of whipping boys? Fortunately for Cotter, the strength of his squad was such that there was no clear discrepancy in quality between most of his players. In any case, he seemed to settle on a middle ground, selecting many first choicers along with some players who had been previously warming the bench.

Not that it would have made much difference in the event. Having been stung so horrifically by the Japanese, the Springboks had been ferocious in their second match against Samoa. Their focus was just as laser-like when they ran out to face Scotland and the physicality they brought to proceedings would have blown just about every other team on the planet off the field, bar perhaps the All Blacks – and even they would have struggled against the brutal green waves that were unleashed at St James's Park in Newcastle.

And so, as predicted two years previously, it came down to the final pool match against Samoa. Rather unexpectedly, however, the South Sea Islanders were out of the running, having lost to both the Springboks and Japan; but in many ways this made them more dangerous as they had nothing to lose and could play as fast and loose as they liked as they attempted to go out of the tournament with a bang. So it was that the packed out crowd at St James's Park were presented with an exhilarating, helter-skelter match played at breakneck speed that produced try after try after try. In an astonishing first quarter, the Samoans ran in three tries between the tenth and twentieth minutes and had it not been for the intervention of the television match official they could have had a fourth. Scotland were reeling, with their restarts particularly woeful, but they kept themselves in the hunt through Greig Laidlaw's boot, Tommy Seymour's first-half intercept and John Hardie's touchdown after a wonderfully driven series of mauls, finishing the half with Samoa leading 26-23.

Finn Russell: It was similar to the first halves we played against the USA and Japan but in none of those games did we ever feel panicked about what was going on. Obviously it wasn't just down to the Glasgow guys in the team, but I think at Glasgow we'd developed an attitude to winning and that the game could always still be won no matter how much time was left on the clock. The run to win the Pro12 after the disappointments of the Six Nations was just what we needed before the World Cup because we were winning tight games and playing good rugby. Like in the semi-final against Ulster, we scored right at the end to win it – and I don't think any of us ever felt that we were going to lose that game even though time was running out. And then we beat Munster in the final a week later and Edinburgh had a great run to get to the final of the Challenge Cup, and Greig [Laidlaw] was on the winning side for Gloucester in that game, so we all managed to get ourselves up after the disappointments of the Six Nations. That was a big change in mindset and showed when we came back against Japan and the USA, and especially against Samoa. I don't think I ever worried that we wouldn't beat Samoa, even though we kept letting them get back in the game.

But there was a lot of pressure on us at that stage and I think that had a part to play in all the mistakes we made, especially in the first half and we struggled to get into our patterns. When we got to half-time and we were still in the game, we calmed ourselves down in the second half and clicked into gear. And although they came back and scored a try at the end in that last play, I never felt like we were going to lose it.

Scotland focused on their strength in the scrum and lineout and looking to take advantage of Samoa's profligate indiscipline, which conceded nineteen penalties throughout the game. Laidlaw would finish the match with five penalties and three conversions to go with his crucial try late in the game for a personal haul of 26 points.

Greig Laidlaw pounces to score the match-winning try against Samoa.

But even with this second-half superiority, it was still harum-scarum to the end as Motu Matu scored late on to leave the game in the balance during the final minutes. Thankfully for Laidlaw's men, Cotter's team in the coaching box, the tens of thousands in the stands and the millions watching at home, Scotland closed out the match for a 36-33 victory to book a quarter-final place with Australia.

In the aftermath of the match, the team's preparation was hit by a hard sucker punch from left-field. Jonny Gray and Ross Ford were charged by citing commissioner Scott Nowland with lifting Samoan flanker Jack Lam at a ruck and driving him head-first into the ground. The pair travelled to Canary Wharf on the Tuesday morning after the game to answer to QC Christopher Quinlan and, after a long deliberation, each were handed three-week bans. It was a hefty sanction, especially in light of various other citations during the tournament when one-match bans were given for what appeared to be much more dangerous – and deliberate – acts of foul play, and the clear evidence that the incident in question looked completely accidental, particularly from Ford's point of view. The SRU announced on the Wednesday evening that they would appeal the bans. Gray and Ford then spent a further day arguing their cases to a three-man appeals panel, which included former Wallaby coach Robbie Deans and Justice Graeme Mew of Canada and was chaired by the Honourable Justice Lex Mpati from South Africa. This trio finally determined that the challenge on Lam hadn't been dangerous because the Samoan flanker 'had not been dropped or driven' into the ground. The bans were repealed, freeing both men to play in the quarter-final against Australia at Twickenham; it was the first time at the 2015 World Cup that an appeal had proved successful in overturning an original verdict. It was a welcome reprieve, but it had muddied Scotland's preparation considerably.

Jonny Gray: We had huge belief going into the game. It was a tough week for all of us – especially for Ross Ford and me – but the togetherness and collective sense of purpose we had worked on throughout the build up to the competition, with our camp in the Pyrenees and so on, helped us deal with that.

I don't really remember thinking much about the incident at the time. We were just trying to clean out the tackle area and I suppose I was so focussed on the game that I wasn't thinking about anything else. When we first heard that we had been cited we took the view that anything could happen and all we could do was carry on as usual. Then, when we got told about the ban, it became all about the team – and helping the guys who we thought were going to be on the park to prepare. So if that meant providing opposition in the line-out then that's what we did. We knew there was going to be an appeal but we couldn't rely on that, so we just had to assume the worst until we heard otherwise.

When the appeal came through we knew very little about it. It was the day before the game and it was really mixed emotions. From a personal point of view, it was unreal to be given this chance to play, but Tim Swinson dropped out of the team as a result and that was a really tough thing for him to go through. I spoke to him straight after and he just shook my hand and told me that if I need anything then he was there. He's a great guy and that just goes to show it. It was the same with Alasdair Strokosh, who dropped out of the squad so that Swinno could cover the bench.

Finn Russell: We trained for the Australia game on the assumption that Jonny and Fordy weren't going to make it. But while we concentrated on that, it was hard for us all not to talk about it. David Pocock had kneed someone and got away with it, Sam Burgess had almost taken Michael Hooper's head off and had got away with it, so there were a few things like that that had happened and I remember watching the incident with Jonny and Fordy at the time and just thinking, 'That's totally fine, that's just a clear-out,' and if anything it was a penalty for Lam holding on. When they first got cited, I said to Jonny, 'Don't worry, you'll be fine, there was nothing in that.'

But they got banned and then they went through the whole appeal process, so they didn't train with us again until the day before the game.

Although Ford and Gray had been a central part of the team for some time and could therefore slip back into proceedings relatively seamlessly, they had still lost several days of crucial organisation, but Cotter had no hesitation in reinstating both to the starting line-up. Matt Scott, however, was out of the reckoning, having failed to recover from an injury sustained against Samoa; Peter Horne took his place – and there was a new back-row combination pressed into service in the shape of Hardie, Blair Cowan and David Denton.

The Wallabies, meanwhile, had lost fullback Israel Folau and flanker David Pocock to injury, but were psychologically in very fine fettle after their outstanding unbeaten run through the 'Pool of Death', which had included victories over England (which had signalled the end of the hosts' part in their own tournament), Wales, Fiji and minnows Uruguay. For many pundits, Australia had become the favourites to lift the William Webb Ellis trophy. The bookies had given Scotland odds of 9-1 to win the match with the most probable Australia winning margin being somewhere between 11-15 points. It was felt that Scotland had achieved their goal of reaching the quarters and that the Wallabies would blow them away as they marched, unrelentingly, to the semis.

Peter Horne: It was a really good week leading up to that because all the pressure had been on us for the previous four weeks to make the quarter-finals and having achieved that the perception outside the camp seemed to be that having reached that goal we would just roll over and let Australia march past us. So that brought us closer together and reinforced our determination.

It was a massive occasion and we knew when we went out there that we were going to take a few people – including the Australians – by surprise. Nobody goes onto a rugby field thinking that they are not going to play well, but sometimes there is a feeling in the team and you know that what is about to happen is going to be a level above. The feeling on the bus was just right, the changing room was electric and I suppose we felt invincible.

Finn Russell: A lot of people seemed to think that by making it to the quarters the pressure was off us, but we knew going into the game that the furthest Scotland have ever gone in the World Cup is the semi-finals; so if we won the game we would equal the best we've ever done, so that brings its own pressure. We wanted to do the same as the team in '91 and we believed that we were good enough to do it, even though the odds were against us after Australia had topped their group and the way they were playing. I don't think any of us felt we had anything to lose, whereas Australia were up with New Zealand as favourites for the tournament, so they had a lot more to lose than we did.

Australia burst out of the traps and took complete control of the opening exchanges. They looked dangerous with every pass, slicing angle or robust carry, and this dominance was rewarded in the eighth minute when Matt Giteau spun the ball wide to his centre partner Tevita Kuridrani, who bounced off Tommy Seymour's spot-tackle challenge to race into the Scottish twenty-two and release winger Adam Ashley-Cooper for the simplest of run-ins.

The omens were not looking good, even with Bernard Foley missing the touchline conversion. But this was a well-worn script at the World Cup and Cotter's team had proved time and again that early set-backs wouldn't hamper their ambition, which they demonstrated, impressively, once again. They swiftly worked their way back into their opponents' territory and won a penalty, which Greig Laidlaw nudged over to get the Scots on the scoreboard.

When in possession of the ball Scotland looked strong on the carry and inventive in attack. On seventeen minutes they pounded their way back into the Australian half, the forwards and backs making yards with every touch of the ball. Finally they found themselves five metres from the Wallaby line; a line that had been breached only twice before in the tournament. As Ross Ford took a short crash ball, Scotland only put two men into the ruck; one of them, Peter Horne, stood over the ball as the defence spread to match Scotland's width. The little centre looked up to see that there were no Wallaby guards and no sweeper present as all defensive eyes were focused on the wider channels. He picked up the ball and darted through the gap to score under the posts before he was mobbed by the Scotland subs and then by the rest of his teammates. Laidlaw's conversion made it 10-5.

Peter Horne: It was the second time we had attacked them. We had a ruck close to their line and I spotted that Will Genia had moved out because they were numbers down. Jonny Gray got a really good clear, which meant I could pick up at the base and nip over. Australia had only conceded a couple of tries during their group matches so when we scored after fifteen minutes it was a real light-bulb moment, when everyone started thinking that we could really do it.

Just a few minutes later Finn Russel unleashed a bomb on Bernard Foley and, unchallenged, the Wallaby stand-off fumbled it forward. Greig Laidlaw exchanged some choice words before the packs engaged. The all-Edinburgh front-row of Alasdair Dickinson, Ross Ford and WP Nel put on the squeeze, the Gray brothers heaved, the back-row kept perfect shape and the Wallabies' scrum, which had taken England's to pieces on the same ground just two weeks earlier, crumbled. Referee Craig Joubert raised his arm and Laidlaw made it 13-5. Scotland, and the rugby world at large, started to wonder if an upset – one that would eclipse Japan's defeat of South Africa – might be on the cards.

Finn Russell: The game plan going in was to target Foley. I put a lot of high balls up on him, we got all the big boys running at him, and pretty much every re-start we put it up on him. The first one we got back; the second one we got back; the third one he dropped – and it impacted on his game because he missed a few kicks at goal in that half. We executed our game plan pretty well, which we hadn't really done that whole tournament, to be honest, especially in the first halves. That game was the first time we executed our game plan well for the full eighty minutes and the whole team played well for the full eighty minutes, it wasn't just ten, twelve, thirteen of us playing well, it was everyone who came on out of the twenty-three.

But the Wallabies were a class act; Rugby Championship holders, they knew how to react to set-backs. After Horne transgressed at a midfield ruck, Foley kicked into the Scotland twenty-two. From the lineout Kane Douglas, Scott Sio and Sekope Kefu carried with brutal efficiency and took play to the Scotland five-metre line. With Australia's heavy runners thundering forward off Genia and Foley's shoulders, the Scottish defence was forced inwards, which opened space on the outside – which was exactly where the ball was sent with crisp accuracy a few phases later for Drew Mitchell to race over for a beautifully executed try. Foley once again missed the conversion.

A few minutes later, WP Nel hit a scrum and knew he had his man on toast. Scott Sio hinged at the hips, lost his bind, twisted in and hit the deck. Nel had remained straight and strong throughout; a rock. Laidlaw stepped up and banged over the penalty. 16-10 to Scotland.

When Michael Cheika took over as Australia's head coach at the end of 2014, one of the weapons he focussed on adding to the Wallaby armoury, as well as an improved scrum, was the rolling maul. It had been a devastating weapon for the Brumbies and the Warratahs in the 2015 Super Rugby campaign and had again been used to good effect in the Rugby Championship and during the World Cup pool stages. Defending the rolling maul was also a known Achilles heel for Scotland. On twenty-nine minutes, David Denton gave away a penalty, Foley kicked into the Scottish twenty-two and from the resulting lineout Australia got their maul rumbling. Scotland were powerless to stop it, legally or otherwise. Had Michael Hooper not touched down after an irresistible series of surges, a penalty try would have surely been awarded, a card probably shown and a straight-forward conversion would have been taken from in front of the posts. As it was, Scotland came out pretty well from the whole passage of play. No one went to the bin – and then Foley missed his third conversion attempt. Like Laidlaw just a few minutes earlier, the demons were muttering in the Wallaby stand-off's ears. Scotland went into half-time 16-15 ahead. No rational

The Scotland scrum marmalised the much-vaunted Wallaby eight.

pundit had predicted such a scenario.

Scotland emerged from the changing room knowing that they would face a green and gold onslaught and that they would have to counter it with a blue one of their own.

But they did not start well. Blair Cowan knocked the ball on at the kick-off and the Wallabies were instantly on the attack, taking the ball into Scotland's twenty-two. And that is when the first of the major controversies in the game occurred. Foley was caught in a tackle and offloaded to Drew Mitchell. Sean Maitland had read the pass and reached out in an attempt to intercept. Had he gathered it, it is likely that he would have been in for a score at the other end. He didn't, knocking on instead. In real time it was clear what had happened and what Maitland's intention was and at first Joubert accepted it as such. Then the TMO intervened, suggesting it was a deliberate knock-down that had prevented a score. Joubert issued Maitland with a yellow card and awarded Australia a penalty. A few minutes later, Australia had a scrum near Scotland's line and took advantage of Maitland's absence with precision, Will Genia sending Mitchell in for his second try down the vacant wing channel. Foley, at last, had found his kicking boots and he sent over the conversion to make it 22-16.

Tommy Seymour: There were lapses and I was culpable for one with a bad read in defence. Sean Maitland's yellow-card, which I personally think was very harsh, is another example. So things didn't go perfectly but we played well and stuck in for the entire length of time, and in the end we showed that we are capable of living with these top teams and winning against them on a good day.

Terrier-like, Scotland would not be shaken. On forty-five minutes Nel won another scrum penalty as Sio was sent backwards and Laidlaw knocked over the points to leave them three points in arrears. This was pegged back nine minutes later, however, when Genia cannily cannoned the ball against Mark Bennett as the centre regained his feet at a ruck. Foley's radar was once again accurate as he stroked over the penalty to take the score to 25-19.

At this stage the Wallabies would have expected to draw away – but Scotland kept playing, kept going wide, kept their ambition. They hassled and harried, their energy high, their intent to keep attacking uninhibited. From a turn-over deep in their half they spun it wide, Denton charged down the touchline, fed Hogg who chipped and then the defence pressed. Australia were trapped in their half, but won a scrum and this time the Aussie pack held firm. Foley hesitated for a few seconds as he weighed up his exit options and then, inexplicably, opted for a chip rather than a booming punt; Russell, having sensed Foley's indecision, pressed up hard and charged the kick down. The Scotland stand-off regathered the ball and only a last-ditch tackle from Genia kept him from scoring. As Russell hit the deck he popped the ball to the chasing Tommy Seymour and the wing crashed over in the corner. The noise from the crowd sent reverberations shuddering through south-west London.

Mark Bennett (Scotland 2014-15, 13 Caps): The support was unreal. There was a great Scottish contingent at every match throughout, but especially at the game against Australia – it felt like the whole of Twickenham was behind us.

The momentum continued to swing back and forth. Australia forced their way back into Scottish territory and a few minutes later Kuridrani wrong-footed the Scotland defence and then powered over for a score, just as he had done during Australia's audacious come-from-behind victory against the Springboks during the 2015 Rugby Championship. Foley converted to make it 32-24 with seventeen minutes left. Was this the moment when the game would be killed off?

Scotland would not die wondering. They worked their way back into Australian territory and won another penalty on sixty-eight minutes. Eight points down with twelve minutes to go, Laidlaw took the penalty and it was 32-27.

Then the heavens opened. The unseasonably good weather that had bathed the World Cup in glorious autumn sunshine at last surrendered to the usual meteorological standard and it began to hammer it down. Dark skies, bright floodlights, pouring rain. Scotland had been here twice before against Australia in recent times, and on both occasions something very special had happened. Would it again?

Australia won possession on their ten-metre line and looked to carefully keep control of the ball in the torrential conditions. Replacement scrum-half Nick Phipps passed the ball out to replacement prop James Slipper at first-receiver, who delayed the pass for a moment and then looked to loop it behind some runners and out to the on-rushing Drew Mitchell. But Mark Bennett had read the pass perfectly and picked it off mid-flight to sprint home under the posts. Twickenham erupted – and then boomed aloud once more as Laidlaw sent over the conversion.

Greig Ladlaw: The support we had all tournament was amazing. Heading down to Gloucester we thought that the Gloucester faithful would probably be supporting Japan [who play in the same colours], but that wasn't the case at all. The Scottish support travelled and filled the place. Then when we drove into Leeds I remember just seeing crowds and crowds of people banked up along the roadside waving their Scottish flags. And then up in Newcastle it was something special. Finally down at Twickenham it was something else altogether. We will probably never see anything like that again – the amount of support we had in Twickenham was unique.

It was, incredibly, 34-32 to Scotland with just six minutes left and they were in the ascendancy. Twickenham was roaring for the men in blue in a way it never has before, nor probably ever will again. The Australian scrum was in dire straits. Scotland looked set to make history. What followed will never be forgotten by those that saw it.

Finn Russell: When Mark went in for that score, we thought we'd won it. There were only a few minutes left. They kicked off to us and although we knocked it on, we got a free-kick at the scrum and we just figured that if we could keep the ball in their half, in that kind of weather they weren't going to beat us.

Stuart Hogg collected a long ball in his twenty-two and sent another howitzer into the night sky. Seconds later, he was clattered by a late hit by Drew Mitchell that sent him spinning over the touchline. In contrast to Maitland's yellow card, neither Joubert nor the TMO had a thing to say about it and play continued. The game could have been settled right there – Australia down to fourteen, Scotland with a line-out in Wallaby territory.

Stuart Hogg: I just about ended up in the front row of the stand.

Finn Russell: That kind of thing happened a lot in that match. Late hits all the time – and nothing ever picked up. But the one on Hoggy should have been a game-changer.

Seventy-seven minutes and fifty-three seconds on the clock and Scotland were awarded a lineout thirty metres out from their line. Everyone watching knew the drill: throw to the front or middle, maul it, kick deep into the Australian twenty-two. But Fraser Brown threw long to David Denton who went full stretch to get his hand to it. He palmed it down as best he could towards his side of the line and as John Hardie went to regather he knocked it on. Josh Strauss, also going for the ball, collided with Nick Phipps and the ball shot forwards to Scotland's replacement prop John Welsh, who dived on it from an off-side position. TV replays would later show that Phipps had grappled for the ball and got a hand to it, meaning that Welsh was accidentally offside and a scrum should have been awarded to Australia; World Rugby issued a statement two days later to confirm as much. But in the heat of the moment Joubert missed Phipps' intervention and signaled for a penalty to Australia.

Finn Russell: Even when they got the lineout, all I was thinking was, 'We're going to win it, we'll smash it down into their half, and we've got this.'

Jon Welsh (Scotland 2012-2015, 11 Caps): The game goes on so fast. There was a scramble for the ball, the Australian guy slapped it back and I went for it. My first thought was, 'Loose ball, let's get on this.' It came off an Australian player and I grabbed the ball, but it happened so quickly.

Things like the ref's call going against you happens in sport. It was a bad call, but the referee made it and you just have to get on with it. We got a bad break, but you can't do anything about it now.

Finn Russell: I remember standing under the posts just hoping that Foley would miss it. I was just thinking, 'He's missed a few in the first half, he might miss this.'

Bernard Foley, with four missed kicks to his name that night, stepped up. In 2009, Matt Giteau's injury time missed-kick had handed Scotland victory at Murrayfield. In 2012, Greig Laidlaw's injury time kick had won it for Scotland in Newcastle. Which way would the pendulum swing? Foley hit it straight and true.

From the kick-off the Wallabies regathered and maintained possession until the clock ran out. Giteau kicked to the touchline and the game was over.

Finn Russell: I don't know what to say about the penalty decision. It was disappointing for us. It maybe should have been a scrum which could have changed the game. But they got the penalty and Foley kicked it well. What can you do after that? It was a real Scottish way of losing. We were so close but didn't get the win. But although we were disappointed we knew we could hold our heads

Stuart Hogg can barely believe it as Australia are awarded the late penalty.

high. We had put in a hell of a performance when just about everyone outside the camp had written us off.

David Denton: I went and met my family and girlfriend afterwards and you could have filled a bathtub with all those tears.

We noticed that Craig Joubert sprinted up the tunnel when he blew for fulltime. I understand that refereeing the game in front of millions of people is tough but the decision he made has affected the rest of our lives and it affected a nation. If he couldn't go back to the TMO to check offside [because of the current rules] that needs to change because it affected us in a big way. Defeats stay with you in a way that victories never do. That game is going to haunt us all for the rest of our lives. I know it is.

Blair Cowan (Scotland 2014-15, 15 Caps): You don't know how much pain we went through to get to that stage of the tournament. We wanted to leave our names cemented in history with something like the World Cup. To have that stripped away like that was devastating. But hell, we were proud of the way we left. I'm not going to cry about that final penalty; I was off the field at the time and you've got to take control of the game for eighty minutes. I saw it up top [on the big screen] but relying on one decision is never going to be enough to beat a side as good as Australia – it's history now and you've got to look at the control of other seventy-nine minutes of the game.

To come that close, to almost make history but yet to fail is utterly devastating and I have no words for how much the gestures of friends, family and fans meant to me and the guys. Everyone was in tears in the dressing room afterwards.

Vern asked us to stand up for our country, stand up for our family and for tradition, and to do our jobs and do them well. We did what he asked, but the game see-sawed and there were things we didn't control and things we controlled bloody well, so to come so close and fall right at the end hurt and hurt a lot. But in the final analysis, we'll heal and we'll come back stronger and better for the experience.

Stuart Hogg: We were bitterly disappointed. We knew coming into the game what we were capable of and we then put in a cracking eighty-minute performance, with just a couple of decisions that didn't go our way. We were that close to a semi-final place . . . It was very tough to deal with.

Finn Russell: Before the game I was thinking about the fact we were a team that went through the Six Nations without a win. Looking back six months before, it was in many ways a similar story to the quarter-final – getting close but not managing to win. But going forward we are all convinced it will be a different story. We believe in ourselves. It's not just about getting close to the best sides. We want to beat them. We showed we can live with the best. For us to go and compete against a top-five side like Australia and only miss out because one decision went against us gives us a lot of confidence. I remember back in the day when I was younger I would be looking up at guys like Matt Giteau and Will Genia and thinking how great they were, but we showed we were as good as them, if not better for spells of the match. We're a completely different team from the Six Nations – we're on par with the best teams in the world now.

Greig Laidlaw: Referees can make mistakes, but that one really hurt us. We didn't want the game handed to us on a plate. We just wanted the chance to close the game out, but we didn't get that.

It was tough to take the way things finished up; we'll never get that back now. It was such an important decision and I certainly feel that he should have been allowed to use the TMO. It was also slightly surreal the way he [referee Craig Joubert] ran off straight after full-time.

Afterwards, it was good to get my head down and just spend a bit of time with my family to try to deal with it. I had various people asking to interview me and get my thoughts on the game but it was one of those unfortunate things that, as players, we will remember forever.

World Rugby coming out to say the referee got that final decision wrong doesn't change the result. There is no point in us sitting around talking a lot more about what has been and gone. The support we got during the World Cup and since we went out was really incredible. I'd never felt it as much, especially on the back of a poor Six Nations for Scotland. To have the support of the nation behind us was something we cherished as a squad and shows how far we have come as a group of players under the coaching staff led by Vern.

Tommy Seymour: Now that I have been able to step back and take time to digest what happened, it probably doesn't taste quite so bitter – but the sense of disappointment hasn't gone. To be so close to doing something so special and not make it is really hard. Nobody outside gave us a chance and you understood why, so we are incredibly proud at what we did out there – and that just makes it harder to live with. In terms of the refereeing, I'm not into slagging people off. As a rugby player you accept that mistakes happen, and I'm glad I play in a sport where we don't harangue officials at the drop of a hat. As human beings you've got to take that into account, and accept that although it has now been acknowledged that the wrong call was made, that's sometimes what happens – and on this occasion it happened at the worst possible time and in the worst possible circumstances.

As a Scottish player I was perhaps looking at it through tinted glasses, but my immediate reaction was that he would award a scrum. Everyone has got a different view point and I can see why some people might have initially thought it was a penalty. Like everyone, I wish that referees could get the call right every time, but that isn't realistic. So, you have to look at how it balances out over your career and you are going to get roughly the same amount of marginal calls for you as against you. Smarter people than I, and higher ranked people than I, have looked at it afterwards and stated their opinions about it. Hindsight is a wonderful thing – the referee didn't have that luxury.

I didn't see the ref run off the pitch. I was on the bench and when Bennett scored his try I was saying to the other lads, 'We're going to win this.' A very close friend of mine had managed to pinch a seat right behind the bench and I turned to him and said: 'Are you going to come to see us in the semi-final?' I was that confident that we were going to be able to see out the game – so my heart just fell out of my chest when the final whistle went. So, I was too distracted with that and the boys around me to see what happened with the referee. When I was told about it afterwards, well, I've always made a point of not bad-mouthing referees – I think we can all make our fair judgement about what we think of his actions. I would say, that was a decision he had more time to think about, and which was more within his control, than the split-second decision to award the penalty.

Peter Horne: I have never been so devastated in my entire life. I had come off with about ten minutes to go and I remember sitting next to Tommy Seymour thinking, 'We're going to win!' Then we were up on our feet screaming at the boys to keep going. And then the way it ended – it was just hard to fathom. It was like a dream.

I felt sorry for Joubert because if it had happened any time earlier in the game nobody would have had a second thought about it. I think we have to accept as players that we should have had the game won by that point – if we had done better in the line-out the referee would have had no decision to make.

It was like someone had died in the changing room afterwards: really flat, a few tears were shed. Vern just said afterwards that he was proud of us as rugby players and as men. He spoke about the whole month and where we had come from. It was a tough way to end the World Cup, but at least you can look back on it now with some pride.

Finn Russell: After the game was over I went into the Aussie changing room and had a chat with Bernard Foley and swapped tops. Just a bit of small talk; we've got Grayson Hart and Taqele Naiyaravoro at Glasgow now who played with him at the Warratahs, so we were just talking about them, a wee bit of chat about the game and so on. It would have been nice to have a beer with them, but obviously they had to recover before the semi-final, so we didn't manage it. Another time.

It was hard watching the Australia-Argentina semi-final; I think that if we had beaten Australia we would have definitely had a really good chance of beating Argentina, especially the way they played on the night. So that was frustrating, thinking what might have been, thinking that we could have been in a World Cup final, which no one would ever have dreamed was possible. It was probably the best chance we'll get to make it to a World Cup final. But you can't dwell on it for long. These things happen in sport and you just have to move onto the next game.

And so it was that Scotland's bravest and greatest World Cup match came to an agonising end. With Argentina in wait in the semi-final after their comprehensive victory over an injury-ravaged Ireland, Scotland would have had their best chance since 1991 to reach a World Cup final – an extraordinary scenario and one that would have been ridiculed before the tournament began. But it is now a moot point, nothing but a ghost to haunt Scottish rugby.

History will look at this moment in one of two ways: either as the greatest missed-opportunity in a litany of agonising narrow losses for the national team, or the marker from which Scotland re-establishes itself at the top table of international rugby. The 2015 World Cup quarter-final will either be considered as yet another heroic failure or it will be a line in the sand from which this team never looks back. A Six Nations title is within reach for this group of players; they have the talent to be history-makers against the Southern Hemisphere giants; and they have the potential to be a major force at the 2019 Rugby World Cup in Japan. There have been many dark days for Scottish rugby, just as there have been many false dawns and promises of greatness that have been squandered. But this team feels different. Time will tell.